OCCULT
PARIS

─────

"With Tobias Churton as the cicerone—or dare I say psychopomp?—the reader is expertly guided in the labyrinthine world of the Occult Paris of the Belle Époque (1871–1914). This is the best introduction to the French occult revival ever written in English."

HENRIK BOGDAN, PROFESSOR OF RELIGIOUS STUDIES AT THE UNIVERSITY OF GOTHENBURG

"Music, art, literature, mysticism—fin-de-siècle Paris had it all in great abundance, and in Tobias Churton's latest tome he uncovers the hidden and not-so-hidden connections between Satie, Debussy, Redon, Rops, Khnopff, Gauguin, Crowley, Lévi, Papus, Mathers, Péladan, Michelet, Blavatsky, Reuss, Huysmans, Breton, and countless others. . . . Eminently readable and filled with meticulous historical details, this is a fabulous depiction of one of the most exciting and fervent periods of creativity in modern times."

JOHN ZORN, COMPOSER-PERFORMER

"A tour de force. A stunning account of fin-de-siècle Occult Paris and its lasting influence on the counterculture. . . . Churton gives comprehensive portrayals of such occult luminaries as Péladan, Papus, and de Guaita as well as a portrayal of their movements and a seminal analysis of esoteric art—in particular the 'Rosicrucian' art of the salons—locating its place in the intellectual, cultural, and political milieu of the Belle Époque. Tobias is as erudite as he is excited and exciting. His scholarship is alive with passion, imagination, humor, and, most of all, humanity. A must-read for students of European history, Art Nouveau, Symbolism, Idealism, Surrealism, and the Decadents as well as for neo-Rosicrucian, Templar and Gnostic esotericists, and modern-day alchemists and magicians."

STEPHEN J. KING (SHIVA X°),
GRAND MASTER, ORDO TEMPLI ORIENTIS

"No one can evoke the feel of a place and an era like Tobias Churton! This is Paris in the Belle Époque, but behind the city of the can-can, Toulouse-Lautrec, and the Moulin Rouge, Churton shows us a Paris of seekers in mysterious worlds—magic, Hermeticism, Kabbalah, alchemy—and of artists, writers, and composers who were also drawn to those realms. The spirit of their compelling quest is stamped on every page of this book."

CHRISTOPHER MCINTOSH, PH.D., AUTHOR OF
ELIPHAS LÉVI AND THE FRENCH OCCULT REVIVAL

OCCULT PARIS

THE LOST MAGIC OF THE BELLE ÉPOQUE

TOBIAS CHURTON

Inner Traditions
Rochester, Vermont • Toronto, Canada

Inner Traditions
One Park Street
Rochester, Vermont 05767
www.InnerTraditions.com

Text stock is SFI certified

Library of Congress Cataloging-in-Publication Data

Names: Churton, Tobias, 1960– author.
Title: Occult Paris : the lost magic of the Belle Époque / Tobias Churton.
Description: Rochester, VT : Inner Traditions, 2016. | Includes
    bibliographical references and index.
Identifiers: LCCN 2016007529 (print) | LCCN 2016008539 (e-book) |
    ISBN 9781620555453 (hardcover) | ISBN 9781620555460 (e-book)
Subjects: LCSH: Occultism—France—Paris—History—19th century. |
    Occultism—France—Paris—History—20th century. |
    Magic—France—Paris—History—19th century. |
    Magic—France—Paris—History—20th century.
Classification: LCC BF1434.F8 C48 2016 (print) | LCC BF1434.F8 (e-book) |
    DDC 133.0944/36109034—dc23
LC record available at https://lccn.loc.gov/2016007529

Printed and bound in the United States by Lake Book Manufacturing, Inc.
The text stock is SFI certified. The Sustainable Forestry Initiative® program promotes sustainable forest management.

10 9 8 7 6 5 4 3 2 1

Text design and layout by Debbie Glogover
This book was typeset in Garamond Premier Pro with Mason and Gill Sans Pro used as display typefaces

Figures 10.11, 10.19, 14.4, and color plate 15 are used by permission of Bibliothèque nationale de France.

Figure 16.7 is used by permission of Ordo Templi Orientis Archives.

Plate 3 inset licensed under https://creativecommons.org/licenses/by-sa/3.0/us

Plate 19 licensed under https://creativecommons.org/licenses/by/4.0/legalcode

Plate 33 licensed under https://creativecommons.org/licenses/by/2.0

To send correspondence to the author of this book, mail a first-class letter to the author c/o Inner Traditions • Bear & Company, One Park Street, Rochester, VT 05767, and we will forward the communication, or contact the author directly at **tobiaschurton.com**.

Contents

Chamonix Mont Blanc

And now away at last I find a town of the Belle Époque,
The feeble frames collapse with time
Replaced by concrete block.
A town 'neath the edge of Damocles:
a constant threat, disturbing wind
On such a scale of ice and rock
Recalls where Sodom's people sinned.

The townsfolk's lives still grate along,
Unsteady, like yon' glacier stones,
Their mem'ries sad ashes of once great Promethean bones,
Incessantly does Nature take her promised ones below
While leaving only debris and Nocturne's afterglow.

Away, away, Gargantua! Return from whence you came,
Leave poets to their emptiness, and widows to their pain,
Remind us not by rising crags of Man's transient, gay façade,
Bruise not our souls with motions fierce:
Malcontent de Sade.

But still we voyage across the seas to worship at your breast,
We cower down and dig our grave by cavernous peak, or rest,
We file past in wonderment and scratch your beaded brow,
And you will weep and quake aloud at those condemned
    to Now.

But are those ermine coronets that crown your kingly head
A barrier, or halt to us who other paths must tread?
For look above and see the skies
Unending: our fraternity,
And grasp the Star that charts the way
While hoping for Eternity!

TOBIAS CHURTON, *AUGUST 1978*

PREFACE

It was once considered the privilege of Soviet commissars to airbrush the images of political or ideological opponents from publicity photographs while expunging victims' names from the leaves of history. This fastidious process usually followed the physical elimination of unwanted rivals by Siberian exile or firing squad. Academics in the Western world are unable to eliminate "inappropriate" minds and stories from the past and would doubtless prove squeamish in the physical execution of political or philosophical correctness. Nevertheless, practical elimination from the historical record, by omission or systematic denigration, is widely practiced. As I write, some students in England seem to be outdoing their tutors in attempting to render invisible historical figures deemed unacceptable to the unquestioning self-righteousness of the latest apostles of correctness. What is regarded by semi-educated persons as "self-evident" depends on what they have been previously informed constitutes unassailably proven fact or truth; the poisoned birds come home to roost. Needless to say, much regarded as self-evident is likely, on unbiased reflection, to be revealed as mere assumption. "Judge not lest ye be judged." Besides, should it not be a primary task in the training of the mature mind to subject what is regarded as "certain" to rigorous scrutiny, as an exercise to broaden the mind? Information is commonplace; understanding is rare. Regarding the subject of this book, information also is rare.

"Occult Paris" is not a subject you are likely to find given airtime on TV, radio, broadsheet, or as a story to be examined in the groves or concrete jungles of academe. Occult Paris's leading figures, influential or even famous for a few years from the late 1880s to the years preceding World War I have been mostly forgotten, or in the case of a handful, find their names and reputations abused in the conspiracy stories that have flourished since the publication of Baigent and Leigh's *Holy Blood, Holy Grail* in 1982. Conversely, in the neat and tidy version of art history, much that you will find in this book tends to be sidelined from attention as we are officially encouraged to entertain a smooth "progressive" transmission of genius from Impressionism and post-Impressionism to the full force of twentieth-century modernism occupied by expressionism, surrealism, and abstract expressionism: a culturally seismic "shock of the new" delivered by art-heroes Picasso, Duchamp, Dalí, et al, before we reach the empty canvas, minimal conceptualism, and alleged "end of history"—or at least, failing an apocalypse—the end of modernism.

Well, *modern* only used to mean "fashionable," and it may come to be seen that what once was regarded as progress was at root an aesthetic variety show stimulated by extreme political and spiritual anxieties. In established art history's somewhat simplistic, and perhaps destined-to-be-outmoded analog for evolution, the artistic movements centered around the word *symbolism,* as practiced by "the Symbolists," tend to be brushed aside as merely decorative accidentals. Symbolists are considered fair game for denigration as reactionary, romantic (damning in itself!), tainted with antirevolutionary—that is, antiprogressive—decadence.

Don't believe a word of it! The revolution entertained, however incoherently, among coteries of Symbolists, whether in paint, word, or music, was essentially a *spiritual* revolution, and for that reason alone, the legacy has been widely ignored or drained of meaning, subsequently reassembled as a scarecrow of scattered contradictions barely resembling humanity planted skew-wise in a distant field to scare the crows of reason off the rich soil of its "culture," which as a result, is little examined in its fullness, notwithstanding its fertility. Spiritual ideas have in the Western world become non-ideas as the bulldozer of logical positivism, behaviorism, and materialist scientism pushes us toward an artificial intelligence. Outside the struggling new discipline of Western

Esotericism, the story is ignored, sidestepped like a murky puddle by automatic, even autocratic, correctness.

To take one example, I am a regular listener of the BBC's third radio channel, devoted in the main to classical music. The channel recently broadcast a "special" on why, from the point of view of neuroscience and behaviorism, music induced certain effects associated with it. Doubtless such studies have their interest, but one could hardly fail to observe the lopsided materialism assumed as the debate's framework. Music with all its incantatory depth, poetic, imaginative, and even spiritual power was stripped to the category of sound that entered the brain. Oh dear! Though few seemed to recognize it, we were landed right back in the mid-nineteenth century where bullish scientists assumed "mind" was a cerebral secretion. For reasons I suspect of "correctness," an examination of spiritual interpretations of music's qualities or even of the spiritual beliefs and preoccupations of composers has not been attempted by this leading outlet of classical music knowledge. Such an attempt you *will* find in this book.

How much longer must we suffer the fallacious description of Debussy as an Impressionist? Here you will see that particular blind exposed as we discover Debussy's deep participation in Hermetism and symbolist literature. Debussy and Satie might never sound quite the same to you again, but if you already grasp the magic of this music, you will need no persuading that these men were aiming very high indeed for sources of spirit, that is, inspiration. Nobody who is inspired is an "ordinary person," and no ordinary person is equal to one inspired by the highest. Inspiration is not the prerogative of the wealthiest, most powerful, studious, or most influential—far from it; nor can inspiration be bought, though its fruits may be exhibited. Wisdom, as Blake tells us, is sold in the desert market where no one comes to buy. It is so often, though by no means always, the "despised" person who is the vehicle for inspiration. To be in-spired is to be filled with the breath of life and to emanate the light of life. This light we need in our collective darkness. Of course, there are many false claimants to this dignity, but we may assess the tree from its fruit.

Occult Paris aims to fill the gap in cultural knowledge that ignorance and materialist hostility to the category of the spiritual has created. And what a place is Paris to find the furniture for this story of a neglected Hermetic movement!—a movement that in the mind of at least one of its leaders, was intended to presage a cultural revolution. "Materialism has had its day," wrote Gérard Encausse ("Papus") at the head of every issue of his fecund magazine *L'Initiation* published throughout the late Belle Époque. It seems Papus, brave and good as he was, was mistaken in this. Materialism is the religion of the West and has made significant strides in the East. We are far from Papus's synthetic, global religion of scientific spiritualism, vitalized and volatilized by combining esoteric traditions embedded in all religions at some level, and toward which he and many other intelligent persons at the time believed the scions of science were heading. In retrospect, Papus undoubtedly pushed too hard and certainly pushed too soon. Joséphin Péladan, Papus's far from uncritical colleague in aspiration, was considerably more guarded. Péladan foresaw an apocalyptic future wherein Latin culture was wasted by aggressive, soulless, Prussianist Germanicism, vulgar and anti-Catholic, scientific in its devotion to the means of killing and subjugating non-Germans to its imperial will. Time would prove Péladan the more accurate prophet, at least of the near future.

Péladan was the reason I came to this book. For all his remarkable qualities, Péladan has endured pretty poor press in the century since his death. His strident individualism and personal eccentricities have cloaked the flame of a vibrant, vital, compelling genius. This genius was brought home to me while writing my last book, *Gnostic Mysteries of Sex*. I had oft written on the troubadours but to my shame had never read Péladan's late work *Le Secret des Troubadours* (1906), which opened a door to my understanding. I seriously considered a biography devoted to Péladan but eventually concluded that he was not, like Blake, an isolated character, but was best seen in all his glory amid the floriate garden of his friends, colleagues, enemies, and friendly enemies. He was a pulse-center of a movement he knew was very likely to fail. A Catholic heretic (I choose the phrase with care), he knew the powers of temptation—his novels' characters fail because they are human. And a

Hermetic movement based on the ideal of human perfection—the ideal of the Heavenly Man linked to absolute deity—is sure to fail, in this world. Grand failures make the best stories, for in the wreckage may be found much treasure: a real, that is spiritual, treasure, far exceeding that imagined by those obsessed with the lost relics of antique mythology.

The bejeweled legacy of "Occult Paris" is waiting to be appreciated. Will humanity ever again witness such a cornucopia of witty, colorful, imaginative, gifted, and spiritually penetrating human delights? I hope to lift the lid on that lost world that only wants finding to prove it is not lost. "Barmy" doubtless, some of its confidences and temporal conceits, but we may, as we read, find it hard to judge too harshly these very human, very lovable souls. We have, I believe, *everything* to learn from their witness, individual and collective.

Given our present discontents and confusion in matters of the spirit, we may see many of our problems solved over a century ago by men and women who, in glimpsing eternity, stepped outside of their own time and are willing, if we let them, to step into our own.

It has been well worth raising this hidden, encrusted jewel, this sunken cathedral, from the dark waters of time to bring it into the light of our common—too common—day. It has been truly my privilege to convey this story, for the first time in its fullness, to the literate world.

Perhaps Victor-Émile Michelet, a signal guide in this story, was right to believe the light should sometimes remain, if not hidden under a bushel exactly, then certainly covered with a very strong lampshade, but it can do sincere seekers no harm to take a peek when the time is right. I take it that you have come to this book because the time is right for you. May it be so for our friends, for our century.

TOBIAS CHURTON,
EPIPHANY 2016

ACKNOWLEDGMENTS

Perhaps the greatest joy in researching and writing this book has been the opportunity to read many a forgotten text, practically all of which were written in the late nineteenth and early twentieth centuries, in French. In that sense, the bibliography constitutes the greater record of those whose assistance in composing this book has been invaluable. Some of these authors, thanks to the strength of their writing and skill in infusing their words with their minds and their hearts, have become to me something akin to personal friends. I felt this most strongly in the case of Victor-Émile Michelet and Villiers de l'Isle-Adam. I also felt something of the presence of Stanislas de Guaita and Joséphin Péladan, whose parting was like the parting of Newman and Keble, among other spirits who must surely find friendships transcending time in the communion of saints that live for the guidance of those bound to earth. Thank you, old friends. Those who understand will not consider me presumptuous in this greeting.

I could not have accomplished this work without my teachers in French. I remember with great affection Nigel Crowther and Bernadette Thornton, as well as the tortures I inflicted on you during the long afternoons of high school. Wherever you are, however you are, you are dear to me, and the fruits of your tolerance are here to enjoy.

Frank van Lamoen and I have been friends now for thirty years: a little time really, but sufficient. As assistant curator of the Stedelijk Museum of modern and contemporary art, Amsterdam, Frank's historical and bibliographical knowledge, and his willingness to assist has been a great boon. I join to my salutations to Frank, Cis van Heertum of J. R. Ritman's *Bibliotheca Philosophica Hermetica,* Amsterdam, for being such a friend to knowledge.

Acquisitions editor of Inner Traditions International, Jon Graham, was the first to seize on the value of this book, ensuring it would not remain a pipedream. Thank you, Jon, for your judgment is sure, and rare. What a blessing it is when the right man is in the right place: for such it is always the right time!

Many thanks are due to graphic designer (GRAPHYK), Paris habitué, and musician Jean Luke Epstein, who functioned as my Paris agent, obtaining information and images while I was waiting for an operation in May 2015.

Regular Skype conferences with artist and Western esotericist Vanilla Beer, now a longtime resident of southwestern Languedoc, and a light in the field, have proved both delightful and vital in drawing out issues and generating inspiration for this project. Vanilla was also on hand to scour the old bookshops of Carcassonne and Toulouse in search of elusive documentation. Thank you, Nil!

I must express my thanks to Péladan scholar and artist Sasha Chaitow, who, while I was in the process of researching *Gnostic Mysteries of Sex,* kindly sent me the following scholarly studies, all of them examining in depth and clearly revealing the philosophies—most notably that of Plato—which imbued Péladan's mind: chapter four of her Ph.D. thesis *Redemption through the Arts: Joséphin Péladan's Platonic Legendarium* (2014); her monograph *Legends of the Fall retold: Péladan's Luciferianism* (Stockholm, Edda Press, 2013); and the papers *How to Become a Mage (or Fairy): Joséphin Péladan's Initiation for the Masses* (published in *Pomegranate: The International Journal of Pagan Studies,* XII, 2; 2012) and *Hidden in Plain Sight: Joséphin Péladan's Religion of Art* (published in *Abraxas Journal Five (Deluxe Edition),* Fulgur Ltd and Treadwells, 2014). Reading Chaitow's analysis of Péladan helped to stimulate a powerful desire to get deeper into the authentic printed texts and, when occasion eventually presented itself, to make more intimate my acquaintance with the period.

Thanks also to my "American friend," Theosophist Renate zum

Tobel who has provided encouragement in difficult times and who has helped obtain antiquarian sources in the States surprisingly hard to obtain in England.

Last but by no means least, I wish to thank my old friend and colleague in the field, Dr. Christopher McIntosh, whose book *Éliphas Lévi and the French Occult Revival* (1972) long ago rekindled my fascination for the subject. His was a marvelous, pioneering English work, and if I have looked further, it is only because I have been permitted to stand on Chris's thankfully broad shoulders.

Ah! I have forgotten the most obvious source of inspiration—we always seem to forget what ought to be most obvious—France herself! This book could not have been what it is but for the welcome I have received in France over the past forty years: memories flood in of sojourns in Paris, Carcassonne, Poitiers, Brittany, Chamonix, Strasbourg, Lyon, Montpellier, Avignon, Annecy, Angoulème, Nîmes, Arles, Narbonne, Perpignan, Toulouse, Lamothe Fénelon, and of course the timeless countryside and villages of the Carcassès, the Lauragais, and the Ariège. One cannot help wondering if France has not learned the wisdom of Victor-Émile Michelet and decided to keep her light under a bushel. For the tourists, of course, there's the Louvre and the Tour Eiffel, which appropriately adorns the cover of this book. In this case, the artful cover is a cover—the true story lives within.

ONE

"Memories Weigh More than Stone"
Edmond Bailly's Bookshop 1888

Paris changes . . . but in sadness like mine
nothing stirs—new buildings, old
neighborhoods turn to allegory,
and memories weigh more than stone.
    (FROM "LE CYGNE"—"THE SWAN"—IN
CHARLES BAUDELAIRE'S *LES FLEURS DU MAL*, 1857)

In the year Vincent van Gogh took his paints and brushes to Arles to paint *Sunflowers* for art's sake, Edmond Bailly established a bookshop at 11 rue de la Chaussée d'Antin in Paris's 9th arrondissement. About a kilometer north of the Seine, this once highly fashionable street, dominated by late eighteenth-century neoclassical "hôtels" had witnessed decades of influential Parisians, some most colorful, entertaining hundreds of guests at a time, whisked in landaus through the street's many pillared portals to elegant ecstasies and shimmering shows of talent and wealth glittering behind stately façades. A recession in the 1860s, however, compounded by the abdication of the emperor Napoleon III amid the horrors of Prussia's military humiliation of France in 1870, ensured that during the ensuing Third Republic, many of the rue de la Chaussée d'Antin's ground floors were commercialized as shops and offices.

Some 600 meters east of the grandeur of Baron Haussmann's freshly constructed *place de l'Opéra,* and running midway between the Louvre, about a kilometer to the south, and the boulevard de Clichy to the north, the area is now best known for what Napoleon Bonaparte considered the "English vice," not of sodomy, but of shopkeeping, with the ironically named *Galéries Lafayette* department store imposing itself at the intersection of the rue de la Chaussée d'Antin with the mighty boulevard Haussmann and rue Lafayette, the latter named after the military hero of the American and early French revolutions. In 1888, Clichy's reddened early-morning eyes had still not opened upon the famous *Moulin Rouge,* but it would not be long before that establishment's shockingly scarlet windmill exterior was smacked in the world's lascivious face. The Moulin Rouge's saucy cabaret and scandalous *Can-Can* would open for business in 1889. In 1888 you would find its most celebrated visual publicist-to-be, Henri de Toulouse-Lautrec, at Edmond Bailly's bookshop.

Twenty-three years old, Toulouse-Lautrec's descent from the village-like atmosphere of Montmartre—no *Sacré Coeur* basilica mounted the grassy hilltop in 1888—down Clichy's streets of rectangular stone setts, to the rue de la Chaussée d'Antin, was a logical step for the budding artist. The year 1889 would see his work exhibited in the "Independent Artists Salon," which, from its dangerous inception four years earlier, at the hands of the *Société des Artistes Indépendants,* was well on the way to establishing itself as the annual fount for all that was new and exciting in French art, flying in the face of Paris's official Salon, run by the *Académie des Beaux Arts* with government approval. *Independent Art* was the thing. And Bailly's little bookshop operated under the sign of the *Librairie de l'Art Indépendant,* and that was where you could find the most extraordinary range of independent intellects and God-given talents in Europe, for Toulouse-Lautrec did not enter the bookshop to be alone.

Erik Satie, another genius who made his way south from Montmartre to the 9th arrondissement in late 1888 was twenty-two when he entered the shop. Born in Normandy, personal tragedy had left Satie with a deep, sometimes wistful melancholy and an underlying spiritual longing that pulsed through his early and most popular musical achieve-

Fig. 1.1. Erik Satie; photograph by Santiago Rusiñol, 1892

ments. Erik Satie smiled wryly in the face of '80s Paris, a conceit of wit that only just suppressed a bubbling enthusiasm for redemptive art. Unknown, Satie had taken advantage of cheap digs in Montmartre the previous year.

In December 1887, Erik and friend, poet, and journalist J. P. Contamine de Latour, approached the famous *Chat Noir* café-cabaret down the narrow rue Victor-Masse at number 12. Already ensconced reciting his poetry at a cabaret in the Left Bank's Latin Quarter, Spaniard de Latour doubtless encouraged Satie to get himself fixed up with a similar gig. Introducing himself to the *Chat Noir*'s wily director Rodolphe Salis as a "gymnopédiste," Satie's unusual demeanor, combined with a fortuitous vacancy, encouraged director Salis to offer young Erik the café band's baton. Satie worked on his exquisitely original series of *Gymnopédies* on the café piano. Practically everyone has heard them today. If they sound uncanny to us in the twenty-first century, imagine their effect on ears accustomed to the tumult of Offenbach, Berlioz, and Beethoven! If this book were a TV documentary, you would hear much of the *Gymnopédies*. But what are gymnopédies and why should Erik sell himself as a gymnopédiste?

The word *gymnopédies* occurs in J. P. Contamine de Latour's poem "Les Antiques" along with the word *sarabandes* with an implication of dancing, in the sense of a play of light. *Gymnos* is Greek for "naked" or "exposed" and *paidia* means "child's play" or "amusement," and the poetic image seems to be of children performing a ritual dance in ancient Sparta, but this is only an image. Satie, like most of those he met at Bailly's bookshop, was concerned with the poetic symbol *beyond* the image. The music of *Gymnopédies* is stripped, for Satie favored absolutely clean sounds, sharp as starlight—no overly romantic mush or gush, but fresh as white water, translucent and cool as a Normandy breeze on the coast of his childhood. Nevertheless, those delicate, tranquil, and at the time musically disquieting, major sevenths strongly suggest an underlying echo of profound, spiritual anguish of yearning. Satie's music wafts us through an aching nostalgia as it finds momentary repose in a cyclic gesture. Defying the fleeting nature of an experience analogous to childhood, a slow, grave rhythm symbolizes with exquisite economy a state of otherworldly innocence touched by the purity, and tremor, of whitest magic, absent from the world.

When only six, Erik Satie's mother died suddenly. Baby sister Diane joined her a few weeks later. People did not seek pat, rational psychological explanations to explain fissures of the soul in those days. When asked about the music's provenance, Satie himself referred to Flaubert's exotic novel *Salammbô*. Set during the ancient Punic wars, *Salammbô's* story, published in 1862, concerns a powerful veil over the statue of a Carthaginian goddess, the removal of which promises death to those who steal or touch it. Satie's reference point is I'm sure, as allusive as it is elusive. Themes of forbidden secrets, violation and exposure, lust and innocence, loss and tragedy, feminine power, spiritual forces, inexorable fate and sudden death underlying the visible "natural" human drama attract everyone attracted to Bailly's bookshop. In fact, the ethereality of the *Gymnopédies* plays very much against the racy atmosphere of the rue Victor-Masse, where the *Chat Noir* was situated at the edge of the 9th arrondissement, some 600 meters southeast of the boulevard Clichy, round the corner from the place Pigalle's not always cheap thrills; syphilis being commonplace. Symbolist artists truly desired a way through the ugliness of the times. The path might come through an embrace of suffering and denial of worldly approval in quest of the spiritual ideal. Some chose to suffer temptation and degradation, others spiritual purging by asceticism and devotion. Satie favored the latter path.

By the end of 1888 he had completed both his *Gymnopédies* and his *Sarabandes*—the latter directly inspired by poems by J. P. Contamine de Latour—and he would play them to his newly acquired close friend Claude Debussy, whom he also met at the *Librairie de l'Art Indépendant* in the rue de la Chaussée d'Antin. Debussy recognized their unique qualities and the two men became close, emotionally and intellectually: poets in sound.

One might have thought twenty-six-year-old Claude Achille Debussy's interest in the rue de la Chaussée d'Antin was pricked by Frédéric Chopin's having taken a room at number 5 in 1833, moving up in the world three years later to number 38 where Franz Liszt attended several of Chopin's soirées, encountering luminaries such as German romantic poet Heinrich Heine and the French romantic painter, Delacroix. Half a century later, in January 1886, while studying at the Villa Médici in Rome, Debussy himself met Liszt and witnessed the great old man play there, shortly before his death. Debussy's contact with the rue de la Chaussée d'Antin probably stemmed, however, from his interest in the arts review, *La Revue Indépendante*. On 9 February 1887, still studying fitfully in Rome, Debussy wrote to bookseller Émile Baron asking for the latest issue. A more direct contact with the address came through Debussy's brother Alfred who, in March 1887, offered *La Revue Indépendante* his translation of a poem: "La Bourdon et la besace" by Symbolist inspiration and English "Pre-Raphaelite Brotherhood" star, Dante Gabriel Rossetti (1828–1882).

In fact, editor Edouard Dujardin ran *La Revue Indépendante* from the same premises in the rue de la Chaussée d'Antin that Edmond Bailly would acquire for his bookshop the following year. Dujardin also cofounded *La Revue Wagnérienne* that catered to the intense enthusiasm for Wagner. It ran from February 1885 to July 1888 and published contributions from many who would gather at Bailly's *L'Art Indépendant*

bookshop. Wagner's music was something of a cult among the burgeoning body of Symbolists deeply concerned with the synthesis of the arts
of word, painting, music, and drama, all claiming hostility to realism
in literature and naturalism in painting. In 1888, poetry by Verlaine
and Mallarmé graced *La Revue Wagnérienne*'s pages. The ghost of
Baudelaire hung over all Symbolist endeavors, crying out for the justification the poet seldom received in his lifetime.

Shortly after Alfred Debussy's Rossetti translation appeared in
La Revue Indépendante, brother Claude heard the first act of Wagner's
Tristan et Isolde at Paris's *Concerts Lamoureux.* He was ecstatic:
"Decidedly the finest thing I know!" Debussy's enthusiasm was shared
by practically everyone who gathered at Bailly's bookshop during late,
crepuscular afternoons in the rue de la Chaussée d'Antin. Musical elixir
for Symbolists, Wagner had myth, magic, daring, originality, roots, thunderous volcanism, and sacred powers of unworldly melodic enchantment:
a controlled, but sometimes volatile marriage of the visceral and the spiritual. In short, music from the chthonic energies of unworldly ecstasy.
Music conjured this life into imaginative being, transporting the listener;

Fig. 1.2. Claude Achille Debussy

indeed Symbolists tended to regard *all* the arts as sharing roots in magical incantation, and if the Symbolists would have their way, their flower too. In this context, Péladan's famous conviction of the Artist as *Magus,* touched-by-the-divine conjuror *extraordinaire,* traversing worlds visible and invisible, was almost too obvious a conclusion for admirers of Gustave Moreau, yet to many ears, the message seemed astounding, reassuring: "telling it like it is." What was being rediscovered was the magical essence of poetry: truth beyond words, beyond reason, beyond explanation, echoes from worlds that could touch but could not be grasped, for what they sought was the spirit of mystery.

Something of Wagner's mythic medievalism and Teutonic underworldliness was shared by the English Pre-Raphaelite Brotherhood's embrace of William Blake's prescient dictum—*Gothic form is living form*—the largely unacknowledged creed of Victorian architectural revival. An adjective that had once meant "barbaric," "Gothic" had been redeemed by perception of the medieval Catholic Church's architectural embrace of the divine-maternal, the mysterious, tempting, oriental *curve:* the very essence of art, according to bookshop *habitué,* art critic, aesthete, monarchist, and Catholic Decadent Joséphin Péladan. So we shall not be surprised to find that Erik Satie will very soon release his *Ogives* (1889): four piano pieces inspired by the curves (*ogives*) outlining Gothic arch windows in Paris's Notre Dame cathedral on the Île de la Cité. Combined femininity and austere spirituality formed a window *through which* we may pass into the light, as to, and through, a symbol, like penetrating an *ikon* of Orthodox devotion: journeying from the organically visible to spiritual vision. A window, of course, works both ways. We see through it as light comes simultaneously through it to us. The visitation of light is suggestive of another world. The bright sky is a symbol of infinity, of boundless values and epic, fraternal ideals. Yet the Symbolists preferred autumnal light: hinterland between the known and the unknown, the clear and the obscure, twixt presence and absence, between life and death. *Who are we? Where do we come from? Where are we going?* Melancholy, longing, nostalgia were preconditions of illumination.

For the Symbolist, Nature, ordinarily viewed, was naught but superficial sense impression, a mirror: mere flesh, not spirit or animating *mind*. Through a genuine ikon, on the other hand, imagination enabled the meditative viewer to slip via the locked gate of the opaque image to the mystery of being. Nobody who has made this journey can see the world as he or she saw it before, nor will be content any longer with the superficial, the shallow reality of the materialist that is conditional, not absolute. Such illumination was eagerly lapped up, if not always fully understood, by Symbolists; its nectar Parnassian, no . . . Olympian and Heliconic, for from the invisible summit of the loftiest poetry came the perspective to see, judge, dismiss, or discriminate and—who knows?—even to transform the huddled, distasteful world below, whose blackened state might yet be subjected to the gold-making skills of the alchemist, that is to say, "Artist."

Rimbaud wrote of the "alchemy of the word." Poetry and painting were never so close as they were among Symbolists: necessarily esoteric, magical in the embrace of the supernatural, occult in penetration of the image. Ideal art evinced a trove of gold existing beyond the world's material image. Those who understood were initiates; thus Péladan and his colleagues embraced Leonardo as an initiate, a "Grand Master." As we shall see, Péladan's declarations about the divine Leonardo are the precise source of the potent *Da Vinci Code* myth.

The Gnostics called the ultimate nature of God *Bythos,* or Depth—as in an ocean or abyss. Understanding of this ultimately incomprehensible reality might require passage through a personal abyss wherein opposites might meet head-on, rendering helpless mere reason's dependency on binary distinctions, as opposites are transcended through mystical congress. One would not see the light until one had experienced the darkness. The miraculous spirit gave new eyes, and thus the means to new art.

Such a prospect of descent into maelstrom we now associate with the works of poets Charles Baudelaire (1821–1867) and Arthur Rimbaud (1854–1891), both resonant stars among the Symbolists and "Decadents." We are therefore unsurprised to find Debussy in 1888 continuing his work begun a year previously on *Cinq Poèmes de Baudelaire,* while his six-part *Ariettes Oubliées,* based on a recent poem by Paul Verlaine—who shot and wounded Rimbaud in a lover's rage in 1873—was published in

Fig. 1.3. Cover to Debussy's La Damoiselle élue
by Maurice Denis, published by Bailly in 1893

January 1888. At the year's end, Debussy will complete *La Damoiselle élue,* inspired by a poem by proto-Symbolist D. G. Rossetti. Published for voice and piano in April 1893 by none other than *L'Art Indépendant* owner and esoteric music theorist, Edmond Bailly (real name Henri-Edmond Limet, 1850–1916), *La Damoiselle élue*'s refined, lyrical, captivatingly curvaceous cover came from the alchemical hand of Maurice Denis, Symbolist of the "Nabi" (prophet) faction, or fraternity, sharing principles of vision with Gauguin and van Gogh.

Perennial descriptions of Debussy as an Impressionist composer, outrageously repeated on classical music programs and recording notes are ludicrously wide of the mark. But then, as now, the world at large finds Impressionism considerably easier to accommodate than Symbolism.

In 1888, while the official Salon had come to accept Impressionists, it looked askance at the new visionaries, and tried to keep Decadent critic Joséphin Péladan out of its galleries.

No, Debussy was no Impressionist, though countless documentaries have used his music to accompany Impressionist paintings, frequently lending them undeserved depth of enchantment to the sentimental uninitiated, while fostering a poppy-stained, summery, romantic image of the Belle Époque: a dry dream. In this regard it is instructive to note that in Debussy's letters to bookseller Émile Baron, sent from Rome in 1885–87, he requested Baron send him Symbolist journals, as well as writings named as "Le chemin de la croix" by Catholic pro-Symbolist journalist, essayist, and poet Charles Morice (1860–1919), and "Rose-Croix," attributed to the poet, esotericist (or "occultist"), Kabbalist, spiritist, and socialist Albert Jounet (1863–1923), himself an active participant in the life of 11 rue de la Chaussée d'Antin.*

---

*See Howat, *Debussy in Proportion,* 167–175. The works named have been sought but not found. I suspect this is because they were not books, but pamphlets, poems, or articles in journals or newspapers. An article by pro-Symbolist journalist and novelist Octave Mirbeau called "Le chemin de la croix" (The way of the cross) appeared in *Le Figaro* 16 January 1888. It concerns the disappointment Mirbeau felt when great artists were granted honors that belonged to military badges ("crosses") and the values of this world. Rodin, who became a Knight of the Légion d'Honneur in 1887, is named. The title is likely to have been a play on the title of a poetry book (1856) called *Le chemin de la croix* by Parnassian poet, Leconte de Lisle (1818–1894). Much admired by Symbolists, Leconte de Lisle was elected to the French Academy in 1886, an event probably alluded to in the punning title of Mirbeau's article.

Charles Morice wrote a positive critique of Leconte de Lisle, along with leading Symbolist writers, in his painstaking 1889 book *La Littérature de tout à l'heure,* 210–14, extolling the Parnassian virtue of *L'Art pour L'Art* or "art for art's sake." Charles Morice's background was quite similar to Péladan's: a highly committed Catholic, bourgeois family from Lyon. Morice knew Mallarmé and assisted Verlaine after Verlaine's traumatic imprisonment, writing a book about the poet. Symbolist-influenced painter Paul Gauguin courted the attention of both Morice and Mirbeau, before sailing to Tahiti in 1891, at the time he attended Mallarmé's famous Tuesday gatherings. Morice collaborated with Gauguin in a number of publication ventures.

The reference to Morice's and Jounet's works appearing in correspondence with bookseller Émile Baron occurs in Francis Ambrière's "La vie romaine de Claude Debussy," 20–26.

*Fig. 1.4. Victor-Émile Michelet
(1861–1938)*

Through Albert Jounet's friendship with the remarkable esoteric poet and journalist Victor-Émile Michelet, Jounet earned his own chapter in Michelet's remarkable book, *Les Compagnons de la Hiérophanie,* where Michelet writes of the gnostic Jounet as one who "always lived in the high zones of the spirit, in the generous innocence of the heart." In fact, Michelet's book, profoundly informed by personal experience of what he describes, as well as by the Martinist conception of the "Tradition"—of which more later—gives us a wonderfully warm, considered and often wry firsthand account of the milieu in and around Bailly's bookshop in the late '80s and early '90s.

A true "son of Hermes" in the sublime sense, Michelet (1861–1938) was an esoteric poet and writer of distinction, perceptiveness, and beauty of mind whose active scope comfortably spanned the occult, gnostic worlds, and the heights of Symbolist art; he knew practically every major figure, as well as many minor figures, of the Symbolist and intertwined Symbolist-Hermetic worlds, writing elegantly and trenchantly about immaterial things that matter. One should always be aware, however, when reading Michelet's reminiscences, that however profound his asides and genteel his comments on art, character, and spirituality may be, he keeps faith to the Hermetic reserve regarding saying too much about the mysteries of the spirit and the truths of initiation, lest, as the movement's arch-progenitor Hermes Trismegistus put it in the *Asclepius,* "they become commonplaces to the rabble." Michelet knows far more than he says.

Reading Michelet's account of the "Hierophany," that is, manifestation of the sacred, or what he significantly calls "the *fin de XIX siècle* movement of Hermetists" one feels the *presence* of much that is not said directly: another life that hovers about the words like a halo or cloud. Sensing this, we may realize just how deep and genuine a commitment to spiritual ideals existed among some of the players in the esoteric drama that unfolded in Paris between the 1880s and the conflagration of barbarity, folly, sacrifice, and untold heroism known as World War I.

Michelet was an initiate.

VICTOR-ÉMILE MICHELET AT BAILLY'S BOOKSHOP

In the Foreword to his *Les Compagnons de la Hiérophanie,* the mature Michelet reflects crisply on his subject:

> In the last years of the last century, a number of young men met, ardent and vibrant, impassioned by the joy of learning of the most arduous studies. All recognized a spiritual fraternity oriented to the quest for the highest knowledge, of the integral gnosis woven under the fabric of time. They undertook to penetrate the secrets of that antique science prudently and necessarily hidden.
>
> Even in the darkest centuries, there were always men enlightened by occulted lights, and even the barbarism around them, in which direction the western world is now rushing [these words appeared in 1937], will not abolish the hatching of illuminated minds. Beyond time and space they are brothers.

Michelet was convinced that the activities of the men he knew and described had joined Paris to the list of historic centers of *gnosis,* such as Plotinus had made of Alexandria; Ficino and Pico had made of Florence; and Robert Fludd and Francis Bacon had made of London. Michelet then names three men at the spiritual helm of the Parisian expression of gnosis. They "deserve the glory" but have never received the publicity: Christian esotericist Abbé Lacuria (1806–1900), Symbolist poet, playwright, and novelist Villiers de l'Isle-Adam (1838–1889), and esoteric theorist and social reformer Saint-Yves d'Alveydre (1842–1909). These men Michelet regarded as the patriarchal lights who guided him and his companions into the luminous world of esoteric truth.

At the center of the center stood Edmond Bailly's bookshop: "This shop united the spirits [or minds] of symbolism with the those of esotericism."[1] It constituted a salon, presided over by the wizened sorcerer-like visage of the esoteric musician, sometime Communard, and author of *The Legend of Diamond: Seven Stories of the Celtic World* (1909), Edmond Bailly (1850–1916): a man, according to Michelet, "with no commercial aptitude but gifted with rare intellectual and aesthetic acuity."[2] In Michelet's words, Bailly was responsible for "some fairly curious verse," reconstructions of history, and a number of interesting esoteric papers on music, belonging "to that category of men whom the gods mysteriously accord a multiplicity of superior gifts, neglecting to add another little one, without which, though secondary, they remain obscure: talent."[3]

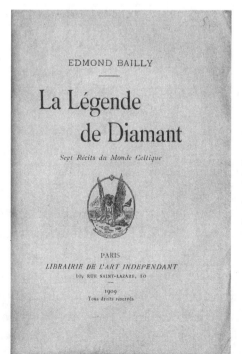

Fig. 1.5. Edmond Bailly,
La Légende de Diamant,
*Librairie de L'Art
Indépendant, 1909*

Fig.1.6. Remy de Gourmont (1858–1915),
drawing by Pierre-Eugène Vibert

Assessing Bailly affords Michelet opportunity to comment on influential Symbolist poet, critic, novelist, and pundit Remy de Gourmont (1858–1915) cofounder in 1889 of the important pro-Symbolist journal *Mercure de France,* and whose aesthetics would in time influence T. S. Eliot and Ezra Pound in the twentieth century. Michelet knew Remy de Gourmont better than those he influenced. While not denying de Gourmont's possession of the essential gifts that constitute "talent," he nonetheless displayed the lack of a no less essential human quality when, as Michelet puts it, de Gourmont "executed" Bailly—a man whom he knew not—with two unjust phrases. "For all his beautiful intelligence Remy de Gourmont only perceived the world of appearances. The sphere of reality was closed to him: a dilettante who could ricochet a volley of ingenious ideas on the surface, but could never go to the depth. Inferior to him in talent, Edmond Bailly was his superior by penetration."[4] The judgment is characteristic in its humanist sensitivity and critical severity of Michelet's observations in general, a sublime talent that makes him the indispensable, providential guide to those of us who have never met, and may never meet, the minds he describes, or himself, and must be content with the crumbs that have descended through time from the masters' table.

For Michelet, it was Edmond Bailly's "interesting mind" that explained why men of such great artistic gifts as Odilon Redon, Villiers de l'Isle-Adam, Stéphane Mallarmé, and Claude Debussy filed into the shop; they all delighted in Bailly's conversation.

Bailly also published a review, *La Haute Science* (The High Science), with the suggestion that occult science was elevated above quantitative science, as theology was once called the "queen of the sciences." Contributors included such "masters of hermetic knowledge" as Matgioï: an intriguing pen name taken from the Chinese *Matgioi* ("eye of the day") by Georges-Albert Puyou de Pouvourville (1861–1939). Matgioï had served in military and administrative capacities on French expeditions into China, where, settled in Tonkin, he was initiated into a secret society by a Taoist master before returning to France to establish Taoism in the West while writing works on China and French colonies in Asia. Bailly's *Librairie de l'Art Indépendant* would publish Matgioï's translation of *Le Tao de Laotseu* (the Tao Te Ching) in 1893.

At roughly the same time Bailly established his bookshop, occultist Gérard Encausse (pen name "Papus") advised "Martinist" magic enthusiast Lucien Chamuel to launch the *Librairie du Merveilleux* at 29 rue de Trévise, about a kilometer east of the rue de la Chaussée d'Antin. *Chamuel* was an anagram of Lucien's real name, Mauchel, Chamuel

Fig. 1.7. "Matgioï" (1861–1939)

being an archangel guardian of the Kabbalistic path of Geburah, reflecting divine strength seeking and seeing God.

Michelet made the point that while the atmosphere in Bailly's shop was less "charged with occult effluvia" than "the house of the rue de Trévise," more artists passed through Bailly's portals. Michelet's observation implies that the Symbolist movement in general, while sincerely accommodating of magic and even "Spiritism," preferred a less exclusive blend of esotericism with the arts, veering toward spiritually sensitive philosophy, inspiring ideas, poetry, and creative theory, rather than practical invocation of angels, evocation of demons, or spiritist séances. While knowledge of esoteric doctrines was regarded as a boon for understanding the hidden scope of the psyche and spirit in the world, there was marginal interest in practicing formal magic as handed down in the *grimoires* of old. In fact, the emphasis was on developing science to spiritual levels, while transposing the spiritual inheritance to scientific levels of application. Magic was part of the armory against materialism. The "magic circle" was now the theater, studio, salon, cabaret, gallery, and concert hall, wherever two or three were gathered together in the name of Art. Nevertheless, *à chacun son goût,* and Chamuel's shop received its fair share of artist inquirers. It was doubtless satisfying for artists to be aware that somewhere in Paris on any given day, someone was searching amid supernatural realms for arcane knowledge inaccessible to telescope, microscope, or motor car—the latter demon patented by Karl Benz in 1886.

The artists would arrive toward afternoon's end. Michelet recalled the erect, enigmatic finger of poet Stéphane Mallarmé (1842–1898) raised in the "dusky penumbra" like that of Leonardo's *St. John the Baptist.* Enjoying distance from his usual auditors—he taught English at a *lycée*—Mallarmé was always gracious, smiling warmly as he developed his speech not much above a whisper with fairness and discretion and just a caress of a light both clear and obscure.

In 1888 Mallarmé's poem "L'après midi d'un faune" had been known for some twelve years. Poet and philosopher Paul Valéry regarded it as the greatest in French literature, a beacon in Symbolist poetry whose

Fig. 1.8. Stéphane Mallarmé (1842–1898)

essence will inspire Debussy's revolutionary orchestral "Prelude to the afternoon of a faun," first performed in 1894. Michelet comments that if Mallarmé "exercised on the so-called symbolist generation an uncontested majesty, this was rather by his speech than by his *oeuvre* which appeared obscure because he claimed to abuse clarity."[5]

The point about Symbolism is that the symbol should never be obvious; if its meaning is exhausted on sight, like an allegory, it has failed. Words do not exhaust the meaning of truth. Symbolist poet Henri de Régnier (1864–1936) held the symbol to be "the most perfect and the most complete figuration of the Idea" or "the expressive figuration of the Idea." The poetic velocity was toward a pure poetic Platonism, a spiritual *religio mentis* ("religion of the mind"). Greek-born poet Jean Moréas (1856–1910), insisted that "the essential character of Symbolist art is never going as far as the conception of the Idea in itself." Allegory then was not symbolism. Mallarmé decreed the Symbolist must resist "too precise a meaning," a Rimbaudian doctrine of reserve almost theological in essence. Pierre Louÿs (Pierre Félix Louis, 1870–1925), author of the Sapphically erotic *Les Chansons de Bilitis*—set to music

Fig. 1.9. Henri de Régnier (1864–1936)

by Debussy in 1897—and a frequent visitor to Bailly's bookshop, was succinct: "One must never explain symbols. One must never penetrate them. Have confidence—oh! Do not doubt. He who has drawn the symbol has hidden a truth inside it, but he must not show it—or else why symbolize it in the first place?" Mallarmé again: "It is the perfect usage of this mystery which constitutes the symbol."

Definitions of Symbolism tend to be vague because a quality of vagueness is of its essence. The poetic-symbolic comes alive precisely at the borderline where matter becomes spirit or is darkened in twilights of otherworldliness. Its art, its magic, is enchantment: to recover stolen soul from the opacity of the world. Michelet remembered a beautiful discussion between kindred spirits Mallarmé and Villiers de l'Isle-Adam. Villiers contested what he considered Mallarmé's error of believing that the "living idea" has no permanent existence, its duration dependent on where it lodges its spirit, and as soon as it is separated, it dies. This Villiers regarded as discordant with Plato's "occult doctrine" regarding the life of the ideas in eternity. A year later, Michelet received a note from Mallarmé, the poet having modified his ideas since Villiers's reproach:

My dear Confrère ["fraternal colleague"],

Thank you for sending your study of "L'Ésotérisme dans l'Art" [Esotericism in Art]. It interested me personally. Because it would be difficult for me to conceive something or to follow it without covering the paper with geometry where the evident mechanism of my thought reflects itself. Occultism is the commentary of pure signs, to which all literature obeys, cast immediately by the spirit.

Your very persuaded,   Stéphane MALLARMÉ[6]

Bailly planned as his editorial debut to publish the Count Villiers de l'Isle-Adam's *Chez les Passants Fantaisies, Pamphlets et Souvenirs*

Fig. 1.10. Auguste Villiers de l'Isle-Adam (1838–1889)

(Among the Passersby, Fantasies, Pamphlets, Memories). However, when the proofs were returned, they were found smothered with black ink corrections. Hardly one "majestic" phrase was definitive. No one, Michelet observes sadly, knew that death was so close to the erratic, much loved Villiers. Michelet joked kindly that if it was the Lord who had called Villiers prematurely—he died in 1889—to the "golden paradise of the beautiful genius," it could only have been to prevent him from revising his work indefinitely!

Chez les Passants was published in 1890 under Bailly's editorial symbol, a curious design by artist Félicien Rops, consisting of a punkish looking, winged female crouching on a very large fish with the rubric: "this fish is not for everybody." No doubt. Michelet recalled how the living Villiers would, while his head oscillated between his shoulders, work his enchanting word while withdrawing a hand from his pocket to cast his hat in any direction leaving the other free to push back the silvery locks that dangled before him as he spoke "and rarely did one interrupt the enchanter." Michelet did not share the view of many contemporaries that Villiers was a crank, mired in a dreamworld. He noticed instead that Villiers had an all-seeing look, valuating both things and men acutely. His pale blue eyes penetrated, Michelet observed, far into the most intimate regions of the world external to him.

Michelet recounted from fond memory Villiers's spontaneity, how he would "surge," always ready to seize the moment and impart his magic to it. Yet though an artist whose actions frequently demanded an adverbial "suddenly," Villiers was nonetheless punctual in formal terms, when he had to be. In this regard, Michelet remembered choosing Villiers as fellow "second," or witness, to a duel that took place in about 1886. The seconds went in a friend's name to demand satisfaction from Jean Moréas. The date in itself is interesting because it was in September 1886 that *Le Figaro* published Jean Moréas's "Literary Manifesto," afterward known as the "Symbolist Manifesto." Moréas announced Symbolism as a movement, distinguishing it from the Decadent: a view not all Symbolists shared, including, I think, Michelet.

Having previously experienced the role of duelist's second, Michelet saw Villiers as one ideally suited to the task, envisaging all eventuali-

Fig. 1.11. Jean Moréas (1856–1910)

ties, untying all complications, with all the superior powers of subtle diplomacy required. While Villiers could appear fleeting, it was, asserts Michelet, because he had been suddenly called on to extricate himself from the jaws of hidden distress, often financial, sometimes romantic in nature. Michelet was adamant, against the naysayers, that Villiers, carrying the enchantment of genius in his heart, lived a happier life than the apparent favorites of fortune: "Leave the vulgar to consider their misery. In Villiers dwelt the world of angels and of gods. O burnt saints with living wounds on some soiled bed, shredded martyrs, persecuted heroes, ridiculed and miserable genius, 'tis you who have the best part! 'tis you who have lived on the borders of the infinite!"[7] This outburst of Michelet's in celebration of his long-deceased friend is extremely telling of the mentality of our movement in general, conveying as it does far more than an encyclopedia entry on Symbolism ever could. It is of the heart.

Michelet remembered being with Villiers in the shop one evening when astrologer and occultist Ely Star (real name: Eugène Jacob, 1847–?1942) invited them, along with Bailly, to dine at his apartment in the heights of Montmartre. An "excellent man," according to Michelet, Ely Star had been a butcher, then prestidigitator with escapologist Robert Houdini,

Fig. 1.12. Camille Flammarion (1842–1925),
French astronomer and Theosophist

before turning to authentic magic and astrology. "He was not very wise, but very intuitive, and his method, if it had made a Selva or a Choisnard smile, drove him to curious results."* The dinner occasion may have been connected to publication of Star's *Les mystères de l'horoscope,* published in 1888 (Paris: Duville) with a preface by Camille Flammarion

---

*Michelet, "La librairie d'Edmond Bailly" in *Les Compagnons de la Hiérophanie, Souvenirs du mouvement hermétiste à la fin du XIX siècle* (Author's translation). Ely Star was a member of the British Hermetic Order of the Golden Dawn, becoming a neophyte on 22 August 1896. His wife, a tarot reader, also became a member that year. Ely Star became high priest at the Paris Ahathoor Temple No. 7, run by Samuel "MacGregor" Mathers and wife, Moina, in September 1899.

Camille Flammarion (1842–1925) was a French astronomer who not only wrote popular science books but also science fiction while involving himself in psychical research. A member of the Theosophical Society and something of a mystic, he attended Lady Caithness's Theosophical gatherings at 124 avenue Wagram where the Gnostic Church was consecrated in 1890.

and a letter from Joséphin Péladan. Michelet's references to astrologer Henri Selva (1861–1952) and Paul Choisnard (1867–1930) reflect the fact that the latter two astrologers preferred a statistical method to justify astrology's validity, whereas Ely Star developed ideas from Éliphas Lévi's friend Christian Paul (ca. 1860), integrating the major and minor arcana of the tarot with the Kabbalist's "Tree of Life," or Sephirotic tree into astrological classification.*

That night, the eloquent Villiers was particularly on form, improvising recitations that bounded from the tragic to the farcical, giving the impression, as Michelet puts it, of being "thrice alive," suggesting a veritable incarnation of Thrice Greatest Hermes himself! Villiers was still speaking late in the evening, continuing in the street till Michelet led him to his door. Michelet had witnessed this "great prodigal of the spirit" applying his working method. A sculptor or freemason of the word, Villiers's method consisted of chipping off the rough edges of the block of his first conception until he had achieved a spoken form suitable to be tried out for his friends. "How many beautiful pages were thus prepared, that death did not permit him to write! While he seemed to us so intensely, so genially alive, the angel of death spied on his gestures. Because each one of us is accompanied from birth by the individual angel of his death, by his *Kere* [female death-spirit], say the Greeks. Recall the tragic moment when Zeus puts in the balance the *Kere* of Achilles and the *Kere* of Hector. *This one is the heaviest.*"[8]

A few days after the dinner with Ely Star, Bailly—who edited a musical journal called *La Musique Populaire*—asked if he could publish Villiers's music composed on Baudelaire's sonnet, "La Mort des Amants" ("The Death of the Lovers"), a piece Villiers sometimes sang to friends. Though he could accompany himself on the piano, he could not write music on the stave. Rather than executing it simply for Bailly, who had taken down the notes, Villiers paid a call on composer

---

*Aleister Crowley would classicize this line of occult symbolism in *The Book of Thoth* (1944). It is significant that Crowley was in Paris in January 1900 with then leader of the Hermetic Order of the Golden Dawn Samuel Mathers at the time Star had just become high priest at Mathers's Golden Dawn Temple No. 7 in Paris, founded in 1893 (the Golden Dawn's first temple was founded in London in 1888).

Fig. 1.13. Augusta Holmès (1847–1903)

Augusta Holmès (1847–1903). Of Irish descent, Augusta's golden hair and proud bosom had aroused in Symbolist-friendly composer César Franck "most unspiritual desires" when she was his organ pupil in the 1870s, initiating jealous anger in fellow organist Camille Saint-Saëns who was also crazy about the "pythoness" Augusta. Franck's wife was equally disconcerted.

Villiers had taken an interest in Augusta in 1865 when she was involved with poet Catulle Mendès (1841–1909) who himself was about to marry Judith Gautier, whom Villiers was also in love with and wished to marry. Villiers then tried to marry Judith's sister Estelle, a consummation blocked by Villiers's mother's Aunt Kerinou since Estelle had neither cash nor position. English readers probably only know Villiers from the famous line "Live? The servants will do that for us," taken from his Symbolist play *Axël,* published after his death. But Villiers *did* live, struggling with a personal sense of eternity trapped in time. Probably happy Bailly's request had given him an excuse to visit Augusta, his luck with her, unfortunately, had not improved with time; she was not at home. So he called on composer Emmanuel Chabrier (1841–1894) who, like Villiers, had contributed to Dujardin's *Revue Wagnérienne.* Chabrier had pioneered the integration of modality with the French harmonic school, along with the use of the pentatonic scale in 1877 (the operetta *L'Etoile*), before César Franck's *Rebecca* in 1880–81, and over a decade before Debussy's well-known experience of the Javanese gamelan at the Universal Exhibition of 1889. The five-toned scale and the writing in antique modes would help to revolutionize music in the *fin de siècle*, because the inner and formal restructuring gave music some of the verbal freedom and mystery characteristic of poetry. On this occasion, however, Villiers's needs were somewhat simpler. Asked by Villiers to write his music, the "fat guy of the Auvergne," as Michelet describes Chabrier, laughed and invited Villiers to confine himself to the art of literature. Chabrier's rudeness may be attributed to depression at a decline in his career, aggravated by the onset of syphilis. Sore vexed, Villiers returned to Bailly's shop, badmouthing Chabrier in "sonorously acid phrases." The next day he moved to other things; Michelet did not forget. Fifty years later the memory of Chabrier's uncouth rebuff made Michelet desire to celebrate "the great music of his [Villiers's] phrases, the most beautiful of the French tongue, that condensed themselves from his thought, derived from the most mysteriously faraway regions of the spiritual world."[9]

It was at *L'Art Indépendant* that Villiers met the novelist Joris-Karl (real name Charles-Marie-Georges) Huysmans (1848–1907), author

Fig. 1.14. Joris-Karl Huysmans (1848–1907)

of archetypal Decadent novel *À Rebours* (Against the Grain, 1884), its decadent, reclusive character Jean des Esseintes being inspired to some extent by real-life aristocrat, poet, and aesthete Robert, Comte de Montesquiou-Fézensac (1855–1921), with something of the personal tastes that permeate Villiers's own novels thrown into the wicked blend. Des Esseintes's character—or, arguably, lack of it—would go on to inspire Oscar Wilde's decadently evil aesthete-horror story, *The Picture of Dorian Gray,* whose eponymous character seems to have been corrupted by Huysman's equally imaginary monster-idol, before going on to culturally congeal into the effete, amoral type evident in the smooth-talking murderer in Patrick Hamilton's 1929 play, *Rope,* made into an experimental thriller by Alfred Hitchcock in 1948.

Huysmans used to drop in on the shop after leaving his office at the Ministry of the Interior, where Chabrier had also worked, as a lawyer, until an experience of Wagner's *Tristan und Isolde* in Munich in 1879 changed his life. Michelet regrets his never meeting Huysmans at Bailly's, though he would meet him elsewhere, as we shall see, in somewhat dramatic circumstances. But Michelet did meet another "familiar of the house" around the same time. The familiar spirit was chemist Louis Ménard (1822–1901) who in 1846 had discovered *collodion.* While collodion's nitrocellulose film found profitable application in both medicine—surgical dressing—and in photography, Ménard himself received neither credit nor benefit.

Fig. 1.15. Louis Ménard (1822–1901), portrait by Émile-René Ménard (1861–1930)

A socialist revolutionary in 1848, Ménard was exiled to London where, in the 1850s, he established a reputation as a classical historian and poet before returning to France to become a painter with the Barbizon artists through the 1860s. Called to care for his sick mother in London, Ménard had to support the Paris Commune (March–May 1871) by pen alone. A respected classicist, Ménard's *Hellenic Polytheism* of 1863 anticipated J. G. Frazer's anthropological approach to religion.

Ménard's translation of the gnostic-occult dialogues of the *Pymander* of Hermes Trismegistus, published in 1866, could be purchased at Bailly's shop, which opened a year after Ménard was appointed professor at the *École des Arts décoratifs,* an important establishment dedicated to the marriage of technique and culture that would play such a role in the revolution of domestic style in the twentieth century—Art Deco being not the least of its achievements. Finding his social and aesthetic ideals in the classical world, Ménard was drawn into the sympathetic orbit of Symbolists who tended to see art as the decorative expression of the soul, from its roots in the ancient world of worship and cult, unifying the interior and the exterior. Art, like life, should be *devoted*.

Bailly wanted to republish Ménard's collection of sonnets, philosophical dialogues and stories, the *Rêveries d'un païen mystique* (Dreams of a Mystical Pagan, 1876), while Michelet was interested in Ménard's personal relationship with college comrade Charles Baudelaire. While Ménard did not share Baudelaire's genius for poetry, he did leave some poems—Michelet draws particular attention to "Empedocles"—that while not being great poetry, certainly expressed "a spirit rich and penetrating." It is typical of Michelet to value what others did not, praising Ménard for having been, as it were, the companion of Neoplatonist mystics Porphyry and Iamblichus in Alexandria, for having invented collodion while playing at chemistry, for his fascination with Hellenic symbolism, in whose pursuit he had scaled halfway the peak of Olympus, before being retarded in his ascent as clouds concealed from him the view of the Olympians, by which Michelet also meant the *perspective* of the Olympian. For Ménard, according to Michelet, had "intelligence lacking brilliance, but which stood firm on solid knowledge," being one of those "who when introduced to the definitive path, walk always close to her, and not in her."[10] "By the clear blue of his eyes, by the triangular construction of his face, Louis Ménard recalled a little Villiers de l'Isle-Adam. He was, however, a singular maniac. He came on foot from the place de la Sorbonne, where he lived in a beautiful house that he owned, to the Chaussée d'Antin [about 4 kilometers to the north], carrying all his corrected proofs, to save himself a sou."[11] Catulle Mendès told Michelet he'd taken Ménard as the model for a miser in his collection of risqué vignettes of hypocritical lusts, *Monstres Parisiens* (Parisian Monsters, 1882).

Ménard's last mania, apparently, was the reform of orthography: the means by which a language is written, including punctuation, capitals, et cetera. "He obliged the typographer to compose his prose in an orthography invented by himself, incomprehensible to others. One scratched one's head to discover which French words hid themselves under an insensate load of consonants and vowels. He must have given himself enormous pains to transcribe the text of his *Reveries of a mystic pagan* in this magma of bizarrely assembled letters. Placid as he was, Bailly tore his hair out when faced with the proofs. What reader would have the courage to decipher these repulsive pages? Louis Ménard, securing his fine head under his long buckled hair, was as obliviously obstinate to disfigure all the words of his prose as he was obstinate to be Republican under the Emperor, as he was obstinate always to adore the divinity of the Homeric Zeus."[12]

A number of Symbolist poets were happy to have Bailly publish their works under the motto borrowed from Baudelaire's publisher Auguste Poulet Malassis *Non hic piscis omnium* ("This fish is not for everyone"), an unlikely marketing rubric today. Michelet praises Bailly's productions. First editions of his *Chansons de Bilitis,* and the *Poésies de Méléagre* by Pierre Louÿs (1870–1925), and the *Poèmes anciens et romanesques* of Henri de Régnier (1864–1936) were much sought after when Michelet was writing in the 1930s, and today more so, being incredibly rare.

One poet who was not seen in the shop but whose work was published by Bailly was the now very obscure French poet and dramatist Louis Ernault (1865–1919). Indeed, Ernault was obscure in his own

Fig. 1.16. Pierre Louÿs (1870–1925)

time. According to Michelet, the poems published by Bailly remained unperceived, "hidden by the walls of the little chapels," and yet they, Michelet tells us, were "the only ones in this so-called symbolist epoch that carried within them the understanding of the symbol. Louis Ernault's *La Mort des Sirènes* [Death of the Sirens] is one of the great poetic works of the French language. Someone will recognize this one day."[13] That day has not yet come.

When the wind of success blew in the Symbolists' direction, it blew them far from *L'Art Indépendant* to less artistic but more commercially assured homes, as Michelet put it. Although Bailly understood human nature well enough, the little exodus from his editorial embrace left some bitterness, but Bailly was without rancor. Only Debussy's somewhat casual departure left him brooding a little. Bailly could hardly forget that Claude Achille Debussy (christened Achille-Claude) had been one of the most familiar visitors to his shop, arriving most days at the end of the afternoon either alone or with his faithful Erik Satie.

Fig. 1.17. Catulle Mendès (1841–1909)

—*What?* Catulle Mendès said to me one day, You don't know the music of Debussy! A collaboration of you and him would be indicated.

Later, a collaborative project was sketched out but went no further. Catulle Mendès had a system:

—Assemble the librettos of all the young composers showing promise. Among them, there will be one who will create a work as successful as *Faust*.[14]

Whether this would have worked immediately in Debussy's case, Michelet had cause to doubt. Debussy assembled an operatic libretto after *Le Cid* by Guilhem de Castro, esteeming it greater than Corneille's:

—What became of your *Cid?* I [Michelet] asked Debussy later.
—Ah! It disgusted me. I abandoned it, and I began setting *Pelléas et Mélisande* to music.[15]

The masterpiece came too late for Catulle Mendès and Michelet to seize the value of the young talent in the bud. As for Michelet's own abortive collaboration with Debussy, it came about in this wise. In 1899, Michelet would write a Symbolist play, *Le pèlerin d'amour* (The Pilgrim of Love), somewhat akin stylistically to the Symbolist Maeterlinck's 1893 play *Pelléas et Mélisande.* Maeterlinck was a friend of Henri de Régnier, and it was de Régnier who opened the door for Debussy to approach the Belgian Maeterlinck, an encounter bearing fruit in Debussy's remarkable opera *Pelléas et Mélisande,* first performed in April 1902 to a mixed but profitable response, while Michelet was still trying to find a home for his *Le pèlerin d'amour.* Parnassian poet José-Maria Heredia (1842–1905; father of Henri de Régnier's wife, Marie) suggested to Michelet *Le pèlerin d'amour*'s being performed at the *Comédie Française,* but a fire scotched that in 1900. Michelet waited for the theater to get going again, but when at last it was put before the selection committee, the play was rejected, whereupon Michelet's childhood friend, André Ulrich, working high up at the Ministry of the Interior, contacted Paul Ginisty at the *Théâtre de l'Odéon.* Ginisty wanted Michelet's play, but only with a score. Michelet, somewhat logically, contacted Debussy whose *Pelléas et Mélisande* was already becoming a cult among *Conservatoire* students and other cognoscenti, and Debussy and Michelet sketched ideas for a libretto between December 1902 and January 1903, the month in which Debussy was promoted *Chevalier de la Légion d'Honneur* as his opera completed its second series on 6 January, after which Debussy decided to commit himself to writing music criticism. Alas for Michelet![16]

Debussy had not always been in such demand. Michelet remembered fondly the many occasions Debussy spent in the backroom of Bailly's shop, where, on an excellent piano, he "played us passages he was working on, and we were enchanted with the glamours of his charming, invertebrate genius. I never heard a pianist play the piano like Debussy." Under strong fingers, "made for kneading the musical dough," Debussy extracted from the rough instrument a voice rich in every timbre. It could be a human voice or the voice of chords of brass or woodwind. Debussy's pale face looked placid but his fiery eyes were

Fig. 1.18. Debussy by the River Marne in 1893

ardent in producing what those who heard him recognized, and inhaled avidly, "this wholly new music, this sonorous powder made to explode the Wagnerian bewitchment that weighed on the atmosphere of the time."[17]

Few who heard Debussy at Bailly's would have believed, Michelet notes, that his music would have so soon been able to impose itself on acceptable taste. He referred to this sentiment when speaking to Debussy shortly after the evening premieres of *Pelléas and Melisande* in 1902:

—I did not believe, I said, that this music would find support so rapidly.

—*Hen!* he [Debussy] replied, It is supported, but not digested. [18]

Michelet remarked that the spiritual stock that was spreading in the esoteric and Symbolist currents, taking in the painting of the school of Gauguin and van Gogh, must have been checked in music. Debussy, however, could express himself in music comfortably, having let himself, Michelet asserts, become "permeated powerfully with Hermetism" . . . *permeated with Hermetism.* This is a highly significant statement about Debussy from a keen, contemporary observer who *knew.* Debussy's esoteric reading and conversation with music theorist Edmond Bailly, who himself studied the esotericism of Eastern and Western music, enabled him to penetrate Indian sacred music through acquaintance with Sufi Inayat Khan and his two brothers.

Inayat Khan (1882–1927) founded the Sufi Order in the West in 1914, teaching universal Sufism even though he left India as a classical musician. Khan told Michelet that Edmond Bailly was the first person he ever knew in Paris. [19] Michelet held Khan in high regard; hardly surprising perhaps since Sufism has been recognized by scholars as the gnosis amid numerous Islamic traditions.

> This fine Murchid [spiritual guide], illuminated by secret lights, consummate musician, who died young in 1927, was only able to know Bailly when he was seeking refuge, after the fall of *L'Art Indépendant,* in an obscure ground floor apartment on the rue St Lazare, at a period when he had some reason for refusing to have anything to do with his old friend Debussy. [20]

It was not Bailly who introduced Debussy to Inayat Khan but another. Debussy made the best of the encounter, finding renewed inspiration there, as he did from the richness of musical ideas of his friend Erik Satie who, as Michelet puts it, was "then too insufficiently accomplished technically to know how to express them."

Fig. 1.19. Ernest Reyer (1823–1909)

—Well! said someone to Erik Satie, Here is a phrase of Debussy's which seems to be from Satie.

—Yes, he replied, It's Satie, but Debussy does it better than me. [21]

Appointed in 1892 as Péladan's master of music for his "Rose-Croix Catholique," Satie had first arrived at Bailly's, Michelet recalls, dressed entirely in corduroys. With the lenses of his pince-nez projecting the fires of his laughing eyes, Satie was, for Michelet and his friends, "such a good companion of the Work of Liberty." He recalled the eccentric composer recounting farcically his visits to the members of the *Académie des Beaux-Arts* who controlled Paris's "official" exhibitions of high art; Satie would present his candidature to the institute at every holiday. This, Satie asserted, was so that he could achieve the goal of preaching to the maintainers of academic authority the cult of the "real and living art." Satie declared that only one of its members fully understood: Gustave Moreau (1826–1898), painter of mythological and biblical imagination, and a hero to many Symbolists, and much later, to surrealists. One voice spoke out for Satie. That voice belonged to Ernest Reyer (1823–1909), opera composer (*Sigurd,* 1884; *Salammbô,* 1890), music critic at the *Journal des débats* (filling Berlioz's shoes), librarian at the *Académie de*

Musique, and a member of the *Académie des Beaux Arts* since 1876. Reyer's music became unfashionable as the 1890s proceeded.

Michelet remembered Satie turning against Debussy in his last years, as he had against many by then. Michelet found the reversal of attitudes amusing. He thought what Satie held most in Debussy's disfavor was Debussy's respect for "la coupole," a reference to the dome of the *Académie Française.* Such ambition was bad form for younger idealists; cult classics rarely get Oscars. Satie complained bitterly: "Claude no longer understands, that the price of living music is something different to being a simple *coupolard*"[22]—a cutting pun on the *coupole* and the French *couard* (coward). One cannot help wondering if Michelet had also experienced a negative jolt from Debussy's ambitiousness when the latter's separation from Michelet's play coincided with Debussy's receiving national honors in January 1903—we may savor the poignant message of Octave Mirbeau's "way of the cross" article referred to earlier: in terms of rewards meted out by the powerful, the cross is not only a badge of merit, but a medal of spiritual capitulation. Had Jesus accepted *their* "cross," he could have avoided *his.* But Debussy was much more of a problem to Satie's reputation than he was to Michelet's, or so we might imagine.

Once one grasps the conceit by which Leonardo da Vinci can be seen as a Grand Master of an ideal order of creative, initiated genius, the fictional ascription of Debussy's name in recent times to the equally fictional Grand Mastership of the Martinistic "Priory of Sion" *ludibrium* makes radiant sense to anyone "in the know." In this manner of perception, Debussy was indeed a grand master, having mastered and transformed music through Hermetic initiation, that is, immersion in divine intelligence invisible to the world and the worldly.

Michelet knew another friend of Edmond Bailly's: Belgian artist of the bizarre, Félicien Rops (1833–1898). Rops would design several frontispieces for Péladan and much else besides of a playfully wicked, graphic, and frequently erotic nature. Known for his "Satanic" women, Rops illustrated Barbey d'Aurevilly's *Les Diaboliques.* His drawing of St. Theresa shows the mystic's "ecstasy" as nothing more than a naked nun

Fig. 1.20 (inset). Félicien Rops (1833–1898)
Fig. 1.21. A self-portrait in Satanic mode, Félicien Rops

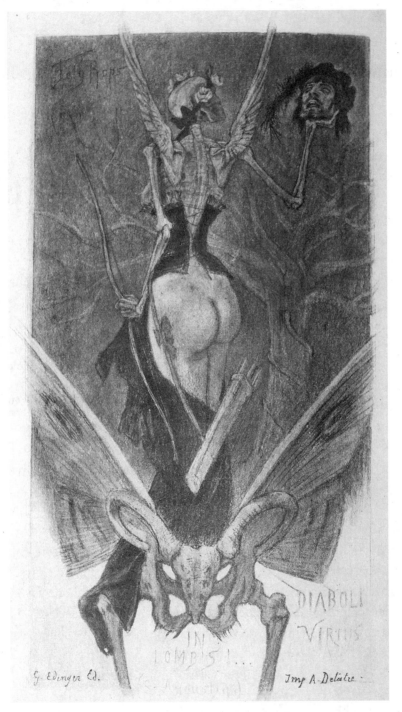

Fig. 1.22. Diaboli Virtus In Lombis! *(The Devil's Virtue Is in His Loins);*
Rops's frontispiece to Joséphin Péladan's novel L'Initiation Sentimentale
(Sentimental Initiation, 1887)

with a dildo up her vagina. Shocking, Rops was an astute humorist of sexual desire and the pornographic temptation of the clergy. Anticlericalism would have stood him in good stead with the secularism of the Masonic Grand Orient of Belgium, of which Rops was a member. Like Satie, who would have the courage to sit himself down on the benches of the *Schola Cantorum* and learn medieval and choral music theory like a schoolboy at an age when most people have left study far behind them, Rops, taking Impressionist painter Corot's advice, joined the pupils of an engraving atelier at the age of forty, becoming thereby a master in etching.

Rops was leaving Bailly's shop one day when painter Edgar Dégas entered. The sharp-tongued painter discerned the engraver's silhouette: "*Voilà!* The Directory of etching!"—"le Bottin de l'eau-forte" implying Rops would work for anyone or anything. The quip, Michelet believed, was unfair. The "aquafortist of Works useless and invisible" was, said Michelet, an artist dignified by his friendship with Baudelaire: quite sufficient praise for a Symbolist of the faith. *Was Rops the Devil?* Michelet joked that Rops did his best to appear so, with a nose strong and brusque, subtle lips, and a goatee beard, and sufficient shock of hair up front for it to resemble two horns. Would Aleister Crowley steal the look from a previous generation of decadent "Satanists"? He would. To maintain the look took a lot of work. Perseverance created an image: Rops was content to be a living symbol of something people wanted.

Michelet delighted in the image of Bailly—who also resembled an old sorcerer—and Rops together, like a couple of witches or devils on the dark mountain called the Brocken, conjuring and making mysteries together. Observing Auguste Rodin with his florid beard one day in his atelier sculpting, Michelet heard him suddenly stop and declare: "These heads asserting themselves as decadent humanity, I leave them to Rops." Michelet added: "—and to Toulouse-Lautrec."

So we return to the painter with whom we began, making his way down to *L'Art Indépendant* from Montmartre. Michelet called Toulouse-Lautrec's art "acute and ferocious," but reserved his last word on Bailly's shop for an appraisal, not of him, but of the most mysterious Symbolist of them all, Odilon Redon (1840–1916). Surprisingly, Michelet never

Fig. 1.23. Odilon Redon (1840–1916)

met Redon, despite Redon's being a friend of Bailly's shop, and according to Michelet, one of the greatest artists who ever frequented the rue de la Chaussée d'Antin.

Lithographer, aquafortist [etcher], he had begun painting at 40, like Titian. This Saturnian visionary of the dark world precipitated himself in the worlds that intoxicate the enchantments of light and color. His name, his work bathed in a halo of obscurity, and the several years that have passed since his death have only ignited a few pale rays of a glory that still await in the future. Certain artists are powerful enough to surpass the limits of their art. They have magnetized their works with the power they have drawn from the great secret springs, and these works emit a mysterious radiance. Thus did da Vinci and Rembrandt in his second style, and lingering between less ample horizons, Dürer. It is to this family of minds that one will have to attach Odilon Redon. Did he not know how a simple bouquet of flowers extracts an intensity of expression exalted to the furthest obsessions?[23]

Fig. 1.24. L'Oeil, comme un ballon bizarre se dirige vers l'infini
(The Eye Like a Strange Balloon Mounts toward Infinity),
Odilon Redon, 1882

Michelet concluded his tour of his memories of Bailly's shop with the melancholy thought that many other remarkable spirits had filed into the boutique of "Independent Art," many of them now forgotten. Forgotten or not, they all found in Edmond Bailly a grand, penetrating and reliable companion in the quest of "the great intellectual adventure."

We now undertake to trace some of the more immediate roots of the great intellectual adventure that was Occult Paris.

Fig. 1.25. Félicien Rops's colophon for Bailly's L'Art Indépendant *publications—Non hic piscis omnium: "This fish is not for everyone"*

TWO

THE BUILD UP

It began to dawn on a number of the "spirits," or *genii,* who frequented Bailly's bookshop in 1888 that they unintentionally constituted what was, effectively, a spiritual movement: a Hermetic, spiritual movement dedicated not to theological or exclusively philosophical doctrines, but to the transformative power of the arts of the imagination. From this nucleus, a new world of perception would emerge, one that, while long forgotten as a movement in its own terms, would not only change the world, or "affect outcomes," as we might say today, as strong beliefs will, but one that I think has demonstrated remarkable capacities to be reborn in or near our own times.

There was never a time in French history, documented from at least the twelfth century onward, when there was no heterodox, spiritual presence, sometimes overt and dramatically controversial (viz: Cathars and Troubadours), sometimes simmering just beneath the surface. We might even choose to revisit the second century CE to find evidence for the active presence of Gnostic teachers in Roman Gaul's Lyon and Rhône Valley teaching Alexandrian doctrines derived from Egyptian poet-theologian Valentinus, as well as Gnostic magic. There is something about France, southern and southwestern France particularly, that seems to stimulate the growth of spiritual heterodoxies of esoteric depth. And yet, we tend to think of France in terms of the Age of Reason and the *Grandes Écoles* stemming from the education reforms of 1794 that created an elite rank of higher education establishments on rationalist, scientific lines. Esotericism, however, has always held a peculiar, even stubborn, place in French philosophical history, despite the fact that its enemies have despised it, seizing the judgment seat to pontificate in an attempt to denigrate its traditions as "rejected knowledge" or outmoded "superstition."

The persistence of esotericism is partly due to the fact that the dominant faith in France, both before and after the revolution, was Roman Catholic. Catholicism operated in uneasy relation to the state until formal separation established state secularism in 1905, following many severe, frequently bitter, and not infrequently violent, ups and downs. While an individual might be critical of official church doctrines, or be indifferent to them, or even risk at certain periods a blatantly anticlerical stance, one did not necessarily have to go from one extreme to another, that is, from absolute faith in the church to atheism. Esoteric traditions provided a tolerant, philosophically oriented region of individual spiritual liberty, centered not on outward conformity and public morality but on the heart and personal spiritual awareness, a principle of revelation, and private morality. This explains in part the remarkable creation and spread of esoteric Freemasonry in France from the mid-eighteenth century onward, though that movement too had been somewhat presaged. A "Rosicrucian scare" occurred in Paris in 1623 when Catholic propaganda encouraged belief that "invisibles" from Protestant Germany were establishing Sabbaths of heretical—and invisible—magi in the name of the Fraternity *Rose-Croix* across the country. While some writers swallowed this fiction, taking the official Catholic line that all magic was heresy and destabilizing diabolism, other writers came to the defense of an enlightened esotericism and made significant distinctions between licit magic, regarded as a divine science, and illicit, or *goetic* magic, based on demonic pacts. The Renaissance in France had ensured respect for the Hebrew Kabbalah in educated circles, as well as for Platonist and Neoplatonist philosophies preserving powerful esoteric indices. Catholic natural philosopher René Descartes (1596–1650) went in search of the Rosicrucians because he suspected they represented a body of advanced cosmic knowledge, and he did not wish to miss out on rare mathematical insight.

Nevertheless, despite strands of esoteric teaching spanning the centuries prior to the so-called French Occult Revival of the 1880s and 1890s, the flowering of overt esotericism and its expression in the fine arts in Paris at this time still requires some explanation, for despite mainstream Freemasonry's humanist presence in nineteenth-century French politics—predominantly on the Republican side—continental Freemasonry's spiritual, esoteric systems, combined with neo-Rosicrucian and associated gnostic traditions, declined during the tremors of the Napoleonic Wars, and were obscure by the time social-ism rose in the 1830s and '40s, in whose cause, whether moderate or extreme, many French cultural figures felt urged to deposit their faith. Strictly materialist science had also ascended on account of the visible achievements and speedy development of new, frequently profitable, industrial technologies. "Progress" displayed an ambiguous visibility that encouraged something like a blind faith in its continuity. As a mar-ket trader once said to me with a slight flush of shame: "You can't see God, but you can see money, so. . . ."

To say that there was a protracted crisis of authority in France from the inception of the Revolution and the execution of King Louis XVI in 1793 is to state the obvious. Political crisis followed political crisis, amid a welter of philosophical innovations, conflicts, fads, and disqui-ets. Governments of various hues claimed to be "right," their exercise of worldly power justifiable, that is philosophically reasonable, sanc-tioned by some superior will, destined, predestined, or "self-evident" according to reason. Messianism was seldom remote from the surface in popular and private speculation. Various political figures attracted messianic glamour, particularly in bitterly oppressed, Russia-dominated Poland, from whose bloody conditions elite refugees poured into Paris between 1831 and 1870, carrying their political and spiritual idealisms with them. It was not unknown for desperate Polish activists for liberty from Russia to wish for, or believe in, Napoleon Bonaparte's imminent return in an apotheosis redolent of Christ the redeemer. Expectation of a "deliverer," a "Lost King" with absolute authority, was widespread.

For many, political questions were not simply pragmatic. Was God partial to one form of government over another? Did a king's legitimacy derive from his being the agent of God's will? Was there a deeper meaning to history? Was history guided by supernatural agencies, or was it all blind forces to which men reacted and struggled to master by light of reason? Was reason sufficient to account for reality and change? Where could "answers" be found? Had the French nation sinned against the church and God by acquiescing in the Revolution? And where did Art and the Artist stand in all of this? Who or what did Art serve? Men who seriously grappled with such baffling questions, men such as philosopher Joseph le Maistre (1753–1821), have tended to be unjustly forgotten as orthodox interpretations of history have established themselves.

It should be held in mind that esoteric doctrines embraced in the period were interpreted in terms of looking "beyond the day." Exponents sought an underlying sense of eternity to the universe: *what has been, is, and always will be;* what is permanent and real, not transitory and passing; what is solid rock, not shifting sand; what is real, not appearance only; what provides repose for the soul rather than distraction and despair. Above all, there is the time-honored promise of mastery of destiny through self-mastery: "a wise man rules his stars."[1] It will be Paul Gauguin, Symbolist, who in 1897 will, on the top left of a masterful painting showing Tahitians in symbolic composition, repeat the precise questions that, according to second-century church father Tertullian, were those that made people heretics (Gnostics):

D'OÙ VENONS NOUS . . . QUE SOMMES NOUS . . . OÙ ALLONS NOUS
Where do we come from? What are we? Where are we going?

POLITICS AND POWER

Anyone seeking principles of permanence would be hard-pressed to find them in France's political history after the blood-soaked, hysterically idealistic, spiritually wounding revolution attempted to eliminate the *ançien régime* for good. Reason, in whose name so much dementia was unleashed, had shown her fruits in unreason on a mass scale. After a decade and a half of chaotic dislocation, murder, war, utopian reform piled on repressive legislation imposed by a police-state armed with summary justice, France's First Republic crashed to a halt when Napoleon Bonaparte seized the Caesarian laurels as emperor of the French in 1804 and declared the First Empire's destiny to be the transformation of Europe on gloriously revolutionary (that is, Napoleonic), scientific, transnational principles, supported by a fiercely nationalistic France. Napoleon's dream finally hit the brick walls of La Haye Sainte and Hougoumont in 1815 when British, Prussian, and Dutch-Belgian troops were victorious at Waterloo. Bourbon King Louis XVIII returned to the throne and France began to pick up the pieces. Church and state recovered a brief, fragile equilibrium.

Dying in 1824, Louis was succeeded by Charles X who, after only six years, amid aggravated divisions in society and critical revolt, was forced to abdicate. Ignoring Charles's wish that his ten-year-old second son Henri, duc de Bourdeaux succeed him, Charles's cousin, Bourbon Louis Philippe, duc d'Orléans, assumed power, promising to rule with greater popular consent. Thus began the Catholic "legitimist" movement in favor of legitimate, "lost" King Henri V of France (known as the Comte de Chambord), a movement that would receive intense support from the family of Occult Paris star, Joséphin Péladan, as we shall see.

In 1848 the continent's capitals exploded like firecrackers in socialist revolts. Succumbing to calls for abdication, Louis Philippe hastily quit Paris. In the heady tumult of a brief period of wild optimism, France's Second Republic was declared. In February 1848, a popular vote secured the state's presidency for Bonaparte's nephew, Louis Napoleon. Predictably impatient with the political system, Louis Napoleon veered quickly from avowed republicanism to imperialism. He wanted France reformed, expanded, and everywhere improved, and he wanted it quickly. Discussion would only frustrate necessity. After appropriate maneuvering, the senate declared a Second Empire, with Louis Napoleon its emperor, in December 1852.

Broadly then, we can now speak of four principal, occasionally porous, political factions at odds with each another: Bonapartists believing in presidential-imperial government by the most able and reasonable dictator, popularly supported; Catholic monarchists favoring the legitimate heirs of the Bourbon dynasty in league with the church; republicans favoring either a secular bourgeois democracy with, or without, a constitutionally constrained monarch; and socialists, agitating for a workers' state or fraternal utopia of some kind. In a small minority, anarchists argued over aspects of a libertarian socialist-type arrangement while wishing to destroy, well, everything to ensure a "new world" of liberty emerged from the rubble of past failures to find its yet undefined form. Time, "humanity," and blessed freedom would tidy it all up, or not, as the case might be.

Louis Napoleon took the bull by the horns—or the cock by the feathers—and shook France up with staggering speed. The very visibility of Louis Napoleon's command-driven structural changes would damn much of them in the eyes of the Symbolist. Massive extension of railroads, construction of termini, renovation of ports, industry, coal mining, social infrastructure and services, and most startlingly visible of all, Baron Haussmann's audacious transformation of Paris's streets and buildings between 1853 and 1869, *symbolized* nothing to the spiritual eye. When the Symbolist looked at the first great "department stores,"

Fig. 2.1. The new boulevard Haussmann intersection with the rue de Mirosmesnil, 8th arrondissement, 1853–70

raised in stately fashion on immensely widened boulevards, he could see nothing behind them but a will to power and a desire to impress through appearances: handsome stage props of political theater.

Baudelaire's poem "The Swan," which opened the previous chapter, captured the poet's own sense of dislocation and dismay at the demolition of most of what was left of medieval, and much of post-Renaissance, Paris. It was not so much a question of maligned grandeur, but of the loss of atmospheres, *depth,* lived-in roughness, pleasing shabbiness, community neighborhoods, nooks and crannies, lamps and shadows, cafés and apartments permeated with ancient "prana," sharing in the lives and deaths of the past that together reflected the poetic inwardness of souls warmed by imagination and spiritual fraternity, despite appearances.

There was "art" in the new architecture of course; there was beauty too in formal, tasteful, spacious rearrangements, but it *meant* very little. Spiritual life was in decay. Pre-Haussmann Paris could be worn like an old, loved coat, ragged but comforting and part of oneself. It had taken many knocks and could take more; it was made for people, not for the "plan." As impressively up-to-date as the grand, tidying changes of the Second Empire undoubtedly were, to the poetic eye they reflected too obviously and opaquely the passing picture show of cold economic history, superficial modernism, whitewashed sepulchers, and window dressing, making the poet feel the transitory nature of existence, encouraging a longing nostalgia where, as *poète maudit* ("accursed poet") Charles Baudelaire put it, "memories weigh more than stone." The wider boulevards also discouraged rebellious barricading of course, easing the path for military repression of public revolt.

Of course, in due time, much of the new—being not without that distinctive French instinct for grace and form—would become familiarly old, and by the time modernist poet-in-the-making Nancy Cunard reached Paris shortly before World War I, she could write enthusiastically: "my mysticism was in those streets," though I should suspect that much of that mysticism came from the residual presence of the Symbolist movement in what was left of the Latin Quarter, by then close to its last legs, but still a tangible ghost unavoidably haunting all the arts nonetheless. But "Ah!" Baudelaire might have added, "You'll never know what you missed!"

And then, in 1870, largely as a result of Prussian Chancellor Bismarck's duplicitous determination, France found herself at war with her pugnacious neighbor. Frenchmen fought bravely the invading "barbarian," but the barbarian was intelligent and had greater industrial resources offering greater destructive power, ruthlessly and effectively applied with scientific indifference to suffering. After the decisive battle of Sedan, when Louis Napoleon, unwell but still leading his troops, was captured, the Empire's defeat demanded the emperor as scapegoat. In March 1871 Old Boney's hardworking nephew was removed while the radical socialist "Commune" of predominantly working-class Parisians took over the capital until May, when its hideously savage suppression left over fifteen thousand "Communards" and National Guard supporters dead, executed, or awaiting execution or deportation to New Caledonia.

Fig. 2.2. Coffins occupied by Communards slaughtered in 1871

The ensuing Third Republic would preside over continued expansion of France's colonial empire, much internal dissension, and a high turnover of administrations whose claims to legitimacy were challenged persistently. The only principle of authority was the fickleness of the ballot box set against the threat of insurrection.

But life went on, placidly for some, if we don't look too closely at *pointillist* Georges Seurat's now universally admired painting *Une Baignade, Asnières* (*Bathers at Asnières*), completed in 1884 and depicting mostly working-class bathers enjoying a hazy summer's swim in the River Seine some four miles out of central Paris (see color plate 14). While workers enjoyed a respite from the grind, summer 1884 saw French forces attacked by Chinese troops following France's assumption the previous year of Tonkin, Annam, and Cochin China as protectorates after securing a treaty at Hue with Indochinese officials, despite China proper's regarding Indochina as a vassal state. Initially acquiescing in the treaty in May 1884, China declared war on France five months later after the French destroyed seven Chinese warships in retaliation for nonpayment of an agreed indemnity. These events explain how it came to be that Taoist evangelist "Matgioï" became in due season an habitué of Bailly's bookshop while promoting Chinese spirituality in Bailly's journal *La Haute Science* after assisting the French administration in Tonkin (see page 15).

Following initial victories against a Chinese army ten times its strength, the French Tonkin Expeditionary Force was defeated at Bang Bo. The ensuing retreat from hard-won Lang Son in March 1885 precipitated the fall of Jules Ferry's administration on 30 March.

If the blood, sweat, and tears involved in French colonial ambitions seem far removed from Seurat's bathers reclining on the riverbank in Asnières's neighboring commune of Courbevoie, so do the smelly industrial buildings spreading from Clichy in the distance. Perhaps Seurat imagined that by treating the industrial realities rather in an analogous manner to that of Nicolas Poussin in *The Finding of Moses* (1638), recommended by tutors at the *École des Beaux Arts*—where the classical structures in the distance are presented as *formal* components of the pictorial, harmonic scheme—the Salon, to which Seurat submitted the painting, might have recognized the seriousness, classical-rootedness, and originality of his work. They did not, even though they had accepted the classical, idealized formalism of Symbolist hero Puvis de Chavannes (1824–1898), a major influence on Seurat himself. It is possible the Salon jurors simply felt abashed by the great size of a painting that not only seemed to obliterate aspects of the reality of the setting, but whose subject, rendered in such an apparently indifferent or undramatic manner (none of the faces addressed the onlooker), was considered beneath the moral interest of the *Beaux Arts,* especially as Seurat observed no class distinctions between the semi-clad figures. Workers lazily enjoying themselves might suggest, God forbid, indifference to hard work! Perhaps they suspected the experimental painting implied a snub of socialist indifference, combined with a subversive mixed-genre challenge to an academic body that had only relatively recently accommodated Impressionism. The Salon might be cool where Symbolism was concerned, but they could read the signs, or *read-in* the signs. *Factories* were not components of formal beauty; they might be necessary facts of life, like lavatories, but they did not strictly belong where Seurat had, as it were, placed them! Unlike Poussin's work, there was nothing either sacred or apparently "classical" in Seurat's bathers; critics would be wrong of course, but Seurat was in a minority of those who could perceive it.

Here Salon jurors might even have shared elements of the Symbolists' own detestation of industrial realism. For here perhaps is one area where we sense the Symbolists' disquiet in the presence of vaunted "progress." The industrial landscape of Asnières was no hazy mirage. When the clouds obscured the sun, and the haze vanished, those belching chimneys, manufactories, and coal-filled unloading bays would have appeared not only harshly real but positively close, encroaching on any patch of unclaimed grass or fleeting moment of leisure. Paris's population had doubled during the reign of Louis Napoleon. Asnières's own population had almost doubled in the ten years between the mid-70s and the mid-80s. The material of the material world looked considerably grubbier and the atmosphere denser in every way; it was recognized as axiomatic that excessive population increase necessitated war or otherwise threatened stability, where it had not already banished beauty.

When we take into account young Seurat's association with two of the most esoterically and spiritually inclined, committed Symbolist painters, Alphonse Osbert (1857–1939)—who took Seurat's pleasure in pointillist techniques toward creating spiritual harmonies occultly—and Alexandre Séon (1855–1917), we might suspect that what Seurat perhaps had in mind in his apparently naturalistic painting was that urge for the idealization of vision so dear to critic Joséphin Péladan, to whose *Salons de la Rose-Croix* Osbert and Séon would regularly submit paintings, as we shall see. We do not know if Seurat would have joined them, for he died at thirty-one, in 1891, shortly before the first highly successful Rose-Croix Salon was inaugurated. For, make no mistake, Seurat has seen the distant factories as symbolic, and placed them *sub specie aeternitatis,* as *forms.* And what they formalize, or give form to, is the idea of Harmony, or opposition in balanced tension: the composition *Bathers at Asnières* thus, arguably, becomes itself a symbol, something permanent, even as the government was falling apart in the wake of war. Seurat's "worker" is classicized, even recumbent, possibly indifferent. Seurat then, mistaken for an Impressionist, as he has been frequently, is *not* painting what *is,* but finally, having closely studied what *is*—the figures and location—in relation to ideal form (classical images and proportion), he is painting what *could be:* one answer perhaps to the question put by Gauguin and the Gnostics, "Where are we going?" If we penetrate *through* the painting we may envision a dreamscape of a real, that is, symbolic, spiritual heaven, alive in the artist's soul, and perhaps that of his bathers as well, enjoying a fleeting break from the System.

DECADENCE

While we can see how the political and social tremors of the nineteenth century were expressed in destabilizing frictions among factions, we should be hard placed to locate the spiritual movement we are discussing within political terms: the Hierophany was not the spiritual or literary wing of a political movement, though it has been argued that it would ultimately foster a curious political movement of its own—"Synarchy." Perhaps only Péladan would go so far as identifying his message closely to a political vantage point, that of the minority Catholic legitimists, although it must be said he interpreted that position in his own and his family's quite idiosyncratic and thoroughly idealist manner. Critic and novelist Paul Adam (1862–1920), a contributor to *La Revue Indépendante* and author of many Decadent novels, would involve himself with the political ambitions of the ultimately disgraced General Boulanger who threatened a one-man coup in 1889, supported both by disillusioned working-class leftists and by aristocrats, but we shall find no point of unity in political groups among those associated with the spiritual movement. Rather we find amid Michelet's Hierophany of Hermetists and among the intimately related spiritually and esoterically committed Symbolists a general disaffection from quotidian issues of government. This disaffection has many aspects, some of which should be quite obvious to us by now.

One important feature that *is* shared among figures in this movement is the appellation *decadent*. Decadence derives from the Latin *decedentia* and has nothing to do with the number ten. The word means quite simply "decay." It is often confused with the term *fin de siècle,* with the implication that odd, disturbing signs spring forth in the last decade of a century, possibly out of a gathered fatigue, excessive sense of self-knowledge, morbid reflection in the shadows and embers of the dying past-present, or grandiose expectations of a new era: certainly the feeling that one is living at the end of something. One of the odd signs of such an era, the reactionary, at least, will tell you, is likely to be decadence. By this the critic may mean anything from *folie de jeunesse* to sexual novelties, irresponsible experimentation, loss of reality, disregard for commonsense values—including family and *patrie*—uncommitted dilettantism, moral indifferentism, dandyism, extrovert aestheticism, unexpected and undesirable arts, drug taking, exotic religions, esoteric mysticism, occultism, astrological portents, apocalyptic excitements, political extremism, delusions of utopia, and hostility to established government, religion, and bourgeois priorities. This potpourri of negatively perceived phenomena comprises the veritable bogeyman of a certain brand of "conservative" or right wing propaganda, supported by those who feel most undermined by the "threat" of Decadence. One thinks not only of the fears stirred up weekly in the old popular Sunday papers, but of British Labor Prime Minister Harold Wilson in 1967 being unnerved by the psychedelic fashion of that year and actually suing a hippyesque pop group from Birmingham, The Move, for affronts to his political dignity, as he saw it. It seems where the 1960s were concerned, Decadence came early, even prematurely, and yet it is arguable that the twentieth century did somehow reach its end in that decade, since most of what immediately followed felt to many like a hangover, punctuated by attempts brave and silly to rekindle the flame: "Apocalypse *Then*" we might say. Or is it simply the case that for many, the sixties was a beginning, an epiphany when Decadence suddenly became *permanently* desirable, even as governments and political activists everywhere desired and desire to suppress the fun, banish the horror, and put the disruptive genie back in the bottle?

Now, it happens that much of what Harold Wilson—or indeed Richard Nixon—and their generation would have ascribed to as being decadent derived initially from French experience of the 1880s and 1890s—the Naughty Nineties as they were called in Britain and America at the time—and the image of that Decadence is a confused and highly misleading one. We might think that a Decadent movement—and such Paris did in fact have in those decades—might see itself as a movement favoring liberalization of everything, free love, liberated homosexuality, psychedelic stimulants, Bohemianism in fashions of dress, hair, music, art, decor, games, entertainment, politics, and a general "live and let live" air of color, spiritual optimism, and personal and social freedom. Well, while there are elements of truth in this characterization, it is really not what the authentic Decadents themselves thought they were about.

It is one of the unfortunate nettles of Renaissance culture that emerged across Europe in the fifteenth and sixteenth centuries that while Hellenistic and Roman culture was raised in scholarly approbation to an eminence, observers had to contend with the unpleasant fact that both of these cultures declined and ultimately fell, for all their brilliances. There was the uncomfortable feeling that a civilization that emulated them closely, or too closely, as Renaissance culture did, might similarly be doomed. Europe, spiritually permeated with residual pagan foreboding of nemesis and Christian apocalypticism never needs much persuading that "the end is nigh," or that some day, a price will be exacted for joys seized from life's fleeting embrace. Moralists tend to have the last word, and it became customary to attribute the ultimate failure or destruction of ancient classical culture to precisely those aspects of it that differed from the moral standards of the Christian Church that triumphed over it even as it succeeded it. That is to say, that falling prey to the temptations of the flesh, whether of sexual incontinence, libertinism, vengefulness, vainglorious power-seeking, or pecuniary avariciousness, the imperium became enslaved to the ever-present forces of decay and destruction, depriving itself of access to the spiritual powers of renewal vouchsafed through Christian moral conversion.

Between 1776 and 1789, English historian Edward Gibbon put a spanner in the works of that doctrine when the six volumes of his *The History of the Decline and Fall of the Roman Empire* made clear his preference for the Roman moral and civic virtues, including Stoicism, as sufficient for august civilized continuity while attributing the empire's fall to a combination of Decadence, that is decay in classical moral virtue, and Christianity itself, subtly indicted for weakening the manly virtues of the Roman citizen with Encratite otherworldliness. The Christian, according to Gibbon, was too focused on the world beyond, citizenship in heaven. The gospel of "love your enemies" had, allegedly, knocked the stuffing out of him. These factors allegedly weakened resolve, and so when the barbarians threatened—as they always did—the structure was in the end too weakened, divided, and timid to withstand serious and protracted onslaught, despite superior knowledge. Indeed, the Christian Church did not lament the loss of imperial Rome, content to take its mantle, language, and surviving structures to further its own theocratic imperialism. The Renaissance of classical culture was the work of scholars often at odds with religious authorities.

In late eighteenth-century France, philosopher-dramatist Voltaire took up a similar cudgel and bemoaned what he regarded as "Decadence," that is, decay, in the familiar civilization of the old regime. The Ancients knew what good taste was, and if decay was to be resisted, a return to classical mores was essential. He wrote to playwright Jean-François de La Harpe on 23 April 1770: "My dear boy, there is no hope of being able to re-establish good taste. We are in every way in the age of the most horrible decadence." [2] Clearly the further away France traveled spiritually or philosophically from "pure" Renaissance classicism, the more it could be seen to be in decay. With Decadence comes nostalgia, another important component for Symbolism: the pained quest for times lost.

The belief that France was on the slippery slope of decline intensified after Napoleon's defeat and the succession of political ructions discussed above. Inwardness and neurotic instability attended lack of firm ground beneath the feet. It was not quite the case that France was something of a headless chicken, or rather, cock, but that the head kept changing in a this-way, that-way flurry of self-decapitation. The guillotine was indeed the profound *symbol* of republican France—a pure product of the Age of Reason—a headless nation. One wonders if this somehow accounts for the Symbolists' near obsession with Salome, the beguiler, and her lust for the bleeding, severed head of prophet of doom, St. John the Baptist.

We are coming to the paradox that those who claimed to be Decadents were in many cases trying to *deal with* genuine decay and its gathering vacuum of spiritual direction, something they felt they had been caught up in, and were perhaps powerless to resist. Much literature, some claiming science on its side, appeared after the revolutions of 1848, alleging the modern European races were in some kind of physiological decline, neurotically cautious, nervous, even perverse. The thin, starving poet with long, greasy hair did not measure up to the statues of Praxiteles. How many artists were fit to be raised to the friezes of the imaginary Parthenon? Industrialization certainly had physiological implications for those suffering overcrowding and polluted, constrained conditions, but the "decadence" began to acquire a twist of new meaning. Rather than fear or bemoan Decadence, why not embrace it as the authentic condition of the times, and even, perhaps, work one's way through it, as Rimbaud would advocate in his personal regime of "disordering of the senses" to spark off a creative alchemy of linguistic invention? By comparison to Baudelaire and Rimbaud's embrace of the abyss, Émile Zola the realist-naturalist writer's acceptance of Decadence seems almost banal. In 1866, he wrote in *Mes Haines:* "My taste, if you like, is depraved; I enjoy very spicy reading matter, decadent works in which a sort of sensitive sickliness replaces the abundant health of the classical epochs. I am a child of my times." A more interesting understanding of what Decadence would mean to many Symbolists may be located in Théophile Gautier's preface to the posthumous edition of Baudelaire's *Les Fleurs du Mal* (1868):

> The poet of *Les Fleurs du Mal* liked what is inaccurately called the style of decadence, which is only art arrived at the point of extreme maturity which ageing civilizations discover in the rays of their setting suns: a style which is clever, complicated, scholarly, full of nuances and investigations, always drawing back the boundaries of language, borrowing from every technical vocabulary, taking colors from every palette, notes from every keyboard, striving to put back thought into that which is the most indescribable, the form in its vaguest and most fleeting contours, hearkening in order to translate them, to the most subtle confidences of neurosis, the avowals of ageing passion which becomes depraved, and the strange hallucinations of obsession turning into madness.[3]

While for many Decadence will be pilloried and calumniated for its daring, box-opening experimentation with androgyny, sexual identity and homosexual love, eroticism, fascination with femininity, and aestheticism, those who began to take up the term with an ironic pride from the first decade of the Third Republic, had a considerably more positive view of their aims. They were conscious of the spiritual decay within the propaganda and manufactured appearances of republican "glory," backed by the bayonet and the bourgeoisie, and would agree with Blake that "God is in the lowest effects as well as in the highest causes," and if Christ could sink so low as to visit the Earth and the earthy, so could they, that they might yet rise with him through the nightmare of the soul. Depraved they might appear to the eyes of the world and the worldly, but those eyes were blind to the riches to come.

New movements need new magazines. In December 1887, Anatole Baju's *Le Décadent littéraire et artistique* changed its name simply to *Le Décadent*, a word now sufficiently meaningful to require no qualification. Poet Paul Verlaine contributed to a magazine that saw its adherents as an *avant-garde* of artistic conflagration and phoenixlike renewal. As one article declared:

> The future belongs to Decadism. Born of the world-weariness of a Schopenhauerian civilization, the Decadents are not a literary school. Their mission is not to found but to destroy, to demolish the old order and prepare the embryonic elements of the great national literature of the twentieth century.[4]

It would seem then that the Decadent, whose disrupted nature was somehow symptomatic of a decay, was not subjected to it in vain, but rather had the self-knowledge, and the faith in the future, effectively *to manage decay,* to take it to the bottom of itself (*Là-bas*) as an immolating rite of cultural renewal. Again, we hear the echo of Blake: "The road of excess leads to the palace of wisdom." And more perversely, an echo of it in the ultimate "bad trip" film, Jean Luc Godard's *Weekend* (1967) in which a hippy guerilla announces amid the carnage of "the civilization of the arse" (Godard's phrase) that he can only overcome the horror of the bourgeoisie with even more horror, as an al fresco cannibal chef shoves a huge fish up a bourgeois captive's vagina. One feels Godard considered that particular fish was intended for practically everyone.

What the determined nineteenth-century Decadent might actually achieve was the creation of a new, challenging class of being. *Bored with bourgeois society?* Join the Decadents. *Disgusted with politics?* Join the Decadents. *Sick of polite art and the Salon?* Join the Decadents. *Can't stand the army?* Join the Decadents. And if you've already asked yourself all of these questions, you don't need to join the Decadents; you're one already!

Strangely perhaps, there were serious writers who saw straightaway the *spiritual* potential of the movement. One of these was philosopher,

esotericist, poet, and all-round pundit Édouard Schuré (1841–1929).
He had followed a now familiar path from initial adoration of Richard
Wagner in the 1870s to immersion in esotericism, meeting Madame
Blavatsky in 1884 and later joining the Theosophical Society. However,
his greatest guide was the French esoteric philosopher, Fabre d'Olivet
(1767–1825), whom we shall encounter in the next chapter. In 1889,
Schuré would publish his most influential work, *Les Grands Initiés*
(The Great Initiates)—the *Doors of Perception* of its time—which made
a systematic study of a series of spiritually enlightened beings, including
Jesus, Rama, and Hermes Trismegistus while examining what it took
to get there . . . to the highest. Individuals and hopefully society needed
to break through the bonds of materialism and realize spiritual reality
was reality, when to quote St. John's Gospel, "I and the Father are one"
(10:30). Initiation was the name of the game. Here is a telling extract
from the book's preface. It could have come from the pen of a kindly,
outspoken Anglican clergyman, reflecting on the spiritual meanderings
of Kathmandu-bound hippies of 1967–69:

> Never has the aspiration to the spiritual life or to the invisible
> world—an aspiration opposed by the materialistic theories of the
> scientists and by fashionable opinion—been more serious and more
> genuine. That aspiration can be found in the regrets and doubts, the
> black despair and even the blasphemies of our Naturalist novelists
> and our Decadent poets. Never has the human spirit had a more
> profound awareness of the inadequacy, the poverty, the unreality of
> this life. Never has it aspired more ardently to an invisible Beyond
> without managing to believe in it.[5]

In 1889 you could purchase the book at Bailly's place in the rue de la
Chaussée d'Antin. Now you can get it on Amazon.

RECOVERING LOST POWERS

Since we tend to think of spiritual movements in terms of conventional saintliness and exclusive concern with religious questions, it may

seem something of a leap to go from Decadent to a movement aspiring "ardently to an invisible Beyond." How could one traverse from being a downbeat poet to a vanguardist of a spiritual movement? While the word *ardent* generally is understood as indicating passion or zeal in pursuit of something, the more pointed meaning is one of burning and glowing, as in flames. Fire purifies, destroys, transforms, presages rebirth. It is a word that springs continually to mind among the Symbolist writers of the period when referring to their friends. The ardent Decadent has powers of penetration like an alchemical blowtorch; having achieved the requisite depth, he becomes, in the understanding of Jean Moréas's "Literary [Symbolist] Manifesto" (*Le Figaro*, 1886) a Symbolist, an apparently higher or more refined aesthetic calling, for Moréas also sensed an incongruity between the Decadent type as generally imagined and the high-minded Symbolist, as Moréas saw him, and wished it to be recognized that Decadent was now an outmoded identity. *Concern with the esoteric* was marked out by Moréas as a distinction of the Symbolist in contrast to the accepted idea of the Decadent. However, not every Decadent Symbolist accepted this, perhaps because the ardent Decadent had distinct advantages for perceiving himself already ranked among elite spiritual revolutionaries.

He possessed the first, essential qualification: ability and willingness to stand outside the common judgment of society, feeling essentially above it. This partly explains the attraction of the movement to aristocrats, who were, in post-Revolution French society, ambiguously placed, their political role and former prerogatives having been completely abolished in the Revolution. It also explains certain aristocratic attitudes adopted or imitated by Decadents of bourgeois backgrounds; nobility of soul counted highly, as did a cool contempt for the opposition, combined with flair for good manners and the habit of dressing as one willed. An aristocrat living on bread and cheese is an ascetic, a triumphant denier of the world, ennobling simple things, indifferent to social aspiration, his sacrifice a sign of inalienable nobility; a poor man eating bread and cheese is a poor man, his pride is defensive. As for the Decadent, he is ennobled by suffering, and suffering included the torments of love, even love denied.

What appeared to those outside the Decadent universe of sensibility as a distasteful glorying in low-life decay was to the ardent Decadent a spiritual position recommended by great initiates: rejection of the world, renunciation of its securities and the price normally paid for them, indifference to worldly standards, beyond the bribery of state promises. The interior life of the spirit has surpassed matter, the outside world has lost its determinative reality. It may sicken, it may amuse. The poet thus attains objectivity: prophetic powers of the real. He may observe decay, offer to society an undesired mirror of evil, and an equally undesired vision of the real. Spiritual psychology thus becomes art's subject matter, sowing the seeds that will germinate as surrealism, expressionism, and abstraction.

The Decadent has another advantage for making the grade in a spiritual movement. He is suspicious of "common knowledge" and bored by thoughtless verbiage. He does not like scientific materialism or mere nature; he seeks enchantment, a way to the depths. He is offended by impersonal rationalism, having inherited the romantic emphasis on personal feeling and truth known by warmth of heart, stirred by beauty. Science for him carries no mystery; it betokens a demiurgic reign of quantity: length, breadth, height, depth, weight, and measure, formulaic digits with no mystery or even, ultimately, meaning. If one knew every fact, one would still have to ask what it *meant,* for there is knowledge of fact, and there is knowledge of meaning: the former vulgar science, the latter *gnosis.* Materialist science speaks not to the soul but already suggests dehumanizing the human experience, ruling by time and dictated motion—making machines and turning men into their acolytes. Thus the appeal of Satanism in Symbolism: transgressive knowledge of occult mysteries, suppressed because feared. Why feared?—for its exposure of the world's lie. For the church had identified Satan with sexual love (that is, humanity) and with thinking for oneself. Perhaps there was more to this ambiguous figure than might be supposed. The attraction of a quest for Man's lost powers follows on the common Symbolist characterization of Lucifer as "bringer of light." Was not the "Beast" Man?

In 1874 Decadent dandy novelist and advocate of Baudelaire,

Fig. 2.3. Jules Barbey d'Aurevilly (1808–1889)

Jules Barbey d'Aurevilly (1808–1889) published *Les Diaboliques* (*The She-Devils*). Péladan would come to admire and imitate both d'Aurevilly's personal style and his literary flirtation with Satanism, mixed with eroticism and mysticism in aristocratic settings. Péladan was also much struck by the work of its illustrator, Félicien Rops. As Michelet observed, seeing him in Bailly's bookshop, Rops looked the part. No admirer of d'Aurevilly's work, the public prosecutor demanded copies be seized for public obscenity and blasphemy. D'Aurevilly claimed in his defense that *Les Diaboliques* was concerned with the battle of good and evil, a battle, one might note, that also concerned Satan.

How does the Decadent become a companion for Michelet's Hierophany, devoted to recovering Hermetic, or hidden spiritual gnosis? The answer is simple. As Blake put it: "poetry, painting and music, the three pow-ers in man for conversing with paradise that the flood did not sweep away." You begin by reading a book, or by seeing pictures, or by hearing music: the right book, the right picture, the right music—at the right time. For every one of Michelet's initiated companions, their gnostic story began with reading a book, or hearing music—predominantly that of Wagner in the first generation—or attending an art exhibition or seeing illustrations in books. These are the first steps to the paradise of genius. Through these encounters, the seeker becomes acquainted with the minds of Remarkable Men. What then normally follows are meetings sought, accidental or providential, with remarkable men physically present. And Paris had quite a few of them in this period.

Following encounter with the sympathetic exemplars while discovering a small community of companions on the way, life becomes a Quest, distinct for each individual, yet taken together, a movement: for the Spirit moves mountains as the aspirant ascends. And the medium for expressing the quest in this period is predominantly Art: the means to spiritual life, pursued through the forest of symbols to the rose garden of delight. And it must be regarded as significant that these three links to paradise, the inner life or genius of every man, appear to the Symbolist as requiring integration and synthesis through magical correspondence: a total art demonstrated at Bayreuth by Wagner, and in past history by the Magus who mastered the laws of the above and below, of sound and image, of word and imagination, who recovered the lost powers of God in Man. Thus Debussy will write a Prelude to a poem by Mallarmé, developing a style that leads to a total visual and aural experience in *Pélleas et Melisande* where painted scenery, lighting, poetry, and music will fuse together into the symbol inherent in Maeterlinck's original story (the same urge would drive film director Michael Powell post–World War II to experiment with what he called the "composed film").

It had not gone unnoticed in the gnostic *compagnonnage* that the traditional sign of the inauguration of the Age of the Holy Spirit, before the end of Time, was, according to physician Paracelsus, the return to Earth of Elias Artista, or Elijah the Artist, whose Art was understood traditionally as Alchemy—transmuting matter—but which was logically taken by the new gnostics, such as Victor-Émile Michelet, as indicating Art and Alchemy as One: the alembic for transformation was the mind of the artist. The gold was the transformative work that emerged from the fires of creativity and the surrender of the artist to the work. To produce "gold" the artist must battle through to the gold within. In Blake's words—he really was ahead of the game!—"what is now prov'd was once only imagin'd." Michelet wrote specifically regarding Elias Artista in his *Les Compagnons de la Hiérophanie* with respect to his friend, poet, and occultist Stanislas de Guaita:

> The Abstract [figure] which invokes the Rosicrucian tradition was named by Adepts, *Elias Artista*. The initiate who takes to the Great Work [of transmutation], according to which mode is appropriate, is an artist, a creator, a poet. He can be compared to the yogi of India, philosopher of the fire and the red Stone, the embodying of the magician's will, metaphysician of real knowledge, poet of beauty; he is an artist. Stanislas de Guaita is profoundly an artist. His beautiful prose, abundant, attests to his metaphysical talent.

The artist who exemplified this surrender most completely for the Symbolist generation was the "damned" figure of Charles Baudelaire whose *Flowers of Evil* poetry book (1857) invited state prosecution

Fig. 2.4. Charles Baudelaire (1821–1867)

for outrages to public morals, resulting in a hefty fine and the official suppression of six of the poems, including "Lesbos," from which these verses come:

> Lesbos, what God to judge you would make bold,
> Or damn your brows so pale and sadly grave,
> Not having weighed upon the scales of gold
> The floods of tears you've poured into the wave.
> Lesbos which God to judge you would make bold?
>
> For us, what mean the statutes of the just?
> Pride of the isles, whose hearts sublimely swell,
> Your faith as any other is august
> And Love can laugh alike at Heaven and Hell.
> For us, what mean the statues of the just?
>
> For Lesbos chose me of all men on earth
> To sing the secrets of her virgin flowers,
> Taught as a child the sacred rites of mirth
> And mysteries of sorrow which are ours.
> So Lesbos chose me of all men on earth.

Here we hear the rejection of the world's judgments in full, lyrical swing. For those who see beauty not in the thing, in the flesh itself, but in the beauty of the eternal idea, reflected in the mire of matter ruled by asphyxiating judgment, and seeing, love it, follow it wherever it may lead, this poem speaks. The doctrine that seems to underlie the stance was associated in late antique times with the gnostic Carpocrates. Carpocrates taught that since matter itself is inherently "evil," subject to decay and corruption, a prison of the soul, once the spirit has come to fruition in Man, he is free to judge whether to use matter as a means to an end, indifferent to its claims and corrosive tendencies, or whether to eschew its depths altogether and ascend through asceticism, diminishing contact with the world through discipline. The orthodox bishop of Lyon, Irenaeus, in circa 180 CE derided such fanciful notions, as he saw them as the temptations of Satan, leading to an "abyss of madness and blasphemy." The Decadent, of course, considered himself "up" for the Abyss; it was preferable to surrender to the world, its dis-conscious mediocrity and narcotic acquiescence.

Baudelaire found alchemical imagery not only a language suitable for freeing the unconscious symbols of the inner life, but useful simply in describing passage through the flames to knowledge. As Rabelais recommended, you had to "Trink" and drink deep. The prize might be expressed as admission into Rabelais's ideal gated community of good sorts, sports, gents, and ladies, with no churls, bores, or hypocrites allowed: the *Abbaye de Thélème* as described in chapter 57 of his French Renaissance satire *Gargantua and Pantagruel.* Rabelais's message written over the Abbey gates: *Fay ce que vouldras,* "Do what thou wilt." The good spirit can do no real harm if it is a freed spirit. In Baudelaire's preface "To the Reader" of his *Les Fleurs du Mal,* he is stimulated by "Satan Trismegistus," an ambiguous initiator of three powers, to open his poetic eyes to the abyss, to avoid hypocrisy, and become aware of the worst, most destructive power, *Ennui:* boredom or indifference, blindness or deafness, to the call of reality.

> Foolishness, error, sin, niggardliness,
> Occupy our minds and work on our bodies,
> And we feed our mild remorse,
> As beggars nourish their vermin.
>
> Our sins are insistent, our repentings are limp;
> We pay ourselves richly for our admissions,
> And we gaily go once more on the filthy path
> Believing that by cheap fears we shall wash away all our sins.
>
> On the pillow of evil it is Satan Trismegistus
> Who soothes a long while our bewitched mind,
> And the rich metal of our determination
> Is made vapor by that learned chemist.
>
> It is the Devil who holds the reins which make us go!
> In repulsive objects we find something charming;
> Each day we take one more step towards Hell—
> Without being horrified—across darknesses that stink.

* * *

Like a beggarly sensualist who kisses and eats
The martyred breast of an ancient strumpet,
We steal where we may a furtive pleasure
Which we handle forcefully like an old orange.

Tight, swarming, like a million parasites,
A population of Demons carries on in our brains,
And, when we breathe, Death into our lungs
Goes down, an invisible river, with thick complaints.

If rape, poison, the dagger, arson,
Have not as yet embroidered with their pleasing designs
The recurrent canvas of our pitiable destinies,
It is that our spirit, alas, is not brave enough.

But among the jackals, the panthers, the bitch-hounds,
The apes, the scorpions, the vultures, the serpents,
The monsters screeching, howling, grumbling, creeping,
In the infamous menagerie of our vices,

There is one uglier, wickeder, more shameless!
Although he makes no large gestures nor loud cries
He willingly would make rubbish of the earth
And with a yawn swallow the world;

He is Ennui!—His eye filled with an unwished-for tear,
He dreams of scaffolds while puffing at his hookah.
You know him, reader, this exquisite monster,
—Hypocrite reader,—my likeness,—my brother!

Reading these lines of power, I immediately recall two statements of perhaps the most outstandingly original artist of the Symbolist period, Odilon Redon. Undoubtedly a visual child of the poet Baudelaire, Redon asks: "Does not art draw all the force of its eloquence, its impact, its grandeur, from the things which leave to the imagination the problem of defining them."[6] "In art, everything happens by submitting docilely to the coming of the unconscious."[7] Redon would probably have been as delighted as one suspects Baudelaire would have been to have read the lines from the Gnostic Gospel of Philip discovered in Upper Egypt in 1945: "Truth did not come into the world naked, but came clothed in types and images, one will not receive truth in any other way." Insofar as the internal life presents itself to us as symbols, Symbolism then is of its essence gnostic, privileged insight that undercuts the world of the "bourgeois" or materialist acquisitor-inquisitor who lives for the tangible and who would, in Ernest Becker's phrase, like to sodomize all mystery out of existence, clinging to his security in the mud to which he has attached himself. The Symbolist has learned that the Decadence, the true decay, is the result of clinging to the corruptible, languishing too long in the mire without ever finding the spirit within it.

To help the Symbolist maintain and develop focus on the symbol, he could find at Bailly's bookshop or in the libraries of his friends, the preserved thoughts of men destined to play the role of spirit-guides in and after their earthly lifetimes.

THREE

Meetings with Remarkable Men

We can see that symbolic powers, occult powers, and
poetic powers emerge from the same source, the same
depths.

GASTON BACHELARD,
PREFACE TO RICHARD KNOWLES'S
VICTOR-ÉMILE MICHELET, POÈTE ÉSOTÉRIQUE

We label these faculties possessed by the Ancients and
cultivated in the Orient as dark, primitive, and inferior.
We happily hound and attack those such as Swedenborg
and William Blake and Victor Hugo who, despite
the scandal it causes, assert they have not vanished,
as madmen or at best imbeciles. As it happens these
abilities are precisely the ones we most need.

PIERRE DHAINAUT, *CHARLES DUITS,
UN GRAND INDÉSIRABLE*

During the 1960s and '70s, British historian Dame Frances Yates
astonished and perplexed the community of historical scholarship by
her reasoned advocacy of the view that a highly significant factor in
promoting the genesis of modern science and its representative the "scientist" was the Renaissance Hermetic movement's veneration for the
Magus. The Magus is concerned with extending his powers over all

aspects of creation, even unto immaterial realms. In analyzing the life of Dominican friar Giordano Bruno in particular (*Giordano Bruno and the Hermetic Tradition,* 1964), Yates demonstrated how the opposition of the Catholic Inquisition created the idea of Bruno as a "martyr to science"—he was burned at the stake in Rome in 1600 as an impenitent heretic—when his actual views were regarded in the main as superstitious claptrap by many nineteenth- and twentieth-century scientists operating on Newtonian lines. Rekindled in Florence after 1460, Yates declared the gnostic "Hermetic Tradition" stimulated the rediscovery of Man as a free-willed Operator in the universe, a cocreator with the divine, to whom no secret need remain hidden. Pico della Mirandola's famous "manifesto of the Renaissance," the "Oration on the Dignity of Man" (1486) began with a quote from the Hermetic *Asclepius,* attributed to Egyptian sage, Hermes Trismegistus: "A great miracle, O Asclepius, is man." Thus "occult philosophy" was not in fact "hidden philosophy"—the deliberate cultivation of esoteric obscurity—but revealed what had *formerly* been hidden to the eyes of the fearful and the ignorant; in another word, *science,* but science with esoteric and spiritual balls. Gnostic science was the vehicle of revelation.

What is truly fascinating about developments in Paris in the 1880s and '90s is that at the very time when many scientists had reached an apogee of materialist certainty verging on hubris—feeling themselves and their experimental methods utterly alien to the figure of the Mage who "dreamed but did not get real results"—at that very moment we find the Magus's position as the desirable ideal and archetype being assumed not *as the ideation of the scientist,* but as the apotheosis of the Artist. The aim? That Art trump Science. New men will embrace the new religion, universal, already hidden in spiritual symbols, which, while the traditions and cultures around them might differ superficially, exist as one in essence.

Esotericism insists there is correspondence between all things. One thing opens a door to another: all rooms are connected. The new religion was at home in the temple, whether of ancient Egypt, Amritsar, the Panthéon in modern Paris, or the contemplative mind in its study, or with like-minded friends in a café or studio. In this religion, the Magus and prophet is not the scientist who limits the universe to measure it, but the Artist who seeks the infinite, the one who accepts the "open secret" of the universe as mystery. The Artist becomes one who reveals the hidden truth, not of matter itself, but of Man and the determinative occult world behind nature. Hail the Artist as custodian of spiritual being, of idealization, of beauty, of essential truth!

The dizzy heights of this realization were given verbal form in sweeping style by Bailly bookshop habitué Joséphin Péladan: "There is no reality other than God. There is no Truth other than God. There is no Beauty other than God."[1] Péladan deduced that the greatest art had necessarily been generated for the Catholic Church and the time had come for the Church to realize that the true hierophant of the mysteries was the Artist, the Magus come to the cradle of the Lord with gifts. *His* return, as it were, was fitting prelude to the birth of the Age of the Holy Spirit, and so the artist was a priest in the true sense. He was sacrificer and bridge-builder between the invisible and the visible, between this world and the world to come: the master of the ikon and of memory. The Artist's business was with the ideal and the spiritual, not with reproducing the visual plane of nature like an ape. Paraphrasing Hermes Trismegistus, Péladan concluded: "Artist, you are Magus: Art is the great miracle." The materialist scientist will only take you further into the endless darkness of matter, progressively enslaving the spirit to rational categories and destroying the divine humanity. The Magus, of whom Leonardo was a shining exemplar, combined search into the quantitative visible world with a no less penetrating search into the invisible and symbolic world, the infinite worlds, the boundless worlds of imagination, not to be confused with merely external fantasies as in the vulgar notion of surrealism or visual whimsicality. He was a man of imagination and his genius transcended his time, perhaps time itself.

So we see the figure of the Hermetic Magus return, and his gift was to justify the position of the artist, to secure him at the heights, or in the words of the late historian James Webb: "It was in the occult that the artist found a definition of his own position."[2] Hermetism made exalted sense of the Artist and his peculiar life and vocation. It thus became desirable for the new artist, who, like Redon, found the "ceiling" of the Impressionists too low for comfort, to explore occult traditions, to partake more fully in the insights of the condemned gnosis. For this purpose, the *L'Art Indépendant* shop in the rue de la Chaussée d'Antin and the *Librairie du Merveilleux* in the rue de Trévise became essential calling points, oases of the ideal freedom. Fountains of inspiration, the shops ordained an apostolate bearing messages into the artists' apartments, studios, informal salons, and café meetings. Symbolism and Occultism conjoined in mutual waves that would rise into an aesthetic flood, rolling through the streets of Paris in an attempt to sweep away the barricades of materialism, to oppose the barbarians at home and abroad with unearthly Beauty and the power of the Spirit. After all the historic, failed revolutions that promoted what was perceived to be Paris's decline into *decadence,* a spiritual revolution was afoot. Its weapon: Art, art in its fullest sense, art perceived as the exercise of the "High Science," that is to say, Hermetic magic.

What in fact were the dominant occult ideas that appealed to the companions of the hierophany—which is to say, the *manifestation of the sacred?*

Other than the broad background provided by the Renaissance Hermetic tradition and its child, Rosicrucian alchemical Theosophy, the ideas that really chimed came from Louis-Claude de St. Martin (1743–1803), Fabre d'Olivet (1767–1825), Éliphas Lévi (1810–1875), Helena Petrovna Blavatsky (1831–1891), and Alexandre St. Yves, Marquis d'Alveydre (1842–1909).

ST. MARTIN

Some readers will undoubtedly have heard of "Martinism." A thought-world of that name coalesced in our period around the works and tradition gathered about the figure of Louis-Claude de St. Martin, a most extraordinary mind.[3]

In 1768, when he was about twenty-five, St. Martin joined the quasi-Masonic Order of Elect Cohens (Priests) of the Universe, based in Bordeaux and founded by the no less extraordinary Martinès de Pasqually (1709?–1774). St. Martin worked as Pasqually's secretary until 1771, learning of an initiated tradition Pasqually identified as one of authentic Jewish Christianity. Pasqually's "Treatise on Reintegration" taught that though in rupture from his primal state as having been made in God's image, Man could be returned to his first estate as a spiritual being. We see immediately the idea so central to mystical Symbolists: the recovery of lost powers, the rebuilding of the link with the source of spiritual symbols.

According to Pasqually, the original Man is man-God and his restoration is redemption from the slough of decaying matter. St. Martin experienced Pasqually's seven grades of progressive initiation before arriving at the highest grade: *Réau Croix,* in which grade theurgic rituals invoked divine energies, "spiritual and intelligent beings," that is, angels. Pasqually's nonword *Réau* suggests, for ill-defined linguistic reasons, "redness," in relation to Adam—made of red earth—and the

Fig. 3.1. Louis-Claude de St. Martin (1743–1803)

red powder of alchemy, spiritualized sacrificial blood, and of course the "rosy" cross. A Symbolist could immediately relate this idea to the work of imagination that made for transformative religious art, such as Delacroix's angels mural for the Chapel of the Holy Angels at the Church of St. Sulpice in Paris that so intrigued Maurice Barrès (*Le mystère en pleine lumière,* The Mystery in Plain Light, published posthumously in 1926).

St. Martin learned that for Pasqually the word *mason* simply meant "man" in his role as a worker or builder of the true human image. Pasqually's mason is thus a creative artist, with *mason* a suitable epithet for painter, musician, or poet. Alchemy was directly linked to the geometry of building, of projection of forms, as it was to music and rhythm and meter and melody and mathematics. Artists found inspiration here too, in the process of creativity and the choosing of appropriate forms to express the living essence of symbols.

According to Pasqually, the first Man was Priest King of the Universe, so he was until his ego (self-reflection) overwhelmed him. To return to universal being as a reflection of God with all-round vision, man must be reconciled to his original spiritual state. For Pasqually's followers, reconciliation ensued through progressive theurgic experience. Manifestations of an apparently supernatural character that attended theurgic rituals were called "passes" or "luminous glyphs." They were to be taken only as signs that reconciliation was taking place. The "Thing," *La Chose,* was the important objective: *that* was the work, or presence, of God. The "pass" signified the presence of the Thing. One had to concentrate on the Thing. As with the Symbolist, experience of nature, however extraordinary, was not to be embraced for itself but only of what was signified beyond it. Likewise, the idea of Woman as Beauty was fraught for those who identified image with essence. Symbolists were fascinated by the image of the questing knight caught up in woman's hair. She signifies beauty—a divine idea—but will entangle the aspiring knight in lower nature should he, content with the image below him, lose sight of the Grail. Image-making is fraught with serious pitfalls.

Theurgic magic was the means for recovering Adam's pristine

pre-Fall faculties. Theurgy could open the eyes of divine vision, to see the underlying order from which the natural order was derived. The natural world had not created itself. Man could never have realized this thought if it had. Man would have no concept of God or spirit unless spirit and God were there within him. Our ideas about these things derive from the primal Ideas themselves, though our grasp of them may be weak or become distorted through inappropriate applications of reason or blind logic, which can operate only on what it knows for sure. But we know very little and cannot know more by believing we know everything or even nearly everything. There is no limit to divine knowledge, however, and the highest knowledge is revealed from within. The Bush of Moses appeared aflame because Moses's mind was truly alight and could see the occult light emanating from the tree's form. The natural order could not of itself provide that which is beyond itself. Such was the fallacy of materialism. Were we material in essence, we should— unable to know anything else—be content. But we are not content; we hunger for God, whether we are aware of it or not. Were it true that spiritual reality is, as materialists maintain, "merely" imagination, then what use imagination in forming science? Imagination is vital in developing rational orders, for what is now accepted as "fact" first existed as imagination, invisible to the eye, apparently "unreal," even a dream, having no measurable dimension. The true scientist accepts inspiration, that is, to be "in-spirited," or enlightened by imagination—literally, to receive divine breath. In the spirit, our blindness fades. Imagination is fundamentally spiritual in nature.

St. Martin's remarkable book *Of Errors and of Truth, or Men Recalled to the Universal Principle of Science* (1775) offered as timely a critique of the dominance of "reason" as William Blake, across the Channel, offered in his *Book of Urizen;* the seers apparently unknown to one another. True enlightenment, or illumination, surpasses reason's reach both in source and conclusion, being a divine gift, not the product of sense experience or of mental calculations, which, while assisting the exercise of science, do not encompass its source. The true cause of everything is an intelligent and active Being. It cannot be objectified or measured, not being an object of our knowing, but is that which enables us to know anything at all. In simple language, it is our "savior" whom we, blind beings, thank not in our acts and will. And yet this knowledge granted from "above" should delight us, for we have the gift of imagination that can free us from many obstacles, and perhaps when the time comes, everything that opposes our true, that is divine, will. Reason unaided cannot begin to imagine what the True Cause is capable of. Reason could not calculate what the visionary has seen, gifted by God in his highest awareness, touched from above with the gift of sight and will. This wine is poured only into new wineskins; one must admit one's thirst and prepare the vessel to receive.

One can imagine the power of these thoughts on any person feeling oppressed by excessive rationalist materialism and whose mind remained flexible and free from that sclerosis of the conscience that afflicts those anxious for the worldly nod of approval: Satan's ambiguous wink. St. Martin taught that the Fall of Man is to be overcome. Man's faculties, which were once a mirror, are currently scattered, fragmented as it were by the impact of the Fall, or crash. His abilities are not synthesized; disordered, they work against one another. Much that is taught as order is, in fact, misunderstanding engendering greater disorder. Reorder the faculties and the knowledge we have will work for us, not against us, and we against one another. For the light of God to be reflected accurately in the mirror of our faculties, they must be reunified by regeneration. Regeneration in turn generates new art and new science. According to St. Martin, human dignity can be rectified through the virtue of the sacrificial act of the *Réparateur,* or Christ the Repairer. What separates humankind from the primal man-God state can be overcome by a first step of faith in the virtue of Christ's act, the self-giving of the perfect, unfallen man: the revelation of our true selves.

The politicians and much of the church ignored the authentic "rights of Man." If Man embraced the work of regeneration, he would inherit his birthright as a son of God: a world renewed, but Man needs to discover and recover what it is in him that is being addressed from above. He must listen with correct understanding of what he is, of what in him is being addressed. Our material-tuned ears will not hear, our material-fixated eyes will not see. Our words are grunts. Our apologies are lies. We must reenter our true nature. Such conceptions informed St. Martin's reading of the potential of Mesmerism, the work that pioneered hypnosis and psychoanalysis led by St. Martin's contemporary, Franz Anton Mesmer, whose work continued to fascinate Europe with demonstrations of "magnetic" hypnotism, linked to mysticism genuine or spurious. Pasqually's views on reconciliation and St. Martin's understanding of the work of the Repairer may be not so far from Jung's concept of individuation, and, let us recognize, Jung was a child of the Symbolist era.

In 1790 St. Martin received a massive jolt after he discovered the works of Jacob Böhme (1575–1624), the "Teutonic Theosopher" who was such an enormous influence on spiritual philosophy and esoteric Pietism in the eighteenth century. Böhme understood that the organ God addressed in Man's restoration to full creative potential was the *heart*. The transformation of the heart was at the core of his many insights into the way God operates in Man and Nature. The dead German showed the living Frenchman, enduring the onset of the French Revolution, that it was the divine *Sophia,* the feminine spirit of Wisdom that enables rebirth into our true selves; she does the work without recourse to theurgic magic. St. Martin began to think seriously about how to save and change the world, caught up as it was in the loss of divine leadership. Embracing the Western esoteric tradition, St. Martin envisioned a government of people chosen by God to lead humanity, their having first overcome selfhood and become concentrated on the divine image through intimacy with divine Wisdom.

Crucially, in terms of Symbolist understanding, Böhme taught a system of dynamic opposites. God is Fire (Father) and Light (Son), or Love *and* Wrath, depending on one's spiritual position. Their contact initiates the first spark of dynamic creativity. Furthermore, the original Man was not male but androgynous. Androgyny fascinated Symbolists who wished to recover a shameless and spiritual sense of the feminine in woman and man, combining feeling and strength. The conception derives from the Gnostic belief that the original Man or "Anthrōpos" was masculo-feminine, whose spiritual nature only split when fallen into the world of manifestation or matter—thus Eve was drawn out of

Adam in his "sleep" or unconsciousness. Matter is based on a binary system, or opposites in dynamic tension. When harmony reigns, the dynamism moves upward to more spirit. When the tension becomes too disturbed in one or another direction, the downward path is taken, generating bad. Man's ideal being is androgynous. Getting caught up in the lust of physical sex alone serves to divide the sexes in cruelties, for man is essentially spiritual and failing to see this, becomes divided against himself and everything around him. When both parties are in love with the ideal, the heaven of an erotic ideal becomes possible, though such remains the ideal, distant goal of a spiritual quest. The spiritual artist ought to seek the ideal in man or woman. These ideas are evident throughout the corpus of Symbolist art where beauty in individuals is always either spiritual or dangerous, if of flesh alone.

Importantly, St. Martin regarded progress on Earth as a by-product or manifest registering of spiritual evolution. This too is crucial. What is real for St. Martin is not history in the sense of what we perceive with the senses: events and changes of every kind recorded in conventional histories—usually influenced by prejudice—but what events *signify*. What appearances in nature signify is the work of reparation, of returning to God's reflection in Wisdom, or of the loss of reparation. Signs point to the world of symbol. History then becomes the expression of symbolic truths in forms, a conception chiming in with the poets' insight as to the value of the ordinary human world at its superficial level, justifying engagement with symbolic schemes expressed as mythology. As Michelet noted, however, the true symbol was rarely grasped in its essence by many of the young artists. They tended to get lost in superficial interest in the mythological, mistaking allegory for symbol, and often concentrated too heavily on the trees of the symbolic forest, missing the *wood,* and above all the spiritual sap. Simply the aesthetic *style* of Symbolist art could be intoxicating and diverting.

The purpose of the ongoing spiritual *apocatastasis* (restitution) was beyond the natural order as we know it, or think we know it, but the visible order would be transformed by the spiritual movement: "on earth as it is in heaven." Significant world events, from this point of view, still had real meaning. If you could read them, they pointed to reality. The more spiritually determined Symbolists attempted to read the world. St. Martin himself interpreted the French Revolution, in retrospect and without denying its horrors, as embodying the quest for right order, stimulated by the spiritual imperative for reconciliation and reintegration. Its horror came from the limitations of its proponents' profound disharmony, their alienation from the intelligent and active Cause. Their violence represented a kind of by-product of long compounded disregard for the True Cause: a kind of punishment. A sacrifice, it foreshadowed a more real liberation of humanity to come.

St. Martin gave the intelligent artist a view of the super-dynamics of the process and purpose of creativity. He also gives us a clue why that word *ardent* was used by Martinists to describe their commitment. From the mystic writings of Madame Guyon and others, St. Martin praised what he called the "hommes de désir." *Men of Desire* are those centered on bringing forth the divine life out from under the fallen condition, thus imitating Christ, incarnating the Wisdom to expiate by personal suffering the sins of the world. One sees this in the heart of van Gogh. Blake called for his "arrows of desire," the will to the highest, to transcend the world and its reasons. The English poet Samuel Taylor Coleridge wrote of the power of the imagination to "disembody the soul of fact," to strip away the familiar film of nature, to locate the symbolic world and give it form, movement.

Observers of Symbolist art are often mistaken in making judgments about the form—the image they see—without making any effort to penetrate it. The work of art, from the esoteric point of view, is not the object produced, but the *whole* art of which the product is a part, and part only. When we enter a house, we do not stop at the door. Disembodying the soul of fact became the very essence of the Symbolist aim, to reveal hidden dimensions to reality: an aim most visible in that split-off group, the Nabis or prophets whose members included abstract pioneers Paul Sérusier, Maurice Denis, and Charles Filiger, who were in 1888 companions of Gauguin in the Pont-Aven school, based in Brittany, before Gaugin's brief sojourn with van Gogh in Aries.

It must be said, however, that on account of Symbolism's high aim, its proponents shot their arrows at an elusive target and often missed entirely. Part of the problem for the original Symbolists was the inherited constraint on abstraction. Representative art always looks like what you see, rather than what the artist might be trying to re-present in a form. For example, in representational art you cannot paint pure space alone. You must, to create space, paint that which limits or obstructs it, thus "creating space." In pure abstraction you can remove all impediments, but only at the cost of identification! And who is to say it is space you have created, if you have removed limits?

Perhaps, from the point of view of the Companions of the Hierophany, St. Martin's key doctrine was that the Imagination is the spiritual part of humanity, that it possesses the vision of all things, and that through imagination, we grasp the spiritual unity of the universe.

FABRE D'OLIVET

We heard in the last chapter how Édouard Schuré, the author of the highly influential book *The Great Initiates* (1889), owed much of his inspiration not only to Wagner but also to a generally neglected French esotericist, Antoine Fabre d'Olivet, who had died long ago in 1825. D'Olivet's curiously original worldview would also be a major influence on Martinist followers of St. Yves d'Alveydre who became something of a distant father-confessor to the Companions of the Hierophany (most especially Gérard Encausse) and who himself took wholesale many of the obscure Fabre d'Olivet's ideas.

Between 1800 and 1805, impacted by the ideas of Pythagoras and his followers, Fabre went through a spiritual crisis. Pythagorean ideas concerning how numbers related to abstract truths about the structure

Fig. 3.2. Antoine Fabre d'Olivet (1767–1825)

of the world and the nature of the soul in the world burst into Fabre's worldview as a profound revelation leading to an embrace of the idea of a Unity behind all phenomena, a unity that was also alpha and omega, origin and purpose of all. Complementing St. Martin's assessment of the value of phenomenal life, d'Olivet emphasized the idea that the life process we live represents a working out of a process of reintegration, where diversity and duality are harmonized into unity. Salvation lay in returning to the One. Fabre then introduced an idea whose impact on Martinism would be massive. Attempting to account for his spiritual experience, and recognizing it was not peculiar to himself, Fabre posited the existence of what he called the "Tradition." We shall meet this word directly in the thought of Péladan who maintained he supported monarchy, *tradition,* and hierarchy, in other words, as he saw it: the Ideal. The esoteric meaning of that word *tradition* is often passed over. It is effectively an initiatic code word. Likewise in d'Alveydre, the Tradition becomes a kind of historical force whose social opponent is anarchy where anarchy is simply understood as *life without the Tradition.*

What did Fabre mean by the Tradition?

The idea is closely linked to the Rosicrucian-Hermetic understanding of the "Dignity" of Man: the restoration of the primitive, that is, original human understanding. Fabre concluded that Tradition must exist in all people at some level, since he had inherited it as a revelation from within himself to himself. Evident in ancient civilizations, Tradition must have been transmitted from long ago. For d'Olivet, this primitive world was not one of unevolved ignorance but of paradisal harmony, pure, original, and profoundly simple. The foundation document of Rosicrucianism, the *Fama Fraternitatis* (published in 1614 in Kassel), declared the revelation of knowledge stimulated by the unseen fraternity of initiated brothers was so that "Man might recover his true dignity and worth." This would be accomplished by Wisdom (*Sophia*), poured out "so richly" on mankind by "the only wise and merciful God"; its signs included the renewal and reducing of "all arts to perfection."[4]

For Fabre the Tradition had to have predated the earliest civilizations (dated at 4500 BCE) since the civilizations were only possible with its guidance, for where deviation took place, collapse would follow. Applying this theory to the nineteenth century, civilization's decay resulted from loss of contact with the Tradition. This is absolutely vital to understand if we are to grasp why the Companions of the Hierophany embraced so many aspects of Rosicrucianism and of Hebrew Kabbalah (meaning "tradition received"), and what their hope for their civilization was in attempting to restore the lost ideal.

Art must represent the Tradition.

According to Fabre, the Tradition's identifiable transmission line was from the Egyptians to Moses, and from Pythagoras and Orpheus to Jesus. Schuré took up the idea as the essential structure for his book *The Great Initiates,* which insightfully saw the Decadents as the seed-ground for renewal of spiritual understanding. Schuré saw its consonance with the esoteric transmission promulgated by Madame Blavatsky. According to Fabre d'Olivet, the great initiates were divine men in full reception of the Tradition, hence Jesus could say: "Had ye believed Moses ye would have believed me" (John 5:46). Having fully realized the Tradition, these men could work the essential task: to bind Will to Providence. By *providence* is meant God's foreknowledge, the mind that sees before we see, expressing God's will to provide what is necessary for the Good.

D'Olivet was familiar with followers of St. Martin. Indeed, the Pasquallian concept of Elect Priests of the Universe complemented that of the bearers of the Tradition, as did that of St. Martin's ideal government of men chosen by God, in love with God, and receptive to God. And that receptiveness included the gift of interpreting aright both spiritual texts and human history and current affairs whose chaotic character tends to cloud even the best ordinary minds. That interpretative task Fabre tried to assist by making it clear in his book *The Hebrew Language Restored* (1816) that usual translation of the Greek Septuagint (Old Testament) was a literal, not esoteric translation. As with the Symbolists, what met the eye was not the essential substance. Somewhat anticipating Éliphas Lévi's idea that miracles had explanations if one knew the requisite magical science, d'Olivet cured a deaf mute by putting the fifteen-year-old Rodolphe Grivel in a "magnetized sleep"—following Mesmer's hypnotic ideas—whereupon he awoke in the mute the "volitive" faculty, that is, *the will,* by drawing it forth by sympathy transmitted in the "universal vital fluidity" posited by Mesmer. Treated in January 1811, the cure hit the newspapers, whereupon Napoleon Bonaparte forbade any repeat since it contradicted what official science believed of Mesmer's theories!

D'Olivet regarded conventional history as a kind of deaf mute, incapable of yielding intelligibility until, as it were, magnetized by understanding. D'Olivet applied his understanding to contemporary philosophical problems. Where Immanuel Kant insisted philosophy was not equipped to assess the truth-value of revealed statements— thus erecting a divide between matters of faith and reason—Fabre assessed Kant as one ignorant of the Tradition by which Man is body, soul, and spirit; Kant confused rationality with reason. Rationality is of the soul, *reason* is of the spirit, according to Fabre. Reason for Fabre is better rendered as "intellect informed by spirit" or spiritual intellect, equivalent to the Greek *nous* or higher reason: the "King" faculty according to Plotinus, and the *neschamah* of the Kabbalist. For Fabre, reason draws on the spiritual source of the universe's intelligibility. It is a mirror of heaven, reflecting the divine mind. It is the means by which humankind receives higher knowledge. Rational statements divorced from this source lack universality. They may be logical within their own terms but are maimed in application, being dependent on sense experience alone. The soul is understood here as the human passions and feeling; the spirit belongs to the higher unity, surpassing ordinary understanding. Spiritual teaching addresses this faculty. The mind receives, and what the higher mind receives constitutes the Tradition.

From d'Olivet's perspective, Kant, along with a vast quantity of post-Kantian philosophy, attempts vainly to submit a higher faculty to a lower one. This explains the sadness inherent in filmmaker Jean Renoir's observation—so dear to Orson Welles—of human behavior: "Everyone has his reasons"—including the corrupt cop of Welles's masterpiece, *Touch of Evil* (1956). Such reasons, derived from the soul, unenlightened by the spirit are insufficient in essential judgments. Here Fabre was offering to artists who came after him the essential tools for combatting the concretion of scientific rationalism that was producing, and is still producing, sclerosis in the culture. And still the churches condemn or are indifferent to esotericism!

In his book *Cain, the Dramatic Mystery of Lord Byron* (1823) written to rebut Lord Byron's popular play *Cain,* which Fabre believed would promote a loss of faith in England when England's problems necessitated faith, Fabre represented Cain as "Will," Abel as "Providence." The separation of Will and Providence is ruinous for humankind, engendering perpetual cycles of conflict between *hommes volatifs* who rely on their own will, and *hommes providentiels* who trust in God's love for humanity. The murder of Abel then is the Luciferian suppression of Providence by Will and is a sign in human history. How history turns out depends on how Man responds to Will, Providence, and Destiny. In *Cain,* Adam and Eve respond to Abel's murder by producing new son Seth. Seth represents Destiny or blind fate, and history then becomes a conflict between sons of Seth who submit to necessity and work with nature through science, and sons of Cain who champion anarchic liberty. The conflict is endless, and though humankind cries out for Providence, the "providential men" no longer walk the Earth. All we have is our limited knowledge of a few such beings, men like Moses, Orpheus, Buddha. Providence can only work indirectly, through channeling humanity's willfulness toward an ultimate apocatastasis: reintegration of Adam and establishment of the Ideal. The *potential* is there in the essence of the individual, like the germ of a seed, but its realization requires an active, guided Will.

The theory is easily compatible with the Symbolist approach to nature and human beings. The ordinary doctor sees only an incomplete human being—an impression—but the good doctor sees health in the completion of the being's potential: drawing forth the hidden will and "magnetizing" the mute capacities. One thinks of Redon's complaint that the "ceiling" of the Impressionists was too low. They saw only what the "vegetable eye," to use a Blakean phrase, could see, and missed entirely the depth, being afraid to look into the abyss.

Symbolist drama reflected Fabre's view that mere history, or "positive history" simply records events without spiritual signification;

"allegorical history" on the other hand, deals with events that may have never happened as presented but that rearranged show the spiritual destiny of humanity, and while "unreal" are more true, encouraging the ardent to make the unreal real, or address the dream as both real and as potential reality. In Jean Cocteau's words: "The unreality of the fable becomes the truth."

Combined with St. Martin, Fabre d'Olivet made a strong case for the establishment of a theocracy. This was and is practically impossible for ordinary democracies since they perpetually exhibit conflict between men of will and men of destiny. Many are taught that democracy ensures liberty. Fabre would defer from this. For him, liberty is the essence of a volitional force reacting against Destiny, and this urge not to submit is a sign of the development of the spark or germ of divine will. When activated in the individual, ordinary will and destiny are put in their place. The aim of illuminated government would be the cultivation of the germ in all people, such being the only justification for the responsibility it bears. Any person receptive to this conception in its depth would look at ordinary dramas of government with at the very least a wizened eye, wise to the delusion of the quick fix in time for the next election, and wary of all but the most banal promises. Of course, in Fabre's day the idea of a government of men chosen by God was more conceivable as a possibility if the King or Emperor could be persuaded of its wisdom as a body of advice. You might persuade an individual such a revolution in government was most desirable; you will never persuade two or more opposed parties to look up to a higher authority, for to do so would expose their essential nature, according to d'Olivet's understanding. Nor, given their willfulness and love of conflict, could they avoid demonstrating their inadequacy. Of course we may justly ask: Who is to know when an individual is God-chosen? Clearly the establishment of such an ideal is a very, very long-term project indeed, but who is to say it has not yet begun somewhere? Fabre d'Olivet had faith that humankind must eventually attain what Christ demonstrated, made possible by the exercise of will trusting in Providence: a leap no doubt into the invisible.

* * *

I think one can detect the presence of Fabre d'Olivet's ideas just under the surface, and sometimes, quite explicitly, in Victor-Émile Michelet's treatment of the cofounder or "reviver" of the *Kabbalistic Order of the Rose-Croix* (1888), Stanislas de Guaita, as a poet. Fabre favored using agricultural imagery to depict the initiation of the human being and his development into knowledge of Tradition. He was very fond of the symbol of the "seed" as containing the potential, even to the extent of retranslating the first few words of the Book of Genesis. Fabre took "In the beginning" in its Hebrew and its meaning as *In principio,* in principle, that is, *in potential.* God's first creation was a potential, a seed that would grow, subject to cultivation. Michelet described de Guaita's early poetry as "youthful gaucheries" that announced "in germ [or seed-like] the depth of this spirit," before referring to de Guaita's poem "The Alchemist" that shows the poet's aspiration "as a disciple of Paracelsus to fulfill the birth-destiny of 'the century of light,' which, he says, is ours. He was at the same time a poet and a passionate chemist engaged in his laboratory."

Michelet goes on to recall how de Guaita's poetry invoked universality, stressing invocation over evocation. Traditionally, in magic, you evoke demons but invoke angels. Michelet says de Guaita invoked, adding: "allegory is not phantasmagoria." He means that devilry consists in uncontrolled thought, and manifests as the merely fantastic, disordered work when thought is not sublimated in the higher light of conscience-consciousness. This leads to a consideration of de Guaita as young man committed to higher order, not demonic anarchy, as his enemies alleged. He then makes explicit de Guaita's participation in the concept of tradition, which one can tell has become a key component of Michelet's thinking, as, when his account was published in 1937, Michelet was leader of the Parisian Martinist community:

> Of a powerfully classical culture, he [de Guaita] guarded the taste of artistic orthodoxy. As much poet as adept, he was a servant of tradition. For an intelligent person, the secret of his creation, is to adapt his personality to a tradition. An art without tradition would

only provide amusement for barbarians. It would be but a passing singing in the wind. A solitary visionary, unattached, with no link to an initiatic chain, can exist, sometimes sublime, but always stumbling, such is a Swedenborg, a Louis Michel [Louis Michel Eilshemius 1864–1941, American artist of visionary scenes]. One of the strengths of de Guaita was his fidelity to the traditions he revealed. He possessed, to a degree rarely attained, the sense of order. Disorder shocked him. . . . He constructed his edifice with the rigor of the good architect, and this "King of Black Magic" is in fact a model of orderliness. It is only in a well-constructed monument that one perceives the arrangement and the details in the penumbra.[5]

The Marquis Stanislas de Guaita, budding Symbolist poet, arrived in Paris from Lorraine in 1880 to be joined by his school friend, writer Maurice Barrès, to pursue literary lives with their friends, Edouard Dubus and Victor-Émile Michelet. According to occultist Freemason Oswald Wirth (1860–1943), who would in time serve as de Guaita's secretary, it was de Guaita's friend, Parnassian poet, journalist, and author of risqué novels Catulle Mendès who introduced Stanislas de Guaita to the works of Éliphas Lévi around the time de Guaita published his occult-inspired poetry *La Muse Noire* (The Black Muse, 1883).[6] Reading Éliphas Lévi was a bombshell for de Guaita. From that moment he began collecting and researching everything he could on the occult and soon built up an impressive library. He believed he had found his true path in life, and in pursuing it soon met Péladan, "Papus" (Gérard Encausse), and Charles Barlet (Albert Faucheux, 1838–1921) who together with their friends would establish their brand of Rosicrucianism in Paris.

We do not know precisely what it was in the writings of Éliphas Lévi (1810–1875) that fired de Guaita up to such a pitch of enthusiasm. One suspects de Guaita was looking to justify a step that was already in him, and something in the accessible reasonableness and warm urbanity of that "Professor of Transcendental Magic" christened Alphonse Louis Constant provided it. De Guaita was not alone in his enthusiasm for the late mage of Montparnasse who had spent his youth as a failed ordinand for the Catholic priesthood followed by life in his twenties

Fig. 3.3. Éliphas Lévi in 1872 (1810–1875)

and thirties as a rampant, romantic socialist and fearless feminist activist convinced his political creed was bound up with a coming age of the Holy Spirit. Ever since the publication of his *Dogme et Rituel de la Haute Magie* (*Dogma and Ritual of the High Magic*) in Paris between 1854–56 inaugurated a run of explanatory books about Magic, Éliphas Lévi had enjoyed a small, devoted following that in the 1860s extended to Great Britain. That following grew markedly with the Decadent movement's openness to occultism and the penetration of Theosophy after 1875.

ÉLIPHAS LÉVI

Perhaps the transformation of activist Alphonse Louis Constant into the Hebraicized version of his name, Éliphas Lévi, can best be seen in a quotation from Lévi's unpublished manuscript of 1870 *Les Portes de l'Avenir* (The Doors to the Future). It shows the canny wisdom and objectivity released in him after meeting the Polish visionary mathematician Józef Maria Hoene-Wronski (1776–1853) in Paris in 1852:

Liberty, Equality, Fraternity! Three words which seem to shine are in fact full of shadow! Three truths which, in coming together, form a triple lie! For they destroy one another. Liberty necessarily manifests inequality, and equality is a leveling process that does not permit liberty, because the heads that rise higher than others must always be forced down to the mean. The attempt to establish equality and liberty together produce an interminable struggle . . . that makes fraternity among men impossible.

What a tragedy this wisdom was not absorbed by the socialist and communist movements in time for the twentieth century—how much misery might have been spared the human race, then and now! Lévi shows a better path for humanity. This path the companions of the Hierophany recognized. Lévi insisted that faith would continue to be a necessity for human beings. Between the known and the unknown, even conventional science always requires faith, since we learn by leaps, and certainty requires experience. Religion provides faith; experience provides science. He identified the highest Reason with God, distinguishing it, like Fabre d'Olivet, from mere rationality and the ability to calculate. This aspect of Lévi's doctrines made acceptance of his esoteric insights easier for the strong Roman Catholic representation in Occult Paris.

The Catholic Church of the late nineteenth century built much of its antiscientific stance on the tradition of miracles in the church, wrought by saints in imitation of Christ. Lévi showed a kind of transition doctrine that accepted the Catholicity of the miraculous while permitting an initiated understanding for adepts. So-called miracles had explicable causes. Those familiar with the fullest science of these causes could manipulate them, even though results appeared as miraculous interventions into the expected, natural order. For the initiated, this demonstrated the unity of all religions. The uninitiated, however, would take such a realization as reason to discard his or her particular faith. The adept should therefore refrain from revealing their innermost secrets to the general public. While this stance might be criticized for obscurantism or worse, it is simply generous good sense. The path to initiation is open to all who sincerely seek it, according to their lights. If we could all make an atomic bomb out of a packet of corn flakes and a lump of sealing wax, it were better we were never told of it. "This fish is not for everybody" and most are content with that.

It is also a stance explaining perhaps why those seeking in Lévi's books actual guidelines to performing magic on a do-it-yourself basis are disappointed. Some have concluded that this was simply cover: Lévi was a charlatan who couldn't actually perform the miracles he attested as being possible in theory to adepts. If he was not an adept, he had no right to speak with authority on the subject. However, it is arguable that Lévi was not trying to reestablish Renaissance or medieval magical practices, but was addressing a new, coming scientific era, attempting to form a rapprochement he believed was inevitable when science and occult doctrines would eventually work in harmony in the appropriate social atmosphere, that is to say, in the New Age of Holy Spirit he believed would begin around the year 2000 when "Enoch" would become precursor of a messianic age. Traditionally associated with knowledge and science, Enoch announced the enslavement of the dark angels that had ruled the Earth. That is why Lévi distinguished High Magic from mere or goetic magic. The training he was providing was predominantly training of the mind, a refinement of attitudes and plenitude of understanding. This would not come automatically and could not be simply acquired by rote. "Many are called; few are chosen" (Matthew 22:14).

There is support for this view, not only in Lévi's writings, but also in testimonies of those who knew him. On 3 December 1861, founder-member of the English *Societas Rosicruciana in Anglia,* Kenneth Mackenzie, interviewed Lévi in his apartment at 19 avenue de Maine, Paris, an event recorded in the journal the *Rosicrucian and Red Cross* in May 1873. Lévi showed the Englishman a prophecy attributed to Paracelsus. It predicted the rise of Napoleon, the downfall of the Papacy—that is, its political power—the restitution of the kingdom of Italy, which took place in 1861, and the ultimate ascendancy of occult sciences as a means of restoring general harmony in society. The prevalence of this idea explains also the enthusiasm for Theosophy that appeared in the year Lévi died (1875), the year in which self-styled "Logos of the Aeon" Edward Alexander Crowley was born.

Apart from philosophical wisdom, there were some essential guidelines left as part of Lévi's legacy for the progress of Magic after his death.

Lévi passed on the traditions of Trithemius, Paracelsus, and Henry Cornelius Agrippa, especially with regard to the idea of Man as a microcosm, a little universe, corresponding in his nature to the formation principles of the universe *in extenso*. The stars are differentiated in space but not in substance. The aim of the adept is the linking of the "above" with the "below," the classic Hermetic-gnostic objective. There exist entities on planes other than the visual, animal, vegetable, and mineral worlds, though these latter worlds have correspondences to spiritual entities. The adept must form a complete model of these relationships through initiation. Communication with these proposed entities is traditionally effected by signs and talismans used with respect to the system of correspondences available. Lévi struggled here with a maimed, unsystematic tradition successors have since refined.

Like Fabre d'Olivet, Lévi regarded the Hebrew language as a fundamental voice of the creative spirit, a language of creation, though its full meaning was in no wise obvious but, again, required initiated understanding. The existing body of reflection on that understanding was of course Kabbalah, received tradition from adepts of old. Moses, it was believed, worked miracles by it that captivated the attention of the Egyptian magi.

Lévi was particularly noteworthy for taking up a casual suggestion of Antoine Court de Gébelin (1725–1824) that while there were twenty-two tarot trumps, there were also twenty-two letters in Hebrew. Lévi popularized the linkage as definitive, bringing into practical application further correspondences between the four tarot suits and four letters of the tetragrammaton (Yod-He-Vau-He: constituting God's name), and the ten numbered cards of each suit with the ten Sephiroth, or emanations of the Kabbalistic Tree of Life, which first appeared during the middle ages. Lévi adapted the inherited system, adding an eleventh sephira, called *Da'ath,* understood as that Knowledge that is true Science, being a reflection and synthesis of the other sephiroth. Lévi's advocacy of the tarot as a codified High Science opened the way for tarot to be used not only as the familiar means of divination, but also as a path to inner exploration, constituting an essential wing of the high magic that could only be worked in a state of exalted or mystical consciousness. Lévi therefore contributed to the development of a magical psychology of personal transcendence that continues to motivate and fascinate.

Lévi's claim that unspecified Rosicrucians and Martinists were in touch with the true tarot encouraged Gérard Encausse and his intimate friends to revitalize these traditions as revived orders of their own making in the light of the enthusiasm of their times. Lévi was therefore instrumental in the formation of the Occult Paris that succeeded him.

In chapter five of the *Dogma and Ritual of High Magic,* Lévi adumbrated a principle that would form a cornerstone of magical practice. He probably derived his idea of the "Astral Light" or "Universal Agent" from Mesmer combined with seventeenth-century Rosicrucianist ideas of the penetration of stellar rays into organic fiber (such as dew), altering its occulted nature. Corresponding to the "primordial light" of divine formation, its terrestrial counterpart is, according to Lévi, the "terrestrial fluid, which we call the Great Magnetic Agent . . . saturated with all kinds of images and reflections." This means the Astral Light is a plastic medium on which thoughts and images can be magically imprinted. The willful soul can affect it. It can dissolve it, coagulate it, project it, or withdraw it: verbs taken from the grammar of alchemy. "It is the mirror of the imagination and of dreams." Artistic interest in this conception was stirred. According to Lévi, the Astral Light "reacts upon the nervous system and thus produces the movements of the body. . . . It can take all forms evoked by thought, and, in the transitory coagulations of its radiant particles, appear to the eyes; it can even offer a sort of resistance to the touch." What might it do to paint, musical notes, or the written word? Could a purely magical art be generated? Péladan thought it could, for it is by use of the imagination that the Astral Light could be manipulated. Here was a means to explore the hidden world of the symbol. Imagination reaches its highest pitch. The idea of magic as a technique of the imagination would inform the basis of magic in the British "Occult Paris" offshoot, the Hermetic Order of the Golden Dawn, whose first Isis-Urania Temple was founded in London, significantly, in 1888. Its leaders, like Mackenzie, were United Grand Lodge of England Freemasons and members of the *Societas Rosicruciana in Anglia* (founded in 1867).

Lévi taught his readers that the Astral Light was in essence the physical soul of the four elements—earth, air, fire, and water—whose subjection by a fifth agent, that is the Will, is symbolized in the five-pointed star, the pentagram. The pentagram then becomes a glyph of power over the elemental spirits when the sign is employed with under-standing, that is, when the will is dedicated to the highest will. This is what is meant by the Magus "ruling the universe," the above and the below, by his enlightened will.

Thus when it comes down to it, or we go up to it, Magic for Lévi is power over self, the means of directing the will. For this to hap-pen effectively, and to prevent the Magus being driven off course, an essential discipline is required: balance and harmony. The Magus is dealing with the opposite currents that hold together the dynamic of the manifest cosmos. The ordinary personal will, or "ego" as we may call it today, is subject to temptation this way and that by its lim-ited vision of its requirements, and the isolating logic of its immediate needs and wants. Thus, power over self is essential, and that is the primary task of the magician in practice. We can see here the gropings toward what is effectively an attempt to produce a scientific religion or scientific interpretation of religion: a gnosis, through practice of a transcendental Art.

The balance between light and darkness, positive and negative, requires understanding of an important gnostic principle to which we have already alluded, since the opposite poles may also be characterized as masculine and feminine. Therefore, Lévi presented his readers with a vital image, or symbol for the frontispiece to his *Dogma and Ritual* (1856).

* * *

It is the symbol of Androgyny, of reconciliation of the opposites: a very appealing symbol to the Decadent imagination. Lévi calls the image *Baphomet* according to the tradition that the Knights Templar respected an image the Catholic antiscience Church associated with the Devil. *Au contraire,* says Lévi the faithful Catholic adept who knows what the church has long forgotten or misunderstood or suppressed, *Baphomet* is the Key. For in this image, as he conceives it, is the symbol of mastery: the resolution of the opposites in a higher unity, pertaining to Man's estate before the Fall into duality, manifestation, and *decay.*

Gnosis is the religion of the Artist, and the Artist is simply Man doing what Man does best: being a joyful cocreator, manifesting light in the dark universe. We may recall Pasqually's view that *mason* was simply another word for Man. Hence, as Aleister Crowley will be inspired to write in 1904, synthesizing all this doctrine and dogma: "Every man and every woman is a star."

Lévi's design for the frontispiece to the "Ritual" section of his two-part book on the High Magic has been used by the uninitiated as an image of the Christian Devil, not surprisingly, and films like *The Devil Rides Out,* based on Dennis Wheatley's black magic chillers, have promoted the view that figures with mixed human and goatish features represent the Evil One. Needless to say, this was not Lévi's intention, though one does sense a little mischief or "shocking the bourgeois" that must have made the image enticing for the Satanist rebels of the Decadent movement. But closer inspection reveals it as a symbol based on the idea of the sphinx, a chimera: half animal, half human, meaning it is neither, but a form for a formless idea, like the cherubs that decorated the Ark, for representations of human beings were forbidden in Israelite worship lest they be thought of as images of God. Lévi was, in my opinion, being provocative as well as profound.

In Lévi's *Book of Splendors,* he asserts that images of this kind point to pure ideas beyond formation. This resonates perfectly with the Symbolist idea: the form of the symbol points to the formless beyond. Symbolist artists were fascinated by the image of the sphinx

Fig. 3.4. Baphomet

and depicted her in many ways, some threatening, some placid, some—like Séon's *Le Désespoir de la Chimère*—hysterical (see color plate 18). For Lévi, his *Baphomet* was a composite symbol of initiation, not a thing.

We see a kind of goat with huge horns between whose horns is the flame of intelligence, the magic light of the universal balance discussed above. The flame is the soul elevated above matter. On the forehead of the goat (*Pan* = the ever-fertile *All*) is the pentagram, with the point at the top representing light and will. His two hands, one pointing up to the white moon of Chesed—sephira of Mercy—the other pointing down in balance to the black moon of Geburah—sephira of Severity or Justice. On the arms—one female, one male—are written respectively, *Solve* (separate) and *Coagula* (dissolve), active principles of alchemical transformation. Baphomet's chest has both female breasts and male hair, below which is a caduceus in place of genitalia, for the caduceus harmonizes masculine and feminine in one, and is the symbol of Hermes's will. Baphomet's wings express the "volatile," another alchemical concept, that which enables flight of one state to another. In short—to uninitiated eyes—a monster. To the initiate—a glyph for the assumption of Man over all his occulted faculties, able to wield the Astral Light at will, the power of the monster Man over himself by initiation. It is an image for a goal and is therefore progressive. By a persistent law of paradox, the beautiful appears at first monstrous, as the hag in mythology is revealed as the maiden. Truth does not come into the world naked, but clothed in types and images.

Androgyny was accepted as a formal ideal for many Symbolist artists, and Péladan regarded androgynous beings as somehow being above the downward-tending, bestial aspects of sex, but one would like to know what Lévi might have thought of the tendency to portray androgyny as something more effeminate and effete than strictly masculo-feminine. One suspects Lévi might have considered these images of "combined opposites" less of a synthesis and more of a mush of confused planes, since androgyny is an idea, a transcendence of opposites, not an alternative sex. Lévi's monstrous image was not intended to gratify aesthetic tastes!

* * *

Lévi's essential contribution to the Occult Paris of the late nineteenth and early twentieth centuries was in effect to redefine Magic as an "occult science" enabling a process of transcendental self-perfecting, a means to connect oneself to a deeper, invisible universe by progressive initiation through symbols and signs. Lévi's *Baphomet* design encapsulated this in a manner both risqué and fashionably provocative.

FOUR

THEOSOPHY
AND THE TRADITION

Hot on the heels of Lévi's contribution to Occult Paris came the Theosophical Society, founded by Helena Petrovna Blavatsky and her colleagues in New York in 1875. The aim of Theosophy as its foundress intended was to integrate the world's esoteric traditions into a new science of spiritual understanding. Its initial interest, however, lay in explaining paranormal phenomena such as table-tapping and spiritist séances with dead or distant persons, automatic writing, levitations, hypnosis, visionary messages, and predictions—all of which had fascinated Americans in particular since the 1840s—in terms of a new science of psychical research, and then integrating newly acquired knowledge, in as scientific a manner as possible, with Theosophical traditions worldwide. By *theosophical* we mean, broadly, accounts of spiritual existence and thought that combined aspects of theology with philosophy into *systems* that could be rationally expressed in series of principles. That word *principle* quickly became endemic to Theosophical discourse. Thus "Christ" would soon become "the Christ-principle": an intended universality removing *terra firma* from Jesus and replacement by an arguably quasi-philosophical abstraction.

The term *Theosophy* also hoped to cover occult traditions stemming from antiquity such as Gnosticism, Hermetism, Neoplatonism, Kabbalah, along with medieval magic, heterodox spiritualities—Catharism, the Theosophies of Paracelsus, Jacob Böhme, John Pordage,

Fig. 4.1. Helena Petrovna Blavatsky (1831–1891)

Jane Leade, William Law, Thomas Vaughan—along with Rosicrucian traditions of interpreting alchemy, Freemasonry, and the tarot. It was expected that Western and Eastern spiritual traditions would find unity in common bonds. The development of Western Esotericism itself partly stems from a reaction to that expectation, a compensatory desire in Western Europe to keep its spiritual traditions from being absorbed into a catch-all, East-meets-West-and-dissolves Theosophy. Indeed, Western Esotericists claim Theosophy as one of their spheres of research!

Madame Blavatsky's personal interest seemed to be influenced by the mythological and spiritual lore she gathered in the southeast of the Russian Empire in her youthful travels and self-education, and from later sojourns in Persia and India amid Hindu and Buddhist literature. Traditions of yoga, Vedantism, the Upanishads, and the esoteric understanding of Brahmanic traditions in general were favored by Blavatsky's closest followers. The overall aim was to challenge Science with the thought that it remained incomplete as a basis for understanding humankind and the universe in which we live, and to establish a Theosophical, higher scientific view of religions and spirituality common to the races of the Earth. Behind this aim was the prevalent belief we have met already in the writings of Fabre d'Olivet, that the disparate wisdoms of the world had a single origin in the Tradition, which, it was imagined, flourished some 7,000 years before Christ in a now vanished civilization. This belief would then be restated in terms that the civilization in fact still existed as a spiritual parent to humankind, whether in the Himalayas, underground, or on an exalted plane of being, or all of these options, depending on the predilections of the believer. Inevitably, with so much weight of baggage, the movement very quickly bifurcated, each group taking what they liked from the immense pot placed before them by Blavatsky's inspiring, imaginative, though often imprecise and sometimes fanciful, writings. It would be the Christian churches, and therefore political establishments, that would feel the provocation much more than materialist science, which felt generally confident to ignore much of the paper onslaught, remaining wary of "heretics" seeping out into the Theosophical maelstrom to "corrupt" virgin science with arcane superstition.

LADY CAITHNESS

The most prominent figure in the diffusion of Theosophist doctrines in Paris in our period was the remarkable Maria de Mariategui, Duchess of Medina Pomar, Lady Caithness (1830–1895). Of a colorful and wealthy background, she was the daughter of Don José de Mariategui, a Spanish nobleman who had married the daughter of the Earl of Northampton. Maria's first husband, Spanish General the Count of Medina Pomar, had obtained the title of Duke of Pomar from Pope Leo XIII before his death in 1868. The widowed Maria retained the title Duchess of Pomar after marriage to James Sinclair, 14th Earl of Caithness. His death in 1881 left Lady Caithness a wealthy dowager living between New York, Nice, London, and Paris, where she owned a considerable mansion named Holyrood at 124 avenue de Wagram in the 17th arrondissment. Now sadly destroyed and replaced by indifferent concrete modernity, the site is about a kilometer north of the place de Charles De Gaulle, with which the avenue de Wagram connects in the south.

In London, Lady Caithness became involved with the spiritualist

Fig. 4.2. Maria Pomar,
Lady Caithness
(1830–1895)

circle of Florence Cook, joining the British National Association of Spiritualists, founded in 1873. In 1876, having become an early member of Blavatsky and Colonel Olcott's Theosophical Society, Maria published *Old Truths in a New Light,* a book much influenced by Christian spiritist Allan Kardec. It tried to reconcile Theosophy, Spiritualism, and the Catholic faith, but enraged Catholic clergy.

Enjoying a powerful interest in the departed spirit of Mary Queen of Scots, part of the reception to the Duchess's beautiful house on the avenue Wagram was modeled on Scotland's royal palace of Holyrood. Spiritist sessions took place in a room dedicated to the Queen of Scots. The Duchess maintained that it was while in Caithness, Scotland, that Mary Queen of Scots appeared to her in a vivid dream urging her to hasten south to Holyrood. Arriving at Holyrood with one servant, she entered into conversation with her royal namesake, an audience concluded with a kiss to Maria's forehead and the instruction to devote herself henceforth to religion, in which service she could rely on the departed queen as guardian angel.

Vouchsafed by higher spirits, Lady Caithness was convinced her task was to promote the "Fourth Revelation," the first three being Moses, Jesus, and the early nineteenth-century spiritualists. Sharing her vision with English seeress Anna Kingsford (1846–1888), the flower bloomed into a dream of a universal religion that would reconcile and reintegrate the masculine and female aspects of the human being: androgyny again!

Originally dedicated to vegetarian campaigns with her close colleague, Edward Maitland, Anna Kingsford studied medicine in Paris for six years. Graduating in 1880, Lady Caithness offered Anna use of her Parisian mansion. In 1883, deeply influenced by Gnostics, Sufis, Neoplatonists, and by Hermetic philosophy—a compound of insights shared with Maitland—Anna Kingsford followed Lady Caithness's recommendation and joined the London Lodge of the Theosophical Society. Anna was soon its president. By 1885, however, she and Maitland had tired of the Society's stress on Indian philosophy determined to pursue ideas of their own. Their new "Hermetic Society" attracted William Wynn Westcott and Samuel Mathers, founders-to-be of the Hermetic Order of the Golden Dawn, to lecture there. Indeed, such was Mathers's and Westcott's admiration for Kingsford that her premature death in 1888 appears to have stimulated their own Order's founding. Lady Caithness's role in esoteric history is then very considerable.

In April 1884 Madame Blavatsky, staying at the duchess's home in Paris, approved her Grace's establishing the Theosophical Society of East and West, intended as the French branch of the international society. The society would attract members from the circle about Gérard Encausse (Papus). Unlike Blavatsky, but like Anna Kingsford, Lady Caithness had little time for Eastern traditions, favoring an esoteric Christianity that denied original sin and conventional Catholic doctrines of Jesus's divinity.

For Lady Caithness and Anna Kingsford, God was both male and female in principle. The era of male priesthood was at an end, and "the perfect way" was now open for women, opposed to the bestiality of men with the power of the feminine Holy Spirit. Published by Maitland and Kingsford in 1882, *The Perfect Way* took its insights into "esoteric Christianity" from Rosicrucian-type traditions that had become bound up with the Theosophy of Jacob Böhme, and with the visions of hell and heaven of Emanuel Swedenborg.

Fig. 4.3. Anna Kingsford
(1846–1888)

Every Wednesday from spring to autumn, a spiritual salon gathered at 124 avenue de Wagram, where Lady Caithness extended her hospitality to some of the leading companions of the Hierophany, men such as Stanislas de Guaita, Oswald Wirth, Papus—who joined the TS in October 1887—and Vice President of the Spiritualist Alliance Albert Jounet, or "Alber Jhouney." Other regulars included Theosophist Annie Besant, Gnostic Church founder Jules Doinel—whose "Sophia" concept would chime in with the Caithness-Kingsford vision—heterodox priest Father Paul Roca (1830–1893), Huysmans's friend, novelist Jules Bois and his mistress, opera singer Emma Calvé, psychical researcher Charles Richet (1850–1930), the astronomer Camille Flammarion, and Abbé Alta, a founder-member of de Guaita and Péladan's Kabbalistic Order Rose-Croix (1888). One might say the whole gang showed up at one time or another.

As if it were necessary to demonstrate the great closeness entwining the leading figures of Occult Paris, one only has to consider how in 1887, when Maitland and Kingsford were in Marseilles, they were approached by Éliphas Lévi's pupil and heir, Baron Guiseppi Spedalieri. The Sicilian Spedalieri not only gave some of Lévi's original manuscripts to Kingsford and Maitland but also Lévi's own copy of Trithemius's tract *De Septem Secundeis* (1567). Spedalieri was even happy to apply its prophecies concerning a final age to Maitland and Kingsford's work, penning a ringing endorsement for the second, enlarged edition of *The Perfect Way* (1887).

According to Richard Knowles,[1] the hospitality did not pass only the one way. In January 1887, de Guaita abandoned poetry to live in a ground floor apartment at 20 avenue Trudaine. On Thursday evenings he would invite guests to gather around the tea table like "alchemists about the athanor." These "faithful to the Gnosis" included Papus, Abbé Roca, Péladan, Lady Caithness—whose guardian angel constantly complained about her unjust beheading at Fotheringay!—Victor-Émile Michelet, Maurice Barrès, and their avuncular friend, St. Yves d'Alveydre. And it is to the teachings of this latter gentleman we shall now turn.

SAINT-YVES D'ALVEYDRE

Born in 1842, known to his friends as St. Yves or the Marquis, devotee of Fabre d'Olivet, Joseph Alexandre Saint-Yves was an elder to Michelet's generation. Since d'Olivet was little known, St. Yves, it appears, took as his own much of Fabre's philosophy, while giving the name *Synarchy* to a hierarchical world order with a God-chosen head. Synarchy was defined in opposition to anarchy, which as we saw earlier was interpreted by St. Yves as a state of society out of touch with the Tradition. In a Synarchic Order, everyone had his place in a tripartite hierarchy, whose order was to be respected, while the whole upward-looking thing was intended to bring forth the finest crop of illuminated beings possible over a period to the benefit of the whole. In time, all members would find their place in the spiritual reintegration process: a restoration, it was believed, of the image of God in Man. The appeal

Fig. 4.4. Alexandre St. Yves d'Alveydre (1842–1909)

was not confined to Roman Catholic monarchists with Theosophist leanings, but such provided the core of St. Yves's following.

After military service, St. Yves had entered political exile in Jersey where he encountered Victor Hugo (1802–1885) and his spiritist séances. St. Yves soon accommodated the idea of guidance from outside his own time and space. From alternative reality planes, St. Yves constructed what he took to be an inspired historical scheme stemming from a primordial legislator for humanity, named Ram, identified both with Abraham ("Ab-Ram"—"Father Ram") and the Hindu Rama, seventh avatar of the Hindu god Vishnu. St. Yves believed he had located the father of all peoples; hence Jews, Christians, Muslims all venerated Abraham while Hindus recognized in the holy figures of the Middle East aspects of their own avatars. Here lies the Theosophical strain that St. Yves was happy to join to the conceptions of Fabre d'Olivet and Louis-Claude de St. Martin. Again, the worldly manifestations might be different, and have become disjointed, but underneath, at the symbolic level, the symbols were of common essence. This conception became part of the Symbolist art sensitivity and spiritual aesthetic, while St. Yves's system acquired an aesthetic flavor consistent with the gathering mood of the time.

Having found his mission in life, St. Yves believed that sense of mission should be shared by professional groups addressed in a series of notable, highly influential "Mission" books. In 1882, *The Current Mission of the Sovereigns* was laid out. The workers received their Mission in 1883, the Jews theirs in 1884.

AGARTTHA

St. Yves seems to have elaborated on Tibetan Buddhist and Hindu legends of a place called Shambhala held to be a pure, peaceful land from which the Golden Age would come as from a root. St. Yves offered his version in a place he called Agarttha, of like import, revealed to him as located somewhere underground in the Tibetan Himalayas. In this place, Ram's spiritual direction held sway through a "king of the world." This conception was akin to the neo-Rosicrucian idea of humanity's destiny being directed by "Secret Chiefs," a sanctuary of spiritual saints. From Agarttha, an oriental Atlantis—though not damned as in the Greek legend—the modern, anarchic industrialized anthill could yet be redeemed should it but accept "Trinitarian Synarchy" as its means of renewal.

According to scholar Joscelyn Godwin,[2] the name Agarttha came through the teacher of Sanskrit who called himself "Hardjji Scharipf" (b. 1838). Lessons for St. Yves, and initially his Russian wife Marie-Victoire, commenced on 8 June 1885. Agarttha mysteriously appeared at the first lesson, when the teacher gave his qualifications as "Professor H. S. Bagwandass of the Great Agartthian School."[3] St. Yves may have heard of an *Asgartha* from travel writer Louis Jacolliot's many books on India published during the previous decade, for Jacolliot knew of a legendary great city of priest-kings, the Brahmatras. Jacolliot was not the only possible source.

Longtime magistrate at Chandernagor Louis Lacolliot (1837–1890) collected many old Hindu tales from his "patch" in South India. One such appears in his *Le Fils de Dieu* (The Son of God, 1873). Giving as its source the "Vedamarga," it refers to Asgartha, "City of the Sun," where Brahmatras ruled over civil and spiritual matters for over 3,000 years before an "Aryan" conquest over 8,000 years before Christ.

Hardjji was delighted to inform the somewhat suggestible St. Yves that the great city persisted and had as its language a primal tongue, Vattan or Vattanian, which St. Yves, already familiar with Fabre d'Olivet's contention that Hebrew was a primordial tongue of divine origin, found irresistible. The teacher slowly familiarized St. Yves with elements of the language, but insisted understanding required slow initiation.

The reverse side of a lesson of January 1886 includes the caption: "Model of Vattanian elements for the Agartthian rite alone for the use of initiates." Papus doubtless overstated the case that St. Yves was initiated by "two of the greatest dignitaries of the Brahmanic Church," one of whom we can be sure of was his Sanskrit teacher. Initially happy to furnish further details of his own initiation into Agartthian lore, Hardjji drew St. Yves on, at least to a point. Eventually, after contributing to St. Yves's obsessive comparisons of Vattanian "Vedic" symbols with Hebrew and Hermetic signs and astrological characters, the teacher seems to have conveniently decided to let St. Yves stand on his own two feet. Obviously St. Yves was concerned with trumping the Blavatskyan mode of finding direct correspondences between Western esoteric lore and that of ancient Hinduism, in an attempt to reconstruct primordial teachings of the Tradition.

In 1886, two years after the *Mission of the Jews,* and after his experience with Hardjii, the *Mission of India in Europe* was written, "taking the lid off Agarttha," as Joscelyn Godwin puts it, though it remained unpublished until a year after St. Yves's death. Europe apparently needed to know of a hidden land under the earth where millions accepted rule by a Brahatmah, a God-soul or Creator-soul, along with a Mahatma (Great Soul) and a Mahanga (Great Limb or Path). The city, St. Yves insisted, went underground at the onset of the present Hindu dark age (the Kali Yuga, ca. 3200 BCE) for protection, and to protect its technology and its system of Synarchy, now lost to the surface races—or shall we say superficial people who can't deal with symbols? However, Agarttha does not despair of those in darkness but dispatches emissaries from time to time, Jesus and Moses among them, as we might expect. When the world accepts Synarchy, many great secrets will be revealed, such as how to stay in contact with the dead and how the spirit interacts with physiology.

St. Yves included in the book open letters to Queen Victoria, Tsar Nicolas II, and Pope Leo III begging them to play their part, even though the Brahatmah would himself have been astonished to hear of what St. Yves had done, and what he knew about Agarttha, for St. Yves was not himself an official emissary, but a "spontaneous initiate," doing what he thought best.

However, he thought better of it, and when the book was just ready for the shops, he destroyed all the copies he could. One, however, had entered Papus's hands, and Papus published it in 1910, a year after St. Yves's death. The reasons for the withdrawal may simply have been fear of facing further critical onslaughts. In July 1885, Victor Meunier's review of the *Mission des Juifs* revealed it as substantially plagiarized from Fabre d'Olivet, while the following year former opera singer Claire Vautier's novel *Monsieur le Marquis, histoire d'un prophète* (Monsieur the Marquis, History of a Prophet) transfigured the real Saint-Yves into the fictional "Saint-Emme," the guilty lover who had seduced her with very St. Yves–like language only to cast her cruelly aside. Jules Bois, who was a scurrilous teller of tales, asserted that the Sanskrit teacher had threatened St. Yves with astral calamities for revealing secrets, but this seems an exaggeration typical of Bois. The fact is that St. Yves was busy organizing important inroads to official circles with a tamer, less fantastic version of Synarchy, and could do without the inevitable ridicule he would have suffered had the world been exposed to what was something like a fit of "enthusiasm" in the sense that eighteenth-century critics of religious visionaries understood the term: people who could not tell the difference between vision and reality, considering themselves beyond criticism.

As Joscelyn Godwin's sane study of Agarttha reveals, St. Yves himself in private and in elements of his poetry ("Jeanne d'Arc," 1890) continued to assert the existence of a "Superior University" with an Ethiopian "High Priest." Of course, in a world of symbolism, cross symbolism can get out of hand with forms and imagination and disparate facts, and meaning, especially if one has dispensed, in the tradition of Fabre d'Olivet and St. Martin, with the superficialities of mere positive history, and feels free to resort to astral traveling rather than buying a ticket from Thomas Cook's. The truth becomes parabolic. If Jesus used stories, why can't St. Yves? Did Jesus ever say anything that was not, in its spiritual meaning, true? Such thoughts doubtless comforted St. Yves as they do his spiritual followers today.

From the Himalaya of his remote mind, St. Yves continued to address business syndicates, politicians, and the opinion-forming classes of society, generally keeping aloof from the fashionable occultism and its schisms in the center of Paris. He made exceptions with the young men around Papus, de Guaita, Charles Barlet et al, who would pay occasional calls on his fine house in the rue Vernet, just south of the Champs Élysées or, later, at his mausoleum-like apartment at Fontainebleau, near to Versailles where he kept a shrine to his late wife who died in 1895, leaving St. Yves in irreparable distress. We know the younger men asked him questions, such as how to astral travel, but found him reluctant to pass on such initiatory information lest they enter spiritual hot water from precocious error—or maybe he wasn't really sure, or had himself got into hot water by his own efforts. They obviously believed in the older man and his visions.

Papus in particular was struck by St. Yves's idea that esoteric ideas could have social and political repercussions of a different order to traditional political engagement, replete with ideas associated with the first Rosicrucian manifesto, first published with a satirical work on the "Reformation of the Whole Wide World" by Venetian Trajano Boccalini (1614) that many of a Rosicrucian persuasion mistakenly took to be part of the original manifesto.

After World War I, when most of the important protagonists were dead, a new generation of Synarchists interpreted the ideas for social change in considerably less spiritual directions, stressing economic, administrative, and sociological applications, and, according to Lynn Picknett and Clive Prince's analysis (*The Sion Revelation,* 2006) these developments were instrumental in the root formation of what currently passes under the name of the European Union. For harder nosed neo-Synarchists of the 1930s, recruitment to the cause of a "United

States of Europe" apparently followed St. Yves's pattern of recruiting future bureaucrats and professional classes in the French polytechnics and *Grandes Écoles,* though in the new order of Synarchy, secretly, on a one-knows-one basis. Such obscure, sinister roots would explain three things about the contemporary EU: the top of the hierarchy's own obscurity; the executive's curiously superior attitudes to democracy, representative government, and national sovereignty; and its apparently benign contentment with a practically static economy in pursuit of a stable, homogenous social control system—not to mention its expansionist tendencies. I think we should know, but doubt if we shall.

If there exists any truth in this, then today's invisible Synarchists have long since betrayed St. Yves's conception of a great spiritual body based on the Christian Trinity so appealing to those disgruntled with secular, republican society.

One does rather wonder what St. Yves made of the Decadent strand in the Symbolist spiritual movement. *Too anarchic?* I should think so. He probably thought it symbolized something.

FIVE

Stanislas de Guaita

I saw a negress generously formed
Whose eyes, full of love, alluring and bored,
Reflected vaguely the trembling stars
Golden buttons on the dark blue coat of the night
I saw a negress generously formed.

Angel of Pain that one can never console
She had in the sky two wings extended
That sometimes she raised as though away she'd fly
In musing about the treasure of sensual pleasures lost
Angel of Pain that one cannot console.

> VERSES 1–2, *LA MUSE NOIRE* (THE BLACK MUSE);
> STANISLAS DE GUAITA, DEDICATED TO LECONTE
> DE LISLE, 1883 (AUTHOR'S TRANSLATION)

Stanislas de Guaita was twenty-two when he felt impelled to write about the figure that inspired him. Unafraid to express the darkness of his vision, he wrote of the "Black Muse" like Marlowe's Faustus crying out: "Tis Magic, magic that hath ravish'd me!" Romantic, de Guaita must have felt fated early on, driven to the shadows by some unaccountable "angel of pain." Though descended from a noble family of northern Italy, de Guaita's great-great-grandfather had married a French baron's daughter, inheriting thereby an imperial estate on the Étang ("pond") d'Alteville, between Dieuze and Mittersheim in Moselle-Lorraine. Entering this world on 6 April 1861, Stanislas was force-fed Catholicism and the virtue of pain by Jesuits first at Dijon, then at the lycée of La Malgrange

("The Evil Barn"!), a barracklike former château, 60 kilometers from home comforts and 3 kilometers south of Nancy. Surrounded by flat, boring grassland extending from the banks of the dull Meurthe River, Stanislas found consolation in literature, whose crepuscular symbols he explored in the company of fellow sufferers and novelists-to-be Maurice Barrès (1862–1923), Paul Adam (1862–1920), and Albert de Pouvourville (1861–1940), whom we last met under his Chinese penname of Matgioï, preaching Taoism in the rue de la Chaussée d'Antin.

Other than literature, and especially Baudelaire—who else?— Stanislas's interest perked up at Latin and science, particularly chemistry: two good subjects for one who would embrace magic and alchemy. But in 1880, aged nineteen, he undertook to study law in Paris where he soon fell in with other aspiring poets in the Latin Quarter. His first poetry book *Les Oiseaux de Passage* (Birds of Passage—Fantastic Rhymes) he published in Paris in 1881.[1]

The book opens with a kind of apology in verse. His poems are, he tells us, like birds of passage that throw their songs into the air, gone as quickly as clouds: "One would say 'Their wing is small, and the gold of their plumage is false.'" This nice touch of self-deprecation is followed by a poem that springs straight out of Symbolist concerns: *L'Idéal et la Forme* (The Ideal and the Form) whose first verse, translated, runs thus:

> You will never obtain, artist,
> A dream that reflects the iridescent
> Seal in the narrow amethyst:
> An ideal crystallized.
> You could die in trying for it;
> Your hard work would be in vain:
> Ah! 'Tis because the form is human
> And the Ideal divine!

Another poem, entitled "The Alchemist," after examining the failure of an alchemist to obtain the philosopher's stone, concludes on a bright, optimistic note, suitable for the bright new era a spiritually enlivened youth could see emerging from the shadows:

> From the cursed century of darkness,
> The century of light is born

The poem is footnoted with a thought that suggests that for de Guaita, as for Papus, the potential of alchemy needed the scientific age to release it: "This alchemist, pupil of the great Paracelsus belongs to the epoch of the Renaissance, but for science, alas!—this epoch, was it not still the middle ages?"

Not all is earnest, or ardent questing, however. "After the Ball" (*Après le Bal*) is dedicated to de Guaita's friend Maurice Barrès and evokes the scene of a pretty girl called Jeanne, going to bed with "golden dreams," a rather philosophical girl, for she says: "It's the Ball which lasts." In the "Ghosts of the Café," the poet speaks up for just recompense for oppressed negroes in the colonies, referring to "European ingrates" who fill the bars with smoke from "divine tobacco" without a thought to who harvests it; de Guaita sees in the smoke the ghosts of those who suffer for it: a powerful image. In "Nothingness" by "a disciple of Bishop Berkeley," he praises the philosopher of idealism for having banished from man the curse of Nothingness, the "archangel of life." The mind is primary; as in the Hermetic philosophy, Mind is creative of reality. Facts are first and foremost facts of mind. De Guaita marks himself out as a classic "head," anti-materialist, content to reside in the infinite regions of his imagination. He was unlikely to find satisfaction in law; he sought the stone of the wise and "a hashish dream come true."[2]

In "Persecutions" de Guaita finds himself with the persecuted, the heretics, the true Christians. He once said that like Goethe, he would rather suffer an injustice than cause a disorder.

> Jesus said: "Christian, never do to others
> What you would not want done to yourself."
> Inquisitors, executioners, satanic apostles,
> You reply: Did he say it?

He cries out that the work of those who have tortured men and women, burnt them to make them believe, that work is the work of "the Pope in Rome." It seems the Jesuits had done their work too well, and de Guaita's stance on those responsible for his education partly explains later differences with his friend-to-be Joséphin Péladan.

Victor-Émile Michelet got to know Stanislas de Guaita in his twentieth year, that is in 1881, when *Les Oiseaux de Passage* was published. For all the errors of his companions, Michelet insists that among them were some who "burnt incense in the poisoned atmosphere of the century." One such was de Guaita who, though dying prematurely at thirty-eight, had nonetheless achieved that rare distinction "of being considered a classic in his lifetime," and would remain so with his "brothers" Fabre d'Olivet, Hoene-Wronski, Éliphas Lèvi, the neo-Pythagorean Abbé Lacuria (1806–1890), and St. Yves d'Alveydre.[3] Michelet says that their respective Venuses (Morning and Evening Stars: a masonic reference), though one appeared in the west—Michelet was born in Nantes—and the other the east (Alteville), they were not unknown to one another on the Mt. St. Geneviève, that is to say, the hill on Paris's Left Bank (5th arrondissment) where the Panthéon ("All gods") stands close to

Fig. 5.1. Stanislas de Guaita (1861–1897)

St. Geneviève's great library amid the Latin Quarter's narrow streets and cafés frequented by confused, energetic but directionless, faithless, and often nihilistic students from the Sorbonne.

In the fevered, malaise-ridden, and often vulgar literary and student swirl about the Latin Quarter, Michelet became acquainted with de Guaita's school friend Maurice Barrès who studied law with little enthusiasm, and the times he was living in more closely. Perhaps Barrès told Michelet of how his hellish, lonely life at Malgrange, with its cold and wet winters, desolate dormitories, and smelly corridors, had been suddenly lightened at the age of sixteen by meeting Stanislas de Guaita who brought for him to warm his inner fires Flaubert's *Salammbô,* and Baudelaire's *Les Fleurs du Mal.* Symbolist in artistic sympathy, Barrès became familiar with the literary coterie around veteran Parnassian poet Leconte de Lisle. Now old, de Lisle held the post of assistant librarian at the Library of the Luxembourg Palace, a few blocks from the Panthéon to the southeast and the Odéon 300 meters to the north. This contact probably explains de Guaita's dedication "with profound admiration" to "the Master CH. LECONTE DE LISLE" of his book *La Muse Noire,* in 1883.

Fig. 5.2. Charles-Marie René Leconte de Lisle (1818–1894)

Until de Guaita's death in 1898, Barrès shared many of Michelet's esoteric concerns, despite a deeper attachment to orthodox Catholicism, which would eventually gain the upper hand—though he never abandoned the mystical sense—combined with what Barrès called "nationalism," the political creed he would make his own from the mid-1890s, and for which he would be "mock-tried" in his absence by surrealist André Breton and Dadaist Tristan Tzara in 1921. Michelet left an unedited manuscript note on Barrès that suggests a muted critique of the "right-wing," socialistic political path Barrès would eventually adopt and promote out of love for his troubled country:

> A tall boy of yellowish-brown complexion, whose flat and elongated feet slowed his gait. He spoke with a voice whose faraway hoarseness allowed one to foresee some revelation of the sensitivity on the subject of which he had to write so much. He spoke on all things with the assurance of those who are anxious.[4]

For his part, Barrès maintained a high regard for Michelet, though distanced himself after de Guaita's death. In 1886, Barrès would write of Michelet in an article in *Le Figaro:*

> Monsieur Émile Michelet whose career began with a splash in the literary set seems to have renounced certain success to disappear into the occult sciences.[5]

It was Maurice Barrès who introduced Michelet to de Guaita at a café close to the Odéon. Michelet saw a young man of powerful neck, blond hair, and very clear face, luminous with dark shades. Both being lovers "of the eternal Muse," they "tu-toi'd" after an hour, that is, they referred to one another in the French language's intimate form of *you* reserved in days past for close friends and family.

The moment Michelet thinks back to how he remembers the young de Guaita, his mind is filled with ideas connected to gnostic alchemy. He remembers an evening he and de Guaita spent with romantic author and chemist-alchemist Albert Poisson. Michelet recalls Poisson, who

Fig. 5.3. Maurice Barrès (1862–1923)

Fig. 5.4. Albert Poisson (1868–1893)

had discovered a fine old volume of alchemy in the bookstalls, hoisting it triumphantly. Elated, this "predestined son of Hermes" (that is, alchemist) revealed its engravings: the mystic nuptials of the King and Queen in the egg representing the athanor until the birth of the royal Child. Poisson would die at twenty-four in 1893: "Both died young without having been able to pursue the work begun, without having uttered the evocative words of which they were depositories."

Michelet was in no doubt that de Guaita was made in the mold of Elias Artista, that he was a poet of beauty, profoundly an artist: "His beautiful prose, of which much survives, attests to his metaphysical talents."

Michelet called "Birds of Passage" the kind of work "all poets write at 20," some of which is published, some hidden, some tossed to the flames, but de Guaita's "youthful gaucheries" announced in seed form the depth of his mind. Michelet also noticed the curious detail that struck this author, how the poem entitled "The Alchemist" expresses the aspiration of a disciple of Paracelsus to fulfill the birth-destiny of "the century of light," "which is, he says, ours." He was at once a poet and a passionate chemist engaged in his laboratory. He was, says Michelet, a "child of Sainte-Claire-Deville," Henri Étienne Sainte-Claire-Deville being chemistry professor at the Sorbonne until 1881, expert in artificial preparation of minerals. De Guaita's books reveal deep knowledge of chemistry. "As with most modern alchemists," wrote Michelet, "chemistry must lead to alchemy, a science immemorially doctrinal, as opposed to the variables of chemistry." Michelet notes how de Guaita had studied toxicology before goetic magic, a preoccupation with dark works alluded to in his second volume, "The Black Muse."

Michelet may not be entirely accurate in relating de Guaita's scholarly analysis of black magic to the somber muse that drove him. The darkness that haunted de Guaita was primarily existential, as noted by a young man who interviewed him in 1894 and who had access to some of de Guaita's correspondence.

De Guaita was more disturbed by despair than by the evil men do. One could comfort the afflicted, but what balm could ameliorate nothingness or ultimate meaninglessness? De Guaita suffered from what Buddhists call "the trance of sorrow," and he "had it bad." On 27 February 1884, he would write to his mother how he suffered an incurable anguish, a strange anguish of thought that a "work of absolute beauty" is yet "destined to perish without remission, first because new books submerge past ones (save in rare exceptions), and then because of cataclysms—deluges, barbaric invasions—which leave nothing, and then because as Philosophy, Science and Religion all agree, the earth must perish one day and disappear entirely. The works of the spirit, having only subjective existence, and not an existence of their own, will disappear."[6] He complained that the Earth was so atomistically tiny in the face of the stars contemplated on a beautiful night, its insignificance made his heart feel an "immense melancholy." The only "double thought" that occasionally brought consolation was that at least he was not a genius, for the author of a masterpiece must surely suffer more! Student Charles Berlet interviewed de Guaita in an elegant hotel room on the beautiful place de la Carrière* in Nancy for a local paper called *Le Chardon* (The Thistle) in 1894. Berlet recalled how the poet's blond hair, blue eyes, beard, and chain smoking projected the epic aura of a prophet. Berlet emphasized de Guaita's almost continual sense of anguish of Nothingness, of man's impotence to scrutinize the "enigma of life," as revealed in the poem "La Prophétie du Squelette" (The Skeleton's Prophecy) in *Rosa Mystica* (1884).

Fascinatingly, Berlet notes that this poem was written in January 1883, as de Guaita was approaching the moment when Lévi's *Dogme et ritual de la Haute Magie* would bring a ray of light into the mystery's depths. We may now begin to glimpse what it was in Lévi that affected de Guaita so profoundly. Berlet observes that the book "invited de Guaita to get himself out of the world beneath which poetry proved unable to take him high enough." This conversion to the positive virtue of the active magus seems very much akin to what Aleister Crowley would undergo over a decade later after his early fixation on poetry and

---

*The place de la Carrière is near the place Stanislas, in Nancy, whence derived de Guaita's Christian name, after the Polish King and Duke of Lorraine who established the Stanislas Academy as a "Royal Society of the Sciences and *Belles-Lettres*" in Nancy on 28 December 1750.

Buddhism brought to him only greater cause for suffering and despair, until he finally embraced "Magick" as *the* way of life." *Magick,* properly understood, we are to believe, takes the wise practitioner beyond the relative being of this world. For de Guaita then, pursuit of Magic was akin to a path of personal redemption, and he would definitively surrender a career as a poet of profound promise and devote his time instead to full-on spiritual pursuits and the exhaustive study of occult sciences expressed in clean, orderly prose.

De Guaita set himself against the superficial aspects of his age as severely as English pundit Christopher Booker divorced himself from what he called the "Neophiliacs" of the plastic-fantastic 1950s and '60s. De Guaita looked at the "brains" of his time pretending to enclose the infinity of the universe within the bounds of their discoveries. Science had set itself up against Faith; the spirit of the time ruined the experience of centuries. The dogma of material progress appeared to have conquered the quest for moral and spiritual perfection. The mechanical game of numbers regulated the destiny of nations, and the terrestrial happiness of the individual had become the goal and purpose of the State. In his introduction to *The Temple of Satan,* de Guaita would write: "The frenzy of disrespect, the monomania of the relative and the fever of individualism: here are the three symptoms of disarray in which the modern world debates itself." The ancient debate of the Magi promised more than the world could offer and offered more than the world.

Michelet informs us that in de Guaita's third collection, *Rosa Mystica* (1885), the mystical tendency that was always a stream in de Guaita's verse spread further. In fact it gushes in lyrical song for an impressive 263 printed pages. The considered preface makes fascinating reading. It is as though most of the precursors, leaders, and sympathizers of Hermetic symbolism in literature had gathered together to hear what de Guaita makes of each one's contribution: Baudelaire, Edgar Allan Poe, Mallarmé—who had translated Poe's *The Raven* in 1876—Charles Morice, Catulle Mendès, Jean Moréas, Barbey d'Aurevilly, Paul Verlaine, Leconte de Lisle, Laurent Tailhade, and—on page 48 of what is a substantial essay on the arts—de Guaita recognizes Victor-Émile Michelet as "a troubling and fluctuating poet who seems a little his own nephew." According to de Guaita, Michelet "has shown himself more penetrating than us. In an estimable study, he has made alternately the analysis and synthesis of the complex faculties of the master." De Guaita is probably alluding to Michelet's study "Esotericism in Art."

What is mysticism? asks de Guaita in the preface to *Rosa Mystica:* "It is the love of our hearts for the dreams of our brains; it is that which makes the vulgar hate, that which makes outlaws of us!" (page 3). There is a strong Lévi-esque touch of ironic paradox to the aphorism. He's taking the Levitical path to Jericho and leaving the wounded poet on the other side of the road. Or as Michelet put it, after *Rosa Mystica,* de Guaita "courageously parted from the divine language [poetry]." For the "High Science must claim the whole man." Though de Guaita ceased his devotions to poetry, he did not cease appreciating poetry, recognizing above all its magic power to invoke the universal truth that exists in the three worlds of the Kabbalists by the "revelation of a rhythm," as Michelet puts it. The poets de Guaita loved were those whose vision took in the circle of a horizon at the visible limits; it had to get beyond the earthy clods that clog the vision. "The limpid language of the French classics charmed his spirit, while not neglecting the graces and audacious efforts of the moderns."

Michelet was particularly impressed by the sense of unyielding orderliness in de Guaita's way of thinking, and in the construction of his books: "He constructed his edifice with the rigor of the Grand Architect. His 'Key of Black Magic' [1897] is a model of organization." Michelet then asks a question of some importance relative to the authority for his creating in 1888 the Kabbalistic Order of the Rose-Cross, since Rosicrucian orders are supposed to be linked directly to authentic lines of transmission with some visible order manifested consistently in time. Michelet, who had every opportunity to know the answer says: "Guaita did not receive from an initiatic center the Word whose mysterious signification he had to seek in himself. His personal effort was his sole guide." Michelet concludes that de Guaita felt morally compelled to establish correct order in the accumulated confusion of occult ideas. He wanted order, system, hierarchy, and tradition. The poem "Les Fleurs vénéneuses" (The Poisoned Flowers) in *Rosa Mystica* hints at the next stage in de Guaita's evolution: to set the "impure rites" of the black magician against the light that will destroy them; these impure rites included what de Guaita regarded as perverted psychic powers employed by "mediums," as well as other abuses of hypnotic powers of suggestion and fascination. The restoration of the High Magian Art was his aim, the synthesis of spiritual and cosmic science.

His first phase of deep study would emerge in part 1 of his "Essays on the Accursed Sciences," *On the Threshold of the Mystery,* published in 1886. The first words of its introduction, which was also published separately in the journal *L'Artiste,* give an immediate idea of what de Guaita was proposing:

> On hearing the sole words "Hermetism" or "Kabbalah" the fashion is to cry out. The looks exchanged at the words range from ironic indulgence to forced smiles accentuating the disdain contorting the faces.[7]

This would have to change. De Guaita observed that from the second to the eighteenth century, the story of the gnostics had been primarily one of martyrdom, persecution, suffering, and extraordinary heroism shown by those who through their agonies transmitted the "treasure of the sacred science," the symbols that today can be deciphered in a new era free of official fanaticism and popular superstition. However, while initiates are no longer burned, they still suffer ridicule with calumnies. Nevertheless, the new gnostic initiates are "resigned to the outrage, like their fathers, the martyrs" of whom "some day" it will be recognized that they were "neither charlatans nor imbeciles." On that day, "Oh Christ, your servants will remember that the Magi prostrated themselves before the royal cradle." It is in expectation of "that hour of Justice and of Gnosis" that de Guaita submits his "Essays on the Accursed Sciences" to the public's impartial judgment.

De Guaita wanted "occult sciences" to be taken seriously. As Michelet puts it: "His decided and robust spirit went straight to the classic masters of the Tradition, French or German: Fabre d'Olivet, Khunrath, Jacob Böhme." Having "discovered the law that nourished his spirit" de Guaita renounced poetry, something for which he never expressed any bitterness, while continuing to enjoy the company of the poets who had encouraged his first forays into art. He had "the blue blood of the intelligence of the heart, the patrimony of the soul." Michelet recognized the true value of de Guaita's achievement, something today unjustly forgotten.

> Already in his taste for order, method, his love of the essential and his horror of missing the target, he methodically established the History of the Transmission of the Doctrine in the West. His fairness saw each of the masters in proper proportion to one another. When he gave me this first volume, he recalled how I said to him, laughing: "Here you are the grammarian of the Mystery."
>
> St. Paul wrote "That which is to be hoped from those who reveal the Mysteries is that which is found true and faithful." Faithful Stanislas de Guaita made it his artistic conscience to clothe the inexpressible in a form so precise as to incarnate the initiatic idea in definitive language. Like Éliphas Lévi he adorned his crucial philosophy with the rose of beauty. . . . No one since Edgar Allan Poe's *Colloquy of Monos and Una* [1841] and *The Conversation of Eiros with Charmion* [1829] revealed how precisely the poet could reveal the primary aspects of the Plutonian palace [the underworld or afterlife] has better evoked the atmosphere of the mysterious domain with more authority than de Guaita in chapter six of his *Clef de la Magie Noire* [Key of Black Magic].

Michelet declares that of the four students from Nancy promised a destiny in the world of the spirit, Stanislas de Guaita, Maurice Barrès, Paul Adam, and Albert de Pouvourville (Matgioï), only de Guaita really measured up to the inner demands of the gnostic path and avoided the temptations of the world's judgment, even though his quiet audacity was arguably premature in lifting the veils beneath which the Black Isis hid herself. Michelet was particularly struck by what Maurice Barrès lost in not learning all de Guaita had to offer him. Even though Barrès admitted the exaltation he felt as an adolescent when, at school, it was de Guaita who introduced him to the "enflamed horizon" of the poets, a few years later, when de Guaita announced he was surrendering the path of poetic fame for new studies, Barrès rejected him sharply: "This is not my genre of madness," Barrès said, smiling. Had Barrès attended to de Guaita's depth of approach, his great artistic talent would, Michelet believes, have found that fixity and certitude he vainly attempted to derive from temporary and superficial doctrines, politically oriented, but then, Michelet observes, Barrès "cornered the market" in appearing other than himself. De Guaita too was inclined to judge Barrès severely, but maintained a long affection nonetheless. Despite discouragement, Guaita maintained his clear and clarifying mission. Though his work could suffer from a didacticism attendant on his "rectilinear mind" of order and measure, there were nonetheless certain concepts that, like a good Symbolist, de Guaita refused to submit to analysis, being content with the symbols. His task was to take the reader to the *threshold* of the Mystery, the experience of it was properly the concern of the individual seeker's will. As far as Michelet was concerned, de Guaita, being a man of strong culture and classical taste familiar with all orders of knowledge, was a trustworthy guide through the "porch of Hermes's temple," which was otherwise encumbered by "all kinds of false prophets and baroque heresiarchs." De Guaita only paid attention to the true masters, the classics of the Hermetic tradition.

Given all Michelet tells us about the instincts and devoted spirit of de Guaita, it perhaps comes as a surprise to contemplate how hard he was hit by the self-aggrandizing personality of the man from Lyon who first burst onto the Parisian art scene in 1883, for by the time *Rosa Mystica* appeared in 1885, de Guaita had been overwhelmed in mind and heart by the novel that in some respects would define the epoch. The human phenomenon that was Joséphin Péladan had published *Le Vice Suprême* (The Supreme Vice) to a widespread rapture he relished to the full. If de Guaita did not believe himself a genius capable of a masterpiece, as he confided to his mother that year of 1884, it is clear that he shared with Barbey d'Aurevilly the view that this twenty-six-year-old unleashed from the south was indeed a genius with proof in print.

The voluptuous novel, with its arresting frontispiece by Félicien

Rops, splashed down at a critical point in de Guaita's life. At a stroke, it synthesized de Guaita's own ardor for the promise of Éliphas Lévi in a work that, if you'll forgive the pun, lévitated theory into imaginative reality. Péladan's main character, the only one of two, as d'Aurevilly observed in his preface, not to typify the traditional vices, is a successful walking, talking example of Lévi's Magus. Péladan's magus, "Mérodack"—invoking in Hebrew the Babylonian divinity Marduk— has fully absorbed and attained to the high ideal of absolute self-control and mastery that the Professor of Transcendental Magic had pointed to. What was even more surprising was that this occult hero was the star of a novel wherein Catholicism beamed off every page like an altar lamp. Somehow the book fused de Guaita's chief preoccupations; he felt he had to seize the moment. Michelet uses the verb *frappa* to describe the effect of the book on his friend. De Guaita was gobsmacked by, in Michelet's words, "a tumultuous beauty, which audaciously created the power of a secret Science in the face of both ignorant vanity and the negativity of the modern intellect."

Le Vice Suprême used a heady technique of seduction to fulfill its subtitle of being an "Éthopée," that is a description whose object is a moral, psychological portrait of a personality. What Péladan was getting at was the debasement of people and art. Mérodack is a "decadent" avenging angel of a society wallowing in moral decay, fleeing from the positive spirit of white, spiritual magic, having abandoned what Péladan believed was the essence of Catholicity in favor of the shadows.

The first five pages of chapter 1 describe the "Princess of the East," lying naked on a bed like a glamorous diva drunk on the blood of the saints in the Book of Revelation, though she is considerably more erotically charged than the apocalyptist dared to make her:

> For she is herself the monster she has vanquished, and invincible as the Omphalus, her soul filled with passion, her body kneaded with desires, she has molded them, with her long thumb, like a voluntary spatula, after a perverse ideal of the modern Artemis. She lived according to one idea: that is her glory. . . . From the height of her

pride she gazes into the distant panorama of the deceased times, and making present her past, resuscitates all her dead life.[8]

There, spread out on the bedspread for the voyeur's complicit eye is decay and corruption whose bosom heaves with a sensuality both tingling and repellent amid silken veils and gaudy drapes and red, red wine. Resistance was futile: readers were gripped by the invitation. De Guaita was gripped, but not by the nude princess. Compare the scene above with this verse from de Guaita's poem "Nihilism" from *La Muse Noire*, published a year before *Le Vice Suprême*:

> My holy dream—my infamous dream
> is to destroy the Universe
> Old accursed body which has no more a soul.[9]

De Guaita was gripped by Péladan's audacity in representing the Tradition in a form palatable to a broad, fashionable audience. Péladan was the "Dan Brown" of the moment. Indeed, it is a fact that without Péladan there would never have been a *Da Vinci Code* for, as we shall see, it was the mighty Péladan who gave to Leonardo da Vinci the luster of a Hermetic adept rooted in the gnostic stream of universal genius, of a "Grand Master" of a Traditional Order wielding a "code" of symbols only fellow adepts could crack. The whole "Blood and Grail/Priory of Sion" fantasy is born out of twisted, mischievous reflection on the people and times we are describing and on Péladan's legacy in particular.

Having referred to de Guaita's first encounter with *Le Vice Suprême*, the first novel of Péladan's novel-series *La Décadence Latine* (The Latin Decadence), Michelet suddenly asks in a manner akin to a lament: "Who, during this period, maintained the Tradition?"

In 1884, the year of *Le Vice Suprême*, Michelet became editor of the review *Jeune France* and did his best to publish work by people he believed mattered: de Guaita, Charles Morice, Edmond Haraucourt, Anatole France (when he was practically unknown), and on 1 November 1885, *Axël*, Villiers de l'Isle-Adam's otherworldly, Symbolist play that

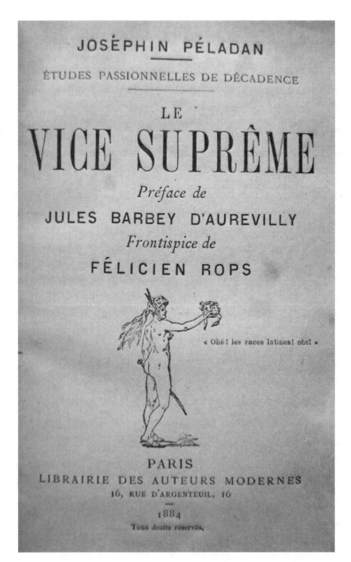

Fig. 5.5. Title page: Le Vice Suprême, *Joséphin Péladan*

Edouard Rod at *La Revue Contemporaine* had refused. Villiers, Michelet notes bitterly, "this magnificent genius" wasn't wanted by editors. He wasn't alone. Abbé Lacuria hadn't been published for thirty years. He would have to die unknown, blind, and poor, Villiers half known, "both in distress and misery. Ah! Destiny and men are hard on the great ones! Ignored, St. Yves d'Alveydre had cast to the wind his *The Keys of the East* and *The Mission of the Jews.*"

ABBÉ LACURIA

De Guaita attached himself indirectly to the still-living Abbé Lacuria's work. Indirectly because de Guaita attached himself to Péladan, and Péladan's master was his elder brother Adrien, and Dr. Adrien Péladan *fils* had been put on the Christian esoteric path by Lacuria's extraordinary work, *Harmonies de l'Être* (The Harmonies of Being[10]).

Lacuria (1806–1890) hailed, like the Péladan brothers, from Lyon where he served as a much-loved teacher at the Oullins seminary into which he put all his money, excelling in mathematics, literature, and music—he corresponded with Gounod and was an early advocate of Wagner—until his ecclesiastical cofounders fell out with him over his reconciliation of faith and science in his book *Harmonies of Being,* first published in 1844, now a very rare classic.

Lacuria left Lyon for Paris in 1847 as a tutor to the Thiollier family. One of the children would grow up to become the famous photographer Félix Thiollier (1842–1914). Tutorial services completed, Lacuria struggled to survive, living in poverty and obscurity first at 11 rue de Fourcy in the 4th arrondissment, then in 1865 in a cold garret filled with books at 11 rue Thouin, close to the Panthéon in the Latin Quarter, where in his old age he would become known by young students of the mystical as the "French Pythagoras," not only a great metaphysician and teacher of Christian esotericism in music and philosophy, but a teller of lovable, fantastic tales of genies, suprahuman worlds, magic, and fairies who, as a priest of the love of God, had made the world his family.

Félix Thiollier left this touching description of Lacuria in his attic room:

> The Abbé was sitting near an old patched table. The furniture consisted of a sofa, dressers, and chairs with disparate feet; a narrow bed was hidden by a green baize curtain. Books and music scores were scattered in all directions; you could see boxes of various sizes filled with brushes, pen holders, or carpenters' tools; paintings provided by friends were hung on the walls; close to the chimney lamp, candle holders, a crucifix, a flower pot of antique form; next to a stove was

Fig. 5.6. Abbé Paul François Gaspard Lacuria (1806–1890)

a grill made out of pieces of wire skillfully tangled and twisted by the master of the house in order to toast bread or chops. An old square piano, almost voiceless, occupied a place of honor; throughout his life, Lacuria expressed a desire to own another; in the meantime, he couldn't resist the temptation of becoming acquainted with all the instruments of Erard and Pleyel he encountered with friends and lingered without troubling assistants; when they expressed their astonishment, he replied: "Mine is so sick that I console myself by attending its healthier parents." . . . If he still had meager fare, he

found a way to be useful to all, especially to his neighbors; he educated a child of the concierge, and conducted a blind man on walks.
He could hardly resist invitations to hear operas by Beethoven,
Mozart, Gluck, Weber and Mehul, which didn't prevent him from
liking Rossini because of his spirit or Boieldieu because his *La Dame
Blanche* [opera] didn't give him a headache. Before the performance,
we went to a restaurant where the Abbé ordered only dishes with
baroque names and seemed quite surprised when the result was not
in harmony with the beauty of the name. Arriving at the theater, he
tried to make himself invisible at the bottom of a seat, and followed
the music and the score with his back to the stage, so as not to be
distracted.[11]

Joséphin Péladan also visited the sage and was dazzled by Lacuria's reply
when he, himself a master, asked the master the source of his inspiring
words:

> "Dare I ask you whence come these clarities? Because I have respect
> for your words."

> "Whence comes the brightness? Is it from the sun, that is to say
> from the star that God has destined for that office, or from a lamp
> that human ingenuity has invented?

> "The spiritual lights [insights] are the fruit of illumination and of
> application at the same time. I who can expect nothing from the
> exterior world receive my substance from the interior world, and if
> I can hardly see forms any more, I perceive other aspects of being."[12]

When Lacuria finally died, in Lyon, in 1890, Péladan wrote of him:

> The admirable man whose name will probably reach the gen-
> eral public for the first time, Abbé Lacuria, has died, blind, poor,
> obscure. I do not hesitate to consider him as one of the greatest pla-
> tonizing and pythagorizing theologians that ever lived. . . . On a cold

afternoon, I ascended to the Panthéon and by the rue de la Vielle-Estrapade, I arrived at 11 rue Thouin. On the top floor, an attic, I knocked; a voice said, "Enter." I found myself in an anteroom full of shelves of old books in order. Looking through the open door, into a second chamber, also lined with books, I saw an unforgettable figure. Beside an old extinct stove, covered with cans of evaporated milk, an old man was sitting in a wicker chair. Accoutred in an old Levite check, feet in an old box of household waste to ward off the cold tiles, the greatest thinker of his time got up: a head fine and beautiful, of surprising aristocracy, much like that of Gobineau but broader and more delicate. . . . The serenity of this genius in plain misery snatched from me tears he did not see because he was, to make matters worse, already half blind.[13]

De Guaita, his mind made up to pursue his studies, and perhaps tired of the Latin Quarter in which old Abbé Lacuria struggled surrounded by books and scores he could no longer read, moved north to 24 rue Pigalle in the 9th arrondissement, just south of Montmartre. There he invited his new friend Péladan to share the apartment, but according to Michelet, Péladan was "of difficult humor and rapidly bruised all friendliness." *Two writers in one apartment?*—bound to be a disaster anyhow, and it is difficult to assess who was the more fundamentally frustrated of the two. They were almost opposite characters.

Péladan moved out and de Guaita moved 300 meters east to what would become his well-known billet, the ground floor apartment at 20 avenue Trudaine, where he built up a magnificent library, drank copiously, and stayed in a great deal. Apart from spending summers at the family château at Alteville, de Guaita would emerge from solitude on Thursday evenings when he joyfully hosted those dinner parties we last heard about with reference to Lady Caithness. Among regular visitants were fellow occultist Gérard Encausse—educated at the Collège Rollin a few doors down the avenue—and the brilliant, sometimes shocking, satirist and poet Laurent Tailhade (1854–1919) who had given Péladan's first novel a pasting in the pages of *Le Lutèce:* "Monsieur Péladan has taken his onaniacal nightmares for reality."[14] Perhaps

Fig. 5.7. Laurent Tailhade (1854–1919)

de Guaita was attracted to opposites because Tailhade was notorious for his anarchist beliefs, and probably ragged de Guaita mercilessly for his love of order! Michelet observed that Tailhade liked to appear indifferent to Hermetic studies, but in fact always had respect for them and for those who maintained them.

Despite the unsatisfactory nature of Péladan and de Guaita's flat-sharing venture, they would nevertheless try once more to join their considerable intellects and energies in a common venture. But before we investigate that bold exploit, we need to get a better picture as to whom Joséphin Péladan was, and just who Joséphin Péladan thought he was.

SIX

THE SÂR

Péladan's follow-up to *Le Vice Suprême* hit Paris in 1886. Entitled *Curieuse!* (Curious!)—which it was—its etched emblem and frontispiece, again by Péladan's favored artist Félicien Rops, and the dedication that follows them, tell us much about its author. The wicked Rops, you will recall, etched the "This fish is not for everyone" colophon for Bailly's *L'Art Indépendant* publications.

Rops's title page emblem continues the decapitating theme established with the first novel. *Le Vice Suprême's* frontispiece depicted a satirical horror scene wherein a headless, skeletal gentleman in evening dress, left lapel splashed with state honors ("the way of the cross"), his right limb clutching his manacled, cigar-smoking skull to his ribs, opens an upright coffin with his gloved phalanges, surrounded by scavenging Poe-esque ravens flapping their ghastly wings in the twilight shadows (see figure 6.2). Inside the coffin, the decomposing corpse of a lady still grips a fan in one hand while raising her skirts with the other. The dress has survived but only the soulless skeleton remains beneath. The phantom duo perform their hideous death rattle upon a plinth depicting an emaciated she-wolf unable to suckle starved and deceased Romulus and Remus, with the inscription *Roma,* after the legendary infants who founded Rome.

The title-page emblem for the Latin Decadence series is almost as garish and shows what looks like a naked Amazon holding up a severed head she has just decapitated (see figure 6.3 on page 136). The caption is blunt: "Ahoy! Latin races! Ahoy!" The barbaric Amazon is presumably Germanic, and the message is at once political and aesthetic.

The politics are clear from the dedication that follows. It is dated 15 November of the fourteenth year of the "MILITARY TERROR." The reference is plainly to the events of 1871 when Bismarck's troops surrounded Paris, France lost her emperor, and the Communards were massacred by order of a panicked French state.

Out and out Catholic Royalist Péladan regarded ideal art, taste, culture, and spirituality as the peculiar gift of the Latin races, and the decline of those ideals as the product of rot within the country and barbarism without. Unless the "Ideal, Hierarchy, and Tradition" were restored, and gloriously, the sky would get darker still, for the barbarian had entered the very citadel of France, while its governing classes were obsessed with sex and money. The she-wolf that had fed legendary founders of Rome, Romulus and Remus, was exhausted, unable to lactate. The children were dead or dying.

Fig. 6.1. Sâr Mérodack—Joséphin Péladan (1858–1918)

Fig. 6.2. Rops's frontispiece to Le Vice Suprême *(1884)*

JOSÉPHIN PÉLADAN

LA DÉCADENCE LATINE

ÉTHOPÉE

II

CURIEUSE!

FRONTISPICE A L'EAU-FORTE DE

FÉLICIEN ROPS'

« Ohé ! les races latines ! ohé !

PARIS

G. ÉDINGER, ÉDITEUR

34, RUE DE LA MONTAGNE-SAINTE-GENEVIÈVE, 34

Fig. 6.3. Title page: Curieuse!

Rops's relatively restrained frontispiece to *Curieuse!* is less straight-forward (see figure 6.4). In the darkness of a forest stands a votive statue of Pan's armless torso, goatlike and bearded. The undergrowth seems to be about to envelop it out of passionate attachment, but a more passion-ate, naked female figure, herself restrained by a series of belts that she is apparently trying to extricate herself from below her bottom, reaches her arms around the stone god's neck and with an intent look, surmounted by laurels, seems to ache to kiss and awaken the frozen statue.[1] The god's phallus is noticeably curved downward and inward; one doubts if her attraction will find satisfaction. However, Pan (= All) is also the alchemical One, the divine principle of the unbroken, ever-regenerating universe. And the All is also fecund, for the all contains all as one; Pan is *Hen* (Greek for "One") and contains *in principio* all possible numbers integrated in harmony. Does the naked girl then allegorize the secret passion for true wholeness in androgynous union, or does she embody the world's vice of trying to drag the ideal down to the level of the flesh and decay? Curious indeed!

The root of the design is I suspect Lévi's design for *Baphomet,* which is an androgynous union of male goat and female body. Rops's design then would symbolize the loss of androgynous idealism and its lascivious consequences, drawn out in the novel. The androgyny theme is plain from the first page of the prologue:

PLATONIC FLIRTATION

—You're staring at me too much, monsieur!

—Isn't that enough?

—Too much, I told you!

—Why, like a sun, do you force one to look?

—Politeness towards a star requires one to be dazzled.

—My dazzle would blind you, princess, if you read my secret thought . . . , for you are . . .

—I am . . . ?

—Androgynous!

—"Androgynous" yourself, monsieur!

Fig. 6.4. Frontispiece to Curieuse! *by Félicien Rops (1885)*

And, brusquely turning her back on him, she continued pouring tea, whilst the strange writer of madrigals returned to his armchair and returned to contemplation.

Like its predecessor, the novel *Curieuse!* concerns a strange figure, Nébo. The name comes from the son of Babylonian god Marduk ("Merodach" in Hebrew). The Assyrio-Babylonian Nebo is equated with the god Mercury, or Hermes, god of alchemical transmutation (*Hen to Pan* = the One is All). The rather effeminate Nébo of the novel becomes attracted to a boyish virgin. Whereas in Huysmans's *À Rebours,* which had appeared the previous year, antihero Des Esseintes perverts through exposure to vice, in *Curieuse!* Péladan inverts the perversion theme by having Nébo unveil all the vices of Paris to the Russian princess Paule precisely to ensure her purity. Nébo anticipates Paule's innate virtue will render her disgusted with the grisly truth of debauchery and precipitate an embrace of her educator's androgynous ideals, that is to say, her spiritual identity.

It is worth noting that in their years of friendly relations, Péladan and de Guaita referred to one another as Mérodack and Nébo respectively, their androgynous ideals perhaps sublimating a sexual passion as Nébo, in the novel, sublimates his attraction for his ideal by educating her. Péladan was of course familiar with the true nature of "Platonic love" from Plato's *Symposium* and *Phaedrus* in which the old philosopher would seek the ideal through the beautiful boy who would thereby be expected to accept the old boy's kisses and caresses, so long as the philosopher had grasped the truth that the proper object of love was the Beautiful itself, the spiritual ideal of which the body is but a temporal, imperfect form. Embracing the Beautiful was the end for which the exploited boy was the transient means, for "time is the moving image of eternity." Hence Péladan's prologue's subtitle: "Platonic Flirtation," and platonic flirtation was precisely Péladan's regular modus operandi. So long as the passion was sublimated into devotion to the sexless or sex-harmonized ideal, which was not bodily but spiritually realized, vice could be transcended. This is the governing principle of Péladan's entire aesthetic vision, and it is securely

Platonist—the "One" is all; *Hen to Pan,* as the Greco-Egyptian Hermetic alchemists put it, symbolizing the idea with a snake swallowing its own tail, forever born and reborn. Theologians who felt Christianity was impoverished, if not impossible, without Plato had long regarded the philosopher as a "Christian before Christ." And Péladan was a Platonist, and a Platonizing Catholic, attracted bodily and spiritually to Androgyny, for in Androgyny, occultly understood, lay the secret key to the reintegration of Man and the vitalization of spiritual culture on Earth. As far as Péladan was concerned, he was in direct contact with the Tradition.

The next important thing we need to know and understand about Péladan is that to which Michelet alerted us in the last chapter. Péladan's older brother Adrien was his master, whose master was Lacuria, whose master was Fabre d'Olivet. Such is made plain in the striking dedication of *Curieuse!* immediately following the title page:

TO MY BROTHER AND MY MASTER

DOCTOR ADRIEN PÉLADAN FILS

Poisoned, 29 September 1895
By the pharmacist WILMAR SCHWABE, *of Leipzig*
Who had sent to him in place of the third
Decimal demanded, a *first* of strychnine, *that is to say*
The death of 1,250 *people.*

Wilmar Schwabe (1839–1917) was the founder of a pharmaceutical empire, noted for its homoeopathic products, that continues to this day. Dr. Adrien Péladan *fils* was a pioneer homoeopathic doctor, self-administering a remedy of his own devising that included the potentially deadly strychnine. He overdosed due to an error in quantity attributed to the ingredient's source. The accusation's untrammeled anger is reflected in the date and place where the dedication was composed. The place: "Bellechasse Prison," Paris. The date: "15 November of the 14th Year of the Military Terror." Péladan, defiant, had missed

Fig. 6.5. Dr. Adrien Péladan fils (1844–1886)

the Republic's 1885 call—law since 1872—for young reservists to serve twenty-eight days in uniform. The punishment was two days in prison. Péladan was in fact allowed to serve only one day behind bars at the Bellechasse barracks. Nevertheless, Péladan envisioned the entire affair in symbolic terms, seeing his brief arrest by gendarmes as a manifestation of the idea of his bare body being manhandled into prison by the authorities that martyred the Communards, the donning of military-conforming clothing a violation analogous to Christ being scourged and jeered at by Roman soldiers. The filthy world had touched him.

Up to his arrest, overcome with grief at his brother's untimely and tragic death, Péladan had been correcting proofs of a piece where he predicted, following his brother's convictions and reading of "prophecies"—such as those of Paracelsus and "Enoch" made by Éliphas Lévi—a coming "Grand Monarch" or "Grand Pope" or even both in one: not the Light itself but a being through whom the Light could be seen, a combination of "Catholic, magus, artist, and saint" who would make manifest the "sovereignty of ideas over forms."[2] While Péladan admitted that this was "only a hope," nevertheless the Almighty, in creating Dr. Péladan, his brother, must, he surmised, already have projected the plan for the awaited "Moses of the future." It was clear Péladan took his brother's death as a sign that the torch of outspoken prophecy had been passed to him, and his aesthetic love of the grandiose and the ancient he shared with his brother was joined to his sense of personal destiny, feeling spiritually joined to an ancient tradition of primordial insight he associated with ancient Assyria, Chaldaean Babylon, and Persia, transmuted into divine philosophy by Pythagoras and Plato, then infused by manifestation of Christ into the Catholic Church, the sole institution capable of transcending the Age of Reason and materialism.

Péladan's ongoing conflict with secular authority was not new. In 1880, the year in which de Guaita began "hanging out," as we might say, in Paris with young friends Maurice Barrès, Edouard Dubus (*poète maudit* and founder of the *Mercure de France*), and pugnacious duelist Laurent Tailhade, twenty-two-year-old Péladan was arrested for protesting laws against unauthorized religious assemblies—Catholic anti-Republican ones in particular—whereafter Péladan informed his court accusers that Catholicism was the only source of Art. He got off with a fifteen franc fine because he was deemed an eccentric no rational person could take seriously. But by 1885 there was quite an audience for an eccentric who aimed his lance at the Age of Reason and his spotless colors at the sacred ideal whose symbol was the Grail.

In his dedication of *Curieuse!* to his deceased brother in 1885, Péladan is, however modest, conscious of the greatness both of his father *Le Chevalier* Adrien Péladan (1815–1890), granted knighthood by the Pope, and that of his brother the good doctor and polymath. He says: "I lack the voice to speak to the desert, and one has imposed on me the mask of vice to hear me speak of virtue." He calls himself a "smuggler" of metaphysics into the pages of a novel. The mystery he has to impart, his brother taught him: "I am only, my Brother, the most known of Your thoughts."

A dreadful death has delivered you from a dreadful life menaced by the barbarians on the frontiers, tortured by the national Barbarians, between the military draft and her rifles, between the [republican] bourgeois of 1872 and their guillotine, there is no longer security for the intellectual man who has become the grand suspect and common enemy; the Recruitment which crushed you in 1871, tortures me in 1885: Catholic and Frenchman. You have been killed by a Protestant German, and I write these lines in peril of death in the jail where the Law and the French Army have thrown me! There will never be on the earth neither liberty, nor justice, nor progress; the battles for the truth will always be lost, however necessary the struggle—the struggle without truce, likewise without hope of victory! God must be for us the ideal that we shall have loved; and eternity will be the realization of our will. Also humanity would be no more than an hour than it ought: "devotee, complete your rosary—artist, your work."

Learning my vocation even from Your life, proclaiming sinisterly of the "Woe" of the prophets on France's last days, I will pursue the enemies of God with the trace of your blood.

You have been rejected and vilified by the [academic] Faculties; I will deny all collectivity; a masterpiece, one law signs itself with a single name. You have been tortured by Recruitment; I will deny the work of blood, I will deny military glory, I will deny nationality. You have been betrayed and sold by the monarchists; I will deny the heredity of the power and the titles.

The Province devoured you; I shall unveil this hypocritical buzzard; I shall proclaim humanism and the dogma of individuality.

I shall renew the doctrine of Enoch, in kissing before the whole world the mule of the Pope, the sole power I shall ever recognize.

Enlighten me, admirable Understanding! As you have enlightened me; and whilst I will ask of those who love me with prayers and masses for the souls released from purgatory, Your protégées,—Magus become saint, make it so my work is a work of charity whose pages be read in heaven by Your new brothers—the Cherubim![3]

This short dedication to his departed brother may tell us more about the real Péladan than perhaps could any other extract from his prolific writings. If one should suppose it the intemperate outpouring of an unbalanced moment in a period of grief, consider that this was placed as the dedication to what was intended to be a popular novel. This is not metaphysics smuggled in, but slapped right in the reader's face: "Take it or leave

Fig. 6.6. Marcellin Desboutin's portrait of
Sâr Mérodack Joséphin Péladan (1891),
Muséee des Beaux Arts, Angers

it—when you get Péladan, you get Joséphin, the brother and the father," and the entire tradition, as he saw it, of legitimate authority, prepared to stand up and suffer ridicule for the sake of the ideal individuality. One can then see why Péladan did not balk at imitating Barbey d'Aurevilly's dandyism. He could be seen better in ruffs and velvet doublets, and medieval fineries, including ecclesiastical cassocks, capes, laced cuffs, and silk stockings and shiny boots with his immense beard, huge staring eyes, and black cloud of hair like the thunderous aura about Horeb into which Moses disappeared to obtain the tablets of the law! His life was his art, his religion his life, and his God went with him.

THE PÉLADANS

You could say Péladan would be both asset and liability to any *Compagnonnage de la Hiérophanie,* but then again, he may have claimed right to the particular use of this unusual word *Hiérophanie* ("Manifestation of the Sacred"), for it appears in the title to his second great series of publications, the first being *La Décadence Latine:* the novels. On the title page to his collection of art criticisms (Le Salon) that first appeared individually in *l'Artiste,* founded by "old romantic" Arsène Houssaye (1815–1896)—as Michelet called him— the phrase "Décadence Esthétique" is followed by the bracketed word "Hiérophanie."[4] Below the word is an emblem depicting a winged sphinx with the heroic epigram *Vives unguibus et morsu* ("You will live by claws and teeth"). The sphinx has very sharp claws embedded in a book, breathes fire, and has the stinging tail of a scorpion. He who gave no quarter expected none.

Joséphin's father Adrien had been made a knight of the Order of Saint Sylvester for dedicating his writings, poetry, and journalism to the cause of the Catholic Church in attempting to secure legitimist governance of France. Adrien *père* was also elected to Rome's *Accademia degli Arcadi* (Arcadian Academy), founded in 1689 to promote arts and letters. And truly, Joséphin's father was in Arcadia, for the Academy's traditional objectives included the desire to return Italian poetry to its golden age when the ideal songs of Virgilian shepherds were evoked, whose muses were Hermes, Pan, and Apollo. The Academy took the pipes of Pan as its emblem. The message of the father was not lost on the son. The family shared a passion for occulted symbols. Joséphin would also attempt a restoration of the paradise lost. His father's sword was his pen, and his sons likewise took dedicated writing as a mark of chivalry in the Grail's service.

Adrien *père* founded a newspaper, *L'Étoile de Midi,* the first of several devoted to the restoration of the Bourbons, a cause suppressed after Louis Bonaparte took power in the 1848 revolts. The family moved to Paris on a meager tutor's wages, before returning to Lyon where conditions improved to the extent that the Chevalier was able to establish a salon of Lyon's intellectuals, poets, and artists at his rue Sainte Hélène home, dominated by poet, humorist, and prominent Lyonnais citizen, Joséphin Soulary (1815–1891) in whose honor little Joseph Aimé Péladan became known as Joséphin, while his elder brother's precocious mind won him the Abbé Lacuria as his tutor. Joséphin regarded Lacuria, as we have seen, as one of the greatest *illuminés* of all time.

Through Lacuria's painter brother Louis, who trained in Ingres's studio and worked at the Oullins seminary school, Joséphin would have become familiar with English Pre-Raphaelitism whose "Order" had been formed in England in 1848 and whose Anglo-Catholic taste for medieval beauties and Gothic chivalries would impact on the Symbolists, not forgetting the incredible impression the image of Rossetti's free-dressing wife, Elizabeth Siddal, who died aged thirty-two in 1862, also made on male and female Symbolist-following imaginations and projections.

When Joseph Péladan was born on 28 March 1858, his elder brother was already fourteen and excelling. At sixteen, Adrien *fils* began learning Chinese before being taken by the study of ancient Assyria, seeking the ancient names of God, being convinced there was an original alphabet and number system shared by humanity. His younger brother in later life was thus inspired to make much of Mesopotamian deities, and encouraged the decorative use of Assyrian forms, rescued from the past by the archaeology of Austen Henry Layard (1817–1894), combined with a general fascination for the doomed Babylon, as in Péladan's tragic play *Babylone* (1895), a fascination shared, indeed celebrated, by Symbolist artists for whom it was hard to choose which was the city best suited to Decadent evocation in word or paint: Carthage, Babylon, or Byzantium, all grand, excessive, erotically charged, overdecorated but frequently topless, shadowy, mysterious, doomed. Their tastes would charge up many an early epic, silent movie whose images spoke volumes, for they derived from volumes that spoke in images— viz: D. W. Griffith's *Intolerance,* 1916.

A friend of Adrien *père,* Chevalier Charles de Paravey (1787–1871), was one of many influential contacts in Lyon. While the former annotated Paravey's "Researches on the Ancient Names of God" (Roanne, 1866), Paravey may have initiated Joséphin's crucial interest in androgyny. Paravey's article "On the Creation of Man as Androgyne and of Woman" was published by Adrien *père* in his revue *la France littéraire, artistique et scientifique* in Paris in 1864. A fervent legitimist and student of ancient mythology and hieroglyphs dedicated to reconciling science and religion, Paravey believed a primordial tradition present in ancient America, China, and elsewhere could be traced to antique Assyria (*Essai sur l'origine unique et hiéroglyphique des chiffres et des lettres de tous les peuples*, 1826). Péladan took it all in. For him, his father's salon, where he heard the graceful sonorities of Latin become Hebrew, become Chinese or Italian, was tantamount to reinhabiting Ficino's Platonic Academy in the fragrant springtime of Renaissance Florence. He was imbued with the sense of unity in tradition, and he already in his childhood had the idea of chastity as the proper mode for the life of high science. In his boyhood zeal, he even forcibly baptized a Jewish schoolmate to preserve the boy from spiritual peril, an act incomprehensible to us now.[5]

Having made a number of still useful studies of the archaeology of Lyon, Adrien *fils,* with his father's assistance, embarked on a tour of homeopathy that would come to dominate his life. Their first treatise on the subject was published in 1869. It was curious, being punctuated with Kabbalistic citations. The penchant for Kabbalah would of course unite Joséphin with de Guaita for a few years. Synthesizing different fields in the course of profound speculation was normal in those days, though frowned on today in our era of specialists who, academically, have cut up the universe of knowledge as if apportioning exclusive properties to acceptable bidders.

Robert Pincus-Witten, an authority on Péladan's Rose-Croix Salons of the 1890s, observed how Joséphin shared the synthesizing tendencies of his father—who synthesized politics with prophecy—and his brother, who synthesized science with the arcane. Péladan's great schemes brought together his twenty novels into the description of the psychology and manners of the period (Latin Decadence), his critical writings into the Aesthetic Decadence (Hierophany), and his philosophical work into seven volumes of the *Amphithéâtre des Sciences Mortes*—the Amphitheater of Dead Sciences—whose title was ironically borrowed from Heinrich Khunrath's *Amphitheatre of Eternal Wisdom* (1595). In fact there was a para-Rosicrucian tradition for this kind of synthesis. It was what Czech educator and mystic Comenius (1592–1670) called "Pansophia," or All-wisdom, which concept informed the minds of several of the original founders of the Royal Society, but the idea of which was lost in the systematic scattering of academic disciplines in the eighteenth and nineteenth centuries.

Joséphin's father filled the 1860s with pro-Catholic works, including an 1863 rebuttal to theologian Ernest Renan's scandalous, stripped-down *Vie de Jésus.*[6] The era reached a fitting climax with Pope Pius IX summoning a great ecumenical council in late 1869 whose deliberations included the formal recognition of Papal Infallibility to bolster up the Church's political clout. Young Péladan was struck by the concept, and to his detriment, imposed it, not altogether ironically, on his own quasi-Rosicrucian system in the 1890s, calling himself Sâr, or King, in the Assyrian-Persian mold (cf. Shah), there already being a Pope. It would perhaps have been appropriate for St. Yves d'Alveydre to write a "Mission pour le Sâr Péladan," except that Péladan knew what his mission was and didn't need any advice from anyone.

Péladan's father predicted the German invasion of 1870 and the family moved out of Lyon, to Avignon and Nîmes. Adrien *père* backed up his support for Bourbon pretender, Henri V (d. 1883), with prophecies. It was during this period that Joséphin conceived his particular hatred for the military, for his elder brother was conscripted, his beautiful hair shorn, and the great mind subjected to the vulgar drilling of sergeants. Joséphin narrowly avoided the draft due to special legislation for seminarists—he attended a series of Jesuit colleges. Discharged after three months, the elder brother led Joséphin before the Papal Palace in Avignon and instructed him to attach himself only to eternal things, to be virtuous, to create, but only ever to serve the church, popular laws being vanities. Not bad advice, methinks, if you don't mind a difficult but meaningful life.

However, young Péladan's idea of serving the "church" was freely interpreted to the degree that he rebelled against Jesuit conformity, emphasized himself as the subject of the redemptive process, and failed his baccalaureate examinations, doubtless dismissing them as signs of surrender to mediocrity, the path of the many. One cannot help seeing a comparison with the young Aleister Crowley, who was born in Leamington around this time. He too would grow up an individualist with a father filled with prophecy and socially exclusive attitudes, and would come to similar attitudes to his senior in years, Péladan (including an early active enthusiasm for monarchical legitimism). Indeed, it is fairly clear that Crowley learned and copied a great deal from the French occultists (even down to book titles), and not only from Lévi, as is well known.

By now, Péladan's brother and father were firmly *contra mundum*, the latter serving six days in prison for writing against the republic's president for not defending the Pope during the Italian revolution, while the brother was shouted down by students at his final oral examinations at Montpellier University, one of whose faculty members, the elder Péladans had libeled for "the most lewd materialism."[7] Adrien *fils* would have to resign himself to operating outside of the academic mainstream and settled into a homeopathic practice in Nîmes, writing books about it, with an increasing interest in gynecological issues such as the nature of the orgasm and the like, while his younger brother, according to Pincus-Witten, absorbed from the dominant males of his family the habit of "courting abuse."[8]

In his *Oraison funèbre du chevalier Adrien Peladan* (Funerary Oration of the Chevalier Adrien Péladan, 1890), Joséphin testified "before the incredulity of the century, that, in 1879, Doctor Péladan . . . told me: I am menaced by dying poisoned by a foreign medicine that I shall administer myself."[9] It proved true, as we know, when insufficiently diluted strychnine sent from Leipzig killed him in 1885.

In 1881, Joséphin's father advised a member of Barbey d'Aurevilly's circle, Charles Buet, to take on his son as a writer on art with a Catholic voice. Buet edited the small-time *Le Foyer, Journal de famille,* and on 21 August that journal published Péladan's first article called, characteristically, "Materialism in Art." He argued that materialism had obscured the proper relation between art and God. Péladan's mission had begun. He observed how the spiritual world's dynamic had moved away from the church and become enthroned in the world of aesthetics. This presented him with an opportunity for which he regarded himself as uniquely qualified, which in many respects, he was. Since Art and literature were on the way to becoming chief repositories of experience of interiority, fountains of spiritual perception, it was Péladan's task to spiritualize and return them to their ideal essence and traditional function. This he could do through comprehending the function of the Symbol, the essence of the eucharist: the intersection of the spiritual and the soul of humanity, where spiritual blood or life is symbolized as wine and taken into substance (form).

In 1894 Péladan would summarize his doctrine in articles one and two of his "Theory of Beauty": "There is no other reality than God. There is no other truth than God. There is no other Beauty than God. The three great divine names are: 1 Reality, the substance or the Father; 2 Beauty, the life or the Son; 3 Truth or the unification of Reality and of Beauty which is the Holy Spirit" (Sâr Péladan, *L'Art Idéaliste & Mystique, Doctrine de l'Ordre et du Salon Annuel des Rose+Croix*, 33).

Like Blake, Péladan saw Art as the divine gift of imagination, our conduit to divine experience and true self-realization. Art for Péladan and the movement he encouraged would be the guardian of the sacredness of the human-divine ideal, whose precious inner life would serve as a barricade against the invasion of value-free nihilism into the vulnerable soul. He believed he understood the potential mind of a universal (Catholic) faith and practice and was prepared to enlighten the church itself if requested. Art could be seen as a form of lived ritual, a communication with heaven, promoting the Platonic trinity of truth, beauty, and goodness. His ideas absorbed fundamental insights in abundance from the mystery tradition of continental gnosis which he regarded as Catholic, for the Catholic ideal had *always* existed, only finding its outward *form* in the genesis of the primitive Christian church, and even that had been born at a price of substance and was therefore subject to development, understood as a reintegration of primal qualities. A conversation between Péladan and England's Cardinal Newman (1801–1890) on the subject and meaning of dogma would have been most interesting.

Indeed, that thought should arrest us a moment, for it is fascinating to observe parallel spiritual revolts against the asphyxiation of materialism occurring in different forms in England and France in the same century. That is to say, France, due to its history, did not experience anything like the "Oxford Movement" that gripped many of the best minds of the Church of England from 1833 onward, and which, until his secession to Rome in 1845, Newman had co-led. That movement was also in many respects an aesthetic revolt against rationalism and materialism toward an ideal of Catholicity that had been forgotten. It gave birth to an aesthetic movement manifest in poetry, literature, design (William Morris), paint and wood and stone in the Gothic revival, the Pre-Raphaelite Brotherhood, and in the architectural creativity of George Gilbert Scott and Catholic convert Augustus Pugin. The difference in England perhaps came with the rootedness of a national Christian faith within hearts and minds, and in scholarship, and a deeper confidence in the polity of the nation as a whole, into which the church was fully integrated, though under sporadic stress. These precious securities were not the possession of post-Revolutionary France in general, and so a spiritual aesthetic movement there was more likely to accrue to a more specifically heterodox, mystical, and occult body of doctrines than in England in the period, though a crossover did begin to penetrate English Bohemia, especially in the brief Edwardian "Indian summer," after Paris's occult, or we may fairly say, gnostic, explosion.

Péladan was in some ways unique as a Catholic apologist in that his concept of the Catholic Church was already imbued with universalist conceptions of ancient, symbolic, and esoteric truths. In this respect, there is something of the Giordano Bruno about him in that he believed himself to be a pioneer in converting the church to its real, obscured self. Bruno (1548–1600) had gone to Rome, misled into thinking the pope would be gratified to hear his plea for a universal Egypto-Hermetic spiritual and scientific revolution in the church, based on the symbol of the sun as our system's center. This hope cost him his life.

For Péladan, centuries of fighting "heresies" head on had coarsened and perverted the church's self-perception. The true throne of gnosis was in the heart of the church, for it was in the mind of Christ. The forerunner of Christ was "Elias the Artist." No grammarian pedant, God was creative. And Péladan knew perfectly well he was himself in many respects better educated, and certainly more intellectually and imaginatively gifted, than most priests, bishops, or cardinals. His self-image and exaggerated individualism insulated him, while the struggles of himself and his family and the works he admired strengthened him. He would struggle "by tooth and claw" if necessary. Curiously, the church could have, but did not, silence him, perhaps because Péladan was always careful to accept as a dogma the authority of the church. A good magistrate will forgive much if he or she sees the defendant truly respects the law.

Péladan's first critical piece came to two conclusions. First, "masterpieces of art are all religious, even among non-believers" (he'd spent March 1881 on a tour of Pisa, Florence, Milan, and Rome), and second, "For nineteen centuries masterpieces of art have all been Catholic, even for the Protestants."[10]

In September 1881, Péladan began contributing his Salon reviews to L'Artiste as he sharpened his arrows in readiness to aim at the annual Salons of the Académie des Beaux Arts. Péladan's work came to the attention of young Michelet who knew the director of L'Artiste, Jean Alboize, and its founder, Arsène Houssaye. Michelet had vivid memories of the septuagenarian Arsène Houssaye, who kept a close eye on goings-on at the journal:

> Péladan had made his literary debut with his "Salon" essays in L'Artiste, directed by his compatriot [from the Lyonnais], Jean Alboize, under the inspiration of the founder, Arsène Houssaye. The old romantic, with his apollonian intuition, recognized the debutant as a born artist. He divined in Péladan the psychologist of the feminine and advised him to write the biography of the demoiselle Marie du Lou, better known as Marion Delorme [1613–1650; Péladan wrote a three-part essay about the courtesan, intimate of political élites and mistress of a Parisian salon for L'Artiste, March–May 1882].

*Fig. 6.7. Arsène Houssaye (1815–1896),
photograph by Étienne Carjat*

Septuagenarian, the elegant seigneur of letters Arsène Houssaye had the lively spirit of youth. I have worked for several months everyday near to the charming mannered old gentleman. I regret that his old friend Baudelaire, having dedicated to him *Les Poèmes en Prose*, had, in a moment of ill humor, lined him up among those called "les canailles" [the scoundrels], that is to say, those who participate in social intrigues. To the eyes of a Baudelaire, an artist who works to serve his faculties dedicated to the ends of fashionable success is a miserable type like a "gaillard" who would traffic his mistress, or more, like a priest who would sell sacred relics. Thus judge those who inhabit the summits where they breathe the perfume of eternity. Arsène Houssaye knew how to pull men to advantage, but he did it with such grace that one could not love him less for it, this old courtier, of this imperial court of which he spoke to me with fire: "My poor friend, you have not known the *décaméron* [Boccaccio's fourteenth-century love tales to be told in ten days] of the Empress: you don't know that this is an attractive woman."[11]

Houssaye's director, Jean Alboize, employed Félicien Rops and was also friendly with Barbey d'Aurevilly and poet and initially naturalist author Léon Bloy (1846–1917) who in 1868 had befriended Barbey d'Aurevilly when living opposite him in the rue Rousselet (7th arrondissement). The friendship led to Bloy's conversion to Catholicism. After arriving in Paris in 1882, Péladan would take full advantage of these connections and those of his new mistress, occult sympathizer, Henriette Maillat (born 1849) who would in due course number Bloy among her conquests before indulging in a brief affair with "Joris-Karl" (actually Charles-Marie-Georges) Huysmans in 1888, her love letters being used for the seduction dialogue of his character Mme. Chantelouve in Huysmans's Satanistic novel, *Là Bas* (1891). Péladan would live with Henriette at the top of a house on the corner of the rue de Seine and the rue des Beaux Arts.

Even before moving to the pages of *L'Artiste,* Péladan had shown a

Fig. 6.8. Léon Bloy (1846–1917)

Fig. 6.9. Pierre Puvis de Chavannes (1824–1898)

distinct appreciation of the art of Pierre Puvis de Chavannes (1824–1898).
Perhaps it helped that the artist came from Lyon. Puvis showed all the
marks of being a Symbolist without ever committing to the movement.
His figures were ideals, classical, unreal but highly decorative, reminiscent of antique frescoes. There was also a chaste quality to the topless
nudes who sparsely populated his rather abstract settings that are more
like stages than landscapes. The laws of nature seldom intrude; the
figures are as apt to fly as to lounge about dreaming by rocks close to
placid seas beneath pale, indeterminate skies. In 1884, Péladan could
have found the artist painting the staircase at the Sorbonne. Another
thing that would have endeared Puvis to Péladan was that the painter

was constantly criticized for the lack of reality in his figures and settings, something Péladan would have regarded as an asset. The mystical ideal was all. Puvis's friezelike composition *Ludus Pro Patria* was the highlight of the 1882 Salon and Péladan was not disposed to question the Salon's taste in exhibiting it.

As Pincus-Witten observed, Péladan's Platonist aesthetic gave him a vantage point from which he could aim his artillery at the official Salon. The simplicity of Italian late medievalism might, he asserted, have been deficient in technical knowledge, but it was in touch with divine realms, unconscious realms, unspoiled by academic discipline cowering beneath the categories of materialist science.

Asked by Alboize to write an article on Rembrandt, Péladan found the artist lacking in the sense of the feminine, unable, unlike da Vinci, to paint the beauty of woman. Latin sensibility was artistic sensibility; the barbarians were at the gates. Nevertheless, Rembrandt's commitment to individualism drove his judge to conclude that Rembrandt's greatness lay in the fact that he copied no one, and no one could copy him. Rembrandt was his own man, inspired and magical: a Magus. Péladan's worship of Leonardo da Vinci erupted again in January 1883 with the appearance of his essay "Le Grand Oeuvre d'après Lionardo da Vinci." *Le Grand Oeuvre* refers to the alchemical Great Work: the transformation of lower orders of being into higher orders of existence. The ideal exists secreted *in potentia* and may be expressed as a visual symbol. Think too much and you will only arrive at a clumsy allegory; nevertheless, clumsy allegories made for perfectly acceptable paintings in the period and not many could tell the difference.

As for the predominant style of Impressionism, Péladan shook his head since it took its cue from the visual plane alone. He emphasized— as did Blake incidentally—the significance of clear lines. This, Péladan wrote in *L'Artiste* in March 1883, had always been sufficient for metaphysical ideas. Such material demanded the clarity of the letter. He would have liked Blake's insistence on "firm and determinate outline" as the honest approach to the artist's conceiving anything. Otherwise one was subject to transient appearance, as edges change in texture according to light and other conditions. Eternal ideas do not change. Mysticism is not misty; it is absolute clarity. Old as it was, this was a daring aesthetic for the time, and most unexpected. Even today, the blurring of the line that came with Impressionism is taken by accepted histories of art as the beginning of modernism, an alleged evolution into which Symbolism and Péladan appear to be unwanted distractions.

Péladan turned his guns on the Salon in May 1883: "L'Ésthétique au Salon de 1883," carried by *L'Artiste* for the following two months. The tirade opens with the famous declaration: "I believe in the Ideal, in Tradition, in Hierarchy." With the coruscating zeal that would typify the critics of the *Cahiers de Cinéma* in the 1950s in their attack on French commercial cinema conventions, and in particular the careful compositions of Claude Autant-Lara, Péladan proceeded to lay waste the neoclassical comforts of the official Salon. Realism in painting was consigned to the same waste pipe as naturalism in literature. Péladan had no problem with representation, but with what was being represented. He wanted the blood of Christ, not cordial from art's altar. Sublimity was acceptable; it cost everything. Better the *via dolorosa* of putting an idea to its extreme at the furthest horizon of realization than enjoying Sunday afternoon with a dog and brush. Conceit, technical excellence for its own sake was smudged out of the picture. Péladan wanted divine action since he believed art was a miracle, coming from the Hermetic miracle that was Man. Nothing less would do. Paris was already full of ordure and debaucheries undreamt by Nero. Full as they were, its drains could still accommodate bad art.

He summarized his view of the worst art as "L'Art Ochloratique." *Ochlos* is Greek for "mob" and playing to the mob was what got Jesus crucified and Louis XVI guillotined. Interestingly, the French equivalent *la foule* was a favorite word in Michelet's vocabulary and was clearly part of the attitude of a group that for all their enthusiasm, knew it was really very small, with the bourgeois barbarians at the door, ready to beat it down if necessary.

With great polemical skill, Péladan would, after debunking the worst the Salon had to offer, make his "Salut aux absents." Those not invited to the official Salon's banquet were welcome in the liberated paragraphs of his printed "Salon." In 1883, salutes were made to the absent Félicien Rops, to Gustave Moreau—another great who refused to be defined as a Symbolist—to Paul Baudry, to Ernest Hébert, and of course to Puvis de Chavannes. Little wonder that in the course of time, organizers would try to prevent Péladan from entering the Salon; he would manage nonetheless most of the time, like penniless lad François Truffaut sneaking in to the cinema to watch *Citizen Kane,* or passing mysteriously through the throng as Jesus passed through the Nazareth mob, baying for the prophet's blood. Before Crowley had a chance to utter that "spiritual attainments are incompatible with bourgeois morality," Joséphin Péladan had already declared that bourgeois art was impossible; like an emperor, art need only ever appeal to the aristocracy or the rabble; the bourgeoisie has a secret loathing for monarchy.

Péladan was not simply throwing stones at the unholy alliance of academicians and Impressionists. He spoke up for the at-the-time still somewhat inchoate cloud of Symbolists starting to find an identity, and for the very close Nabis (prophets) of what is known as the *Pont-Aven* school for their delight in the Brittany coastline, which became for them a kind of Galilee full of the meek and pure of heart to which the spirit of Christ and heart of art responded.

Péladan fired off another barrage in the autumn. The Salon organizers were asked by Antonin Proust, minister of arts to exhibit three paintings by Manet, who had recently died and was Proust's friend. They would only allow one, so Proust withdrew them all. Péladan was in like a bulldog. He didn't like Impressionism, but Manet, he wrote, was as significant to art history as schisms were to the history of religion. Manet at least was an artist, which is more than could be said for half the jury members! He accused their opposition of turning what could have been a master into a reactionary!

Pincus-Witten takes the sensible view that had Péladan muted his androgyny theme, he might have been able to capitalize on his brilliant critical invective for considerably longer, but that was like asking Oscar Wilde to quit England on the Channel Ferry rather than face the ignominious trial that would destroy his reputation and his health, if not his soul. Péladan did not know when to stop because his horizons were ideal and very personal. Prose poems about da Vinci's androgynous *John the Baptist* in the Louvre did not open the eyes of the enemy; they brought him ridicule of the predictable type. Péladan could envision a new age when he and what he stood for would make perfect and obvious sense but he was probably considerably further from its realization than he knew, if indeed he cared.

While some Decadents might have taken the symbol of the Androgyne as a basis for erotic exploration of the homosexual kind, Péladan took it seriously as an aspect of the divine. The Hermetic *Asclepius* is quite blatant in saying that "God is bisexual" having the full masculine and feminine potentialities within him. Therefore, androgyny was a kind of imperative of spiritual and religious art and an ideal aesthetic symbol that had to be stated because Péladan believed it to be not only true, but as Hermes Trismegistus would say, "of all truth" whether one liked it or not. Péladan knew how much the vulgar enjoyed fighting and war, in spite of themselves, and he seems to have grasped that this was somehow a result of an aesthetic *and* biological imbalance, a war with sex, a war in the soul derived from enforced division of the sexes. Realizing this, he was content to induce a crisis in the patient, if he could.

Péladan, to his credit, had his eye on "Le Groupe des Indépendants," one of whose founders was the Belgian Fernand Khnopff. They had their first exhibition in May 1884. Seurat and Redon were there. Péladan would give the survivors access to the *Salons de la Rose+Croix* when he launched that enterprise in 1892. Then there was the Belgian Symbolist group, "Les XX," which included Jean Delville, another outstanding contributor to Péladan's later ideal Salons. Delville would come to promote Péladan's aesthetic revolt in his home country. These artists painted from spiritual experience.

The year 1884 saw Péladan launching more rockets into the bosom of academic art, along with great praise for Puvis de Chavannes who was exhibited there ("Le Bois Sacré") and an appreciation of Huysmans's *Au Rebours,* the hit novel that included a favored description of Gustave Moreau's *Salomé.* Péladan reckoned Zola's time was now up, which is to say, naturalism was on the way out—so he thought—Huysmans having decamped to a new kind of literature, the Symbolist kind, of sorts.

Publication in 1884 of the sensational *Le Vice Suprême,* set Péladan up for his own turn under the critic's scalpel. He didn't do so badly. Public notice of his first novel did bring him the attention of Stanislas de Guaita. De Guaita's love for the book did not prevent him from going through the first and subsequent editions, listing grammatical errors or stylistic lapses.

Catulle Mendès's recollection that it was he who brought de Guaita to Éliphas Lévi was contradicted by Barrès who held that it was reading Péladan's novel that introduced de Guaita to Lévi.[12] It is difficult to tell which encounter proved more fateful or indeed fatal for de Guaita. The marquis wrote to Péladan on 3 November 1884: "I have just read your beautiful book *Le Vice Suprême,* and reread it several times . . . it seems genial to me, the hermetic gust which blows through your work."[13] De Guaita wrote again a fortnight later: "It is your *Vice Suprême* that revealed to me (to me, sceptic, although respectful of all holy things), that the Kabbala and High Magic could be something other than a trick."[14]

Until 1888 when de Guaita and Péladan formed the *Ordre Rose+Croix Kabbalistique,* Péladan kept himself busy writing further striking critical essays on the arts, artists, and official Salons—when he could get in—always favoring Puvis de Chavannes and Moreau with praise, and Rops with employment (frontispieces for his novels *L'Initiation sentimentale,* 1887, and *À Coeur perdu,* 1888), while also developing his association with Fernand Khnopff who executed the cover to Péladan's novel *Istar* (1888) and frontispiece to Péladan's short story collection *Femmes Honnêtes:* "Honest Women" (1888).

Just why Péladan participated in de Guaita's pet project, a renovated Rosicrucian Order, has never been satisfactorily explained. As Michelet noted: "Péladan was of difficult humor and discouraged friendlinesses. He did not stay long in the rue Pigalle [with de Guaita]. Nevertheless, when de Guaita founded his *Ordre de la Rose-Croix rénovée,* he made Péladan one of the six members of the Supreme Council. Péladan was not the man to accept that another than himself was his Grand Master.

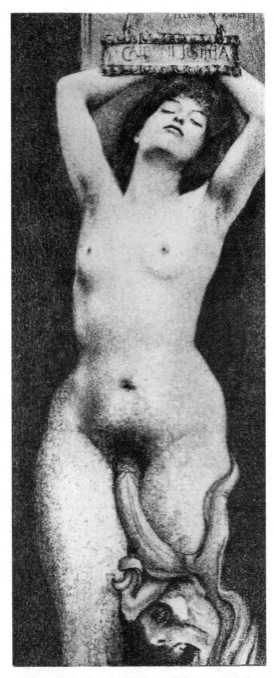

*Fig. 6.10. Fernand Khnopff (1858–1921),
design for frontispiece of Péladan's novel* Istar
(La Décadence Latine, Éthopée, vol. 5), 1888

Already he took the title of Sâr, which would weigh so heavily on his name and unhappily also on his work."[15]

We had better examine the new Kabbalistic Rosicrucian Order that provided opportunity for the first serious rupture within the burgeoning world of Occult Paris.

SEVEN

THE KABBALISTIC ⊙RDER
⊙F THE R⊙SE-CR⊙SS

There must have been something in the air, something that made different individuals at roughly the same time try to do similar things. The spark ignited in 1888 when Stanislas de Guaita assumed Grand Mastership of a renewed Order under the "Rose-Croix" banner. In England, Rosicrucian Freemasons inspired by Anna Kingsford's Hermetic reading of Western esoteric sources established the secret Hermetic Society of the Golden

Fig. 7.1. Sigil of the Kabbalistic Order of the Rose-Cross, based on the Hebrew tetragrammaton and the letter Schin, representing spirit, or "fifth element"

Dawn. Back in Paris, Gérard Encausse (Papus) organized a society for "esoteric studies" that met at Chamuel's *Librairie du Merveilleux* in the rue Trévise. Meanwhile, tensions persisted in the Parisian Theosophical Society, patronized by Lady Caithness, as members differed over Madame Blavatsky's emphasis on Indian philosophy and religion, differences Anna Kingsford had sown the seeds of.

It was probably Anna Kingsford's sudden death in February 1888 that provided the spark for the British Golden Dawn. The Golden Dawn's foundation documents—forged—were alleged to have come from a Nuremberg Lodge of Rosicrucian adepts with links back to the "original" Rosicrucian Fraternity that had announced its existence (!) in the manifesto called the *Fama Fraternitatis,* published in Kassel in 1614 (see my book *The Invisible History of the Rosicrucians*). The German link to London was falsely ascribed to one "Anna Sprengel." The "Anna" was probably William Wynn Westcott's devoted reference to admired seeress, Anna Kingsford.

It is significant that the English Order chose a link to Germany, not Paris. This suggests to me at least that the regular Freemasons of the *Societas Rosicruciana in Anglia* (founded in 1867) who established the mixed membership Golden Dawn and claimed to be in direct line to legendary founder Christian Rosenkreutz were aware of French motions toward reviving a specifically occult order, and did not wish to be subordinate to it. Since the emergence after 1716 of London's Grand Lodge, leading members have been extremely sensitive about jurisdictions and recognition issues, asserting primacy in the discomfiting face of competing Masonic fraternities.

Be that as it may, there is also the sense that the time had simply come when some Order of the kind had to happen: a solidification of awareness that had been coalescing, as materialism encroached further in the wake of mass production and mechanized warfare amid the unnerving consequences of Darwinian evolution theory and geology's explosion of the biblical time frame.

Was there strength in numbers on the occult level? Or was it rather a question of discrete evangelism? With so much occult enthusiasm being generated, in Paris especially, the question would naturally arise as to who was in charge, or "How can I join?"—difficult questions when such strong personalities were involved. Had Stanislas de Guaita been less systematic and more intuitive in his thinking, I suspect he might have thought twice before sharing ideas for a Kabbalistic Rose-Croix with Péladan in late 1887. However, it might have been as much a question of pooling enthusiasms at that stage. For by late 1887, Péladan, after two or three years of literary notoriety, was probably looking to consolidate his position, and being apt to toy with enthusiasms, probably encouraged de Guaita and his organizational priorities. Beside, if there was going to be an occult fraternity, he, Mérodack, leader of the young gods, had better be on the ruling body. If de Guaita wanted to do the paper work, so much the better, Péladan probably thought—to begin with. It is unlikely Péladan took the idea altogether seriously, perhaps for the very reason that de Guaita may have been seeking his active participation. What do I mean by this?

I mean that a Rosicrucian Order traditionally had to demonstrate its lineage in a similar manner to that of the "laying on of hands" in the church. Authority came from linkage to the original spiritual spark, either in the past or via some otherworldly mandate. Without supernal authority, without that seat in heaven, as it were, without preternatural guidance, one was merely establishing a sect, which by definition is something "cut off" from something else, as in the case of willful schismatics. While de Guaita himself doubtless felt inspired to offer systematic shape to the "new" occult awareness, to establish order, which, as we have seen, was a basic drive in his makeup, he had the problem of justifying authority within the Order.

"Fail not of an heir" is a primary Rosicrucian adage. Of whom, or what, was de Guaita's order the heir? Who was passing on the requisite linkage with the spiritual dimension? Eighteenth-century Rosicrucian and Kabbalistic Orders had been at pains to demonstrate that they were subject to higher authority, "unknown superior," bodies of adepts, in distant refuges or assumed to unearthly planes of existence to exercise influence on significant matters on Earth. Without contact with such dimensions, what was the point of an occult order? How could the order be recognized by spiritual beings, attentive to the spiritual activities of men and women on the plane of manifestation (Earth)? Such beings had either to choose someone who became inspired as a result, and could therefore inspire others, or they would have to recognize one charged to the work by "one of their own," lest the Order fall into error and evil.

De Guaita, respecter of tradition, must have been aware of the risks in establishing such an Order. Michelet was of the view that de Guaita simply took it upon himself out of the logic of his activities and in the purity of his spiritual motives. That is, since there was in 1887 no known competing Order in France to object, might it not be a God-given duty to revive the old tradition for the sake of Tradition, and that that desire to renew the tradition constituted in itself the genuine spiritual impulse necessary to launch it? And if his friends encouraged him, could he resist the responsibility? And if he did not do it, might not some perverse person do the same? Besides, had he not been led spiritually from despair to the light of Éliphas Lévi? Or was it, as enemies surmised, the "Black Muse" that was leading him on?

It could have been Péladan's initiative. It was Péladan, after all, who saw himself as spiritual heir to his recently deceased brother's life and legacy. In his 1892 book, *Comment on devient Mage* (How to Become a Magus), Péladan himself stated that his brother Adrien had been an "initiate" of a Rosicrucian Order in Toulouse, associated with Adrien's fellow spagyric doctor, Catholic legitimist Vicomte Louis Charles Édouard de Lapasse (1792–1867). The intriguing background to this fact was first brought to scholarly attention by Gérard Galtier, in his studies of "Egyptian" Masonry and French neo-Rosicrucianism.[1]

VICOMTE LOUIS CHARLES ÉDOUARD DE LAPASSE AND THE ROSE-CROIX OF TOULOUSE

Born into the worst year of the revolutionary Terror, the vicomte's family kept their heads down and raised the boy in the bosom of the church. Following army service and study of law in Toulouse during the last years of Napoleon's empire, the Vicomte de Lapasse was—come the Restoration—employed as secretary to his relative, the Marquis d'Osmond, king's ambassador, which profession took him to London in 1815, Hanover in 1818, Berne in 1824, and Naples from 1828 to 1831. Opposed to Louis-Philippe and the Orléanists who seized power in 1830, the vicomte worked in Paris for a decade from 1832 on legitimist journals. Having failed to found a bank, Lapasse embraced his passion for occult sciences, particularly in medicine, studying in Paris and Montpellier. Back in the Toulousain by 1846, he practiced spagyric medicine. Recognized as a worker of medical miracles, he offered a "drinkable gold" freely to the poor. To heal the poor *gratis* was a stipulation of the first, early seventeenth-century Rosicrucian manifesto, the "Fame of the Fraternity." Inspired by discovery of the "whole and unspoiled" corpse of "frater C.R." described in that document, longevity was Lapasse's great interest. His ministrations ensured his mother lived to nearly one hundred, and doubtless played a role in his election to Toulouse's municipal council in 1865.

*Fig. 7.2. The Vicomte Louis
Édouard de Lapasse (1792–1867)*

Around 1850, the vicomte formed a Rose-Croix fraternity with like-minded friends from Toulouse otherwise concerned with the region's archaeology and Hermetic practice and history, which went back in part to an extant (though renamed) medieval society founded to preserve the art of the Troubadours—the *Académie des Jeux Floreaux,* of which Lapasse became "Mainteneur" in 1867. One of the vicomte's Rose-Croix brethren was writer Firmin Boissin—born in 1835 and a friend of Jules Barbey d'Aurevilly—in whose book *Visionaires et illuminés.* (1869) we find a description of a December evening in 1839 when Countess d'Albanès played hostess to the Vicomte de Lapasse, Charles Nodier, Ballanche, Dr. Koreff, the Comte d'Ourches, Baron Brice de Beauregard, Madame de Hautefeuille (under the mystic name of Anna-Marie), the Chevalier Scèvole (son of Jacques) Cazotte, the Abbé Loubert, and the poet Adolphe Dumas, from whom Boissin obtained the story. Conversation revolved around mystical heretic Guillaume Postel, alchemist Duchanteau, the Rose-Cross fraternity, the Martinists, the Marquise de la Croix, the Avignon "illuminés," and the Abbé Œgger. The vicomte cut into the conversation by announcing his receipt of the "Divine Essence of the Brothers of the Rose-Cross," revealing a flask of rock crystal filled with the elixir of long life. This Lapasse said he carried with him always, having inherited it from a wise hermit on the outskirts of Palermo. According to Boissin's account, the vicomte never missed an opportunity to rehabilitate the Rose-Cross and he was taken as the last descendant of the celebrated confraternity.

Manuscripts surviving in Lyon indictated a "Scottish Grand Master, Knights of the Sword and the Rose-Croix" degree operated during the 1760s in Bordeaux and Lyon, where its chief creator, Freemason and friend of Louis-Claude de St. Martin, Jean-Baptiste Willermoz (1730–1824) had founded a "Sovereign Chapter of Knights of the Black Eagle Rose-Croix" in 1763. Lapasse obtained initiation abroad, however. The process seems to have begun in Germany. While a "Scottish Rectified" Rite Lodge deriving from Willermoz survived in Frankfurt, Boissin considered it was through diplomatic familiarity with Bavarian aristocratic circles that Lapasse was introduced to disciples of Catholic mystic and imperial librarian Baron Karl von Eckartshausen, author of *The Cloud upon the Sanctuary* (1804), whose visionary assurances, incidentally, would launch the occult career of Aleister Crowley in 1898. German adepts may have recommended Lapasse seek out a disciple of much-maligned Inquisition victim, Palermo-born Alessandro Cagliostro (probably born "Guiseppe Balsamo," 1743–1795), proponent of an alchemical system of Freemasonry believed inherited from ancient Egypt. While Lapasse served as ambassador in the Kingdom of Naples from 1828–1831, his 1843–44 voyage to Sicily, recounted in Boissin's *Excentriques disparus* (1890), may have provided the decisive encounter with Cagliostro's alleged disciple, for it was in Sicily that initiation into understanding of the true "Rose-Croix" by one "prince Balbiani" of Palermo took place. The "prince" may refer to a grade in an Egyptian Masonic rite, such as the "Sovereign Grand Prince" of the 1816 Statutes of the Rite of Misraïm (Hebrew for *Egypt*). As we shall see, Balbiani was scathing of the use of the expression *Rose-Croix* in Masonic orders. There is no record of an aristocratic or princely Balbiani family in Sicily.

Balbiani's alleged master Cagliostro had informed the Inquisition in 1790 that *his* alchemical knowledge came through a Neapolitan prince. Chief candidate for this role must be Raimondo di Sangro, Prince of Sansevero (1710–1771), military strategist, genius-inventor, devoted alchemist, freethinker, and Grand Master of Neapolitan Freemasons, until Pope Benedict XIV's bill *Providas* condemned Freemasonry on 18 May 1751. Cagliostro's friend Chevalier Luigi d'Aquino (1739–1783), a dominant figure in post-Providas Neapolitan Masonry and exponent of Templarist and Rose-Croix rites was also a knight of the Order of Malta, and it is often assumed Cagliostro learned alchemical healing from a member or members of that Order while residing in Malta.

The important thing to bear in mind is the distinction between symbolic Masonic rites and medical knowledge involving practical alchemy. It is the latter that concerned Édouard de Lapasse. In search of it, Lapasse took advantage of Balbiani's recommendation to the Comte d'Ourches that the vicomte access the count's extraordinary library of ten thousand books on magic, magnetism, and occult medicine in Paris. Living in St. Germain, just west of Paris's center, and enrolled as a medical student at the university, Lapasse immersed himself in the

Comte d'Ourche's library. Lévi's *History of Magic* describes the Comte d'Ourches somewhat jocularly as a man who learned magnetism from hypnotizer and magnetizer Abbé José Custodio de Faria (1755–1819), one of the three faces of the Count of Monte Christo in Dumas's novel. According to Lévi, the Comte d'Ourche's house in St. Germain was filled with broken furniture: detritus of spiritist levitations! There, Lapasse familiarized himself with alchemical works attributed to Paracelsus, Mercure Van Helmont, Robert Fludd, and many other exponents of the secret art.[2] Thirteenth-century doctor and alchemist Arnaud de Villeneuve particularly intrigued him. Author of a treatise on the conservation of youth, and teacher at Montpellier's great medical school—considered the true Rosicrucian Fraternity's base by Rosy Cross enthusiast and Paracelsian alchemist, Adam Halsmayr in 1612— Villeneuve had died in 1313 journeying between Sicily and Provence. Lapasse followed in Villeneuve's footsteps, visiting the medical schools of Montpellier and the great Salerno medical school in southern Italy. In his book on longevity, *Considérations sur la durée de la vie humaine et les moyens de la prolonger* (1845) Lapasse relates how from 1843 to 1844 he undertook a retreat at Sicily's Monreale Benedictine monastery, experimenting and perfecting his own medical theory.

As Galtier observed, the practical success of the vicomte's treatment of epilepsy, tuberculosis, rheumatism, among other ailments, and his expertise in longevity ought to dispose us to taking his theories seriously. Rooted in the alchemical-medical mainstream of the original conception of the *Fama Fraternitatis*—which first appeared as a manuscript in 1610—Lapasse was determined to show scientific efficacy in the Rosicrucian secret, writing in his "Essay on the Conservation of Life" (1860; p. 59):

> There existed a more mysterious science professed by the Rose-Croix, a secret society of which some adepts still exist today. The secret of the Rose-Croix, as far as one can conjecture it, involved a kind of pantheism which confounded the material element and the intelligent principle [or principle of intelligibility: God's creative mind]. The adepts positively assert that their secret may be found

in all places and *in all things,* that their gold is not vulgar gold, that their quintessence is the soul subtilized of all that has form and substance. A false doctrine in an absolute sense; but true and useful if one only applies it to matter, and if it helps to demonstrate the unity of creation, as the basic identity of all bodies, which only vary in their attributes by the laws of movement.

Lapasse further reported in his "Essay on the Preservation of Life"[3] how Prince Balbiani had explained to him that Masonic Rose-Croix degrees were not to be confused with the supernal brotherhood of Christian Rosycross itself:

I pass as Rose-Croix and by this title they believe me to be a Freemason. This is a mistake. Freemasonry has given to one of its grades the title of "Rose Croix" [usually understood as the 18th-degree Chevalier Rose-Croix of the "Ancient & Accepted Rite"].

The profane confound the upstart masons with this "dark dignity," with the brothers of the Rose Croix whose institution goes back to the 15th century. The vulgar fool themselves. The real Rose Croix are beyond the masonic associations. The original Rose Croix called one another amongst themselves "Edelphes" . . . they had to keep under oath their doctrine hidden from the eyes of the vulgar. . . . They had found a new idiom to express the nature of beings . . . they were committed to hastening the reign of the Pure Spirit.[4]

This statement dismisses any suspicion that Lapasse's Rose-Croix initiation was derived from Willermoz's Masonic Rose-Croix degree or, indeed, any other directly Masonic lineage. Besides, as Catholics, de Guaita and Péladan avoided *regular* Freemasonry and could not have worked "high" Masonic degrees such as the 18th degree of the A&A Rite unless they were first regular Freemasons. Péladan was always scathing of regular Freemasonry, many of whose French members were secularists and republican. This fact might have made the idea of a renewed Rosicrucian fraternity even more attractive to esoteric

Catholics. The Rose-Croix legend predated the official establishment of regular Freemasonry, and its imaginary founder came out of a Catholic monastic education, with a spiritually ideal purpose.

As Galtier deduced from the rare evidence for the Toulouse Rose-Croix in the writings of Lapasse, Boissin, and Péladan's novels, *Le Dernier Bourbon* and *La Vertu suprême* among other fragmentary sources, this fraternity did not hold temple assemblies with grades and rituals. Yet while an individual devotion, it was not *symbolic* but practical, involving medicine freely offered—in the case of Lapasse and Adrien Péladan—or organizing salons of art in Joséphin Péladan's case. The Rose-Croix was a path of experimental individualism, somewhat at odds with Catholic orthodox conceptions in that aspect, but still respectful of the Tradition represented by the church and legitimate monarchy. Its essence concerned initiation of the interior being into a legitimate divine gnosis of nature.

Lapasse's quotation above from the obscure "prince Balbiani" offers a fascinating clue to understanding Lapasse's orientation with regard to the authentic Rose-Croix. One of the alchemist-doctors who particularly excited Lapasse was David de Planis Campy (1589–ca. 1644), "Chirurgien du Roy" (King's Surgeon), also known as David *l'Edelphe*. This "Edelphe" was devoted to the alchemy of rejuvenation, and anyone familiar with the *Fama Fraternitatis* will know that its hero Frater C.R. greatly desired not only the rejuvenation of the body but also the rejuvenation of the church:

> And although that as yet the Church was not cleansed, nevertheless we know that they did think of her, and with what longing desire they looked for: Every year they assembled together with joy . . . and joined together by God, and the Heavens, and chosen out of the wisest of men, as have lived in many Ages, did live together above all others in highest Unity, greatest Secrecy, and most kindness one toward another.

Lapasse worked for legitimist journal *Le Rénovateur* (the Renovator), a term messianic, alchemical, and Pasquallian-Martinist. Alchemist

David *l'Edelphe* sought the "universal medicine." In a rare Paracelsian, magical, Kabbalistic, Pythagorean, and spagyric-alchemical work *Le Demonsterion de Roch le Baillif Edelphe medecin spagiric,* by Roch Le Baillif de la Rivière (Rennes, 1578), I discovered a key definition of the word *Edelphus* in its glossary of spagyric-alchemical terminology "which the ancients used amongst themselves to keep the secrets of the hidden alchemy": "*Edelphus, est qui iuxta naturam elementi pronosticat*" (p. 131). The Edelph is none other than "he who prognosticates close to nature's elements." This is *precisely* what Paracelsus was famous for: throwing out books of theory unrelated to reality, getting his hands dirty—hence chiurgical medicine: literally "hands-on medicine"—learning from nature, not imposing theories despite nature; accepting the "Book of Nature" or *liber mundi* as bearing the signature of the highest creator. This was the high science and "haute magie." Furthermore, it was a distinction of Frater C.R.'s journey to the East that studying with the wise of Fez, he encountered "the Elementary Inhabitants": spiritual creatures dwelling within the elements delineated by Paracelsus as gnomes (earth), undines (water), salamanders (fire), and sylphs (air). Now we can understand the critical distinction Lapasse attributed to Sicilian hermit Prince Balbiani, a distinction enabling Lapasse and his circle to claim what he believed to be an authentic Rosicrucian role and tradition fundamentally superior and essentially distinct to that spuriously assumed by any Masonic or para-Masonic body.

Hailing from Brittany, Roch le Baillif (or Bailli; 1540–1598) was an early advocate of Paracelsian medicine. Accused of dangerous quackery, Roch was tried in 1579 by a Faculty of Medicine in Paris indifferent to the value of his cures. He avoided condemnation but was ordered to cease practicing, which he did not. When Paris was struck by plague in March 1580, le Baillif's offer of cures was rejected; he left the city for Rennes. One can see immediately why Lapasse and Adrien Péladan *fils* took the name "Edelphe" as the proud name of the true Rosicrucian healer. The true Rosicrucian Brotherhood was a body of healers, working amid the world's blindness and therefore "invisible." The duty of a Rose Cross Brother, according to the *Fama,* was to heal the sick, gratis. This is precisely what Lapasse did in Toulouse and this alone would qualify him a place in the fraternity's invisible "House of the Holy Spirit," inaccessible to persons claiming to be Rosicrucian brethren on account of holding Masonic degrees, however high-sounding. Medical student Papus would have been extremely interested in the story too, for he too, in the end, would devote his life exclusively to serving the sick, gratis for the poor.

The conclusion is clear enough. Lapasse was an initiate because he operated as an Edelph, a spagyric-alchemist doctor in the same hope of the cleansed church as Frater C.R., with the same open mind toward Nature's Magic, its secret will to cure of itself, and to cleanse itself. *This* was the essential initiation of Adrien Péladan! It was passed on to him in spiritual principle by Lapasse's living example, unseen by the world at large. Adrien's younger brother applied the analogous principle *to Art:* locate the hand of God in creation—perceived by Paracelsus as the "signatures in things" or *Signatura rerum* in Jacob Böhme's 1621 book of that name—the signs of the divine in things or matter, analogous to Péladan's understanding of the "ideal" or "symbol," secreted beyond the visible form, that could by art be given ideal form. Perfect art should cure, that is banish, inhibiting darkness, for ideal art introduces into the world occulted power from beyond it.

When indicating his particular right to use the term Rose-Croix, Joséphin Péladan included the names of some of Lapasse's Rose-Croix coterie. Apart from his own brother Adrien, the brethren included Toulouse journalist and councilor Firmin Boissin (1835–1893), Eugène Aroux (1793–1859), and Arcade d'Orient (1790–1877). From study of Lapasse's fellow workers in operative alchemy, Galtier has identified other probable associates of Lapasse's Rose-Croix: Texerau de Lesserie, who, once content with the alchemists' orthodoxy, followed Lapasse into Hermetic studies; Toulousain Hermetist and occultist Ferdinand Rouget, author of works on alimentary hygiene, spiritism, magnetism, and physiognomy; and de Lesserie's nephew, the encyclopedic-minded author of "Essay on Medical Zoognosis" (J. Martel Ainé, for the faculty of medicine, Montpellier, 1856), Dr. Louis-Antoine de Montesquiou-Laboulbène (1803–1896), in whose château Lussac,

Lapasse died in 1867. The doctor came from an ancient Agenais family intimately connected to the old Catholic and noble families of the Tarn, Albigeois, and Aquitaine north and south, as can be seen from a funeral invitation that I obtained recently from a dealer in Toulouse: that of Anne Marie Louise Raymonde de Montesquiou-Laboulbène who died, aged nineteen on 20 March 1884 at Lussac (Villefranche du Queyran, Lot et Garonne, between Toulouse and Bordeaux). The list of invitees to the funeral is illuminating as a cross section of historically committed Catholic nobility in the region. Dr. Louis-Antoine's grandfather was Jean Joseph Laboulbène (1698–ca. 1772), knight of the Royal and Military Order of St. Louis (reserved strictly for Catholics), Agen consul, and captain of the Chablais regiment of his Royal Highness of Savoy.

We can now examine the evidence for Péladan's claims to authority for initiating a new Order with considerably deeper understanding than hitherto. In his crisp, instructional book *Comment on devient Mage* published in 1892, two years after he had departed De Guaita's Order and proclaimed his own, Péladan makes his claim as follows:

> By my father, the Chevalier Adrien Péladan, affiliated since 1840 to the neo-Templary of Genoude [Abbé Antoine-Eugene Genoude], [and Jacques Honoré] des Lourdoueix—who for 50 years held the pen to the light for the Church against the Protties [Protestants], for the King against the intriguers—I belong at once to Hugues des Païens [cofounder of the twelfth-century Knights Templar]. By my brother, Dr. Péladan, who was with Simon Brugal [pseudonym for Firmin Boissin], of the last branch of the Rose+Croix, said of Toulouse, like the [plural] Aroux, the [pl.] d'Orient, the [pl.] viscount de Lapasse—and who practiced occult medicine, without remuneration—I proceed from Rosencreuz.

Péladan concludes the introduction to *Comment on devient Mage* with a "Commemoration of Firmin Boissin (Simon Brugal), Commander

Fig. 7.3. Firmin Boissin (1835–1893)

of the Rose+Croix of the Temple, Prior of Toulouse and Dean of the Council of 14, dead in the arms of the Church":

> To all those of our Order and to those of intellectuality, we summon in great sorrow the demise in God of our Commander and Prior of Toulouse, Firmin Boissin. We lose in him our Dean; he had received the accolade *Rose+Cruxienne* from the members of the last branch of the Order, that of Toulouse. In 1858 he received Rose+Croix brother Dr. Adrien Péladan, and with the death of the illuminated doctor, we [royal we, meaning *I*] legitimately became the Grand Master of this extinct [*éteint*, or "faded"] Order that we have revived [*ranimé*, or "restored" or "renewed"]. . . . We commend it to your prayers . . . and to your memory. Amen.

Gérard Galtier has suggested that the renewal of the 1888 Order of the Rose-Croix may just as likely have come from Péladan as from de Guaita, despite de Guaita's Grand Mastership having always been assumed as reason to believe the initiative was his.[5] Galtier takes his clue from letters that passed between de Guaita and Péladan in 1886, some eighteen months or so before it was believed de Guaita and Péladan discussed establishing an *Ordre Rose+Croix Kabbalistique*.[6]

In a letter of 12 August 1886, written from Nancy, de Guaita signs with what Galtier calls his "initiatic name" Nébo, while "*tu-toi*'ing" Péladan, whereas a preceding letter of 1 April 1886, written in Paris, uses the formal *vous* and is signed "de Guaita." In the August letter, de Guaita adds the expression "Ta Créature" ("Your Creature") before his signature. For Galtier, this proves an initiation took place between April and August, adding for good measure that use of the Rosicrucian "+" conceit to indicate a friend of Péladan's in the same letter shows an existing brotherhood: "I did not tell you that I'd received . . . a long letter, friendly and wise from your friend Bois+Sin."[7] While I agree with Galtier's view that the required authentic Rosicrucian affiliation came through Péladan, I don't think these references prove the revived Order existed in 1886 or that de Guaita was formally initiated into it.

Christopher McIntosh, looking at the same letters, observed that there is simply a gathering of enthusiasm from de Guaita who begins to "break out of his shell" in stages after his first encounter with Péladan, an encounter de Guaita respectfully sought after he had read *Le Vice Suprême* in 1884.

In his first letter to Péladan, de Guaita attributes his occult awakening as much to Péladan's novel as to his own "superficial" reading of Lévi: "it was owing to your [Péladan's] book that I undertook the study of Hermetic science which seems to me, at first sight, so beautiful and fecund in sublime symbols. . . . In a fortnight, Sir, I shall be back in Paris. If you will be so kind as to permit me, I shall come to ask for some advice to guide the researches which I hope to make."[8] After Péladan's invitation for a meeting, de Guaita wrote: "You do me a great kindness in offering to let me have a chat with you about hermetism, something which I have wanted to do for a long time. I do not claim until now to have been anything more than a mere admirer of the higher sciences, who has studied them attentively and perseveringly; it will therefore be a great joy for me to be able to talk with a true initiate—who is greatly my senior in cabalistic studies."[9] He takes it that Péladan is already an initiate, that is, on the inside of occult knowledge, whereas he is on the outside. Péladan has obviously not "renovated" an Order at this stage; he has learned from or through his brother, though de Guaita would not have been aware of this, certainly at this stage.

Having met Péladan, de Guaita expressed his submissive appreciation: "I am grateful to you for having sacrificed several precious hours . . . you have pleased, interested and obliged me."[10] McIntosh notices the teacher-pupil relationship developing from the very beginning. It is not long before de Guaita is virtually gushing, even anxious for Péladan: "I am very uneasy about you and would be greatly comforted to see you again. You are becoming very seldom seen."[11] He allows Péladan's enormous ego every opportunity to envelop him: "I know, I sense, that you are an intelligence superior to mine . . . you have the genius of spontaneity and synthesis; I have the talent for patience and analysis."[12] In these words we see the idea of a wish for collaboration in germ.

As often happens in such relationships, the talented pupil, in trying to negotiate a position in the relationship of value, and to maintain self-possession, begins making moral judgments about the admired one, expressed as a friend's best wishes for the welfare of a friend. It is the friendship relationship that counts. For example, when in *Curieuse!* Péladan opened the book with a salvo against Germans— the pharmaceutical magnate who "poisoned" Adrien *fils*—de Guaita, who lived close to the German border, begged his friend to weigh his hatred for the bad against good Germans such as Mesmer, Goethe, and Albrecht Dürer. I can imagine that cut no ice with Péladan! Then de Guaita started experiencing disquiet over Péladan's lively amorous adventures: "Your soul is perpetually haunted and obsessed by ridiculous sentimental cravings. Can you not live one week without your being preoccupied with these futilities?"[13] De Guaita was, nevertheless, happy to be informed and would make complicit-sounding inquiries as to whether Péladan had done the deed with one or another lady in his life: "What news? Daphne? Linga-Yoni?"*[14]

In 1886, as we have seen, de Guaita started signing his name *Nébo* when writing to "Mérodack." While Nébo is a form of *Nabu,* Babylonian god of Mercury, seen as a son of Marduk (Hebrew: "Merodach"), the

---

Linga-Yoni is a reference to Hindu terms for the sexual organs.

Babylonian Jupiter and king of the young gods of Babylonian mythology, we should not forget that Nébo is also the wise love-sublimating hero of Péladan's second novel, as Mérodack was the hero of the first. Both men are spiritual educators, and while de Guaita was expressing appreciation for the education afforded by Péladan (Mérodack) to his mercurial "inferior" (in genius), he also feels that he too—as Nébo was Mérodack's disciple in the novel—is now ready to take on an educative role of "virgins," or pure hearts, in need of protection, as Nébo performs that service for Russian princess Paule Riazan in *Curieuse!* This may of course have simply meant that the younger de Guaita was now involved with a lady himself, or had taken it on himself to steer his friend from the snares of precipitous loves. The names Mérodack and Nébo begin to be accompanied by symbols, such as an Indian lingam and yoni symbol, signifying sexual union, as well as planetary sigils, Chi-Rho Christian monograms, and Hebrew letters, signifying numbers.

PÉLADAN AND THE TEMPLARS

While we have a better idea of the essence of what constituted Péladan's "Rosicrucian" initiation, his claimed link to Templar-founder Hugues des Païens, used to invoke a Templarist lineage, requires elucidation. It is most likely the case that as with Adrien Péladan *fils's,* Édouard de Lapasse's, and Fermin Boissin's "Rosicrucian" identity, the existence in Toulouse of any formal para-Masonic organization with regular summonses, special-dress meetings, formal initiations, and so on, was probably unnecessary. Rather one may picture a coterie of empathetic friends, adepts operating in the laboratory with practical alchemy, not symbolic rituals, spiritually dedicated to making symbols manifest in individually oriented, beneficial action. One has to understand the real power of the symbol as providing a spiritual context for action.

For example, it has been thought that Péladan's reference to the "neo-Templary of Genoude and Lourdoueix" to which his father had been affiliated since 1840 indicated a formal Templarist Order of Palapratian descent, that is to say, the neo-Templarist and Johannite Church revivals launched in Paris in 1804 and 1812 after founder

Bernard-Raymond Fabré-Palaprat (1773–1838) allegedly discovered documentation purporting to reveal an unbroken line of covert Grand Masters operating after the official dissolution of the Order of the Temple in 1314 through Masonic Lodges (see my *Invisible History of the Rosicrucians*). However, as Galtier argues, the Palapratian Order was Bonapartist, or Orléanist—supporters of Bourbon Louis-Philippe who replaced the legitimate Charles X in 1830—and liberal, whereas Adrien Péladan *père,* Abbé Antoine-Eugène Genoude (1792–1849), and Jacques Honoré des Lourdoueix (1787–1860) were Catholic legitimists, supporting the abdicated Charles X.

Genoude played an important political and journalistic role through the suppressed legitimist paper *La Gazette de France,* against the Philippe d'Orléans-headed "July Monarchy" crisis in 1830, advocating national royalism and social amelioration by universal suffrage. Lourdoueix, novelist, journalist, and supporter of Genoude's generous and moderate legitimism, advocated state pensions for workers.

Both the Abbé de Genoude and the Baron of Lourdoueix were friendly collaborators with the Vicomte de Lapasse on the legitimist *Gazette de France.* Approaching death in 1849 Genoude chose as editor in chief Louis-Adrien Péladan *père.* As the "Pope's liege-writer" as his son described him, Péladan *père* increased the circulation of Genoude and Lourdoueix legitimist journal *l'Étoile du Gard* with inflammatory writing. This precipitated a relaunch as the bigger *l'Étoile du Midi* in November 1850, successful in securing popular support for Catholic tradition in the Midi until the legitimist cause collapsed with Louis-Napoléon's coup d'état just over a year later, when the broader populace of France chose imperialism.

If they were not affiliated to Palapratian neo-Templarism, Galtier surmises the neo-Templar formulary to which Péladan's father was affiliated was likely to have been a secret society of neochivalric Catholics and legitimist Royalists, believing in primordial hierarchies, that is, lines of traditional descent of divine duties exercised by sacred rulers—the meaning of *hierarchy*—linked to the divinely created cosmos, or as Péladan declared, they believed in "Tradition, Hierarchy, and the Ideal," which he summed up in the one key word *Hiérophanie:* the manifestation of the sacred. This was the Great Idea whose promulgation was the Great Work and that constituted the sacred trust and essence of Péladan's initiation. In his particular case, his "arrows of desire" would in due time be shot from the quiver of Art for the sake of the Ideal.

Péladan's novel *Le Dernier Bourbon* (p. 5) gives us a substantial account of how he envisaged the difference between a Catholic "Templar" organization and a Catholic Rose-Croix organization, and notably, how they could be combined. In the relevant scene the character Marestan speaks to Mérodack of a character ("Elohil") who represents Péladan's father:

—"It belongs to the neo-Templary of Genoude, of Lourdoueix, who failed due to the timidity of the clergy and the weak will of the comtesse de Chambord."

Mérodack then asks:

"Why were the last Rose-Croix not united to the Templars? Only Simon Brugal [Boissin] remains, does he not, with Dr. Phégor of the Toulouse branch, which thirty years ago included the vicomte de Lapasse, Arcade d'Orient, Aroux, Antarès, Brugal?

The Rose-Croix were gnostics, alchemists; their research into truth worried the strict and literal Catholicism of the Templars. The two currents could only blend in the hands of a Grand Master capable of balancing equably the Rosicrucian liberties, the individualism which inspires them and the obligations of the Templar. The Temple presents the qualities and faults of the Company of Jesus, it takes its strength from the collective; the Rose-Croix puts its force into the individual.

In fact, interrupted Mérodack, the one subordinates itself to the Church and the other shares solely in itself. The Templar appeared exclusively modern and Christian; the Rose-Croix dates from much longer ago, it complicates or completes the notion of the remnants of the orient. They are as different as the priest is from the Magus. The thinking of the first confines its experience to evangelical evolution; the second weighs its decision in a cosmic fashion, ecumenical. . . .

We can now see the analogy of Péladan's inherited position with the "Tradition" of Fabre d'Olivet and the call of d'Alveydre's and Papus's "Martinism" for a revived, reformed, social-spiritual structure as a hierarchical bulwark against anarchy. Understand this, and you will understand what the essence of Pierre Plantard and his pals' Priory of Sion game was all about. When authors Michael Baigent and Richard Leigh observed that surreal performance from without, they were driven to explain the attraction of the colorful, too-colorful package, resorting to the idea of an organization that cleverly, perhaps fiendishly, employed archetypes. The attraction to any part of the Priory tapestry simply lies in the power of symbols. Symbols surpass the rational faculty, seeking rest in, and response from, the soul. This was the point about the legitimist position: republicanism has nothing for the soul; it is not rooted and is always unstable. Divine government speaks to our deepest nature. Symbols express the language of magical religion. Its opponents instinctively fear—and therefore dismiss—it as a result.

Péladan's statement in *Comment on devient Mage* regarding his lineal authority contains a few, easily missed extras. His brother, he says, was "with Simon Brugal [Firmin Boissin], of the last branch of the Rose+Croix, said of Toulouse, as *les Aroux, les d'Orient, les vicomte de Lapasse* [my italics to emphasize the plural *les = the*]." Péladan is referring to Eugène Aroux (1793–1859) and Arcade d'Orient Vial (1790–1877).

Government official Aroux wrote *Dante, Heretic, Revolutionary and Socialist* (1854) where, in pretending to denounce the heretical Fidèles d'Amour—the "Faithful to Love" fraternity mentioned in Dante's *Vita Nuova*—Aroux apologizes for them. Galtier judges this typical of the Toulouse Rose-Croix, "constantly navigating between heresy and orthodoxy"[15]: a statement certainly true of the Sâr.

Aroux was not himself from Toulouse; he lived in Rouen. Nor was he a legitimist. While working as an advocate, he was part of the liberal opposition to Charles X, supporting Philippe d'Orléans, whose cause he supported in parliament. However, he lost his post as King's Prosecutor in 1832 for blurring distinctions between church and state, misjudging the 1830 Charter principles. In his *Mysteries of Chivalry and of Platonic Love in the Middle Ages* (1858), Aroux showed, without ambiguity, favor for the Cathar *perfecti,* believing them holders of Neoplatonic doctrines shared with the Troubadours. He also posited the existence of a "Massénie du Saint-Graal" that survived within Freemasonry.

One can see that, like Péladan, Aroux had to negotiate a special path between Catholicism and heterodoxy, and while clearly of the latter persuasion, his views influenced Péladan's, particularly with regard to Dante, whom Péladan saw as a patron of his Rose-Croix art projects, as well as the Troubadours and Cathars: a perspective evident in Péladan's *Le Secret des Troubadours* (1906). Péladan saw Dante and the rose at the center of his heaven in *Paradiso* as the immediate predecessor of Christian Rosenkreuz, responsible, at least in part, for the rose in the Rose-Croix. It would be interesting to enter the labyrinth of Péladan's soul to see precisely how he simultaneously reconciled the idea of Dante as a kind of heretic and as one of the glories of Catholicism. Yet here may lie the key to Péladan's ultimate hope: the revivifying of the Catholic Church through esoteric understanding and experience of gnosis, as being the hidden flower of the faith, yet to bloom in its fullness. Such or something like it may also have inspired the creator or first creators of the Rosicrucian mythology, who, though initially Lutheran Protestants, were neither uncritically so, nor willing to be satisfied with a Christian church or Body of Christ divided forever.

Born in Perpignan in 1790, the strangely named Arcade d'Orient Vial remains obscure, despite prodigious literary output in the fields of physics, magnetism, alchemy, theology, and spiritualism—explained by rules of mechanics.[16] Inspired by Böhme and Spinoza, Vial also wrote on vegetarianism and prophecy, correctly predicting the end of the Ottoman Empire and the return of the Jews to Palestine, while declaring the revolutionary Terror of 1792 as the evil time when the temporal power of the Roman Church was broken, with 1,000 years thereafter under the sign of the apocalypse. In his *Destinies of the Soul* (1846), he defended reincarnation with reference to the Bible and the church fathers. D'Orient was violently opposed to socialism and regarded Voltaire as the Antichrist of the eighteenth century, much as Blake did in England.

Arcade d'Orient Vial also wrote visionary poetry like Milton's and Klopstock's, while earning a good living as a jeweler, financing his books yet living frugally close to St. Sulpice in Paris, where Genoude trained as a priest. A great friend of extreme legitimist writer Antoine Madrolle,[17] he loved and assisted the poor of the area. They called him "the man of the good God." Most enigmatic, Arcade d'Orient trod, like Aroux, a peculiar path between orthodoxy and spiritual affirmations of a non-orthodox character.

Galtier speculates there may be a misprint in Péladan's *How to Become a Magus* where it gives 1858 as the date Boissin "received" Dr. Adrien Péladan as R+C. If the date was 1878 originally, then, conceivably, Arcade d'Orient Vial could have been Grand Master before him—for Vial died in 1877—and Vial may himself have succeeded the Vicomte de Lapasse in that role after *his* death in 1867, as Aroux had been dead for eight years before then. The use of the French plural *les* before the names of Aroux, Arcade d'Orient, and de Lapasse may suggest they were all "one thing" or shared a specific role, or were entitled to use the first person plural, as the true sovereign is never spiritually alone and speaks with divine sanction. Boissin, described as "Prior and Dean," was presumably not then Grand Master, but it is speculation as to whether this little fraternity had, or needed, a Grand Master. Authority in a true Rosicrucian fraternity does not come from titles, and the exemplary figure of Christian Rosenkreuz eschewed them, being brother among brothers. It is arguably a pity that Joséphin Péladan did not likewise.

Galtier further speculates that Boissin played a sort of "Grand Conservator" role and hoped Dr. Péladan would work to renovate the order, a task undone as a result of premature death in 1885. This might then have made brother Joséphin a suitable "heir" for the task. But the Sâr was not a doctor and could not heal the sick gratis, and if we must in his case interpret that role symbolically, then it is likely that such a reinterpretation was Péladan's alone and not something placed on his shoulders by an anxious Prior. Furthermore, there is nothing in the establishment of the Ordre Rose+Croix Kabbalistique of 1888 to suggest a revival of the spirit of Lapasse's friends, or the good advice taken from "prince Balbiani," whoever he may have been. Heirs, however, have been known to cause revolutions if sufficiently inspired, and Péladan was. He may have had the seed of a conception in mind he found ill at ease with developments within the Kabbalistic order, but that is to jump ahead of the story.

Where Galtier may really have a point is where he recognizes in the curious or ambiguous position of the Toulouse group regarding the Catholic Church a symbiosis with Péladan's own position, which most commentators are far from grasping, being tempted to join the throng and throw stones at the "foolish" Sâr, who may turn out to have been not the wrong kind of "fool" at all. Galtier summarizes the R+C position *vis à vis* the church as being one of conserving the Catholic institution as representative of the divine Order, body of Christ, and vehicle of tradition, while recognizing that the institution required, as the *Fama* unambiguously suggests, revivification of its dogma by gnosis and esoteric science: the holy embrace of Sophia, divine Wisdom. Author of the Rosicrucian ludibrium, or "serious joke," Johann Valentin Andreae (1586–1654), was working for a *second reformation* of the true Catholic Church. Such had not yet happened.

The case of Firmin Boissin helps us to see what kind of Rosicrucianism Péladan had inherited from his brother. Born in the Ardèche, Boissin left his teaching job at Cavaillon for Paris. There he mingled in literary circles, rubbing shoulders with Jules Barbey d'Aurevilly and Constant Thérion. His novel *Jan de la Lune* (1887) was a success. His chief income being journalism, he became editor of *Le Messager de Toulouse* in 1871, a Catholic monarchist journal. In 1887 he was elected to Toulouse's Academy of Jeux Floraux ("Floral Games") and quickly promoted the Occitan language and medieval culture, forming an "Athénée des Troubadours" responsible for lectures on the *langue d'Oc,* the language celebrated by Dante and consolidated by

Troubadours—Joséphin Péladan would publish the Sophianic *Secret of the Troubadours* in 1906. Boissin was a member of several Catholic chivalric Orders, including the Order of Isabella the Catholic, an honor shared by Salvador Dalí.

Péladan calls Boissin "Commandeur de la Rose+Croix du Temple, Prieur [Prior] de Toulouse et Doyen [Dean] du Conseil de 14 [of the Council of 14]" while in his 1900 book *La Vertu Suprême,* he says that Boissin—using what might be a symbolic name of "Simon Brugal," though Brugal was Boissin's mother's maiden name—was a transmitter of the secret tradition of the Troubadours, the Cathars, and the *Massénie* ("House") of the Holy Grail. Quite a character!

And yet, whatever seeds the Toulouse friends may have planted in Joséphin's fertile soul, it is difficult still to see the Ordre Rose+Croix+Kabbalistque as being their bloom. There does not have to be a single motive, of course, and there are yet other factors to consider, for we have rather lost sight of Stanislas de Guaita.

DE GUAITA AND BOULLAN

De Guaita's decision to become the walking encyclopedist of the occult would take him into some very murky areas, though he would not enter them deliberately.

Abbé Joseph-Antoine Boullan (1824–1893) was a defrocked Catholic priest who had turned away from a promising career as a literate supporter of the church to involve himself with the strange, somewhat sickly cult of Eugène Vintras (1807–1875).

Believing himself Elias, forerunner of the messiah and spiritual patron of the Carmelite Order of monks and nuns—officially abolished in France during the revolutionary Terror—Vintras had founded a sect, the Carmel Éliaque church that claimed miracles of bleeding hosts and the spiritual benefits of sexual rites combined with prayers. Elias, or Elijah, was the prophet who called down fire from heaven; the original Carmelites had a controversial reputation for passionate visionary states. With devoted sexual partner Julie Thibault, Boullan took over a portion of the Vintrasian ministry after Vintras's death in 1875.

Fig. 7.4. Abbé Boullan (1824–1893)

This was familiar territory to Boullan, for Thibault simply fulfilled the role formerly held by his former sidekick, Adèle Chevalier. Adèle had become Boullan's assistant in 1859 in what he called the "Society for the Reparation of Souls." Accused of fraud and indecent practices, an ecclesiastical investigation of their activities had resulted in three years imprisonment for Boullan (1861–64). Jailed in Rome, Boullan wrote a confession that emerged after his death through Joris-Karl Huysmans who used Boullan as the chief source for his shocking novel of modern Satanism, *Là Bas* (Down There, 1891). From Boullan's confession we may learn, and rather wish we hadn't, what was unknown to curious occult researchers in the 1880s: that he attributed miracles to consecrated hosts mixed with excrement, and that on 8 December 1860, he sacrificed a child fathered on Mlle. Chevalier on an altar in a black mass. Boullan always denied he was a Satanist, just misunderstood by the ignorant—and persuaded Huysmans of the same. Boullan undoubtedly subverted the good for his own ends and comfort. Denial, nonetheless, became a way of life. He liked his work and wasn't going to give it up.

Boullan's journey to Vintras in Lyon in 1875 was preceded by episcopal excommunication after Boullan purloined a sacred relic from Argenteuil to cure an epileptic: a curious dilemma for the professional moralist, to be sure. Vintras, meanwhile, still performing his services to suffering humanity in a cope with an inverted cross displayed on its front, was on his last legs, and when they and his heart collapsed in December 1875, the door opened for Boullan's takeover of Vintras's rites: the "Provictimal Sacrifice of Mary" and the "Sacrifice of Glory of Melchizedek," fanciful, ironic names for "redemptive" sexual stimuli conceived as liberating rituals. Julie Thibault would be perpetually on hand to restore her master's spirits.

Boullan was still at it ten years later; somehow he always got away with it, despite what was already known about him, which was distasteful enough. His self-affirmations were always modest and plausible; he didn't need to play the scholar, he had the tools, those of the born con-man and self-deceiver, and Thibault was dark and devoted.

Possibly the first of the Parisian occultists to investigate the rumored-to-be miracle-working Boullan was Joseph Paul Oswald Wirth (1860–1943), a young Swiss familiar today to students of the tarot, in which study Wirth excelled. Initiated a Freemason in 1884,[18] Wirth practiced a form of hypnotic healing he called "curative magnetism." The principle seems to have been that by which Fabre d'Olivet awoke the "volitive principle" in the deaf mute, for which outrage Napoleon had ordered Fabre to cease his activities and leave healing to the professionals who habitually failed, with theory on their side. Wirth met Boullan in August 1885 and began a long correspondence with the voluble provictimist.

It appears that Wirth attended Lady Caithness's Theosophically oriented salons at Holyrood, 124 avenue de Wagram, as did, occasionally, Stanislas de Guaita, though the two did not meet until 1887. When they did, it was due to Canon Roca's recommending Wirth to de Guaita, Roca being a regular attender at Lady Caithness's court. Heterodox priest Father Paul Roca (1830–1893) was an admirer of St. Yves d'Alveydre and of Vintras's writings; he was the Christian "brother" of de Guaita. It is reasonable to conjecture then that when de Guaita decided to contact Boullan by post toward the end of 1885, it stemmed from Wirth's talking about Boullan either at Holyrood or to St. Yves d'Alveydre, with whom de Guaita had been acquainted since 1885.

Encouraged by Boullan's postal response, de Guaita visited Boullan and Thibault in Lyon in 1886, returning to Paris with a copy of the rite of "the Sacrifice of the Glory of Melchizedek." In thanks for this perhaps, de Guaita inscribed a copy of his own work on magic to Boullan: the introduction to what would become de Guaita's *Essais des sciences maudites,* entitled *Au seuil du mystère* (On the Threshold of Mystery), published in *L'Artiste* that year. Social etiquette apart, de Guaita realized something was amiss in Boullan's ministry. He informed Péladan that Boullan fell "into deadly error with regard to Spiritual Marriages."[19] Doubtless wary of exposure at the hands of the bright young man bearing a gift, Thibault later informed Huysmans that she felt an evil intent emanating from de Guaita so intense as to make poor Boullan sick: either pure deception or a classic case of projection. Boullan began to feel uncomfortable at the new scenario of earnest young men in Paris who might prove immune to his charms. He was right to be concerned. De Guaita saw it his duty to pass judgment on Boullan, but needed what would effectively serve as a united tribunal of magi to judge the case. Boullan, for his part, would cunningly affect to present his poor innocent self as the victim of black magicians operating under the cloak of respectability in the capital!

But what made de Guaita think it was his responsibility and that of his friends to "deal with" Boullan? The answer may be found in nearly everyone's favorite magic book—Péladan, interestingly, did not like it—Éliphas Lévi's two volume *Dogme et Rituel de la Haute Magie.* Not only in those two volumes did de Guaita find ample confirmation for what he thought Boullan was up to—projecting "fluid" forces to imprint his evil will on his female dupes; Boullan had been employed to exorcise nuns allegedly possessed while in fact accomplishing the opposite—but also the duty of the true magician to *judge* such matters with the means whereby such evil could be combatted. In short, it was no good expecting the conventional law of the land to deal with a Boullan, for the law did not recognize the "reality" of magical forces and could not therefore observe what for the magician was evident. Furthermore, de Guaita was aware of the traditional Rosicrucian promise that the good work of the brotherhood was of value to rulers if they could but seize its usefulness. Péladan, for example, would write an open letter to the French President recommending his clairvoyant skills: "I have the means of seeing and hearing at the greatest of distances, useful in controlling enemy councils and suppressing espionage."[20] Here in the Boullan case was a means of establishing the scientific and social validity of the "accursed sciences." And this appears to have been de Guaita's chief motive in establishing an orderly "revived" *Ordre Rose+Croix+Kabbalistique*. Besides, it was no good going it alone with a character like Boullan; one needed the collective resources of a dedicated force of white magic. It would be a test, and so indeed it transpired, though not at all as de Guaita imagined.

As for the right of serious occultists to judge such cases, de Guaita and his friends needed only to consult an important supplement to Lévi's classic on magic: his explanation of the *Nuctemeron,* attributed to first-century magus Appolonius of Tyana. The *Nuctemeron* outlines in twelve "hours" the "intelligences," demons or "genii" that may be pressed into the highest God's service, turning, as Lévi puts it, "night into day." This Hermetic tract in Greek, Lévi found in a Jewish work on the "life and death of Moses," published in Amsterdam in 1721. According to Lévi's interpretation, the work was a systematic series of twelve steps, or "Herculean labors" to initiation, the means of establishing a perfect equilibrium. Where there is disharmony, the magus must reestablish harmony, keeping the opposite poles apart.

In the first "hour," "in unity," the "demons sing their praises to God, losing their malice and their anger." The seven "geniuses," or "demons" of the hour are named. The first should strike the reader. He is called "PAPUS" and is of course the source for the name taken by Dr. Gérard Encausse with which he signed all his occult works, for *Papus* is the "génie" of medicine, which is to say he is "doctor." The second genius (inspiring spirit) is "Sinbuck" who is "judge." Lévi explains:

> It is necessary to become the *doctor* and the *judge* of oneself to vanquish the wickedness of the necromancer. To conjure and despise the genius of scandal ["ZABUN"], to triumph over opinion which

freezes all enthusiasms and confounds all things in the same cold palor as makes the genius of the snows. Know the virtue of the signs and thus be able to link together the genius of the amulets ["MIZKUN"] to arrive at the "dignity" ["HAVEN"] of the mage.[21]

De Guaita saw establishment of spiritual equilibrium as the first duty of the Rose+Croix fraternity and the Boullan case accelerated his path toward it. In 1887, possibly as much out of genuine concern for one in touch with Boullan and his black magic as to obtain more information, de Guaita contacted Oswald Wirth. How this came about is a little story in itself, related by Wirth in his memoirs:

Practicing at that time curative magnetism, I was treating a sick woman who went to sleep under my influence and imparted her visions to me. . . . I was struck by the tone of exceptional conviction with which she said: "I see a letter with a red seal carrying armorial bearings. You will receive it; it is very important for you."

I wanted to know who was planning to write to me and with what intention.

"It is a young man of your age, but shorter than you, blond, clear-skinned, with blue eyes. He is very learned and is interested in the same things as yourself. He has told me about you and is anxious to make your acquaintance."

A few weeks later arrived the predicted letter with the red heraldic seal:

"Sir, My excellent brother [note], Canon Roca, has talked to me about you in terms which make me extremely anxious to make contact with you.

"If it would please you to come and visit me tomorrow, Saturday, at six o'clock, we can dine together informally and that will give me the opportunity to make your acquaintance."[22]

Stanislas de Guaita gave his address as 24 rue de Pigalle. When they met, Wirth was impressed by de Guaita's knowledge of magnetic healing.

Wirth also received from the marquis a pointer toward understanding the tarot as a magical system, which study led to Wirth's *Les Vingt-deux clés kabbalistiques du Tarot* (22 Kabbalistic Keys of the Tarot), submitted to de Guaita for approval and published in 1889. Wirth would become de Guaita's secretary and fervent supporter.

In May, de Guaita felt he knew enough to denounce Boullan as a vile sorcerer, though nothing further was projected until the Rose+Croix Order was properly established.

THE ORDER

The first thing to be noted about the *Ordre Kabbalistique de la Rose-Croix* is that it was not really an attempt to revive the fraternity as first described by "the brothers" in the *Fama Fraternitatis* or their follow-up manifesto, the *Confessio Fraternitatis* (1615). That fraternity anyway was imaginary and symbolic, devoted to healing the "sick," that is the spiritual divides across Europe, whose body was suffering from the outflow of a limited Reformation that had set Christian against Christian with Christianity, and science, the losers. Nor did the Order attempt a revival of eighteenth-century German neo-Rosicrucianism, such as that of the Gold-und-Rosenkreuzers, who until their demise celebrated elaborate, Masonic-style rituals, owning Lodge rooms and even a system of alchemical laboratories for manufacturing the "universal medicine." Nor was it an adjunct of high-grade Masonic Rose-Croix degrees such as existed in the Ancient & Accepted Rite (18th degree) and in the Rite of Misraïm (46th degree, 1816 Statutes). As far as we can tell, the Order, led by a Supreme Council—a term borrowed from the Ancient & Accepted or Scottish Rite—devoted itself to education, particularly education in Kabbalah, including applications of the Kabbalistic systems *gematria, notariqon,* and *temurah* to tarot and astrology. It was also interested in the symbolism of Freemasonry and the relation of Western esotericism to Eastern spiritual traditions. What individual members did with the knowledge they acquired was their own high responsibility, but the Order operated as a checking device on members' activities, imposing discipline and duty, inculcating a high sense of sacred responsibility in a genial atmosphere.

The Christian orientation of members was heterodox insofar as they believed generally speaking that the life of faith could deepen into expanding realms of spiritual knowledge and awareness through lives of initiation. The purpose of this knowledge was to raise the individual to reintegration with the divine humanity—cosmic consciousness—and in so doing, serve the greater good of humankind. It was all highly idealistic, indeed, the ideal was its goal, the symbol its path.

Unfortunately for de Guaita's purposes, whenever an attempt is made to establish the ideal on Earth, spiritual warfare is unleashed; problems occur with tedious insistence that may either make or break the devoted, for while equilibrium is, as Lévi argued, the magician's aim, the fulcrum of life on Earth is never completely still, and the spirit bloweth where it listeth, and fools grow like weeds.

However, it started well enough, with three grades of initiation that emphasized the Order's educational character. The grades were unpretentious: baccalauréat, licentiate, and doctorate of the Kabbalah. This in itself was pioneering and one senses de Guaita's personal priorities, his desire to establish the "accursed sciences" on a respectable knowledge base. However, there was as yet no existing academic discipline by which the process could be seriously assessed. There is in the occult tradition the fundamental idea of "correspondences" that flies in the face of modern academicism, for in the magical and spiritual realms, "everything connects" and the virtue of the magician is to make links between orders of nature and spiritual dimensions beyond the visible. In the late nineteenth century, materialist science as preached in the academic faculties was extremely intolerant when roused; little has changed there.

In due course, Aleister Crowley would be able, as it were, to "mark" a person's vision or astral journey as might a don judge an oral examination, but a don whether in Oxford, Harvard, or the Sorbonne would be hard-pressed to judge the validity of a journey along the sephirotic tree for accuracy, since the vantage point of judgment required esoteric initiation, which, by definition, surpasses rational analysis. Nevertheless, one could have established a distinction between theory and practice, while our contemporary academic discipline of Western Esotericism generally contents itself with matters of history and explication of philosophy, both of which can be assessed according to existing academic strictures.

For those joining the Order, the licentiate in Kabbalah required library study of the classics of occultism, after which the student could seek spiritual communion with the Divine through meditation, before spreading the word among the uninitiated. Jean-Pierre Laurant has described the functioning of the initiatic society as "chaotic."[23]

It is unlikely that the Order's first Supreme Council of twelve known and "unknown" members—perhaps the core group awaited an epiphany of celestial genius to enter its portals—would have impressed many outside of the magic circles of Bailly's bookshop, Lady Caithness's salon, or Chamuel's Librairie du Merveilleux. However, the dominant figures were all interesting people. Not only de Guaita and Péladan stood on hand to guide aspirants to knowledge of their unknown dimensions, they were joined on the Supreme Council by "demon" of medicine, the dynamic Papus, Marc "Haven"—the name of the *Nuctemeron*'s demon of dignity taken by Dr. Emmanuel Marc Henri Lalande (1868–1926)— the Abbé Alta (real name Dr. Calixte Mélinge who took his name from a rare, good character in *Le Vice Suprême*), François-Charles Barlet (real name Alfred Faucheux), Paul Sédir (real name Yvon Leloup), and the writer Paul Adam. There seems to be no absolutely certain list of members of the council. Regarding an order statute of 1891, Michelet reproduced the additional names of Martinist Julien Lejay and Oswald Wirth as Supreme Council members. Joanny Bricaud in his account of the Boullan scandal (*J.-K. Huysmans et le Satanisme,* 1913) includes the name of socialist and spiritist, Albert Jounet (who wrote as "Alber Jhouney"). Maurice Barrès's name has also been included. It is usual to say that the council consisted of six known and six unknown members, with the latter six being symbolic, but the list above gives us eight. Some accounts include Paul Sédir but not Paul Adam, and vice versa. Some account of the discrepancies may be discerned from Michelet[24] who also clarifies the "role" of the six unknown members:

These last [unknown members] had the mission of re-establishing the Order if hostile powers should destroy it. In reality, the six unknown members never existed. Of some six known members, of whom one was a prematurely dead writer's wife, I will only name the dead. They were, with the Grand Master de Guaita, Paul Adam, Papus, A. Gabrol, H. Thorion, Péladan. This one, having demitted, was replaced by a woman. Another was replaced by Marc Haven. Two men came late who were in plain maturity of age, Barlet, and another member, Alta, who was a priest; all the rest were young. There was lots of juvenilety. Beside, de Guaita, meditative and sedentary, ruled his Order rather in the manner of the Old Man of the Mountains, Hassan-Sabah, who during 35 years of rule, only once left his room to go out onto the commanding terrace of his marvelous castle.[25]

What were these men really like? We can get an insight into some of them through the firsthand experience of Michelet, beginning with the writer Paul Adam.

PAUL ADAM

Influenced by French authors Jacques Cazotte, Joseph de Maistre, Balzac, and de Guaita, the novelist and historian Paul Adam, author of *L'Époque* and *Le Temps et la Vie,* had, like Maurice Barrès, been at school at Nancy with de Guaita who had influenced him, though not so much as he had Barrès. Adam had a foot in both the Symbolist and esoteric camps, having joined forces with Jean Moréas, the author of the "Literary [Symbolist] Manifesto" of September 1886 to write the novel *Les Demoiselles Goubert,* a not altogether successful attempt at a Symbolist novel, also published in 1886, not long before being called into the Rosicrucian Order. Michelet tells us how "in his search of knowledge his avid spirit had explored the world where arcane glimmers vibrated. He possessed a 'certitude,' reflected in the subterranean meanderings of his work, sagely ordered."[26] Michelet says he was one of the three or four minds of the Symbolist generation who really grasped what a symbol was and could thereby vivify his work with that perception; the others apparently only acceded to the "threshold of allegory." Adam swam deep into "the oceans of gnostic intellectuality" and knew how to penetrate beyond appearances.

Possessed of prophetic powers, Adam could read into the subterranean wefts beyond nature on "which were embroidered the events of 1914 and the following years." That is to say, he predicted World War I and subsequent events. His skills derived, Michelet tells us, from a deep knowledge of the secrets of history often neglected by the ignorance of historians afraid to incur the scoffing of peers should they delve into the powerful wells of influence that emerge in the East and Far East out of secret societies. Adam could discern between the "marionettes" visible to the profane world and the real powers that move events. He was familiar with "egregores," that is, occult forces, thoughtforms that develop momentums of their own, taking history with them; what the modern world calls simply "forces" without asking too much more about what these forces actually are. "These forces are beings, living and

Fig. 7.5. Paul Adam (1862–1920)

determined, that an anterior terminology named Angels, or Demons, or Egregores [the Greek *egregoroi* means "watchers"]. Or by other vocables, according to how a time or race designated their evident reality."

Paul Adam relied on an occult conception of the significance of numbers for the structure of his work: "If one agrees with the great Pythagoreans, the Fathers of the Church, and the great Arabs, that numbers are the *Noumena* [objects known without the senses], one quickly comes to perceive how their real life has been noted by all in a chain of high intelligences, from St. Irenaeus to Claude St. Martin to Lacuria. This life of numbers is inscribed on the 78 leaves of the Tarot, that is to say, on the symbolic substratum of all human knowledge." Paul Adam constructed his stories, the lives of his characters, the twists and turns of his dramas that link them into logical sequence, on the tarot. His dramas are the eruptions of invisible reality, symbolized by any manner of combination of the tarot's seventy-eight cards. And if this all sounds implausible, Michelet reproduced a letter in his *Companions of the Hierophany* in which, in the most charming French prose, Adam congratulated Michelet on having penetrated his secret: that yes, the tarot had been for him a constructive key, indispensable to a "thousand intutitions": "I remain a docile disciple having received the highest recompense of his zeal, that of your approbation. Paul Adam. June 1919."

The prosaic account of Paul Adam is that he was a French novelist whose novel *La Force* (1899) opened a series on the Napoleonic Wars and whose sociological novels also gained public attention.

BARLET

Barlet was the pen name of Albert Faucheux (1838–1921), who also wrote his name as Ch. Barlet, Ch., F.C., or François Charles Barlet. In 1885 he joined the Hermetic Brotherhood of Luxor, founded in London by Max Théon. He was one of the first Frenchmen to join the Theosophical Society, but left it with Papus in 1888, after having joined with Papus, Péladan, Paul Sédir, Lucien Chamuel, de Guaita, and Augustin Chaboseau in Papus's brainchild, the Groupe Indépendant d'Études Ésotériques.

Fig. 7.6. Barlet
(Albert Faucheux, 1838–1921)

That group would become the Hermetic School, with Barlet one of its
seven councilors. He would write for Papus's journal *Initiation* and go on
to participate in one esoteric task after another, combining his activities
with a great love and appreciation of painting.*

Michelet recognized in him the type of individual who is content in
the penumbra of life, rather like the clergyman described on his tomb as
"a venerable and discrete person." He was involved in practically every
esoteric circle of his day, often being roped in against his better judgment to groups who only wanted the honor of his presence. He had
a saintly nature that could not refuse a service, even to the undignified. Self-effacing, he wrote tersely and exercised considerable authority, established on encyclopedic knowledge, sure science, and personal
uprightness. He possessed what were called in the eighteenth century
vertus, which means more than what "virtue" suggests today: real,
fecund, erect strength. Before he died, Michelet overheard him say to

---

*In 1890 he became a bishop in Jules Doinel's Gnostic Church. After de Guaita's death
in December 1897, Barlet became Grand Master of the Kabbalistic Order of the Rose-
Croix. He would hand the documents and grades of the Order to René Guénon, who also
obtained de Guaita's library. Barlet was a member of the first Supreme Council of the Martinist Order (Papus's creation) from March 1891. He was Director of "Cosmic Review"
1901–03, wrote two volumes of *Cosmic Tradition* (1903). During 1900–01 he visited Max
Théon (Louis-Maximilian Bimstein, 1848–1947) at Tiemcen, Algeria. Barlet wrote *The
Synthesis of Aesthetics: Painting* (Chamuel: Paris, 1895); *The Art of Tomorrow: Painting
Then and Now* (Chamuel: Paris, 1897); and *St. Yves d'Alveydre: Our Teacher* (1910).

a wife of a friend: "I beg you, do not call me a master. I am only an old student." Indeed, he spent his long life in studies that never made their way to paper, but which would furnish any conversation with wonders and enlightenment, speech flavored with gentle complaisance and spirituality that made the interlocutor complicit in the sensation of being lifted up to a higher realm. He knew far more than he would write. "The gods," said Shakespeare, "make of us that which we make of torches: we do not light them for themselves." The gods, asserts Michelet, served Barlet as they did St. Yves d'Alveydre.

Michelet recalled the Sundays he spent at the "great gentleman" St. Yves's "little palace of Versailles," with his elegant words keeping himself and those around him in high spiritual regions. According to Michelet, his voice, like that of Villiers de l'Isle-Adam, was the most powerful he ever heard. Barlet's voice was always of simple expression, "a calm river glittering with sequins of gold."

Michelet observed truly how "one belongs to an intellectual generation not by age, but by affinities." Although Barlet was older than the young men who first gathered at Bailly and Chamuel's Librairie du Merveilleux, his was a necessary voice, making a vital contribution to the journal *L'Initiation*. Working as a registrar at Boulogne sur Mer, and coming to Paris for holidays, Michelet wondered how Barlet could have found the rare works necessary for his studies.

As he was in the 1880s, he was in his last days: looking round the market at the Buci crossroads in the 6th arrondissement (St. Germain-des-Prés), with a string bag containing three or four vegetables comprising his whole nourishment. His hair and beard might have become cloudy, but his black eyes were always aflame, and his fast gait testified to the perpetual youth of his spirit spreading through his limbs. "His ever youthful eyes had cast into the world ideas of a passionate and charitable curiosity." Barlet had a synthetic, not analytical mind, and so was able to assemble from vastly separate sources concepts and knowledge that would baffle the specialists of today. He had great knowledge of myths and legends from around the world and, having paid attention to their profound significations, could reduce them to essentials "as one reduces fractions to the same denominator."

Michelet has left us a fragment of Barlet's prophetic powers:

I will always have in my memory one of those conversations which was so prophetic. I met him on the place Saint-Michel in the first days of July 1918. It's easy to recall that at this time, the situation [World War I] was quite worrying. We awaited the last blows of the battering ram of the formidable German army.

—*Eh bien,* I asked Barlet, have you drawn up [astrologically] the scheme of events? What do you predict?

—Yes, he replied: the aspects are very good. Venus, who is our protector, is about to enter a favorable position. The second fifteen of July will be good for us, and will mark the beginning of success. In August, the situation will be better and in September better again, and even better in October. I see the end of the war before that of the year [the Germans officially surrendered in November]. But I do not see the peace before two years. There is a point, he added, on which I am disappointed: Russia. I have been concentrating on the strength of Nicolas II [tsar of Russia] and found the death of the Tsar [at this time everyone was ignorant of the tsar's murder].

We spent an hour forcing ourselves to follow from the "other side" the concordances with events that overturned the entire planet. The sublime seer of the Iliad showed the process of the war simultaneously on the terrestrial plane and on the plane of secondary causes. Things always take place in the same manner. We try to follow the conflict of cosmic forces weighing on the conflicts of men, "inclining" some things, necessitating others. We wanted to see the movement of the Hierarchies of the invisible world. That day, I left Barlet, fully convinced of the favorable process of events.

A regret grips me today: that is, that all the intellectual riches crammed in by Barlet, the greater part will not have found a place in his published work. I know he dispensed his thought in articles here and there. There are so many people who are too occupied informing people in order to have the time to learn something; Barlet was too occupied with learning to have the time to inform.[27]

It is one thing for me to write about the members of the Kabbalistic Order of the Rose-Croix. It would be quite another to have heard them speak: so much is lost.

High Summer 1888 ⁓

While Gauguin leaves Paris to paint at Pont-Aven in Brittany, Bailly bookshop regular Claude Debussy receives a cash gift from financier and music lover Étienne Dupin. Debussy takes the money and travels to Bayreuth to hear Wagner. He listens to *Parsifal* and *Die Meistersinger,* and he doubtless sees there the outstanding figure of fellow Wagner devotee, Joséphin Péladan, likewise come to worship at the Wagnerian shrine. For both Frenchmen, the experience is unforgettable.

In Péladan's work *Le Théâtre complet de Wagner* (1895), he says it was that summer when: "I conceived at that time, in a single flash, the foundation of the three orders of the Rose+Croix of the Temple and the Grail, and resolved to become so far as concerned the literary theatre, a disciple of Wagner."[28]

Péladan didn't share his intentions with de Guaita. He must have known deep down it would mean the end of their collaboration. He had seen the Grail knights in a *tour de force* of artistic synthesis, and he had seen his future. And he had seen suddenly, glimpsed anyway, what a new Rosicrucian Order could be, what it needed to be. It could not be something like a museum of the past, however comforting. He was not going to waste his legacy, his brother's initiation on anything less than something culturally explosive. Like the original conception of the fraternity, the draft must taste as fresh as it did at source. He could see a totally different concept of a magical order and its place in the world; it would have to burst out of the bookshops and on to the great stage of life.

Péladan must have returned to Paris, looked hard at the R+C+K, listened to talk of Freemasonry and Eastern religions and old books and asked himself: *Is this the best I can do with my brother's legacy? Is this the work for Sâr Mérodack Péladan?* Is not Péladan linked in spirit through time, beyond time, to Baladan, *Merodach-Baladan?* And was he not a Chaldaean prince who usurped the Babylonian throne in 721 BC, who maintained Babylonian independence in the face of Assyrian aggression? What more "authority" did one require? For what did Merodach-Baladan mean? "Marduk has given me an heir." The Master, the brother, Adrien Péladan, would not fail of an heir. Mérodack Péladan was the heir. All hail!

And all hail was let loose. . . .

EIGHT

Papus

Incedo per multam merdam.*

MARTIN LUTHER

Late August 1888 ︵

Imagine Bohemian Joséphin Péladan, large-eyed and full of hair, topped by a broad brimmed akubra hat, in corduroy breeches and suede boots and a loose fitting mustard-colored jacket over a sportsman's shirt and ample tummy, hauling his case beneath the vast arched window of the Gare de l'Est on a very hot, early summer evening, after a long train journey from Munich. Beneath the heavy air, sweetened by smoke of steam locomotives wafting in from platforms inside the station, Péladan hails a hansom cab, driven by a sun-kissed woman, seated above and behind the main cab. Péladan calls up to her his destination: 29 rue de Trévise. The driver pulls a lever, the door is unlatched, and Péladan lifts his case inside and hauls his large frame into the cab as the single black horse steadies itself, waiting for a gentle pull on the reins.

The cab heads west, hooves echoing noisily on the stone setts, strewn with cabbage, horse muck, cigar butts, and waste paper. After 50 meters it crosses the busy boulevard de Magenta, a broad, airy Haussmanian, tree-lined thoroughfare, packed with cabs, horse-drawn water wagons, rattling dairy carts, distillers' carts, coal wagons, carts of fruits and vegetables, haulage carts overstuffed with wicker baskets, a heavy wheeled

---

*"I advance through much shit."

Fig. 8.1. Joséphin Péladan

brewer's wagon advertising "Bière Moritz," and crisscrossed with men and women in clothes colorful and drab, in hats tall and flat, with faces subdued and tired by day after dusty day of unrelenting heat.

On the other side of the boulevard, the cab takes the narrow rue de Chabrol. It heads west some 500 meters toward the 9th arrondissement. Being so narrow the five-story houses on either side, lined with elegant wrought-iron balconies and pretty flowers and not a little washing hanging out like flags from the upper floors, seem to fall into each other like a magical gorge painted by Böcklin. To the left, in the shade afforded by the low, glaring sun, looking fazed after a long day getting longer, a lampshade seller hovers in a felt hat, frockcoat, checked shirt, and little dicky bow that matches his coat-hanger-like moustache. His beige moleskin trousers hang baggily above bare feet in well-worn leather slippers. The basket hanging down his back is full; his day's work is not over. To the right an old, bearded man in a grubby, flattened bowler cranks his wheel-mounted hurdy-gurdy while a young boy in a tattered gentleman's smoking jacket sings in sweet soprano Pluto's pastoral song by Offenbach. A baker in a white beret, pale short-sleeved shirt with an apron down to his bare shins and feet, listens with an enormous cigar-like loaf of bread held tight under his arm. Its dark crust shines in a blade of sunlight.

As the cab nears the street's end at the junction with the boulevard de la Fayette, Péladan hears the screeching of a mobile knife-grinder. A moustachio'd workman in huge leather overtrousers and a flat cap with a leather peak, presses a glistening fishmonger's knife to a huge spinning wheel, mounted on a barrow, watched by a grinning market-porter, dressed in a sail-like cotton overall, wide open at the chest and blown out by a middle-aged stomach, shaded by his trade's massive, flat saucerish sombrero of a straw hat.

Emerging from the stone grip of the rue de Chabrol, Péladan blinks as shafts of dappled light cascade through the trees of the great boulevard, making pearls of empty glare on the hot sidewalk. The cab turns left onto the quietening thoroughfare. Toy shops with charming dolls and puppets, ladies outfitters, bakers, hatters, bric-à-brac sellers, and vegetable shops, stacked high with baskets of cauliflowers, potatoes, aubergines, garlic, peppers, and tomatoes, are closing down as the café life begins to warm up, though many habitués are away in the country or at the seaside resorts. On every street corner, an impassive flower lady stands holding erect hyacinths before a basket of lavender, lilies, and roses. With their ample smocks covering collapsed bosoms, they resemble pious widows, because they probably are.

The cab pauses at a junction. In homburg and raincoat: an epitome of optimism misplaced, a poor Jewish salesman approaches the cab window clutching cheap umbrellas. His bearded face smiles at Péladan: "It must rain soon, monsieur!" "Then you will need your umbrellas!" quips Péladan as the cab pulls away, past more peddlers and overdressed nannies taking groups of sweet, uniformed children for an evening stroll into the little park at the place Montholon, watched over by a city park attendant in military style kepi with dress sword to the side of a bright blue jacket over dazzling white trousers. He impresses the children with his swagger and slightly comic authority.

Turning left into the narrow rue de Trévise, Péladan snaps out of a passing reverie, opens the hatch above him and tells the driver: "Numéro 29, madame."

"Oui, monsieur. Vingt-neuf."

Number 29 rue de Trévise is on the right a little way down the street from the junction with the boulevard: a fine, pale stone, five-story house. Its ground floor has been taken by Gérard Encausse's younger friend Louis Chamuel, for a bookshop, publishing base, and meeting center.

"Deux francs, monsieur." Péladan pays the driver through the hatch with a fifty centimes tip, and the driver frees the cab door. The street is hot and very dry. As the cab pulls away, leaving the steaming residuum of the horse's repast behind it, two young faces come to the window of the *Librairie du Merveilleux*. Seeing Péladan standing in the street with his case, they smile. The thinner one unlocks the front door of the shop. He has a dark complexion, a long face, and a curious pendulous beard that falls from either side of his full lips like a pair of money-bags or bull's testicles meeting at the gorge of his chin. He is Lucien Chamuel, twenty-one, mystic to the marrow. He has put up the cash for the enterprise. Chamuel greets Péladan with a warm, moist handshake and beckons him inside.

The shop seems more full of alchemical equipment than it does of the "books of the marvelous" that have given the establishment its name. There are rusting aludels and dented retorts and old crucibles and alembics scattered about the floor and, hanging from spare moments in walls encrusted with tomes old and new, framed engravings of magical and Rosicrucian provenance. In the left corner is a solid writing desk

Fig. 8.2. Lucien Mauchel
("Chamuel," 1867–1936)

where whoever is managing the shop sits to survey casual customers in quest of novelty. Incense from a most exotic source smolders in a corner and the man whose youthful, energetic bulk presides over the proceedings is twenty-three-year-old medical student and born entrepreneur Gérard Encausse, olive-skinned with a squared beard, gypsy eyes, and slightly sinister eyebrows. He is called "Papus," pronounced as you would a Native American baby.

Gérard-Anaclet-Vincent Encausse was born 13 July 1865 in Corogna, Spain, the son of a French father, Louis, who tried to sell his self-invented medical equipment to the people of Spain's Basque region from a caravan. Gérard's mother, Iñes Perrez-Vierra, was a Spanish gypsy. Papus believed the visible inheritance of gypsy blood in his ardent black pupils that gazed far into the mysteries accounted for his spontaneous intuitions, prophecies, and skills in tarot and chiromancy. Michelet recalls a moment in their youth when studying chiromancy together,

Fig. 8.3. Papus (Gérard Encausse, 1865–1916)

Papus said to him, showing his hand: "See: I will die aged 53 years"—a fair prediction.[1]

Of southern French origin, Louis Encausse failed to make an impact in Spain and so brought his skills to Paris where, with a certified physician, he opened a clinic near the dusty lanes of Montmartre. There, Gérard, a mischievous boy who avoided scholastic discipline, grew up, eventually enrolling at the Collège Rollin, where he failed to make the grade. He did not lack intelligence by any means, possessing as he did rapid powers of assimilation, immediately grasping the most abstruse concepts that, according to Michelet, could then be incarcerated into rather gross formulae accessible to the vulgar. Michelet calls him a "born vulgarizer." He might have called him a "born salesman" but that perhaps would be too vulgar.

Michelet's judgment of Papus was astute as well as appreciative. He tells us that certain very rare men are able to supplement by their intelligence faculties they otherwise lack. Though "entirely denuded of that artistic organ that Goethe esteemed indispensable to seize the domains of Art" Papus came to comprehend a work of art by his intellect, thus entering a world ordinarily only penetrated by grace of aesthetic gifts. "His militant ardor carried him joyfully into the struggle." He took blows with a smile and rendered them back likewise. He had natural leadership qualities, with an "obliging camaraderie" combined with organizational gifts and a talent for uniting others.

Having failed at school, he took night classes in medicine, volunteered for military service, and in 1885 embarked on a crash course in occultism having, he said later, realized through his medical studies that a spiritual order, unheeded by science, operated even in the strictly biological sphere. He outlined his realization in a short memoir, "How I Became a Mystic" (*Comment je deviens mystique*), published in the journal founded by his friend Lucien Chamuel in 1888, *L'Initiation*:

They told me: "These mineral salts, this earth, having slowly decomposed and been assimilated by the vegetable's root, will *evolve* into the vegetable's cells. In turn, this vegetable, transformed by the secretions and fermentations of the animal's stomach . . . will be transformed into the animal's cells." Reflecting on this I realized one of the critical factors in the problem had been forgotten.

Yes, the mineral does evolve, its essential principles becoming the material elements of the vegetable cell, but only if the physico-chemical forces and the sun aid the phenomenon. Superior forces by their evolution have to *sacrifice* themselves to the inferior forces' evolution.

The digested vegetable does indeed become the material basis for the animal cell, but only when the blood and nervous force (superior forces in evolution's ladder) sacrifice themselves for the vegetable cell's evolution. . . .

Each step of the series demands the sacrifice of one or more superior forces. Evolution as a doctrine is then incomplete, only recognizing one side of the facts, ignoring the other. Bringing to light the law of the struggle for life, it forgets the law of *sacrifice* that dominates all phenomena.

I held firmly to this idea I had brought to light and deepened my understanding in days spent at the Bibliothèque Nationale . . . where alchemical works, old magical grimoires and the elements of Hebrew occupied my attention. My future was mapped out while colleagues devoted years to passing their exams. I found what I thought was my discovery in the works of Louis Lucas [Papus wrote of Éliphas Lévi's friend Lucas in his work *L'Occultisme Contemporain* (Paris: Georges Carré, 1887)], then in Hermetic texts as also in Kabbalah and Indian traditions. It was a question of language: where we write HCL, the alchemists showed a "green lion"; where we write $2HCL + Fe = FeCL_2 + H_2$, alchemists portrayed a warrior (Mars = Iron) devoured by a green lion (acid).

Thus I could read the old grimoires more easily than some of the works of our pedantic chemists. I also learned the analogical method, little known to our philosophers, by which all sciences may be grouped into a single synthesis. It shows the ancients have been libeled by the infinite historical ignorance of today's professors.[2]

Michelet first encountered the young medical student in 1887 at the time when Félix-Krishna Gaboriau, a young Breton of ardent and intransigent convictions, joined his energies to a small inheritance and published a Theosophical review called *Le Lotus*. The review was alone in welcoming the first occult effusions of Stanislas de Guaita, Barlet, and Papus, though their work was received with a certain reserve, accompanied by slightly acid editors' notes. The reason was that the "shadow of a strange Russian medium, Mme. Blavatsky, weighed as heavily through the pages of *Le Lotus* as did Gaboriau's own spiritual ardor."[3] This comment of Michelet's gives us a perfect insight into the tensions that persisted between Theosophists and enthusiasts of the Western esoteric traditions. Catholics in particular were uncomfortable with the Theosophist tendency to equate Jesus with Hindu conceptions of avatars and gurus. While Vedantism and related strands of Eastern philosophies were interesting, and sometimes made for enlightening comparisons, they were neither central, nor even necessary for the specifically "occult," that is Hermetic and Rosicrucian enthusiasts. Hindu philosophy was felt by them to be too drily philosophical, remote, verbose, bloodless, pseudo-universalist, and insufficiently magical, astral, and viscerally spiritual, which is to say romantic, to those raised on, and fond of, the Western Christmas and Easter celebrations, with their colorful immediacy and warmly charming, childlike blend of spiritual magic and high paganism. The rift persists to this day.

Papus found himself in polite tensions with Félix-Krishna Gaboriau, but before leaving Félix-Krishna's Isis Lodge to form his own Theosophical lodge, called "Hermès," Papus took part in a *soirée* organized by the revue *Le Lotus* in a room of *Véfour,* celebrated café in the Palais-Royal at 8 rue de Montpensier near the rue de Rivoli in Paris's 1st arrondissement. Michelet helped in setting it up, but was greatly disappointed by Gérard Encausse's public speaking début. He was "badly gifted," indeed, rarely had Michelet heard a speaker more painfully fumble for his words. Michelet reckoned Papus should at once renounce any ambition to oratory.

Michelet, however, had forgotten about the prodigies wrought by will and by training, and the next time he heard Papus in public, he was struck by his clarity, even though his grip on the audience was won at the price of a degree of vulgarity that nonetheless suited "a middling audience." But so impressive was Papus that Michelet hardly dared wait for another blow of the smiling fat man's trumpet.

He did not have to wait long. Living in modest chambers close to the Gare de l'Est, Papus, on Sunday mornings, held a literary get-together with a coterie of five or six former schoolfellows of the Collège Rollin in the avenue Trudaine. There was the philosopher Weber [not the famous Max Weber], the writer-to-be Georges Polti (1867–1946), Émile Gary, and a young student from the Vendée, Lucien Mauchel (Chamuel). Despite the quarter's commercial nature, this little literary set was ebullient, full of burning intellectual ardor. "Pythagoras annexed it to his school," commented Michelet on what was in fact a school of mystical and philosophical initiation. The group necessarily attracted like-minded and sympathetic spirits to their number. Michelet was obviously taken up into the experience: "There was the marvel of discovering a source of acquaintances differently dressed, differently passionate, differently grandiose, all enraptured in a magma of scholarly sciences promising universal enlightenment. And these studies by which we perceived immense horizons were yet treated with contempt, damned! But we, we were going to restore the world; we were going to reveal to the modern world that which the great initiates of antiquity knew! And *this* was our Error."[4] Though Michelet pleaded their spirit of generosity be recognized by posterity, it would have been better, he reflected in his maturity, had they listened to the experience of old Bernard Fontenelle (1657–1757) who was almost one hundred when he said: "If I had a hand full of truths, I would be careful about opening it." "It is said that one must not put one's light under a bushel. So be it, but it is certainly necessary to cover it with a very strong lampshade. Thus assert the Masters in all ages."[5]

Papus looked for ways to unify what had been initiated, beginning a life characterized by a perpetual struggle to group his scattered forces, forming one body after another in the search of an organizational spearhead. Instead he created a quiverful of irregular arrows, dependent on his personal bowstring.

One day he said to Lucien Chamuel: "Several thousand franc notes would suffice to create a publishing house of occultist works which could stand up perfectly." A little later, Chamuel rented the shop in the rue de Trévise that became the Librairie du Merveilleux. Providing a center for radiating antique ideas in renewed form, it soon attracted a crowd of distinguished minds as well as the fashionable and the snobs. Michelet reflected wryly that wherever the fashionable and the snobs passed, disaster followed.

In 1888, Papus and Chamuel's monthly review of elevated studies, *L'Initiation,* appeared. It would run for an impressive twenty-five years. Wildly animated, Papus simultaneously created the *Groupe Indépendant d'Études ésoteriques* in an anttempt to unite all the minds of the occult world.

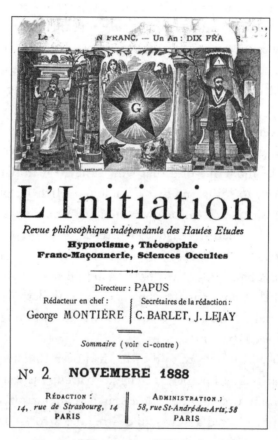

Fig. 8.4. L'Initiation, *"The independent philosophical revue of high studies," 2nd issue, November 1888*

Papus loved having people around him. And what people! The group consisted of young poets, writers, artists, polytechnicians, doctors, and divers sages, among whom were Péladan, Stanislas de Guaita, alchemist-chemist Albert Poisson, Barlet, Georges Polti, Émile Gary, parapsychologist and military engineer Colonel Albert de Rochas (1837–1914; author of *Undefined Forces,* 1887), Paul Adam, the publisher Lemerle, Paul Sédir, Marc Haven, Abel Haatan, Henri Selva (pen name of Jewish astrologer Arthur Herrmann Vlès 1861–1944), Chaboseau, and "other precious companions avid for intelligent nourishment."

Parallel to *L'Initiation,* Chamuel's imprint created a little weekly, *Le Voile d'Isis* (The Veil of Isis), while Papus asked Michelet to run

Fig. 8.5. Le Voile d'Isis, *1st issue, 12 November 1890; note the headline, "The Supernatural Does Not Exist": typical eye-catching salesmanship from Papus.*

Fig. 8.6 (left).
Léon Bazalgette
(1873–1928)

Fig. 8.7 (right).
Augustin Chaboseau
(1868–1946)

a little literary review, *Psyché,* with help from Augustin Chaboseau (1868–1946) and, just out of school, Léon Bazalgette (1873–1928) who would go on to write biographies of Walt Whitman and Henry Thoreau.

According to Michelet, Papus had "the gift of ubiquity." He seemed to be everywhere, organizing conferences, reunions, societies, while at the same time involving himself in the closed circles of the Martinist Order, which he refounded, or de Guaita's Ordre R+C+Kabbalistique, all the time drawing toward him all kinds of people of varying talents and levels of interest.

Somewhere in everyone, Michelet observes, exists a curiosity about the mysterious world. Most are onlookers of mystery. They like to lean over an abyss for an instant, like hasty tourists. Others will climb the slope of Vesuvius to the crater or travel to the rue de Naples to linger in the *musée secret,* the secret cabinet of Pompeii's erotica. Papus recognized the latent curiosity and fomented it by giving out the assurance that pursuing this intellectual movement toward transcendence brought social success. He understood his market and pursuing it was ready to adopt Luther's vulgar dictum, *Incedo per multam merdam:* "I advance through much shit." But, as Michelet comments: "Must not all director-innovators accept this ineluctable necessity?"

People wishing to know what the occult movement was all about gathered at the Librairie du Merveilleux, where in a decorated room at

*Fig. 8.8. Papus (seated) at the rear of the Librairie du
Merveilleux, before a lecture for his* Groupe Indépendant
d'Études ésoteriques *(note the blackboard in the foreground)*

the rear of the building, lectures, talks, and discussions were held under
the auspices of Papus's *Groupe Indépendant d'Études ésoteriques,* which
soon became the *École Hermétique,* while all these activities were practically interactive at this stage with de Guaita's *Ordre Kabbalistique de la
Rose-Croix*: precisely the same steering names appear in both, which has
been confusing for researchers favoring tidyness.

Papus wanted to evangelize and while neophytes were forthcoming,
he also attracted some of the finest writers of the day. Villiers de l'Isle-
Adam, Catulle Mendès, de Guaita, Péladan, and poets from the Chat
Noir cabaret offered their talents to the pages of Chamuel and Papus's
L'Initiation, quickly establishing Papus and his circle as an unavoidable

feature of the Belle Époque's mystical and magical explosion, whose main problem, as a movement, in retrospect, was to try to find a clear direction, for very soon the movement accreted so many aspects, traditions, and priorities, as well as competing bodies and individuals, that the Hierophany, with all its intimate companionship, began more to resemble at certain points an undisciplined parliament in its constitutional infancy than a concerted movement with an achievable objective. Nevertheless, it had its effect.

Regarding himself as a manager of men as well as a successful entrepreneur, Papus saw it as good policy to make full allowance for the beliefs and ignorance of what Michelet calls "the vulgar." This, for Michelet was a policy whose limits should have been set, since all artists and philosophers who made concessions to the mob decapitated themselves. Michelet noted one particularly outrageous stroke in the direction of vulgar popularization that offended the genuinely spiritually minded supporters of the movement. Papus put a headline in the *Voile d'Isis:* "THE SUPERNATURAL does not exist." Papus knew "like us" says Michelet, that if the supernatural does not exist, then the "natural" would exist no longer, for one is only the symbol of the other. Papus was prepared to attenuate spiritual conceptions to bribe the denials of common opinion. Papus would, as he put it, "gild the pill" to be everybody's friend, or everybody's friendly neighborhood occultist, cheapening the goods in the process and obscuring the difficulties of the path.

Papus took it upon himself to try to persuade leading figures as well as up-and-coming figures of the validity of the occult sciences. One such was the writer Anatole France (1844–1924), whose name was just beginning to pass beyond the obscurity into which it had long lain, despite having written five or six books, later celebrated.

Michelet had often met Anatole France in the Luxembourg Gardens on his way from the Senate Library where he worked as supervisory clerk with librarian Leconte de Lisle. Appointed director of a "luxurious" review, Anatole had taken on two very young collaborators: Michelet and Maurice Barrès. Knowing France's tendencies, Michelet

Fig. 8.9. Papus as "magus," by Octave Denis
Victor Guillonet (1872–1967)

informed Papus that the literary critic would not go in the direction
Papus wished to lead him because, while he was charged up with a spirit
of brilliance, it did not extend beyond literature. As Michelet put it:
"I did not see the gracious and superficial dilettante descending into
hermetic profundities."[6]

"—Oh!—said Papus—I will gild the pill for him!"

Papus, who was at the time a nonresident pupil of Dr. Luys at the
Hôpital de la Charité at the corner of the boulevard St. Germain and
the rue des Saints-Pères—then headquarters of the French National
Academy of Medicine—took Anatole France to see professional

experiments in hypnosis. From there, Papus took France's curiosity on a walk to "the fringes of Hermes's domain." He didn't get far, but got something from it. Put in the direction of the Paracelsus-saturated novel by Abbé Villars (1635–1675), *Le Comte de Gabalis,* Anatole France proceeded to write his *La Rôtisserie de la Reine Pédauque* (1893), which in fact criticized belief in the occult. Michelet tactfully recognized the novel was agreeable, pleasant literature, but lacked the scope of the Abbé de Villars, murdered in 1675 in a family feud, though some have attributed his death to his novel's revealing Rosicrucian secrets.

As literary critic of the newspaper *Le Temps,* France wrote in 1893 in response to the claim of the Collège de France that it was open to all knowledge, even novelties, and that one could be educated in everything there: "I wish they would create a chair of Magic there for Monsieur Papus." So while Papus got *something* for his efforts, Michelet observed that you cannot *make* someone see the spiritual world. While France enjoyed the gift of "a very nice talent," he was "incapable of making the first steps in the grand spiritual palaces" as was demonstrated, in Michelet's opinion, by France's reflections on the poetry of Stéphane Mallarmé.

Papus continued to propagandize among literary types and journalists, titled princesses, and theatrical and musical stars. The center of awed Symbolist gaze, Sarah Bernhardt, perhaps the greatest stage star of them all, received his philosophical attentions with gratitude, as did Augusta Holmès and opera singer Emma Calvé, the latter being the most curious about what Michelet calls Papus's "facile word." Papus would attend gatherings where fashionable figures met their public. Augusta Holmès, who would hold auditions of her music that she did not herself accompany, invited Sarah Bernhardt, knowing what a draw she was. Both attracted and hesitant, La Bernhardt said: "Put my name on the program, but please don't if I don't come."

"So many minds were solicited by the atmosphere of Mystery! They came to inhale an instant, then pass, passing affairs. Artists, writers, politicians filed past. The Librairie du Merveilleux saw the different files of different élites, pass by. This was a mob."[7]

*Fig. 8.10. Actress Sarah Bernhardt (1844–1923),
photograph by Paul Nadar*

There was still one project, among all his other efforts to spread the word, that preoccupied Papus's attention. He was determined to create an educational system in Hermetic studies. Michelet was sceptical. Not believing in systems of education except for the provision of rudiments, he took Bernard Shaw's quip as axiomatic: "When a man knows how to do a thing, he does it; when he doesn't know, he teaches it." "Nothing is initiated except by itself," maintains Michelet. "The profound knowledges are not transmittable." Nevertheless, Papus's various attempts at establishing a faculty of Hermetic studies was a "happy initiative" since official education determined to maintain itself in strict limits. It was, on reflection, a good thing to manifest an independent education that was audacious and lively, helping young intellects to discover for themselves vast horizons conventional education shuts out. Michelet gave the example of Alexandre Mercereau (1884–1945), Symbolist poet who inspired cubism, whose generosity established for a while the Abbaye de Créteil (1906–08), based on Rabelias's Abbaye de Thélème, which, sadly, died without sufficient support, though Michelet's old friend, Léon Bazalgette, joined it.

Papus's Hermetic School gave opportunities for most of Paris's occult figures to give talks: Paul Sédir, Barlet, Marc Haven, and alchemist François Jollivet-Castelot (1825–1893) all contributed. Papus himself took a special interest in hypnosis, as part of his medical studies—he would not obtain his doctorate in medicine until 1894—attending Faculty of Medicine talks and demonstrations at the Hôpital de la Charité, Collège Rollin, and the Saltpêtrière Hospital where nervous maladies were treated. Once he found his stride, Papus discovered he was especially skilled in popular exposition. His *Traité élémentaire de science occulte* (Elementary Treatise on Occult Science) was published in 1888 while still a student. He followed it up with his *Clef absolue des sciences occultes, le tarot des Bohémiens* (Absolute Key to the Occult Science, the Tarot of the Bohemians, Paris, Ernest Flammarion, 1889). These books helped students make a start.

PAUL SÉDIR AND MARC HAVEN

Regarding Paul Sédir, Michelet relates a nice story about his first, startling appearance at 29 rue de Trévise. Michelet, Papus, and Chamuel were all present. A very young man, thin and light, presented himself, declaring at the top of his voice:

—*Voilà!* I want to do occultism.

Michelet couldn't stop himself laughing, so gauche did the lad appear. Seeing at once a useful person, Papus refrained from laughter:

—That's very good, my boy. Come to my place on Sunday morning.

He did, and that Sunday Papus began the boy's education.

The first matter was the young Breton's real name. It was Yvon Leloup. Papus changed it to Paul Sédir, "Sédir" being an anagram of *Désir,* a very significant word in the system of Louis-Claude de

Fig. 8.11. Yvon Leloup
("Paul Sédir," 1871–1926)

St. Martin, who wrote of the "L'homme de désir": the Man of Desire being one keen to realize divinity in his life, ardent in retrieving the divine image, dedicated to reintegration. The world is redeemed by the reparatory response of the Men of Desire. Paul Sédir responded in like manner to his master's teaching, and very soon his half-Breton, half-German roots showed themselves in the way he attacked the most arduous studies. Michelet knew he had misjudged the young man and was properly impressed. The results were plain. Within a short time, Sédir was an encyclopedia of knowledge, so impressive in fact that even the severe Stanislas de Guaita admitted him to the inner sanctum of 20 avenue Trudaine to enjoy the marquis's library. He would become a Doctor of the Kabbalah in de Guaita's Order.

Michelet reckoned him a superior student to his master, for Papus tended to be a butterfly. He wanted to embrace every branch of the tree of science, but when one branch called for too close attention, Papus's gaze would flit onto something else. He could be the same with people. Papus would fuss over an individual, then, for no apparent reason, direct his attention elsewhere. A new acolyte would then have the pleasure of the large man's briefly concentrated interest. Papus regarded his gypsy intuition as his best asset and he followed its dictates without always realizing, as Michelet puts it, that intuition was not intended to travel alone.

Sédir, on the other hand, would never leave a subject till he had grasped it from head to tail. This zeal made him a better lieutenant than a captain, and with the bookishness came a lack of personality. Michelet noticed that while serving as Papus's aide-de-camp, Sédir generated his most interesting studies, but when left to his own devices, he was less assured and became prey to "pseudo-mysticism." Michelet does not explain this, presumably not wishing to cause offense, but we know that Sédir involved himself with Jules Doinel's neo-Catharist Gnostic Church—formed under the auspices of Lady Caithness in 1890—wherein he was consecrated as Tau Paul, Gnostic bishop of Concorezzo. In 1897 he joined Marc Haven's *Fraternitas Lucis Thesauri* (FLT), a novel spin on Rosicrucianism. Then, in 1897, he met the Lyon mystic "Monsieur Philippe," Papus's peasant guide also: Nizier Anthelme Philippe. The effect on Sédir would be even more pronounced than on Papus.

Sédir had a vision and realized for himself the vacuity of magical orders and esoteric wisdom and, quitting all associations, devoted himself exclusively to a Quaker-like ministry of "Spiritual Friendships," loving his neighbor and seeking the kingdom of God. Out of all this activity, not to mention his involvement with François-Jollivet Castelot's Alchemical Society of France and the Ancient & Primitive Rites of Freemasonry (Memphis and Misraim), it is difficult to know what in particular might have qualified for Michelet's use of the term "pseudo-mysticism." It is often the case that people who acquire immense amounts of knowledge value it least, for with all knowledge comes, as the biblical book of Ecclesiastes reminds us, an equal measure of vanity—and "much sorrow."

Two more young men presented themselves to the Librairie du Merveilleux with similar intentions to Sédir. A young student of medicine, Emmanuel Lalande, from the Champagne Sénonaise, turned up with his pal, Thomas, who was studying to be a pharmacist. Calling himself Marc Haven after the *génie* of dignity in the *Nuctemeron,* Lalande desired to master Hermetism; his friend Thomas, who called himself "Abel Haatan" would become one of the deepest of the astrologers. Both of a meditative character, they were more inclined to look inward than to expand, and however high they flew, Michelet informs us, neither felt the need to recount in literary form their spiritual adventures. Hence, neither one is as well known as merit might have made him. Such seems consistent with Haatan's name, for "Haatan" is the *Nuctemeron's génie* who hides treasures. Haatan died young, leaving only an estimable treatise on judicial astrology to a world in which astrology earned little but contempt. Astrology is the antique science for studying correspondences that exist between different planes of the universe; it has been ladled with pitch due to the notion that it is wholly concerned with daily predictions or obsessed with individuals' birth details.

Both Galen and Paracelsus—two physicians normally considered

Fig. 8.12. Emmanuel Lalande ("Marc Haven," 1868–1926)

at odds—indicated it was difficult to practice medicine with great efficacy without astrological knowledge that touches on all sciences.

According to Michelet, Haven buried the artist within him. He once gave Michelet an example of his etched poetry which Michelet recognized as the work of an artist lacking only a little in technique and experience, but Haven wrote little more than a doctroral thesis study of Arnaud de Villeneuve, the physician who so fascinated the Vicomte de Lapasse, Péladan's brother's Rose-Croix initiator. Haven also wrote a wise preface to the seventeenth-century French alchemical text *Mutus Liber,* the "Silent Book" that taught a method for preparing the Philosopher's Stone with the aid of divine génies and angels. Marc Haven also wrote two books on founder of Egyptian Freemasonry, Cagliostro, alleged master of de Lapasse's Sicilian initiator, Prince Balbiani, though one of the books was in fact a veiled portrait of Papus's revered Monsieur Philippe, whose daughter Marc Haven would marry. Haven regarded Philippe as something of a reincarnation of Cagliostro, or of the master spirit that was incarnated *in* Cagliostro.

Michelet was by no means uncritical of the ubiquitous Papus, and his testimony is vital, for Papus is normally only confronted today as a name, a being who seemed to head so many "secret societies" one might conclude "Papus" was simply a code name for some malefic invisible, dedicated to spiritual subversion: an accusation of a type he certainly suffered in his lifetime after the Russian royal family took an interest in what had influenced their ancestors at the time of Bonaparte, namely, Martinism. Martinism will always be closely associated with Papus, for in 1891 he established a "Supreme Council" that allegedly reestablished an Order of Martinists, still active in essence today. Michelet was careful, however, to understand Papus's true significance in the movements of his times, and he keeps his most penetrating criticisms to expounding the weaknesses not of Papus but of the movement as a whole.

A survivor, Michelet recognized that between 1885 and 1890, two spiritual movements, close both in tendencies and bases of support, attempted to shake up deleterious beliefs then fashionable in France, and which, I may say, are still fashionable in the English-speaking world today. These beliefs may be designated as scientific materialism and its successor, literary naturalism. Against these foes were ranged the parallel movements of Symbolism and occultism. Their interest to us today, apart from intrinsic fascination, is that the battle still rages, except perhaps that the war is waged in a variety of different ways. However, one means of conflict still stands: literature, however that literature may be absorbed.

Writing in the 1930s, Michelet had become convinced by experience that the movements of Symbolism and occultism were unable to keep their extravagant promises. Partly as a result of that, Michelet was able to look at Papus with a degree of objectivity, even though he was himself involved in the movement. Why did they not fulfill their promise? According to Michelet, acute on this subject, there was a failure to push, or grow to the source, base, or fount of their spiritual quest. He says the Symbolist poets in the main did not even seek to perceive the *life* of symbols. They knew of them only as appearances. Michelet asks: "But what great poet ever expressed himself other than by the symbol?"

Michelet's companions in the Hierophany were, he says, like all other men in their passions, their weaknesses, their errors. They were distinguished by the height of their ambitions and, to their credit, only exalted their work, not themselves. "Even the little social manouvres of a Papus or the buccaneering of a Péladan tended to highlight their works, not their persons."[8] Michelet felt that at the time he was writing, it was still premature to assess the value and significance of men who for most people were long forgotten, perhaps risible characters allegedly drenched in superstition. It was hard for Michelet, who had powerful memories of their words and their gestures to disengage them from his personal feelings or from the "embers" that were still laid against them by an arrogant and uncomprehending posterity.

I hope we today can better appreciate than could the society of the 1930s the character and value of Michelet's companions of the Hierophany. Michelet had this to say of Papus, a génie of medicine, and of his times:

Of these figures, the most characteristic of them was Papus. His personality, though complex in appearance, was very simple in reality, but already in his time he was very diversely judged. No doubt in the future he will be legendary, like Cagliostro or the Comte de St. Germain. This great smiling boy, with his sad, malign eye, was at once the passionate animator and the latent destroyer of the occultist movement to which he dedicated his forces.[9]

NINE

Rosicrucial Differences

We believe in neither progress nor salvation; for the
moribund Latin race we are preparing a final explosion
of splendor to dazzle and mollify the barbarians who
are approaching. The last enthusiasts of this world, we
come among the tavern crowds braying the Marseillaise
to intone a final hymn to the Beauty which is God, and
thus earn the right to gaze one day upon the mystic rose.

My lust for the ideals of the past has violated the
tombs in which the miracles lay sleeping, and my
debauchery has had knowledge of some very young ideas
that will not develop for another century.

JOSÉPHIN PÉLADAN, INTRODUCTION, *GESTE ESTHÉTIQUE,*
CATALOGUE DU SALON DE LA ROSE+CROIX

The story of the falling-out of Stanislas de Guaita and Joséphin Péladan
and the creation of a second Rosicrucian Order claiming primacy in
Paris—sometimes called the "Wars of the Two Roses"—usually focuses
on incompatible differences between the latter men in temperament
and attitude. With benefit of hindsight, I think we can see a build up
to the rupture that, now we have a better understanding of Péladan's
motives in particular, makes the split appear inevitable. There were concrete issues and other persons involved; we can't just put it down to an

ego trip on Péladan's part, as Oswald Wirth, for example, would assert in his memoir of de Guaita.

Published by Lucien Chamuel in 1895, Péladan's book *Le Théâtre complet de Wagner* asserted that the grand idea of a new Rosicrucian Order came to the Sâr in a flash during a performance of Wagner's *Parsifal* at Bayreuth in summer 1888: "I conceived at that time, in a single flash, the foundation of the three orders of the Rose+Croix of the Temple and the Grail, and resolved to become, so far as concerned the literary theatre, a disciple of Wagner"[1]—and this despite his having just committed to coheading the governing council of twelve with de Guaita of the Rose+Croix+Kabbalistique in May of the same year. It is almost as if seeing *Parsifal* crystallized a doubt already in his mind. Perhaps getting out of Paris and into a foreign country where something radically new was happening artistically opened his inner eyes to the creation of spiritual theater. Perhaps it was in perceiving the sheer contrast between the excitement, magic, and wonder of the knights of the Holy Grail as revealed on Wagner's massive stage, and the familiar group of serious-minded Frenchmen forming a governing council in prosaic Parisian cafés and apartments that turned the key.

Péladan was committed to absolute idealism in Art and nothing less would satisfy him. The Ordre Rose-Croix Kabbalistique (R+C+K) was essentially an educational institution, albeit of a peculiar kind, but Péladan had little time for directed education; it just wasn't his style or his mission. De Guaita was, as we have seen, struck by Lévi's idea that the magician's task included warring with Satan's servants of disharmony to establish equilibrium. In de Guaita's book *Le Temple de Satan* (1892), into which he poured his knowledge of black magic, partly based on his experience of the defrocked Abbé Boullan, de Guaita informs us that the governing body of the R+C+K unanimously judged Boullan guilty of Satanic evil on 23 May 1888. Exposing Boullan was clearly a priority policy for de Guaita at the time Péladan headed for Bayreuth.

We do not know Péladan's own view on what amounted to a pious vendetta against perverse Boullan, a figure already condemned and excommunicated by the Church, but I suspect we can fairly imagine Péladan's asking himself why members of a Rose-Croix system should function as an inquisition. Did not the Catholic Church already provide such facilities, though less fatal in modern than in previous times? Péladan wasn't really interested in such murky matters. Perhaps he may have suspected what de Guaita's intended provocation might stir up in Boullan's strange mind. Was it right for artists to get mired in such stuff? It could all prove unpredictable at best, tiresome at least, ruinous at worst—and was it not a distraction from the main challenge of the times? So he probably thought, for in Péladan's own mind, there were far bigger fish to fry. What, anyhow, had Boullan to do with Art? Besides, de Guaita was unable to control the novel currents flowing into the esoteric movement. While the Sâr continued to express commitment to the aesthetics and ethics of Art through critical articles, eccentric burlesques, and trenchant observations in *The Salon,* stranger, doubtless to Péladan more questionable, phenomena were occurring within spiritist circles seeking guidance from "beyond."

As Debussy and Péladan joyed in their seventh heavens over Wagner in 1888, an official at the library at Orléans named Jules Doinel discovered among the city's medieval records an account from 1022 concerning the trial and burning at the stake of Canon Stephan (Étienne) d'Orléans, identified by Doinel as a precursor of the independent, heretical "Cathar" Church, but at the time regarded as a "Paulician" heretic (heretical designations were interchangeable at the time). The so-called Albigensian Heresy of the eleventh to thirteenth centuries had already entered the realms of romantic mythology through the agenda-heavy, sometimes-historical works of Naploéon Peyrat (*Histoire des Albigeois,* 3 vols., Paris 1872–78) when Doinel found personal significance in the ancient manuscripts of a persecuted true believer. Doinel declared to his Theosophist and spiritist friends in Paris that he, Jules Benoît Stanislas Doinel du Val-Michel (1842–1902), had been chosen by the "Aeon Jesus" to reestablish *the* Gnostic religion in France on the lines of the extinct Cathar Church. Further guidance came from now spirit-being *Parfaits* ("Perfecti") of the Cathar Church, such as the extremely late Cathar leader Guilhabert de Castres, who allegedly graced a series of séances with his spiritual presence and wishes.

Fig. 9.1. Jules Doinel (1842–1902)

In 1889, with the new era of Papus's eclectic openness campaign beaming out from the *Librairie du Merveilleux* and the pages of the journal *L'Initiation* now having real effects, Doinel's enthusiasm caught on. Symbolist, poet, civil servant, and Fourierist Fabre des Essarts became excited at the formal return of what he called "Esoteric Christianity," that is, gnosis. But is not gnostic knowledge supposed to be as secret as Hermetic wisdom? Is it not supposed to be, well, *hermetic:* sealed from the profane? Ah, but to secrete a manifest spiritual experience, would that not be to underestimate the spiritual power and purpose of the new age, the coming age of the "Paraclete," widely expected in esoteric circles, when the Holy Spirit would reveal the secrets of the centuries, and with them, the full unfolding of man's spiritual nature: gifted with vision to conceive of the world as symbol and so transcend the world's gross material grip?

The long-since condemned Cathar message that gross matter was Satan's work chimed in with the Decadent insight deriving from Baudelaire that the world, whose values should be disregarded, was an abyss into which the soul had been thrust, or might choose to be thrust, with the symbol of exiled man as Lucifer bringing light into the darkness. Faced with a condemned world of decaying matter and its concomitant, "bourgeois" materialism, there were two gnostic options for conduct: transcend matter by asceticism, by resisting worldly lusts and by, for instance, pursuing Art as a sacred duty, or, alternatively, accept the worldly facts and "do what one wanted" with the knowledge that the spirit would remain uncontaminated since one knew already and all the while that the spirit's true home was "beyond." Life could be a purging, a realization of its vanity by realizing its vanities in practice, progressively unburdening oneself of cosmic accretions in what Aleister Crowley, who picked up on this Decadent path, would describe two decades later as "redemption by sin." Needless to say, the Catharist route favored ascetic abstention and purity of life, but there were other currents about to merge into the neo-gnostic current. Did sex have spiritual value? There were certainly early Gnostics who believed so and practiced accordingly, such as those who took first-century magician Simon Magus and his consort Helena as their idols. For them, the idea of androgyny, so dear to Péladan, held a key, though differently cut to Péladan's Platonist ideal, where virginity represented the spiritual and moral perfection.

Joining forces with Doinel, Fabre des Essarts was not only struck by the fundamental gnostic idea that the redemptive spiritual light secreted within the gross being of men and women should be brought forth, but also by the idea that male and female identities could be progressively harmonized, correcting the double standards of the world where a man succumbing to temptation is a Don Juan and a woman a harlot. In 1889, Fabre des Essarts shared this vision of male and female spiritual complementarity with Lady Caithness at Holyrood on the avenue de Wagram. Already far advanced in considering an equal spiritual role of women as a priority, and regarding women as potentially superior in spiritual sensitivity, it was Lady Caithness's guardian angel, Mary Queen of Scots, who had persuaded her that spiritual woman's liberation was a keynote of the age of the Holy Spirit. She therefore approved of Doinel's gnostic church initiative. In 1889, des Essarts wrote a *Catéchisme éxplique de l'Église Gnostique*—a gnostic catechism—and Doinel backed it. The Gnostic Church was born, or as they thought it, reborn. That which the Catholic Church had long regarded as the great heresy was now out in the open. And it was, significantly, linked to circles around the R+C+K. Alarm bells rang in the Vatican's precincts.

Like the Vatican, Péladan also recognized that Papus and Chamuel's

L'Initiation supported the latest manifestations of esoteric spiritual life. First issued in October 1888 with Barlet's, Lejay's, and Sédir's assistance, *L'Initiation*'s issues of November 1889, April 1890, January, June, and August 1892, all featured articles promoting Doinel's *Église Gnostique* and its long departed doyens, the first- and second-century CE heresiarchs Simon Magus and Valentinus. Doinel, self-consecrated bishop of the church with the sanction of Lady Caithness responding to invisible sponsors from heaven, organized meetings at the *Librairie du Merveilleux*.

It was very soon apparent to Péladan that Papus had a specific agenda of enlightened eclecticism, in tune with the fashion of the moment. Édouard Schuré's extremely influential, bestselling book *Les Grands Initiés* (The Great Initiates) appeared in 1889 with a message that Papus could have composed himself. Moses, Rama, Orpheus, Jesus, Hermes Trismegistus, Socrates, were all initiates of something marvelous they held in common. Only the darkness of men's minds had rendered their common spiritual bond into a collection of competing sects. *Also sprach* Schuré, friend of Wagner and Nietzsche.

Papus's intention with *L'Initiation* was to assemble every group and tendency related to Hermetic knowledge and treat all equally as shafts of the light of universal initiation, which initiatory light was being made available for the new age of the spirit. In Papus's outlook, the greatest eclecticism was a sure sign of reintegration.

In February 1890, Papus published a *Declaration to Our Readers and to Our Subscribers* in large letters at the head of *L'Initiation*:

> The idea that has presided since the founding of *L'Initiation* is that of absolute Tolerance. . . . We wanted to demonstrate to members of the Theosophical Society, to the Western Kabbalists [presumably referring to de Guaita et al], to those fervent for spiritism [such as Doinel and Lady Caithness], with Magnetism [such as Oswald Wirth], or the other branches of Occultism, that one doctrine identical in many points gathered them together in a common aim.
>
> . . . We desire, before all to strengthen the growing army of all those who struggle against the false conclusions of Materialism already well shaken. . . . We destroy religious hatred by unveiling the

unity of all the cults in a sole Religion. We destroy philosophical hatred in proclaiming the unity of all doctrines in one very Science.[2]

What actually happened was that all those party to the "initiation" expressed their own beliefs with perfect freedom. Papus's psychosomatic medicine was followed by the gnosis of Doinel, then by de Guaita's historical, Kabbalistic work, then some alchemical discourse by the amiable, reclusive chemist Albert Poisson (1868–1893) and others, and then bulletins concerning spiritist, magnetic, and hypnotic healing, parapsychological, Theosophical, and Masonic meetings, spiced with symbolist poetry, and so on. The spirit believed to be behind all of these manifestations or ideals became through variegation rather vague. Was a spirit a dead person or what was truly alive in the living? What then was a spirit in alchemy, and in what sense were any of these things spiritual, let alone holy? What the various schools did have in common most definitely was a denial of positivist materialism, or the closed world of material cause and effect, and assumptions of spiritual authority in the Roman Catholic Church. Esoteric traditions were taken as higher sciences, accursed by those bound to what Blake called "the vegetable eye." There was, the review murmured, if you looked for it, *another kind of church or authority altogether:* both real and "coming" as all these scattered traditions were assembled like the menagerie for Noah's Ark. Tumults of barbarism were widely expected and only the spiritual doctrine could survive in the crucible of cosmic and global evolution and catastrophe.

Fig. 9.2. Jules Doinel; the writing says "T [tau] Jules, év. gnos. (éveque gnostique = gnostic bishop)

The Catholic Church was quick to recognize what it could only regard as subversive encroachment on its claimed preserve, despite Péladan's sincere desire to bring consciousness of the value of occultism to the church—or *back* to the church—and vice versa. Promulgated by Cardinal Mazzella on 14 May 1891, *L'Initiation* joined the *Index* of publications prohibited to Catholics. "Gnosis" was specifically mentioned as the fundamental provocation in the "Congregation of the Index's" deliberations. *L'Initiation* printed a response to the Catholic proscription entitled "The Gnosis and the Inquisition": "That which menaces the hierarchy is the reconstitution of the gnostic episcopacy and the Albigensian or Cathar assembly, with a definite episcopal seat, Montségur." The article was signed with a gnostic episcopal tau: "T JULES, bishop of Montségur (Jules Doinel)" (*L'Initiation*, July 1891, p. 143–47).

From this point, no Catholic could read *L'Initiation* without staining his or her conscience and imperiling their soul. Such condemnation would doubtless work in the review's favor in some areas of opinion, while the review strove to appeal to different categories of cultural engagement: the "initiatic" core, the philosophically minded, devotees of the *lacunae* and fringes of science and new discoveries, and of course the literary sets; they all had their own section in *L'Initiation*. The review published *L'Hespérus* by Catulle Mendès, the fantasy stories of Debussy's friend Charles de Sivry, as well as the poetry of Victor-Émile Michelet, Robert Scheffer, and Albert Jounet, whose work also graced the pages of Michelet's superior review, *Psyché,* published for nine numbers from November 1891 to December 1892. While Michelet's publication raised literary standards without cheapening its contents, *L'Initiation* brought the occult into mainstream intellectual discourse, at a price of subtlety. It was essentially a form of propaganda, though it gave freedom of individual propagation.

We must therefore take into account Papus's significant influence when trying to understand Péladan's breach with what had been, in part, and perhaps by spiritual authority, his own Order. Papus was a leading member of the R+C+K and Papus was quite a whale to invite into any aquarium. The pages of *L'Initiation* and the weekly *Le Voile d'Isis* made abundantly clear to readers the success and scope of his activities, for they were reported regularly. In April 1890, for example, readers of *L'Initiation* learned that the adepts of the *Groupe independent d'Études Ésotériques* had at their disposal, annexed to the *Librairie du Merveilleux*, a library, a lecture room, and a conference hall with 180 seats. By July of that year, the group had more than 350 members, with plans for the inauguration in December of eighteen study groups. By June 1891, the group could boast fifty-five local lodges in France and as far away as Argentina. Little by little, Papus was transforming the group into a University of High Studies, with exams for licentiate and doctorate diplomas in Kabbalah.[3] Students from all over France and elsewhere joined in enthusiastic local gatherings and were invited to meet Papus personally at 29 rue de Trévise where he made himself freely available to all comers for several hours of every week. Michelet would remark that Papus's eventual slowing down in the twentieth century was a result of overzealous outpouring of his youthful energies in the eighties and nineties.

On 11 November 1891, Papus's friends would present him with a diploma of honor, signed by, among others, Camille Flammarion, Laurent Tailhade, Prof. Luys (hypnosis expert), Émile Goudeau (poet and founder of the Hydropathes literary club), Michelet, Gary de Lacroze, Jules Lermina (author of *La Magie pratique*), and de Guaita. In May 1892, Papus and Chamuel, like Paul and Barnabas, left Paris to

Fig. 9.3. Jules Lermina (1839–1915), libertarian and spiritually anarchistic contributor to L'Initiation; *author of exciting, popular Edgar Allan Poe–like and futuristic fantasy fiction; began journalistic career in 1859; was arrested and imprisoned several times for socialist opinions and defended by Victor Hugo*

visit their Belgian branch where they would conduct a series of conferences. Péladan, who had left the show by then, would make his own
lecture tour of Belgium six months later.

While much of the above had not quite unfolded when in June 1890
Péladan publicized his departure from the R+C+K through a letter
published, significantly, in *L'Initiation,* he doubtless saw it all coming
beforehand. Papus's "Declaration" in the February 1890 issue alone
would have sufficed to confirm Péladan's suspicions. He could obviously envision the omnivorous Papus taking the R+C+K into his super-
eclectic occultist fold as well. While de Guaita was clearly content to
pool resources with Papus's sincere enterprises, Péladan was not. The
time had come to part. Mindful, with the recent death of his father
Adrien *père* in March 1890, that he, the Sâr, was son and heir to a peculiar tradition of his own, Péladan drew the line, politely, but as directly
as he could. In June 1890, every reader of *L'Initiation* was presented
with news of Peladan's distaste for what the Kabbalistic Order of the
Rose-Croix was now linked to:

> My adherence, fruitful until now, would henceforth become sterile.
> My absolutist nature isolates me from your eclectic work. I could not
> take occultism in its entirety with me to Mass, and I refuse to rub
> shoulders with spiritism, masonry or Buddhism.

Péladan not only asserted a knowledge of occult matters superior to all
but the five other known members of the R+C+K's Supreme Council but
also made clear his unique angle: "You come from free thinking toward
Faith, I leave the Vatican toward the occult."[4] Christopher McIntosh
observed that Péladan's reference to Masonry probably reflected his attitude to the Masonic enthusiasms of de Guaita's friend, Oswald Wirth
(*Eliphas Lévi and the French Occult Revival*, p. 171). There was little love
lost between Wirth and Péladan. Wirth's memoirs give the false impression de Guaita held Péladan in contempt from the start. Wirth himself
severely criticized Péladan, most likely because Péladan was vocal in his
dislike for the things Wirth most valued, Freemasonry among them.

Fig. 9.4. Oswald Wirth
(1860–1943)

On page 384 of July's issue, "Le Gérant" (Manager) "ENCAUSSE" ameliorated the breach on behalf of the *Ordre Kabbalistique de la Rose+Croix:*

One of the six known members of the Supreme Council of Twelve, Monsieur Joséphin Péladan, having demitted at the start of June to found *l'Aristie,* the Council has decided to offer his chair to one of the six unknown members of the same order.

In consequence, our Brother Alta, Catholic priest, doctor at the Sorbonne, and Grand Chaplain of the Order, passes from the occult Section to the recognized section of the Supreme Council: this section finds itself henceforth constituted by the six known members whose names follow in alphabetical order: Messieurs Agûr [Péladan will give this name to a potentially debauching homosexual admirer of "Samas" in his novel *L'Androgyne,* published the following year, 1891, p. 173], Alta, Barlet, de Guaita, Papus, et Polti.

As for the seat of the occult section, left void by the transfer of our Brother Alta, a new member, secretly elected, occupies it at this hour.[5]

On page 486, the review's directors defended it against the charge—probably Péladan's—that it was too eclectic. *L'Initiation* maintained that it was neither occult nor spiritist, but like an army, success required there be cavalry, artillery, and infantry and that they should never be confused.

Péladan's idea of the *Grande Armée* understood one thing: it needed a Bonaparte, not a council to command it. The reason given above for Péladan's departure, that is, that he left to found *l'Aristie,* refers to three "mandements" or pastoral letters that Péladan added to the 19th edition of his review *Le Salon,* dated 14 May 1890.[6]

The title page first announces the critical commentary on what Péladan calls the "Salon National" and the "Salon Jullian." The "Salon Jullian" is a punish skit on establishments where students who had failed entrance exams to the *École Nationale des Beaux-Arts* were sent to improve their drawing, such as the *Académie Julian,* conceived by Péladan as a lapdog of the former school, yet out of whose "failures" had emerged brilliant artists of the likes of Bonnard, Vuillard, Denis, Valloton, Ranson, and Sérusier—the latter four Nabis, or symbolist "prophets."

The year 1890 had seen a ruction in the official Salon that broke the grip of the *Société des Artistes Français* resulting in the first Salon of the *Société Nationale des Beaux-Arts,* a more progressive Salon headed by Puvis de Chavannes, Rodin, and Eugène Carrière.

Fig. 9.5. Eugène Carrière (1849–1906), self portrait

Plate 1. The Collège Rollin, avenue Trudaine (9th arr.), where Papus
was educated, now called the collège-lycée Jacques-Decour
(photo: Jean-Luke Epstein)

Plate 2. Formerly the ground floor apartment of Stanislas de Guaita,
20 avenue Trudaine (9th arr.), allegedly haunted
(photo: Jean-Luke Epstein)

Plate 3. The former site of *Le Chat Noir* cabaret 1885–1896 (see inset), 12 rue Victor-Masse (9th arr.), where Erik Satie performed (photo: Jean-Luke Epstein; inset: Mu, Cc-by-sa 3.0)

Plate 4. Satie's first decent flat (1888), 50 rue Condorcet (9th arr.)—until he ran out of money (photo: Jean-Luke Epstein)

Plate 5. Site of Chamuel's *Librairie du Merveilleux* and Papus's numerous esoteric operations, including *L'Initiation,* 29 rue de Trévise (9th arr.) (photo: Jean-Luke Epstein)

Plate 6. Site of 11 rue de la Chaussée d'Antin (9th arr.): Edmond Bailly's *Librairie de L'Art Indépendant* bookshop where the stars of "Occult Paris" gathered (photo: Jean-Luke Epstein)

Plate 7. A top floor room at 6 rue Cortot, Montmartre, for Erik Satie from 1890–1898; here he wrote *Gnossiennes* (photo: Jean-Luke Epstein)

Plate 8. The original *Cabaret du Chat Noir* at 84 boulevard Rocheouart, created in 1881 by Rodolphe Sallis and moved to 12 rue Victor-Masse in 1885 (photo: Jean-Luke Epstein)

Plate 9. Artist Paul Ranson's studio, 25 boulevard du Montparnasse (6th arr.), was the meeting-place of the "Nabis" or "prophets," including Sérusier and Maurice Denis (photo: Jean-Luke Epstein)

Plate 10. The exterior of 1 place de L'Odéon, formerly occupied by the *Café Voltaire,* described in Balzac's *Les Martyrs ignoré* (Ignored Martyrs) and once the haunt of Verlaine, Moréas, Gauguin, and Mallarmé (photo: Jean-Luke Epstein)

Plate 11. The Gustave Moreau National Museum, 14 rue de la Rochefoucauld (9th arr.): a mecca for lover of Symbolist art. After turning his home and studio into a national museum in 1895, Moreau inhabited the first-floor apartment (photo: Jean-Luke Epstein)

Plate 12. Gustave Moreau,
Oedipus Wanderer (1888),
Musée de la Cour d'Or

Plate 13. Edmond Aman-
Jean, *Dame en rose*
(1898), former collection
Alain Lesieutre, Paris

Plate 14. Georges Seurat, *Une Baignade, Asnières* (1884),
National Gallery, London

Plate 15. "Apparition," musical adaption
by Edmond Bailly of a poem by Mallarmé,
Bibliothèque Nationale de France

Plate 16. Poster to advertise Edmo
Bailly's independent art publication
11 rue de la Chaussée d'Antin, 189

Plate 17. Manuel Orazi (1860–1934), *Black Mass*. Born in Rome, Orazi worked in art nouveau illustration (Pierre Louÿs; Baudelaire) and poster work in Paris. In 1895 his occult-inspired *Calendrier Magique* (*Magic Calendar*) appeared.

Plate 18. Alexandre Séon, *Le Désespoir de la Chimère* (*The Chimera's Despair*, 1890) caused a sensation and was twice exhibited at the Salons Rose-Croix

Plate 19. Fernand Khnopff, *I Lock My Door Upon Myself* (1891), Neue Pinakothek, Munich (photo: Yelkrokoyade, Cc-by-sa 4.0)

Plate 20. Alexandre Séon, *Portrait of Péladan* (1891), Musée des Beaux Arts, Lyon

Plate 21. Fernand Khnopff, *Lèvres Rouges* (1897)

Plate 22. Joséphin Péladan, *L'Androgyne* (1891), with frontispiece by Alexandre Séon

Plate 23. One of the scurrilous anti-Masonic journals attributed to conman "Léo Taxil," *Les Mystéres de la Franc-Maconnerie* (The Mysteries of Freemasonry); he has used Lévi's androgynous "Baphomet" to imply the Devil (photo courtesy Gallica Digital Library)

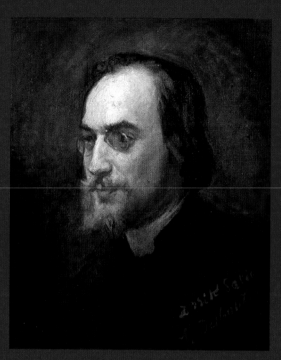

Plate 24. Marcellin Desboutin, *Portrait of Erik Satie* (before 1900
Les Maisons Satie, Honfleur

Plate 25. Maurice Denis, *Self-portrait with His Family in Front of
Their House* (1916), Galleria degli Uffizi, Florence

Plate 26. The grave of
Papus, Père Lachaise,
division 93, Paris
(photo: Jon Graham)

Plate 27. The grave of
Joséphin Péladan, Paris
(photo: Jon Graham)

Plate 28. Pierre-Cécile Puvis de Chavannes,
The Dream (1883), Walters Art Museum, Baltimore

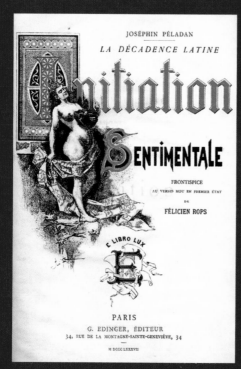

Plate 29. Félicien Rops,
cover for Péladan's novel
L'Initiation Sentimentale,
1887

Plate 30. Félicien Rops, frontispiece to
Péladan's novel *À Coeur Perdu,* 1888

Plate 31. Carlos Schwabe, poster
for the first Rose-Croix Salon, 1892

Plate 32. Erik Satie, *Sonneries de la Rose+Croix* (1892), with a design from Puvis de Chavannes "La Guerre": the battle was against vulgar materialism; the sheet music edition was funded by Antoine de La Rochefoucauld

Plate 33. Alphonse Osbert, *Vision* (1892), Musée d'Orsay, Paris (photo: Rama, Cc-by-sa.2.0-fr.)

Péladan's joke was to see the main, official Salon as a school where good artists received perverse correction—if they were any good—or deserved correction if they conformed to official standards. Péladan's palliative for the sickness, as he saw it, in the art world, was of course the conception first announced on the title page of *Le Salon* as "la Rose Croix Catholique à l'Aristie." *L'Aristie* is a transliteration into French combining the Greek *aristos* ("best") and *eidos* ("kind" or "type"), so the Order is the Catholic Rose-Croix *to the best or ideal kind. Aristocracy* means "government by the best."

After sixty-four pages of frequently blistering satirical criticism, we find the "Tiers-Ordre Intellectuel de la Rose-Croix Catholique, Syncelli Acta" consisting of a pastoral letter to those of the Arts of Design, a letter to the Archbishop of Paris, and an "Excommunication of the 'Rothschild woman.'" A *syncellus* is a "Vicar General" or first assistant or confessor to a bishop or patriarch, and his *Acta* are his diktats.

Those concerned with the arts of design are saluted in the names of Plato, Leonardo da Vinci, and with benediction "in Our Savior Jesus Christ." Péladan's "Syncelli Acta" are effectively "Bulls" from the Pontiff of Art who signs himself "To the Cross, by the Rose, to the Rose, by the Cross . . . SAR MÉRODACK," the personification of Tradition, Hierarchy, and the Catholic Ideal. His Eminence the Archbishop of Paris is then addressed by the "tiers-ordre intellectuel catholique" (intellectual Catholic triple-order) whose organization lies hidden the better to enlarge it. Péladan's "triple-order" "despises the imbeciles of Masonry with the treasures of the Rose-Croix and of the *Veheme* ["Ardent"]." The Order is purely Catholic and absolutely Roman and not to be confounded with Hindu imports. Péladan then draws attention to a barbarous importation in Paris of bullfighting in the rue Pergolèse, whose moral pollution invites women in search of orgasms to go there to satisfy their lusts and where these lusts are indeed satisfied by the bloodthirsty entertainment. He signs himself "SAR MÉRODACK" as the Archbishop's "suffragan [or *syncellus*] according to the exoteric hierarchy."

The third mandement concerns Baroness Adèle de Rothschild who has demolished an historic chapel of the style of Louis XVI at the château of Beaujon that she has bought. By the rules of the Rose-Croix, she has committed sacrilege in destroying a temple of religion. "We" of the "Tribunal Vehmique" ("Ardent Court") excommunicate "her infamous name." This social excommunication is kicked off by the declaration that the family La Rochefoucauld will not receive her, a name soon to loom large in Péladan's activities.

I think we see here a kind of wry Sârist comment on de Guaita's conception of a court or tribunal to judge Boullan. If the Rose-Croix has any jurisdiction of a moral kind, it should be expended not on fighting medieval battles with sorcerers, but with defending the cause of sacred beauty, for where beauty is, there is God. The black villains of modern reality, according to Péladan, are the destroyers of Latin culture, the barbarians of lust, corrupted by money, and enflamed with materialist arrogance. It may be suspected that de Guaita did indeed get the message, for on 24 May 1890, shortly after the publication of the pastoral letters, even before Péladan's announcement in *L'Initiation,* de Guaita wrote to Péladan expressing dismay about the contents of *The Salon:* "I, Stanislas de Guaita, having received a mandate from the Supreme Council to speak in its name, appeal to your loyal friendship, begging you to publicly clarify the misunderstanding which cannot fail to ensue."[7]

While de Guaita's appeal doubtless precipitated Péladan's public notice of departure of June 1890, it was not the sole stimulus, for three days after de Guaita's letter, de Guaita's friend Maurice Barrès wrote a front page review in *Le Figaro* that referred to Péladan's *mandements,* as well as to de Guaita's recently published *Seuil du Mystère.* Headed "Les Mages" (the Magi), Barrès exhibited his personal distaste for Péladan's "satins and lace with mutton sleeves, his beard of superb black" while offering high praise to de Guaita's new work. Barrès's article can hardly have improved relations between the two men, for like much journalism, it personalized an ideological rift. As in subsequent press attacks on Péladan, his eccentric appearance provided the core while his immense critical creativity was largely ignored.

In August 1890, Péladan finally outlined what the founding of what *L'Initiation* called "l'Aristie" and the pastoral letters the "catholic intellectual triple Order Rose-Croix" actually entailed. *L'Initiation* was chosen as the announcement's mouthpiece, probably in the interests of recruitment as well as clarification.

THE ORDER OF
THE CATHOLIC ROSE-CROIX,
THE TEMPLE AND THE GRAAL

The new "triple intellectual Order" *Rose+Croix+Catholique* was "for Romans, Artists, and women." Save Péladan, its governing council included no names familiar to readers of *L'Initiation*. Aristocrat Count Léonce de Larmandie sat side by side with the young "Count of Tammuz," that is, artist and artists' patron, Antoine de La Rochefoucauld, fervent admirer of the Nabis. The council, that is to say, "les Magnifiques" had elected Péladan Grand Master and consequently, "le Sâr Joséphin Péladan is hierarch of the supreme hierarchy." Having invited Papus, as editor of *L'Initiation,* to sit in on society meetings— rather like inviting someone to watch a banquet—Péladan elaborated on his conception in a floridly inscribed parchment that appointed his friend Gary de Lacroze as second-in-command:

> Under the Tau, the Greek cross, the crux ansata and the Tiara of Chaldea, before the Grail, the Standard and the Rose Cross, We, Grand-Master of the Order of the Catholic Rose Cross, the Temple and the Grail, detained in Barbary to elaborate the constitution of the order, do hereby designate to you our friend Commander Gary de Lacroze as Archwarden of the Province of Paris for the reception and preliminary selection of candidates. . . .
>
> Do not forget, friend Commander, that only science or genius can compensate in our order for the absence of worldly position.[8]

The Order's task was to accomplish "works of mercy" in preparation for the reign of the Holy Spirit. Works of mercy meant essentially the encouragement and appreciation of works of art. Refined aesthetics would apparently lead to a refined sense of ethics. Decorating the walls of the world with beauty would heighten people's sense of truth and goodness as well, for in the Platonic trinity of Goodness, Truth, and Beauty, each participated in all, and all in each. Vulgarity had no place in the ideal divine scheme.

Péladan received initiates at his large apartment in the stately rue Notre-Dame-des-Champs, in Montparnasse in the 6th arrondissement, ironically close to the Catholic *Collège Stanislas*. For the ceremony, Péladan would don a monk's robe with a rosy cross embroidered on its front before putting ten questions to candidates in a musical voice while gesticulating with flourishes of rings and fingers:

> *Who are you?*
> *What is your void?*
> *To what does your will tend?*
> *How do you realize yourself?*
> *By what force?*
> *Declare your attractions and repulsions.*
> *Define your glory.*
> *State the hierarchy of beings.*
> *Name happiness.*
> *Name sorrow.*[9]

Péladan formed his idea of the candidate's potential from the answers given—a process that must have prompted moments of hilarity solemnity would have been hard-pressed to suppress. Successful candidates entered at the bottom of the hierarchy as servants of work, whence they could advance by ascending grades of equerry, knight, and commander. Commanders were assigned a correspondence to one of the *sephiroth* on the Kabbalistic Tree of Life. De Lacroze was to be inspired by Tiphereth (Beauty, balance, spirituality) whereas Comte Léonce de Larmandie was Commander of Geburah (Rigor).

In addition to Count Antoine de La Rochefoucauld and Count Léonce de Larmandie, Péladan brought Elémir Bourges (1852–1925) to the feast, celebrated for his incest-themed novel *Le Crépuscule des dieux*

Fig. 9.6. Léonce Comte de Larmandie
(1851–1921)

(The Twilight of the Gods, 1884). Bourges believed Naturalists in literature "had belittled and deformed man."[10] Michelet recognized that Péladan had united four remarkable personalities for his Order, but Péladan had poor retention skills. When the Order began to attract press notice and ridicule, Bourges "soon fled for refuge on a sofa in the reading room of the *Bibliothéque Nationale* where he read everything."[11] Bourges, at the time, was a fastidious and rather dandyish dresser, which ostentation belied a pessimistic nature, somewhat afraid of the life he could render so well in frenetic form. Michelet recalled Bourges's sourness of tone when he observed Michelet reading Casanova's *Memoirs* one day: "At least he really *lived*. We, no!" Michelet considered Bourges a "despairing thinker" but chose to remember rather the graceful smile with which he welcomed his friends.

Count Léonce de Larmandie (1851–1921) came from a family of medieval knights, and of himself said chivalrously: "I was not made to be a leader, but to be an excellent lieutenant." In this, Michelet believed him right. He had a great round head on stocky shoulders, with clear, candid eyes, and the demeanor, Michelet felt, of a good dog in quest of devotion. He was loyal to Péladan as far as he could be, though was poorly compensated for it, and would eventually separate himself from a man who did not know how to hold a friend. He nevertheless never failed to admire Péladan and his artistic achievements, which he documented in his vital account, the *L'Entre'acte Idéal* (Paris: Chacornac, 1903), which tells of the five successive years of Rose-Croix Salons of which he was ever the enthusiastic agent, even when Péladan seemed hardly interested, as occurred toward the end of the series.

Émile Gary de Lacroze was, according to Michelet, "a metaphysical and aesthetic head of rare profundity."[12] The Commander of Tiphereth, author of *Les Hommes, Leurs Formes, Leurs Natures* (Men: Their Forms, Their Nature, Paris, 1900), was a meditative personality who had the gift of penetrating a subject from such an acute angle that while little understood by those who heard him, his acuteness yielded access to "limitless horizons." He could ruminate on a subtle aesthetic question or issue of transcendent psychology for months. Michelet remembered that at the time he quit editing the *Gaulois* daily paper,[13] Gary de Lacroze decided to call on Michelet at 1 a.m. for a walk on the Left Bank. He spoke a great deal while they walked together. When Michelet objected to a statement, Gary said: "Ah! I hadn't reflected on what you said there. I shall do so. Goodnight!" Some three months later, he came around again at about the same time: "I've reflected on what you objected to the other night, and here is my response." He then embarked on a demonstration of "captivating interest" pursued for 3 kilometers of nocturnal streets. "Such was Gary: a mind who goes to the end of his thought." He would join another singular, original, and penetrating "child of Pythagoras," Georges Polti, to write a rigorously constructed, "stupefyingly talented," *Théorie des temperaments* (Theory of Temperaments, Paris: Georges Carré, 1889). Polti, of course, stayed with the R+C+K after Péladan split.

Above the commanders in Péladan's order was an "Archonte," who was, according to Michelet "a young gentleman of generous spirit and fine character, apprised of art," Count Antoine de La Rochefoucauld (1862–1959). Michelet recalls La Rochefoucauld's first entering the

Librairie du Merveilleux, having met and been charmed by Péladan. Péladan's speech could seduce, being one of the few whose improvised speech was the equal of literature, a similar current of improvisation informed the current of his pen, notably demonstrated in his *Prométheïde* wherein Péladan claimed to have discovered the two lost plays Aeschylus intended to join his *Prometheus Bound.*

Another commander appeared briefly only to disappear again: Saint-Pol Roux (Paul-Pierre Roux, 1861–1940), author of *La Dame à la Faux,* a play published in the *Mercure de France* in 1899 and performed by Sarah Bernhardt. Michelet describes him as a "soft provençal dreamer" who went to live on the Brittany coast whose wildness stimulated the tempests of his imagination. "Proclaimed leader of the School of the *Magnifiques* [Péladan's name for his commanders, and a name that stuck to Saint-Pol], he was brave against the scoffers [of Symbolism], and the scoffers were wrong, for it is a fine thing to inculcate a taste for grandeur."[14]

Saint-Pol Roux was a personal hero of surrealist leader André

Fig. 9.7. Saint-Pol Roux (1861–1940)

Breton, after World War I. Breton dedicated his poetry collection *Earthlight* to him and wrote to him, expressing his and his surrealist colleagues' sense of the critical importance to surrealism of Saint-Pol and of the esoteric tradition he supported and alluded to in his work:

> I have long been outraged [wrote Breton] by certain literary customs and weary of seeing so many men willingly stoop to anything for honors, and as ever, the noble and selfless attitudes—from Baudelaire to you—completely unknown and prey to what can best ruin them.[15]

According to the late James Webb, Saint-Pol Roux distinguished Symbolists from Naturalists thus: the Naturalist counts the grains of sand on the shore; the Symbolist rejoices in the beauty of the sand itself, and goes beyond the image to the source of beauty, the Ideal beyond.[16]

Saint-Pol Roux, of the first septenary of the Commanders, signed the first pastoral letter of the Rose-Croix aesthetic, written in Péladan's style and dated 15 May 1891:

ACTA-ROSAE CRUCIS
LA ROSE-CROIX DU TEMPLE

Under the Tau, the Greek cross, the Latin cross, before the *Beauséant* [sign of the Templars] and the Crucified Rose.

In Roman Catholic communion with Hugues de Païens and RosenCreuz, the SAR PÉLADAN master of the Order of the Rose-Croix of the Temple, assisted by a septenary of commanders LL. SS. GARY DE LACROZE, COMTE DE LARMANDIE, COMTE ANTOINE DE LA ROCHEFOUCAULD, ELÉMIR BOURGES, SAINT-POL-ROUX, SAMAS

Ordains

In the name of Jesus, only God, and of Peter, only king;

To all those who hear the 12th verset of the second chapter of Bereschit [Genesis] at the risk of being rejected by the Order forever,

To concentrate their effort of light on the artistic plane,

To this end and from this hour are created, the remaining secret institutions.

LA ROSE-CROIX ESTHÉTIQUE

Expressed in Paris on the Feast of the Ascension of the Redeemer, and signed by the seven:

SAR PÉLADAN, GARY DE LACROZE, DE LARMANDIE, DE LA ROCHEFOUCAULD, ELÉMIR BOURGES, SAINT-POL-ROUX, SAMAS

The seventh signatory "Samas," the name of the Assyrio-Babylonian sun god, was probably imaginary, for Samas was also the name of the hero in Péladan's new novel, *L'Androgyne,* the object of homosexual lust of a certain young man named in the novel as Agûr, which name also features on the new Supreme Council of the R+C+K, following Péladan's departure.

The aims of the Order from the aesthetic point of view are now indicated:

> The Rose+Croix does not confine its solicitude to painting and sculpture; the *Soirées de la Rose+Croix* will be consecrated to the fugues of Bach and Porpora [Nicola Porpora 1686–1768], and the quatuors of Beethoven, to lectures with two pianos of Parsifal. One evening will be given to the glorification of César Franck, the greatest French musician since Berlioz.

July 1891's issue of *L'Initiation* carried a skeptical review signed by "Pierre Torcy" of a work attributed to the "Commander of Geburah," Léonce de Larmandie, entitled "EÔRAKA, Notes on Esotericism," a kind of manifesto of Péladan's new order. The author of the article tears its pretensions and questionable assertions to shreds. *Rose Croix* and *Catholique,* Torcy says, are as mutually averse as cat and dog (p. 177). This attack appeared in the same issue in which Doinel reported the Catholic Church's condemnation of *L'Initiation*. Since, Torcy argues, the *Confessio Fraternitatis* of the "original" *fratres* of the Order (published in 1615) unequivocally declared the Pope "Antichrist," how could a Catholic Rose-Croix be taken seriously? Likewise in claiming a Templar heritage, how could they blithely ignore the fact that the Templars—"themselves initiatic sons of the gnostics issuing from the essenes" (p. 178)—were suppressed on papal authority? The writer concludes: "The Rose-Croix *tout court* and Martinism are therefore the only Orders actually qualified to speak in the name of Christian esotericism."

Just to make the point of view of the review absolutely clear as to the limit of its tolerances, the July issue carried a supplement dated "August 1891" headed with the emblem of the R+C+K: a cross with a rose in each quarter surmounted by a pentagram in which were the letters of the Hebrew tetragrammaton and the fifth letter *schin,* signifying the spiritual manifestation of Jesus and the completion of the "Name" in Royal Arch Freemasonry.

THE SUPREME COUNCIL OF THE ROSE + CROIX

Considering that a demitted member of the Council, Monsieur Joséphin Péladan, has founded, in August 1890, a schismatic sect, under the name of the Triple intellectual order of the Catholic Rose-Croix R+C+C+;

Considering that this sect, in which M. Péladan is proclaimed Grand Master and Arch-Magus, is attached to intransigent Ultramontane principles, infeodation of the Holy Seat &c. . . , diametrically hostile to those of our times professed by the illuminated Brothers of the Rose+Croix;

That which suffices, in effect, to convince one of it, is to re-read the symbolic *Manifesto* and the *Confession of the Brothers R+C,* such as one finds in Latin published at Frankfurt in 1615, by the Frater VALENTIN ANDREAE: *Fama fraternitatis, Roseae-crucis, &c.,* and in the French work published in Paris, in 1623, under the title: *Instruction to France on the truth of the story of the Brothers of the Rose-Croix* (by Gabriel Naudé) or again in the *Methodical Treatise of Occult Science* (Paris, 1891), where Papus reproduces them *in extenso;*

The mandate continues accusing Péladan's Order for its ultramontane character that contradicts the ancient and authentic R+C, which is in no wise contradicted by the renovated R+C as revealed in the Concordat published on pages 159–61 of de Guaita's *Seuil du mystère*. Since in Péladan's "Letter to Papus" published at the time of his novel *Coeur en peine* (Heart in Sorrow) the author wrote that he "had separated himself from everything that is not my R+C+C+ in which I am Arch-Magus . . . not wishing to interrupt the good commerce of friendship with the Messieurs of the R+C+K, I must break all doctrinal rapport and solidarity with them" (*Coeur en peine,* p. 323–24).

The mandate proceeds to charge Péladan with doing nothing to banish the confusion in the public mind as to which is the "orthodox" Rose-Croix and which the schismatic, thereby creating a deplorable picture, giving the Rose+Croix a bad name and creating a situation that must be addressed having been allowed to fester too long. "Because of all these things" the mandate ordains two "Articles." The first promises a short note to indicate precisely the essence of the R+C and the tendencies of Rosicrucian knowledge in all periods. With this will come a precise summary of the circumstances motivating the retreat of Péladan and the foundation of the R+C+C+. The second article indicates that this note will be publicized so that everybody who is interested will see it.

The mandate is dated 5 August 1891 with the names of the Supreme Council affixed with the Hebrew letter *aleph* under each name surmounted by a Masonic "fire" glyph consisting of three dots like a pyramid, indicating an illuminated society: de Guaita, Jacques Papus, F.-Ch. Barlet, Paul Adam, Julien Lejay, Oswald Wirth.

The mandate was followed by a history of "Elias Artista" in the context of the Rose-Croix and then a chapter devoted to Péladan himself. How could this man "excommunicate" the "Rothschild woman" in the name of the Rose+Croix, thus implicating de Guaita's Order in potential scandal? Was not the Rose-Croix grade in Masonry invented by the Jesuits to impede the development of Masonry? And is not the same motive behind Péladan's efforts, that is, to forestall a growing movement of genuine spiritual esotericism and send it scuttling back to its historic oppressors and sworn opponents? Since Péladan had not consulted with his colleagues on the Supreme Council, he obviously considered he could speak for all. Such arrogance! He must have known the confusion he was sowing by not mentioning in his printed pastoral letters that there was another body of R+C Brothers. Speaking for "all" he has insulted all, from the administrators of Fine Arts to the "imbecile" Freemasons, to a lady of the Rothschild family. Péladan is called the "Panurge of Occultism," "the *enfant terrible* of mystery," and finally, after recognizing his very precious talents, a "bon fumiste" (a good mystificator). The piece was signed by de Guaita, Barlet, and Papus.

The drawbridge, you could say, was up.

And yet, still anxious to resolve the issues, de Guaita wrote personally to Péladan on 13 August:

> My dear friend,
>
> I hope that my book gives you as much pleasure as the androgyne [*sic;* Péladan's novel] gave to me: the reading of it reminded me of some of the most picturesque years of my life at college, *apud patres jesuitas.* [Evoking his Jesuit-led education suggests the use of the word *picturesque* was ironic; he probably objected to the strict morality of the book as well as linking his thoughts to the anti-Jesuit supplement to *L'Initiation. L'Androgyne* includes a fanciful account of Péladan's Jesuit education wherein he calls himself Samas.] Thank you also for so graciously sending me your *Gynandre* [another Péladan novel]. Everything that comes to me from you reminds me of a past which is a precious memory to me.
>
> I only regret that the provocations, more or less indirect of your R+C+C+ force us to protest energetically against it. It is important to make known to the students of occultism that its doctrines are the very opposite of all the Rosicrucian traditions, and that we can have nothing to do with the acts of willful madness which you have been perpetrating in increasing numbers for a year under the label of the Rosy Cross. Furthermore, your *Letter to Papus* and your Declaration of "Exodus" contain errors of fact we must deny, remembering the principal events of your breaking away and subsequent founding of your R+C+C+.

I strongly regret that the provocations of your attitude have driven us to such explanations, which always have an unfortunate effect.

Yours

Guaita[17]

Péladan apparently wrote back to de Guaita, expressing a conviction that all this fuss was quite unnecessary and that they should meet to sort any misunderstandings out. De Guaita's response was fairly curt:

My dear friend,

A conversation would not smooth out anything: for it is not a question of misunderstanding between us; it is a question of proclaiming solidarity before the public, who believe all of us to be involved in your acts. As to your final statement: "you desire aggression for the sake of aggression," let me tell you that I find that strange, when what you refer to is a very belated response to a series of gratuitous aggressions on your part.

Yours, and *bon voyage.*

Guaita[18]

On 23 August 1891, *Les Petites Affiches* (The Little Posters) inserted the following notice, conforming to the law concerning societies. This perhaps may be seen as Péladan's way of clarifying himself before the public:

9256–BY ACT UNDER PRIVATE SIGNATURES

Monsieur Joséphin Péladan, Comte Léonce de Larmandie, Gary de Lacroze, Elémir Bourges, 19, rue de Naples;

Monsieur le Comte Antoine de la Rochefoucauld, 19, rue d'Offément, Paris,

Have formed between them a society of collective name having for its object the organization of exhibitions of the Fine Arts.

The reason and the social signatures are:

ASSOCIATION DE L'ORDRE DU TEMPLE DE LA ROSE+CROIX[19]

Péladan had now only one way to go: to his own Salon, where he could experience the criticism he had meted out to others. Then again, Péladan's *Salons de la Rose+Croix* themselves constituted critical gestures in plastic form, and the entire, extraordinary exercise was undoubtedly as symbolic as was his bull-in-a-china-shop Rosicrucian Order.

TEN

The Salon
of the Century

Artist, thou art priest: Art is the great mystery; and if
your attempt turns out to be a masterwork, a divine ray
descends as on an altar. Oh real presence of the divinity
resplendent under these supreme names: Vinci, Raphael,
Michelangelo, Beethoven, and Wagner. Artist, thou art
king; art is the real kingdom. When the hand draws a
perfect line, the cherubim themselves descend and take
pleasure there in themselves as in a mirror. . . . Drawing
of the spirit, outline of the soul, form of understanding,
you embody our dreams, . . . Artist, thou art magus: art
is the great miracle and proves our immortality.

Who still doubts? Giotto has touched the stigmata,
the Virgin appeared to Fra Angelico; and Rembrandt
has proved the resurrection of Lazarus. . . .

Miserable moderns, your course to nothingness is
fatal; fall under the weights of your indignity: your
blasphemies will never efface the faith of works, O
sterile ones!

You could some day close the Church, but the
museum? Le Louvre will officiate, if Notre Dame is
profaned.

Brothers of all the arts, I here ring the bell to fight;
form a holy militia for the salute of idealism. We are
few against all, but the angels are ours. Our chiefs are

the old masters in the heights of paradise, who will
guide us towards Montsalvat. . . .

Oh you, who hesitate, my brother, do not
misinterpret or confound the fire of Faith with the cry
of the fanatic.

This Church so dear, the sole august thing in this
world, banished the Rose and believed its perfume
dangerous.

JOSÉPHIN PÉLADAN, PREFACE TO *GESTE ESTHÉTIQUE,*
CATALOGUE DU SALON DE LA ROSE+CROIX, 7–11

Other than Péladan's magical will, the person most responsible for
getting Péladan's dream successfully into the Gallery Durand-Ruel in
1892 was Count Antoine de La Rochefoucauld. But here lay obscured
another fissure in Péladan's ideal edifice, for while La Rochefoucauld,
an artist himself, was enthusiastic for Péladan's primary ideals, he
had his own special tastes, tastes he wished to see promoted by the
Rose+Croix+Catholique.

La Rochefoucauld was in sympathy with the Pont-Aven school
of independent artists. Among those who gathered to paint in the
spiritually congenial southwest coast of Brittany were Maurice Denis
(1870–1943), Paul Ranson (1864–1909), Charles Filiger (1863–1928),
and Paul Sérusier (1864–1927). Gauguin sojourned with them in 1888,
leaving as winter approached to stay, fatefully, with van Gogh in Arles,
before returning to Paris to share his ideas with Symbolists Aurier,
Morice, Redon, Carrière, Moréas, and Mirbeau in the Café Voltaire in
the Odéon district, attending admirer Stéphane Mallarmé's Tuesday
gatherings, while working toward his own Symbolist universe.

When not in Brittany, the three ex-students of the *Académie Julian,*
Denis, Ranson, and Sérusier, would meet at Ranson's studio on the
boulevard du Montparnasse on Saturdays. Out of their discussions
came a kind of manifesto, written by Maurice Denis and submitted
to the review *Art et Critique* in 1890. Denis wrote of his dream of a
brotherhood (the prophets or Nabis) whose aim was not to copy nature

Fig. 10.1. Paul Gauguin in 1891

Fig. 10.2. Paul Sérusier
(1864–1927)

Fig. 10.3. Maurice Denis,
drawing by Odilon Redon

but to visualize their dreams *through* nature in order to recover spiritual vision. Nature served only to stimulate awareness of the symbol, for the spirit surpasses matter, and it is *that*—what Martinists would call "The Thing" or *La Chose*—that alone is worthy of brush and canvas. Strangely, John Lennon would come to an analogous conclusion in early 1969, when, in discussions with the other Beatles as to their future, he gave out that "God is the gimmick," meaning that the essence of what he believed the Beatles should work for was cosmic consciousness, and while the music had obvious commercial value, that was not what it was essentially about; Beatles was a means to an end, a "medium of communication."

Jean Cassou has expressed the Symbolists' challenge to prevailing representational forms thus: "By reacting against the positivist spirit of its time, Symbolism found the way to discover the right language for man to recover his faith in the imaginary and the unreal."[1] While this comment might be applied to the decadently grandiose visions of Gustave Moreau, that last word *unreal* hardly applies to the austerity of the Pont-Aven school whose associates were seeking mystical, or "higher" reality in and through paint. It is not surprising that it would be this initially obscure wing of the Symbolist bird that would create the flight path for the revolution of abstraction.

Péladan himself assisted the process toward artistic revolution, for he believed the artist was bound to look *through* nature in search of the ideal idea that corresponded to the symbolic language of the soul and then to give that experience ideal form, or, to use Coleridge's words, "to disembody the soul of fact." This idea of abstraction—for you "abstract" the *idea* from the object—was central to Péladan's thinking but curiously latent in his actual appreciation of different pictures. This was because his idea of abstraction was based precisely on Plato's distinction of time and eternity—time being eternity's "moving image"— distinctions best evinced in the works of da Vinci, in Péladan's view. When the Symbolist reaches the essence of the task, he should be able, like a magician or alchemist, to *abstract the Idea* that is eternity from its *image,* time, or the products of time. In the hands of a great artist, for example, a ruin—an image that might otherwise suggest *decay*—may invoke eternity, the ideal world beyond time and space. The tension between the decay and loss, and the idea of eternity, creates the drama of the artistic event: the invisible *point* of the painting.

Spiritual forms were still for Péladan essentially anthropomorphic, corresponding to the visual creation, though idealized: "God saw that it [the creation] was good." Man is made "in the image of God." The example above demonstrates Péladan's difficulty in embracing complete abstraction from the visual plane. If creation is somehow redeemed through vision, one wants to see the created matter transformed, idealized—not denuded or "minimalized."

Péladan's idea of the ideal was highly influenced by the Italian Renaissance and Hermetic revival of the Quattrocento that stressed human form as the ideal form of divine beauty, and androgynous form as the spiritual ideal—hence Péladan's great love for da Vinci's *John the Baptist*. One was unlikely to be tempted to fall in love, worship, or risk all, for a triangle! *Magnum miraculum homo est!* Geometry for Péladan, as for most occultists, referred to the essential construction or plan of a work, divine or symbolic proportions implicit to a great work. To replace a great painting merely with its geometrical lineaments would have been the aesthetic equivalent of stripping the Venus de Milo to the bare bones: What was the point? The difference between a skeleton and a truly ideal form was *life:* "the Word was made flesh and dwelt among us."

However, it only remained for new artists to decide there *was* a point, and that ideas could be expressed in abstract forms that had life of their own, for the bonds that bound paint to identifiable objects to dissolve. The first step only required a transition of interest to Plato's inherited tools of creation, the five primal geometrical solids. Once sacred geometry, such as the "golden section," and symbolic numerology were combined, the path opened to the revolution in form and color, mentalized and spiritualized, we know as "Abstract Art." We may therefore deduce that abstract art, while obviously "modern" on the stylistic, visual plane, was derived through an esoteric perception of Pythagoras, Euclid, medieval religious architecture, and occult traditions. Pont-Aven habitués Sérusier, Denis, Ranson, and, to some extent, Charles Filiger (regarded by Breton as a proto-surrealist) believed forms derived from these sources possessed their own ideal beauty, holding the secret keys to ideal form.

The revolution of abstraction must have seemed very distant at the time from what was exhibited under the auspices of the *Salons de la Rose+Croix* from 1892 to 1897, but in fact, it was already there, just under the surface. The sad thing perhaps is that while Péladan could grasp the revolutionary idea intellectually, he could only envision it in forms with which he was largely already familiar. This would mean that as the 1890s movements surged toward the colder lights of the twentieth century, Péladan's objects of devotion would come to look rather old fashioned, and he, unjustly, with them. It would be abstract, spiritual pioneer Wassily Kandinsky (1866–1944) who would recognize and state the seminal importance of Péladan's critical genius and pass on the torch of spiritual idealism in painted form. In his book *Concerning the Spiritual in Art*, Kandinsky wrote: "The artist is not only a king, as Péladan says, because he has great power, but also because he has great duties."[2]

Exercising those great duties would be an enormous trial for Péladan through the 1891–92 period. June 1891 saw Péladan compelled to take Léon Bloy and Léon Deschamps to court over a dispute stirred up in the pages of Léon Deschamps's review *La Plume* the previous year. It centered on the fact that Bloy, close friend of Barbey d'Aurevilly—who had died in 1889—accused Péladan not only of having significantly darkened the last days of Barbey's life, but also of having dishonorably exploited his contact with Bloy and the Barbey circle.

What in fact had happened in 1889 was that Péladan had informed an old flame of Barbey's that the old man was dying, whereupon the woman arrived at Barbey's house demanding, in very poor taste, money owed to her. When it transpired Péladan's indiscretion had precipitated the unexpected scene, Bloy refused Péladan access to pray at his friend's bedside, informing Péladan that Barbey, having tired of Péladan's antics, regretted giving his first novel the boost of an endorsement.

The hearings, covered by *La Plume*, commenced on 15 June. Péladan insisted Bloy had falsified circumstances around Barbey's death. In October the judgment found against Péladan and Bloy crowed his satisfaction in November's *La Plume*. By that time, Péladan had already burned his boats with old friends at *L'Initiation,* who might otherwise have supported him through the interminable trough of ridicule that followed the judgment, though *L'Initiation* did print one letter in the otherwise critical July 1891 issue from a country subscriber who lamented the dispute between Péladan and Papus's review, admiring all parties and calling for a spirit of ideal love and charity among men who were so important and who had spiritual responsibilities to those attracted to their cause. The editorial comment was that publication of the reader's letter proved the review's impartiality! To be fair, *L'Initiation* had certainly given Péladan a hearing, but had remained unmoved by what it heard. We shall see why shortly.

Péladan delivered a final word to *L'Initiation* on 17 February 1891, published in full in the April 1891 issue: the first article in a sequence followed by de Guaita on modern sorcery (again aimed at Boullan, though not naming him), and an article by gnostic bishop of Montségur, Jules Doinel, which sequence gives one a flavor of the time.

The "Avant-Propos" is headed by Péladan "MANDEMENT [Pastoral Letter] from the Sar Péladan, master of the catholic Rose-Croix, to Papus, president of the Esoteric Group and Director of *L'Initiation.*" Péladan goes right to the point of what separated him *essentially* from his old colleagues. It is the overexpansion, as Péladan sees it, of *Papus's* eclectic doctrine—not a personal dispute with de Guaita as has usually been thought. Péladan disapproved of Papus's policy, and a defensive Papus responded with an attack, as we saw in *L'Initiation*'s August 1891 "Supplement" in chapter 9. Papus could not stomach what Péladan here declares:

> *Salut,* Light and Victory in Jesus Christ only God,
> and in Peter sole king.

> *Très cher Adelphe,* [Note the French version of the Greek for
> "Brother" does not have the idiosyncratic initial *E* of the keyword

Edelphe used by the Vicomte de Lapasse for genuine Rosicrucian physicians, as directed by "prince Balbani." One wonders whether Péladan's use of *A* was because he was unaware of the specialized, Paracelsian connotation of de Lapasse's *Edelphe* taking it merely as an archaic spelling of Adelphe.]

A year ago, I wanted to leave your eclectic works; at your request, I accepted to figure, at the head of *L'Initiation,* with the quality of Roman Catholic Legate.

Today, the divergence of our paths has become such that my intransigence generates your expansion whilst my orthodoxy would suffer from your compromises.

This Catholic rigor that I manifested three times in *le Figaro* does not permit me to stay any longer as consort to a group where Cakya-Mouni [Buddha] usurps our Savior Jesus Christ.

That which for you comes under the rubric of *comparative religion,* I rather call *sacrilege.*

Regarding doctrines, the expansive mode divides us again: you would open the doors of the temple that I would like to close.

The implacable hierarchy that I recognize, you sacrifice to a proselytizing movement that I admire, but which I cannot associate myself with.

I therefore quit today and forever the work accomplished together.

Henceforth, I give my entire self to my *Rose-Croix catholique.*

Among yourselves, you often forget that I am the dean of works of this renewed magic wherein you occupy such a great place.

Among my own, one never forgets that you are one of my highest peers.

From this moment, the Church possesses the occult as I bring it to her, in my person, one of the six gnostic lights of the hour.

I go, with my brothers [*adelphes*] to wait for you before the Eucharistic altar, in the palace of *ardent fire;* and I hope one day to welcome you there with inexpressible *laetare* [rejoicing].

That this same light that we seek, you by numbers and diffusion, me by *l'aristie* and occultation, shining equally on our workman's hands.

Materialism has found in you an invincible adversary, and, whatever the mutual and disparate necessities of our realizations, I salute your glory with my catholic enthusiasm because your initiates will become our faithful, as our faithful are your initiates.

Differing missions, one dedicated to disseminating truth, the other to the aestheticization of the truth. And *verbum caro factum est* ["the word was made flesh"]; and that the Absolute realizes itself, by you or by me, or by others *non nobis sed mominis tui gloriae solae*, ["not for us, but only to the glory of thy name"] said the Temple;

Ad Rosam per Crucem, ad Crucem per Rosam in êa in eis, gemmatus resurgam: ["Achieving the Rose through the Cross, achieving the Cross through the Rose in her in them, thus adorned I will be resurrected"] sings the catholic Rose-Croix in the name of that I salute you from heart and from spirit.

SAR PÉLADAN. This February 17 1891.[3]

As it turned out, Péladan only just got into the review before the Vatican took it out of his hands and placed it on the Index. The Catholic hierarchy got very close to putting Péladan's own works there too. A provincial Catholic congress held at Malines in Belgium accused Péladan of dishonoring the faith, along with Baudelaire, Barbey d'Aurevilly, and Paul Verlaine. Doubtless flattered by the company, Péladan's response was to excommunicate (!) the congress's constituents in his "Ardent Execration of the Malines Catholic Congress," published by Dentu in Péladan's *Règle* of the Rose+Croix Salon in 1891, cosigned by "Le Grand Prieur [Grand Prior], A. De la Rochefoucauld."

Péladan readers were greeted in May 1891's *Salon* review not only with lengthy, rather over-the-top praise for the Sâr's skillful portrait artist, Marcellin Desboutin—to whom Péladan's new Sapphic novel *Gynandre* or the "Woman-Man" was dedicated—but a preview of some of the artists who would feature regularly in the *Salons de la Rose-Croix*.

Close friend of Seurat and Aman-Jean and trained in Lehmann's studio, Alphonse Osbert's style fitted perfectly the "mauve" decade's crepuscular vision of intermediate life states. Influenced by the classical

Fig. 10.4. Frontispiece by Alexandre Séon for Péladan's novel
La Gynandre *(The Woman-Man), from the catalog to the*
first Rose-Croix Salon 1892

compositions of Puvis de Chavannes, Osbert employed his own pointillist technique that placed his subjects somewhere between life and death, time and eternity, making the viewer question his own perspective on both states.

Fig. 10.5. Hymne à la Mer *by Alphonse Osbert, from the 1892 Rose-Croix Salon catalog*

Fig. 10.6. Fernand Khnopff (1858–1921), self-portrait

Fernand Khnopff, described by Péladan in *Le Salon* (*Dixième Année*, p. 23) as "so intense and subtle" had provided the almost kinky St. Sebastian–like frontispiece to Péladan's *Istar* (1888). Khnopff, his name resonant of an Egyptian curse, will provide a style practically emblematic of the Salons collectively and of the era, the very definition in form of the phrase "the late antique": mysterious, arcane, intellectual, haunted, and remote, a world where classical Roman and Greek certainties of logic melt in the monstrous seepage of conquered, chthonic spiritualities in the form of Middle Eastern chimeras, some erotic, others inscrutable. *Burn your togas! The Age of Reason has had its day!*

Péladan was likewise drawn to Alexandre Séon's ability to paint the nightmares of genius. He had executed the cover for *L'Androgyne*, described in the *Salon* of 1891 (p. 40) as a work set above "the strange rocks of Bréhat, licked at by the waves, there rolls in the sky in place of the moon, the head of the androgyne Samas, stupefied by the sexual enigma."

Séon's unforgettably weird and disturbing *Le Désespoir de la Chimère* (*The Despair of the Chimera*—see color plate 18) shows us a kind of demented sphinx, most unhappy at her polymorphous incongruity as she screams like a strangled cock through lips stained with rouge on the edge of a coastal cave, the waves of time and space eroding its sense of existence. A midday nightmare at the seaside, it would appear as a shocking "Rosicrucian" vision at the third *Salon de la Rose+Croix*.

Péladan shared with all ancient civilizations the fascination for combined beings, firstly of men and women, boys and girls, but also of humans and animals, the most obvious examples being Pan and of course the Sphinx. Such combinations had great symbolic value, lost to the anthropocentricity of the modern world where different "classes" of being are kept apart. Being more concerned with soul than body, occult systems looked for the correspondences between them, while alchemists saw magic in combinations, seeking volatility.

Péladan expressed admiration for the Swiss artist Ferdinand Hodler who caused a sensation at the Salon with a painting reminiscent of Fuseli's famous *Nightmare*. De La Rochefoucauld went to Switzerland in 1892 to persuade Hodler to exhibit for the Rose-Croix. The artist sent his *Les Âmes Deçues* (Disappointed Souls, see figure 10.7). Péladan would have noticed a resonance with Breughel's blind leading the blind, for its five seated men with heads in hands all suggest a posture of penitence, though to this author the highly stylized image is more prescient of the condemned "Waiting for Godot," for a genuine penitent should never be disappointed, nor would resort to a bench like a waiting room for hell.

Péladan's *Rose+Croix Ésthétique*, drawn up on May 1891's Feast of the Ascension and appended to the 1891 *Salon* critical publication, spelled out the aims of the *Salons de la Rose+Croix*. Addressing his "Magnifiques" in the Order, Péladan creates the *Règle* or "Rule" of the Salons to come. The use of the Rule comes straight from medieval monastic or chivalric orders where each was governed by a Rule. Theologian and founder of the Cistercian Order, Bernard of Clairvaux drew up the Templars' Rule, for example. In conformity with Péladan's ideal artist as priest, magus, and king, the Magnifique must live a dedicated life by adhering to a Rule. The new group is given its aims, predicated on

Fig. 10.7. Les Âmes Deçues *by*
Ferdinand Hodler (1853–1918), from
the first Rose-Croix Salon catalog, 1892

the infallibility of the Sâr with the benefit of intercession with God
of the effectively canonized Balzac (author of the androgyny-inspired
novel *Séraphîta,* 1834), composer Wagner, and painter Delacroix, whose
angels in St. Sulpice provided daily devotional inspiration:

> To insufflate theocratic essence into contemporary art, especially
> aesthetic culture, such is our new path.
> To ruin the notion attached to facile execution; to extinguish

methodological dilettantism, to subordinate *the arts to Art,* that is to say, to return to the tradition which regards the ideal as the single aim of the architectonic, the pictorial or plastic effort. (*Salon,* p. 55–56)

For Péladan, this amounted to "holy war" against philistines and materialists, and that is why his Order takes the name of the Temple, as well as the Graal. When in the early twelfth century St. Bernard of Clairvaux called together his "poor knights" to the Templar Rule, he thought of them as "Maccabees," that is, holy warriors fighting for Zion against the heathen. Judas Maccabaeus led the second-century BCE revolt against Greek domination of the Holy Land. His name meant "the hammer." Desiring to give the art world's academicism and limp Impressionism a thorough hammering, Péladan summoned to order his "Maccabees of Beauty." In bringing forth this level of mythic power, Péladan began to initiate his remarkable attempt to extericize the occult and create from art, by and through art, the locus of a new, or revived, spiritual religion that could change the world without from within. Oscar Wilde, residing in Paris in late 1891 while writing the risqué symbolistic classic, *Salome,* must have been listening. James Webb wrote, with respect to Wilde: "The idea of the [Wildean] aesthetic movement was essentially a corruption of the doctrine of the French Symbolists" (*The Occult Underground,* p. 166). *Salome's* French translation was the work of Symbolist intellectual and *Gil Blas* journalist, Marcel Schwob (1867–1905), who would perform the same service for Aleister Crowley's *Rodin in Rhyme* in 1903. Crowley often took his cue from someone else.

When *Les Petites Affiches* carried the legal announcement of the *Association de l'Ordre du Temple de la Rose-Croix* on 23 August 1891, there was great public interest, satisfied by Péladan on 2 September with a popular version of the aims of the Order in *Le Figaro* called *Le Manifeste de la Rose+Croix.* A fascinating article, its second paragraph expresses the effort precisely in terms of, and as an illustration of, the thought of Fabre d'Olivet, who spoke of the sacred, transformative union of Will with Providence. Clearly Péladan saw himself as one of the "hommes providentiels" that Fabre d'Olivet believed to be incredibly rare, and who saved the world from oblivion:

> Such a fuss [journalistic interest in the Order] bears witness that our *Will*, blessed by *Providence,* will polarize *Necessity* with *Destiny.*
>
> The Salon de la Rose+Croix will be the first realization of an intellectual order that originates, by theocratic principle, with Hugh of the Pagans [cofounder of the Knights Templar]; with Rosenkreutz [legendary founder of the Rose-Cross brotherhood] by the idea of individualistic perfection.
>
> The infidel today, he who profanes the Holy Sepulcher, is not the Turk, but the sceptic; and the militant monk [Templars were both monks and knight-warriors] with his motto "ut leo feriatur" [Templar motto attributed to St. Bernard of Clairvaux: "Let the lion be beaten down," the lion being the animal passions] can no longer find a place for his effort. . . . The Salon de la Rose-Croix will be a temple dedicated to Art-God, with masterpieces for dogma and for saints, geniuses.[4]

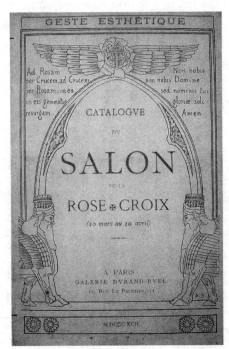

Fig. 10.8. Title page: catalog, first Rose-Croix Salon 1892

To get an instant sense of what Péladan was driving at, we need only look at the catalog for the first Rose+Croix Salon that came to pass in March and April the following year, that is, in 1892. The catalog's pages consist mostly of drawings exhibited. In Alexandre Séon's frontispiece for a new edition of *Le Vice Suprême*[5] reproduced on page 64 of that document, we see the startling image of a Paris blown apart, devastated and flattened on a terrific scale worse than the Germans' World War I bombardment of Liège; indeed, the scene seems chillingly prescient of Hiroshima's annihilation. Only two identifiable objects are standing. One is what's left of the Eiffel Tower (constructed 1887–89), either because it is depicted as partially obliterated by war, or simply not finished; the other is a standing cross on a hill occupying the foreground. On the cross, nailed up by abundant black hair is the severed head of Joséphin Péladan, like the prophet-Baptist. His eyes gaze into ours. He sees us, and we see the void. *What void?*

Below the severed head is an inscription: *FINIS LATINORUM*. This is the end of the Latin world, Latin culture, Latin idealism, Latin beauty,

Fig. 10.9. Alexandre Séon's new frontispiece to Le Vice Suprême, *from the catalog to the first Rose-Croix Salon 1892*

Latin faith, even Latin decadence in the form of the decapitated Sâr. If the barbaric enemy, by implication the Germans, has not completely wiped out the massive iron Eiffel Tower, it is because Péladan sees its iron hubris as in a sense "one of their own." The viewer will have been aware that the place where this offensive Tower of Babel was erected for the World's Exhibition of 1889—an erection opposed by hosts of writers and artists—was the Champ-de-Mars: the field of Mars, god of war, and the Champ-de-Mars was where the official Beaux Art Salons were held. Péladan sees what all this means. *Fight* for the spiritual culture of idealism—the Holy Graal—or look forward to the wasteland whose iron sign, devoid of symbolic value, is already towering over an apostate Paris, forcing us to see its significance!

That is what all Péladan's posturing is fundamentally about. One could write pages on Péladan's sometimes curious laws that were printed to govern conduct both within the Order and at the Order's manifestation in the Salons, but while these laws had meaning, they were not, I think, to be taken entirely literally, as so many have, concluding that Péladan was a dotty eccentric. The rules were fundamentally an aesthetic abstraction from the rules of the militant monks of past times, whose ardent fervor for Christ, the living Word, had been forgotten by the skeptic, the materialist, the relativist, and the smiling pragmatist who cuts cards with the Devil who flatters him and invests in Krupps mechanized warfare in the name of "profitable industry" at any price to save money.

Péladan's first three "constitutions" should suffice of his symbolic transformation of medieval language and charitable intention, which one might describe as ironic parody were those words not alien to Péladan's nonskeptical, passionately ardent yet playful spirit:

I - The lay order of the Rose-Croix of the TEMPLE and of the GRAAL is a confraternity of intellectual Charity consecrated to the accomplishment of the works of mercy according to the HOLY SPIRIT, which it exerts to augment the Glory and to prepare the Reign [of the Holy Graal].

II - Soulfully, it gives hunger and thirst for the IDEAL to those whose only guides are instinct and interest; and that is the orientation of others towards the light.

Hospitalize the errant and indecisive hearts, comfort them and reveal to them their path; and that is the discernment of vocations.

Clothe with beauty and with means the imperfect or weary aspirations; and this is a correction of the specializations.

Visit the sick of will and cure them of the dizziness of passivity; and this is a cure for moral anaemia.

Console the prisoners of material necessity and obtain for them cerebral life; and this is a mental charity.

Redeem the captives of prejudices and emancipate opinion, of the country, of the race; and that is an abstract accomplishment of another.

Bury the august dead in pious commemorations and repair the wrongs of destiny; and that is of the ideal sculpture.

III - Spiritually, it [the Order] instructs those who ignore the Standards of Beauty, of Charity, and of Subtilty, following their functions, and that is the Board of intellect.

Retake from every holder of social power the attacks against the Standard and the tradition; and that is the Ardent surveillance.

Counsel those who are in danger of the sin against the Holy Spirit in misusing their faculties or their gold; and that is the fraternal correction.

Console the Holy Spirit of human stupidity in enlightening experience by the mystery of faith; and that is a concordat between religion and science.

Personally support all the troubled in order to have the right to defend the idea; and that is abnegation to the profit of the Word.

Pardon to all his offenders, but not to the offenders of Beauty, Charity and Subtilty; and that is the chivalry of ideas.

Pray to geniuses as saints and practice admiration, before being illuminated; and that is the meeting-point of culture and mysticism.[6]

These words constitute about a fifth of the *Constitutiones Rosae Crucis templi et spiritus sancti ordinis* that opens: "We, by the divine mercy and the assent of our brothers—Grand Master of the ROSE+CROIX DU TEMPLE ET DU GRAAL; In Catholic communion with JOSEPH OF ARIMATHEA, HUGUES DE PAYENS and DANTE"—and which draws toward its close with the 35th constitution, in which we learn that the, presumably otherwise "invisible," brotherhood "manifests itself annually in March–April, by: first, a Salon of all the arts of design. Second, an idealist theatre, until it can become hieratic. Third, auditions of sublime music. Fourth, clean conferences to awaken the idealism of the worldly."[7]

It ought to be clear from the above that Péladan's Order was essentially a conceptual Order, a kind of ideal Church of Aesthetics, a House of the Holy Spirit of Art, stubbornly set within the Catholic communion and knowingly beneath an ecclesiastical hierarchy that has not asked for it, nor will understand it. In no wise was Péladan's intention to compete with de Guaita and Papus's Order. Being ideal, and practically "virtual," it sets itself above such considerations. In fact, it is in spirit much closer to Johann Valentin Andreae's original "ludibrium," or serious fiction, of an "invisible brotherhood" bringing healing wisdom to the starving souls of broken Christendom, than subsequent historical attempts to incarnate that conception in Masonic or para-Masonic forms. As Péladan says, it is a confraternity, and confraternities were formed by laypeople to gather about objects of beauty or sacredness performing works of mercy as being useful and sanctified by God. Indeed, confraternities represent the probable factual origins of Freemasonry, before the Reformation split the Catholic Church. Importantly, the text defines the "orthodoxy" of the Order as "Beauty," the Platonic ideal expressed in the Book of Genesis when the Elohim sees that the creation is "good." Goodness and Beauty, relate to Truth (the Ideal), where Beauty is the path, and Goodness the life; thus: "I am the way, the truth, and the life" (John 14:6). This is the way to the heavenly Father. Hence, Péladan can speak of "Art-God."

THE MANIFESTATION

The *Figaro* article trumpeted the artists Péladan wanted and expected to see at the R+C Salon: "the great Puvis de Chavannes," Dagnan-

Bouveret, Merson, Henri Martin, Aman-Jean, Odilon Redon, Knopff, Point, Séon, Filiger, de Gusquiza, Anquetin, the sculptors Dampt, Marquest de Vasselot, Pezieux, Astruc, and the composer Erik Satie.

Having been a regular visitor to *Le Chat Noir* (though its director, Rodolphe Salis did not like Péladan, a dislike reflected in the attitude of *Le Chat Noir*'s eponymous periodical) and to Bailly's bookshop in the rue de la Chaussée d'Antin, Péladan was in an excellent position to entice the practically unknown young genius and *Vice Suprême* admirer Erik Satie into the fold as official composer ("maître de chapelle") to the Order.

Satie's formal connection with the Order dates from 1891 when Satie wrote about a minute of music known as the *Première Pensée Rose+Croix*. On 28 October of the same year, Satie signed the manuscript of his short "leitmotif" for Péladan's tenth *Décadence Latine* novel, *Le Panthée* (The Panther). The score was reproduced in facsimile on the book's frontispiece, along with an etching by Khnopff. Satie then wrote a hymn, *Salut Drapeau,* at Péladan's request, for his play *Le Prince du Byzance*. More works for the Order would follow. The *Figaro* article trumpeted the composer of the trumpet fanfares that would open the Salon: "Among the idealist composers that the Rose-Croix will shed light on, it is proper to mention Erik Satie again, of whose work one will hear the harmonic suites for *Le Fils des Étoiles* and the preludes to the *Prince de Byzance*."

Having secured a "house composer," Péladan promised to go to London to secure the participation of Burne-Jones, Watts, and five other Pre-Raphaelites. Germans Lenbach and Böcklin would also be invited.

The Salon would not accept all subjects. Unacceptable were "all contemporary, rustic or military representations; flowers, animals, genre history-painting, and portraiture-like landscape." Landscape was only acceptable if it reflected the genius of Poussin, presumably because Péladan recognized in Poussin's works ideal, symbolic, and occult value, rather than simply attempts to render the countryside "as it was" or even "as it felt." Welcome was "all allegory, legend, mysticism, and myth and even the expressive head if it is noble or the nude study if it is beautiful. You have to create BEAUTY to get into the Salon de la Rose+Croix."

The arbiters of acceptability would be the Magnifiques of the Order, but the final word was for the Sâr, because in a proper Order, someone has to have the last word, and it should be the Master's, as in all works of Art. In respect of which, portraiture was out, unless it was a portrait of the Sâr, itself a commitment to the Ideal. "The 10th March 1892, Paris will be able to contemplate, at the Durand-Ruel Gallery, the masters of which it is unaware; it will not find one vulgarity." Should there be any profit from the shows, it would go to the costs of republishing the *Treatise on Painting* by Leonardo da Vinci, "the divine Leonardo" whose work was "so necessary to artists."

"Contrary to what one reads in the papers, no work by a woman will be accepted because in our renovation of aesthetic laws we faithfully observe magical laws." Impossible to swallow today of course, but the tradition behind the proscription of women's art came from the traditional magical axiom of the feminine as passive, serving as muse and receiver, and the masculine as creative and generative (the king-magus role), the male as sacrificer of creative seed (the priest-role), the female as nurturer, and the prejudice that the lone or independent female seeks to dominate the male when in company, thereby imperiling individuality, the cornerstone of the Order. To which strictures, Susan Sontag, Germaine Greer, Yoko Ono, and many other women would doubtless cry: "Bullshit!" Not all *that* long ago, but different times, for sure.

As it turned out, Puvis de Chavannes declined to support the event, as did academicians Dagnan-Bouveret and Luc-Ilivier Merson. Art historian Robert Pincus-Witten reckoned the latter two, being market-leaders in academic religious art, declined to jeopardize their position with the controversial outsider, Péladan.[8] Puvis de Chavannes actually protested "with all my strength" in the evening's *Figaro* that his name was being used to bring others to the event, but he was an influence through his pupils Séon and Osbert. After that rejection, Péladan cooled toward his onetime art hero.

Antoine de La Rochefoucauld was doubtless disappointed that Maurice Denis did not exhibit with the Rose-Croix, though the Pont-Aven school was represented by de La Rochefoucauld himself, his brother Hubert, and by Émile Bernard and Charles Filiger. Apparently,

Fig. 10.10. Drawing of Alexandre Séon by Puvis de Chavannes, Musée des Beaux Arts de Lyon.

Maurice Denis would not subscribe to an aesthetic that included both allegory and Symbolism within categories of the Ideal. According to Denis, the symbol "suggests ideas by beauty alone."[9] Perhaps surprisingly, Odilon Redon preferred to be out, and neither Félicien Rops nor Gustave Moreau appeared in the two first *Salons de la Rose-Croix;* pupils of Moreau would enter the third.

Less surprising was the attitude of much of the Press. While *La Revue Indépendante* praised highly Péladan's use of Plato's *Symposium* in his aesthetics,[10] critic Gonzague-Privat dismissed Péladan in *L'Evénement* (November 2, 1891) as "the only Frenchman with the right of addressing the Ideal in familiar form. . . ."[11] Predictably, *La Plume* struck hard on 15 November when S. Mueux cast the socialist hatchet into Péladan: "We equally mock the Thaumaturges as the Myths, the Myths as much as the Magi, the Magi as the Saints, the Saints as the Angels, the Angels as the elves, the elves as the sorcerers, the sorcerers as the alchemists, the alchemists as the occultists, the occultists as the Knights Templar, the Knights Templar as the Free-Masons, the Free-Masons as the Illuminates [etc.]."[12]

Nevertheless, as Pincus-Witten has observed, Péladan was truly in touch with an "urge" deeply set in the period. François Paulhan's 1891 book *Le Nouveau Mysticisme* cited Péladan along with Huysmans and Bourget as significant mystical influences, while G. Albert-Aurier's classic assessment of Symbolism in his "Le Symbolisme en Peinture, Paul Gauguin," which appeared in the *Mercure de France* (February 1892), and which indicated the five necessary features of Symbolist

Art, corresponds closely to Péladan's theories, though not in all parts. Aurier's categories are now established, that is, that Symbolism is: (1) Ideological; (2) Symbolistic (idea expressed in forms); (3) Synthetic; (4) Subjective (objects are not merely objects, but signify ideas); and (5) Decorative in function. According to Pincus-Witten: "Péladan's attitudes and actions demand reappraisal because, in theory, they relate to aspects of that which is most modern in their period. The crucial difference between Aurier and Péladan is that Aurier had the genius to recognize these principles in the art of Paul Gauguin whereas Péladan's were applied *a priori* to a host of less illustrious and, in many cases, inept artists."[13]

I wonder what Péladan would have said in his defense concerning the last sentence. The "inept" may only be seen as such in retrospect. Péladan was trying to encourage young artists to the cause. It is not unheard of, when opening up a new continent, to say: "Bring me your rejects! I can mold them! We have the dream!"

Posters for the event appeared in Parisian streets in early 1892. Reproduced many times, Swiss Symbolist Carlos Schwabe (1866–1926), designer and printmaker, had made a big hit with Péladan, for the catalog of drawings for the exhibition contains eleven of his works, all resembling Pre-Raphaelite influenced illustrations in works of fantasy and mythology, set in medieval times, though Pincus-Witten regards them as Botticellian. Ten came from *L'Évangile de l'enfance,* published the previous year in the *Revue Illustrée.* Schwabe produced a gem for the poster (see color plate 31). The theme is ascent from the mire of the world toward the ideal. We see a nude mired in the material swamp, slime dripping from her fingertips. She looks half asleep as well as literally "half-soaked." She gazes vaguely to two defined female figures on a celestial staircase—Schwabe's inspiration may just have been Blake's *Jacob's Ladder.* The lower female hands a lily to the transparent-seeming figure slightly above her. She is Idealism, and holds a heart in her hand. She receives a beam of light directly from above. She then is the Greek *nous,* or Latin *intellectus,* the "higher reason" that is spiritual mind.

Lilies and roses, flowers of the Virgin, are strewn on the stairs. The

Fig. 10.11. Carlos Schwabe's illustration from L'Évangile de l'enfance, *Salon Rose-Croix catalog 1892*

Ancient & Accepted Rite's 18th Rose-Croix degree employs similar stage settings as the knight-mason's voyage reaches its climax. The picture is framed by crucified roses on altars familiar to any Knight of the Pelican and the Eagle. The design is basically allegorical and emblematic rather than strictly Symbolist. It works.

In fact, it worked almost too well. On opening day, Thursday 10 March 1892, the police had to stop traffic between the rue Montmartre and the Opéra, until past five in the afternoon. Larmandie counted 274 carriages; more than 22,600 visiting cards were left. According to Larmandie's record: "The real, the only food, was an immense enthusiasm, an unshakeable faith in the certitude of an apotheosis, the deep-rooted belief that a new life opened for art and that we were the predestined workers of a regeneration without precedent."[14]

It had taken three days and three nights to hang the exhibition, with no time to stop to eat, hence the remark above about what drove the organizers. Two thousand press invitations went out, and many invitations to private individuals. The Salon provoked extraordinary levels of curiosity. Larmandie was gratified by the number of French nobles who came to gaze: "the premier 200 names of the French Armorial."[15] Government ministers, the count of Münster, poetess Anna de Brancovan, Comtesse de Noalles, Lord Dufferin, the Duke of Mandas, Count Radziwill, two Gramonts, Montesquiou, Maillé—they all wanted to know what was happening.

Though he had declined to exhibit, Puvis de Chavannes, a friend of Alphonse Osbert (who did) came to see, as representative of the National Society of Fine Arts, as did Gustave Moreau. Even the Naturalist opposition, Émile Zola, came for an hour. The Society of French Artists held aloof. Verlaine arrived, leaving a *bon mot* before he left: "Yes, yes, agreed, we are Catholics . . . but sinners."

"Clearly correct," added Larmandie![16]

In the light of the collective sin, we may note the gallery opening was preceded by a Solemn Mass of the Holy Ghost celebrated at 10 a.m. at the church of Saint Germain l'Auxerrois at 2 place de Louvre, where the "Prelude," the "Last Supper of the Grail," the "Good Friday Spell," and the "Finale of the Redemption" from *Parsifal* by the "superhuman

Fig. 10.12. Gustave Moreau, self-portrait

Wagner" were played. The Mass was preceded by "three fanfares of the Order composed by Erik Satie for harp and trumpet."[17] The organizers and their special guests then took carriages a kilometer north back to the gallery at 11 rue le Peletier, close to the junction with the boulevard Haussmann in the 9th arrondissement, 400 meters or so east of Bailly's bookshop.

Entering the gallery Durand-Ruel, normally no friend to Symbolists, but temporarily won round by La Rochefoucauld's charm and wallet, visitors were first confronted by a long corridor in which was hung a large Manet. This attracted jeers from many "idealists" who had cottoned on to the idea of a regrettably "low ceiling" of vision attempted by Impressionism. Nevertheless, the objects of so much Impressionist delight were everywhere: the gallery was filled with flowers. Those who arrived in the first two hours were charged a hefty gold *Louis* for the privilege of ingesting their fragrance at its purest; the rest paid twenty francs, worth roughly thirty dollars at today's prices, and enjoyed the fragrance of one another, confronted with dozens of pools of eternity, or at least the palpable longing for it.

The works on show conformed to Aurier's idea that Symbolist art should be decorative, for decorative art allows for abstraction and representation both, and their combination kept symbolism in its romantic swaddling bands from the coming austerity of "pure," rigorous abstraction that hit the art world like a sermon from John Calvin as the twentieth century unrolled its barbed carpet.

Here are the painters and sculptors who exhibited at the first Rose+Croix Salon, many now forgotten, but caught in this moment of history on the rue de Peletier, glowing briefly, like flies in amber: Edmond François Aman-Jean, Atalaya, Émile Bernard, Gaston Béthune, Émile-Antoine Bourdelle (sculptor), Jean-Louis Brémond, Eugène Cadel, François-Rupert Carabin, Maurice Chabas, Louis Chalon, Alexandre Charpentier, Albert Ciamberlani, Pierre-Emile Cornillier, Émile-Antoine Coulon, Jean Dampt (sculptor), Vincent Darasse, Jean Delville, André Desboutin, Marcellin Desboutin, Rogelio de Egusquiza, Charles Filiger, Eugène Grasset, Edmond Haraucourt, Ferdinand Hodler, Icard, Isaac-Dathis, Georges-Arthur Jacquin, Fernand Khnopff, Leon-Charles de LaBarreDuparc, Lambert Fovras, de La Perche-Boyet, Antoine de La Rochefoucauld, Hubert de La Rochefoucauld, William Lee, Paul Legrand, Georges Lorin, Lowenberg, Edouard de Malval, Henri Martin, Baron de Massy, Charles Maurin, George Minne (sculptor), Auguste Monchablon, Auguste de Niederhausern-Rodo (sculptor), Charles-Jean Ogier, Alphonse Osbert, Lord Arthur Payne, Jean-Alexandre Pézieux, Armand Point, Gaetano Previati, Emile Quadrelli, Emile-Paul de Raissiquier, Pierre Rambaud, Richard Ranft, Raybaud, Léopold Ridel, Lensbaron Arild Rosenkrantz, Emmanuel de Sainville, Léopold Savine, Carlos Schwabe, Alexandre Séon, Albert-Gabriel Servat, Léon-Julien Sonnier, J. M. Stepvens, Tonnetti-Dozzi, Jan Toorop, Albert Trachsel, Félix Vallotton, Pierre-Théo Wagner.

Of the artists who exhibited at the first Salon Rose+Croix, Pincus-Witten regards Séon (1855–1917), Osbert (1857–1939), and Armand Point (1861–1932) as most representative of the "hard-core Rosicrucian style,"[18] but I doubt if he would object if we added to that hard core Fernand Khnopff (1858–1921), Jean Delville (1867–1953), Jan Toorop (1858–1928), and Émile Bernard (1868–1941), whom he and posterity regard as important artists.

It is not, however, altogether clear what we might mean by a "Rosicrucian artist." The guidelines for entry, though they resisted

Fig. 10.13. Émile Bernard
(1868–1941), self portrait

realism—Péladan had declared the Order's intention to *"ruin Realism"*—were quite broad, from the religious and mystical, to the mythical and the dreamlike, with the overall caveat of idealism, beauty, symbolic and allegorical spiritual value. Perhaps there is simply something particularly graphic and original about the seven named artists above that we, through seeing their works in books dealing with the period or its occult aspects, cannot help linking with Péladan's intended movement. Posterity seems to judge them anyway as being about the best artists of the crop, able to create images of great power, suggestiveness, and distinction from the complex and sometimes ambiguous aims of Péladan: aims that were after all, characterized by a certain aggressive destructiveness, though his armory was intended to be the undeniably beautiful. Here of course we encounter the eye of the beholder, and the strangeness of many of the images, and their occulted subject matter or inspiration, makes it hard for some people to see them as unequivocally beautiful. I expect in time, a few other names than those familiar to us will emerge with a hidden gem or two. Evolution in art is one thing; evolution in taste is another.

The arbiter perhaps should be whether the artists themselves were committed to Rosicrucian spiritual or occult, gnostic principles, and

here it gets very difficult, for not only did Péladan transform the meaning of the word *Rosicrucian* into a broad Catholic aesthetic, but we
also find many other Symbolists who did not exhibit, but who were
moved by the esoteric spiritual currents of the time in different ways
at different times. Paul Sérusier, for example, was spiritually involved
with Christian esotericism and the Rosicrucian traditions, but he did
not wish to associate with Péladan's "brand." Similar remarks apply to
Maurice Denis.

There is nothing dreamy or symbolic about Alexandre Séon's superb
oil portrait of Sâr Joséphin Péladan, now in the Musée de Beaux Arts,
Lyon (see color plate 20). It shows him in a pleated gray robe with wide
sleeves that might last have been aired 400 years earlier, in profile, his
hands gently by his side, attending as it were to some ideal conception
off canvas. It radiates the man's idealized character projection wonderfully and is perfectly representational, full of immediacy and calm,
though co-exhibitor Félix Vallotton found it embarrassing, partly on
account of Péladan's dress. Séon's other works for the Salons tended
to be his disconcerting illustrations for Péladan's novels; they too have
that very curious, slightly off-putting yet intriguing characteristic of the
"Décadence Latine," chimeras abounding.

The Belgian Jean Delville is probably the most directly accessible
"Rosicrucian" artist, arguably because of his almost photographic, or
fantasy-cinema, draftsmanship combined with precise imagery, his
works having since appeared on record sleeves and books of magic. It
is interesting that the almost blazing, magically transfixed face and
electrified red hair of his startling *Portrait of Mrs Stuart Merrill* (1892)
has provided the cover for Jullian's book on Symbolist art *Dreamers of
Decadence,* as well as anthologies of occult poetry. Oddly perhaps his
quite brilliant crimson dip into hellish streams of human lava, *Satan's
Treasures* (1895), which combines magic, mystery, eroticism, and dream,
was used as a very effective record cover for a collection devoted to Satie,
Ravel, Fauré, and Debussy issued in the late '70s. I say "oddly" because
the sleeve notes seemed to be under the impression that these composers
were all somehow Impressionists, when the cover spoke loudly of that
Symbolist Occult Paris I here describe!

Fig. 10.14. (top) Portrait of Joséphin Péladan by Alexandre Séon; (bottom) Alexandre Séon frontispiece for Péladan's novel L'Androgyne

Fig. 10.15. Jean Delville (1867–1953); the artist dressed for Masonry

Delville was certainly Rosicrucian in philosophical outlook, if by that term we imply the mélange of late nineteenth- to twentieth-century neo-Rosicrucianism of the Theosophically imbued strain. A member of the Belgian Group, "Les XX," he split with former colleagues in 1892 over his commitment to Péladan's style of idealism. He then copied Péladan's outlook, from Wagner to the Pre-Raphaelites, to Leonardo with the new Belgian group *Association Pour l'Art.* Delville undoubtedly desired to see the world awaken to the value of esoteric tradition. Under Russian composer Scriabin's influence, he would become a convinced Theosophist, and later a disciple of Krishnamurti. Delville contributed three works to the 1892 Salon, among which *Le symbolization de la chair et de l'esprit (Symbolisation of the Flesh and the Spirit)* is quintessentially Symbolist in feel. It depicts a male figure trying to rise, amid swampy weeds of dark emerald, from the grip of the female figure whose peachlike erotic bottom is prescient of Gustav Klimt's in-your-face "Red Fish" posterior of 1903, though Delville's "flesh" figure has a serpent's tail: all a little obvious, perhaps, and more allegory than symbol with not a little hint of erotic misogyny, or having one's Jesuitic cake and eating it.

Émile Bernard of the Pont-Aven school would grow to resent the attention given exclusively to Gauguin as the latter took certain Pont-Aven sensibilities to the level of fame, while the pioneers languished in relative obscurity, Filiger in particular. Bernard contributed to the first Salon, *Christ Carrying the Cross,* an *Annunciation,* and *Christ in the Garden of Olives,* works displaying a folkloric style, curved contours, and flattened perspectives, all informed by deep feeling. The designs would have made outstanding medieval friezes and tiles.

Like Bernard, part Dutchman, part Javanese Jan Toorop (1858–1928), born in Java's Poerworedjo, promoted respect for the work of van Gogh, an effort assisted by his being chosen president of the First Section (Fine Arts) of the *Haagsche Kunstring* in December 1891. In 1884 Toorop had journeyed to London with Symbolist poet Émile Verhaeren (1855–1916), there to be influenced by the Pre-Raphaelites and charmed by William Morris's art and socialism, as was Rops. Returning to Paris, Toorop met Péladan and Redon.

Fig. 10.16. Jan Toorop (1858–1928),
photograph by Willem Witsen

Inspired by mystical Theosophy, magic, fantasy, and religious ideals, Toorop hoped to make the *Haagsche Kunstring* a focal point for promoting *Nieuw Kunst,* the Dutch equivalent of Symbolist-dominated art nouveau or the Austrian *Jugendstil.* Familiar with Khnopff, Ensor, and other Symbolists, Toorop organized an exhibition of *Les XX* and the split-off *Association pour l'Art* in July–August 1892, the latter in association with Jean Delville. Péladan would come with Paul Verlaine to address the new Dutch and Belgian artists in November. Toorop contributed two works to the *Salon Rose-Croix* in March 1892 (nos. 175–76: *l'Hétaire* and *Une generation nouvelle*), and began work on his remarkable *The Three Brides,* highly influenced by Péladan's blend of Catholicism and Rosicrucian alchemy, and painted in a unique angular style, blended with art nouveau arabesques and symbolic figures sacred and profane, influenced by Javanese puppetry and spirit forms. Toorop became a Roman Catholic in 1905.

Alphonse Osbert's phenomenal, and very large, portrait—or vision—of Saint Geneviève, called simply *Vision* (see color plate 33),

Fig. 10.17. Paul Verlaine in the Café François in 1892,
photograph by Paul Marsan Dornac

could be the gateway to the aesthetic that emerged from the first Salon and that can still communicate with us its compelling yet simultaneously repulsive force. *Vision* was, however, not quite ready for the first R+C+C+ Salon, which had to be content with Osbert's *Hymne à la Mer,* a work touched by the spaced mystery of Puvis de Chavannes, but considerably warmer. In a golden light, more dawn than dusk, a nymph with a lyre holds her hand out toward the lapping waves, touching the air, casting a spell of her longing, sung for the infinite, the sublime, the eternal. She is like a column, dignified, the pleats of her Grecian dress like flutes of a votive pillar. The painting could be an illustration of the first verse of Rimbaud's unforgettable proto-Symbolist poem *L'Eternité* (1872):

> Elle est retrouvée.
> Quoi?—L'Eternité.
> C'est la mer allée
> Avec le soleil.
>
> *She* [or "it"] *was found again.*
> *What?—Eternity.*
> *It's the sea gone*
> *With the sun.*

Osbert was an associate of the *Salon des Indépendants,* from among whose number several contributed to Péladan's dream: Bernard, Filiger, and Séon. Osbert has been called one of the "Nostalgiques" by *Indépendant* historian Gustave Coquiot, along with the Swiss Albert Trachsel who exhibited at Durand-Ruel's sole excursion into the Rose+Croix aesthetic in 1892. Osbert borrowed a pointillist technique from his recently deceased friend Georges Seurat, who in his last days allegedly regretted departing from symbolist poetics for more realistic subjects, ironically blaming J.-K. Huysmans for the fatal transmission, while Huysmans himself had made the reverse conversion to symbolist-decadent modes, resulting in full Catholic conversion. When the critic Fagus criticized Osbert's work as being literary, Osbert defended Idealism: "art lives only by harmonies . . . it must be

the evocator of the mystery, a solitary repose in life, a kin to prayers
. . . in silence. The silence which contains all harmonies . . . art is
therefore, necessarily literary, according to the nature of the emotions
experienced."[19]

Nostalgia is a clear characteristic of the works displayed: nostalgia not
only for times past of idealism, romance, spiritual mystery, classicism,
the antique, but also personal nostalgia for moments when touched
inwardly by the elusive Absolute, and perhaps above all, that peculiarly
gnostic nostalgia for spiritual home, somewhere to fly to, not of this
world. But the yearning for that which is just out of touch, or even
remote, inaccessible, can make one feel rather sick as well as painfully
comforted by the hint of a presence with its glint of fugitive hope. Is
there not something a little sickly in Khnopff's chimeras? Perhaps it
was a quality within his sister's face when juxtaposed with chimeras
and the fatal stillness of the compositions. She appears time and again
in Khnopff's works, and probably in the *Sphinx* he provided for the
1892 Salon. His art, even when bathed in unearthly quietude, seems to
presage some oncoming catastrophe, like electric air and amber light as
birds stop singing before a storm, for which all the artistic evidence from
the late antique and Byzantine worlds testifies: the crumbled empires,
whose art, once loved in function now sits clean on museum pedestals
or mildewed as garden ornaments. The world in which the winged head
of the god really meant something has been destroyed: its testimony
mute as a stringless lyre. If its spirits would speak, it would be in the
darkness of a séance *chez* Lady Caithness. There is an enormous tension
in the best works of the Rose-Croix Salon; the shadows are advancing.
Péladan himself was aware that the effort might constitute as much a
last stand before barbarism smashed the decadent banquet as the dawn
of an Age of the Grail. Those who hated the aesthetic dismissed it as
superficial in its mystical objectives and as unwholesome in its forms,
the peril of youthful indulgence in *introspection*. Péladan hated the
army, which contempt he transformed into a valuable aesthetic rule: a
"patriotic" painting does not have to be a military subject, but rather a
very good painting that gives credit to its place of origin.

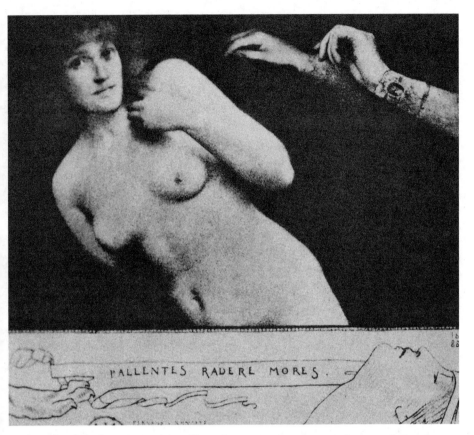

PALLENTES RADERE MORES.

Fig. 10.18. Fernand Khnopff's Pallentes Radere Mores *(Immoral People Turn Pale under the Lash of Satire), frontispiece to Joséphin Péladan's* Femmes Honnettes! *(Honest Women!)*

Perhaps one of the most direct statements of the value of the 1892 Salon's approach to painting came from one whose work was exhibited there, Swiss painter and Nabi, Félix Vallotton (1865–1925). Vallotton entered the Salon with a heavy, skeptical heart, writing that: "Not much good is to be expected from Péladan and his crusade. The Sâr already has amply proved that he only knows how to be dangerous to the causes he represents."[20] The experience of the Salon transformed Vallotton's perception of Péladan:

Instead of the anticipated mystification, the open-minded visitor was astonished to find a well-arranged hall, nicely composed, wherein

very good work appeared with dignity with no other showing-off
. . . a breath of youth and life, so that, whether one wanted to or
not, sympathy was won; all the works shown, even beginners' works,
denoted audaciousness and sincerity. The air that one breathed on
entering there bore witness to so much faith and loyal effort that we
were impressed as by a bravura melody.

One can be utterly indifferent to the Sâr, the sweet inoffensive
Sâr, for his manias, for his costumes, and his ridiculousness, but
after the smiles one nevertheless owes him a debt of gratitude for
having put before the public the chance of judging so much valiant
and tangible work.[21]

Vallotton seemed to recognize there were two Péladans. This anyway
was the conclusion of Paul Verlaine who would travel with Péladan to
Bruges, Ghent, Antwerp, and Louvain in November 1892, as Péladan
evangelized the Rose+Croix cause to enthusiastic Dutch and Belgian
artistic idealists. Verlaine appreciated the man of profound talent, but
distinguished him from the doubtless sincere but overbearing "sec-
tary" that delighted in being regarded as Sâr and Magus. This distinction has, interestingly, been made of Aleister Crowley, who with
hindsight, seems to have been in some respects a curiously English
replacement for the declining Sâr of the Edwardian era. In short,
Péladan's error may be seen as his having demanded, rather than commanded attention. Such was his own assessment of his personal failure as the 1890s drew to an end, though as with so many things, time
will tell.

Whether it was a result of La Rochefoucauld's getting tired of the
Péladan self-promotion or some deeper cause, we cannot be sure, but
the unhappy rift that opened up between the two men before the first
Salon was over would reflect badly on Péladan. When a man's friends
leave him, what have the enemies left to prove?

The obvious causes of the rift came out of organizational differences, chiefly with regard to the soirées that began on 17 March and
that Péladan had planned with great care, even to the extent of forming

La Rivière

Fig. 10.19. Alexandre Séon's La Rivière, *clearly influenced by Puvis de Chavannes, from the 1892 Salon Rose-Croix catalog*

his own theatrical company to add a Wagnerian totality and synthetic sparkle to the proceedings. For the Salon was intended as a complete artistic gesture: in paint, in music, and in dramatic word, for the three combined opened the path to the reintegrated spirit.

However, as we have noted, there had developed a kind of ideological rift as well. The Commanders all realized that the Symbolism reflected in the Salon had two main schools. First there was a kind of "impressionistic" symbolism, nature-sensitive, obviously religious, almost pietistic, favored by the Nabis; then there was what was recognized as a kind of "English" Symbolism, or more particularly, a classical kind.

The latter reflected enthusiasm for Puvis de Chavannes, Gustave Moreau, Leonardo, and of course the Pre-Raphaelites. The "Archonte," La Rochefoucauld, who would support the struggling Pont-Aven artist

Fig. 10.20. La Prière *by Charles Filiger (1863–1928)*

Charles Filiger with a stipend in gold *Louis,* was personally committed to the Nabis, and obviously asked himself why he did not favor
them alone. When the "classicists" seemed to dominate the argument,
he was upset.

Another cause for annoyance was that the Gallery had been leased
in La Rochefoucauld's name, meaning he had legal rights to direct the
Salon artistically. He did not have to submit to the "Grand Master," and
as an aristocrat from a distinguished family, he of course would never
have taken the Order hierarchy any more seriously than he had to. If he
had to pay, it would be for all that he believed in, or not at all.

Things began to get seriously out of hand when the Archonte
became fully aware of the costs of the musical soirées, which he was
expected to pay alone.

The *Soirées de la Rose-Croix* opened on Thursday 17 March, with
seats for 200 at a price of twenty francs. According to the program,
first the audience would be entertained by a performance of Palestrina's
Mass of Pope Marcello, sung a cappella by forty voices, to be followed by

Fig. 10.21. Judith Gautier
(1845–1917)

a speech in praise of Palestrina by the "SÂR," after which a fragment of the one-act opera *La Sonate du Clair de Lune* (libretto by Judith Gautier) would be sung by the composer of its music, Benedictus. Judith Gautier (1845–1917), Théophile Gautier's daughter and estranged wife of Catulle Mendès, enjoyed a long-running relationship with Dutch composer Ludwig (Louis) Benedictus (1850–1921).

Judith was a friend of Wagner while her partner Benedictus had successfully conducted Wagner's music in Paris in 1882 and 1889. The opera featured Beethoven as its hero. The climax of the evening would be Péladan's own play *Le Fils des Étoiles* (The Son of the Stars), a "Kaldaean Wagnérie" ("Kaldaean" meaning of the culture of the Chaldaean Magi of ancient Babylonia). The three acts of this play would be accompanied by "an harmonic suite" by Erik Satie.

Péladan was apparently so proud that his play had been turned down by Jules Claretie of the *Comédie Française* on 3 March that he printed Claretie's amiable rejection letter in the program for all to see. La Rochefoucauld obviously saw this curious demonstration in different terms when the actual performance attracted bad notices. The Archonte refused to pay the large sum required for the billed repeat performances of the play and musical score on the second soirée of 21 March and what would have been the fourth soirée (undated on the program).

Furthermore, for some unknown reason, perhaps due to the perceived adulterous relationship of Judith Gautier and Benedictus, La Rochefoucauld refused to have conductor-singer Benedictus involved at all. The first night did not feature the Gautier-Benedictus opera fragment. Clearly, this high-handed override is where the aristocrat's legal status as artistic dictator really got Péladan's goat, for the Sâr was forced into having Benedictus smuggled into the now rescheduled second soirée and announced as "our Capelmeister," a title he had already given to Erik Satie in an inscribed copy of one of Péladan's *Salon* reviews. Péladan was faced with the unpleasant news that the third night, dedicated to Wagner, had, a week before the performance, been taken out of Benedictus's hands and given by La Rochefoucauld to the famous conductor, Charles Lamoureux. It was rescheduled for 5 April.[22] The Count tried to assure Péladan that Benedictus had left of his own free will. Péladan was understandably beside himself and declared La Rochefoucauld "anathema," excommunicating him from the Order before starting legal proceedings.

On the night of the Wagner concert, what appeared to be a bearded man entered the gallery during the "Siegfried Idyll," asking for Commander Larmandie, but Péladan had ordered Larmandie "to retire immediately and definitively from Durand-Ruel, treacherously rented in the name of La Rochefoucauld."[23] Catching sight of the count, the bearded man began showering him with insults: "La Rochefoucauld, you are a felon, a coward, a thief."[24] A scuffle ensued, with the bearded man being thrust through a glass door that shattered, bringing the orchestra to a standstill, whereupon the audience stood up and an attempt was made to arrest the instigator of the fracas. In the mêlée, the man's beard got pulled off, revealing a Magnifique of the Order. It was Commander Gary de Lacroze, and the police took him away, much to the delight of "Willy" (Henry Gauthier-Villars), the *Chat Noir's* "Ouvreuse [Usherette] du Cirque d'Eté," arch-critic of Satie and Péladan, who observed the goings-on with relish. Willy—soon to marry twenty-year-old novelist Colette (author of *Gigi*) in 1893—would continue attacking Satie for over a decade. According to Gauthier-Villars's account, La Rochefoucauld reassured the discomfited audience: "Ladies and Gentlemen, that was a friend that Sir—not Sâr—Péladan sent over to interrupt the performance."[25]

Fig. 10.22. Sidonie-Gabrielle Colette (1873–1954);
in 1893 she married Henry Gauthier-Villars, under
whose name her first four Claudine novels were
published; they separated in 1906, divorced in 1910

Willy was far from the only journalist with an interest in the *Salons Rose-Croix*. For the record, Firmin Javel submitted a well-considered, detailed, and almost entirely approving review of the Salon to *Gil Blas* (11 March 1892), picking out Khnopff, Bonnard, Séon ("very remarkable"), and Henri Martin's tiles for special mention. Anquetin, Brémond, Marcelin Desboutin, Trachtel, and Hodler ("five aged men, almost naked, sitting on a bench and appearing very unhappy, but well ugly") also impressed the critic. Javel also found Émile Bernard's *Christ in the Garden of Olives* and his *Calvary* moving, while works by Chabas, Dathis (*Anaesthetized Sleep*), Point, Aman Jean, Bourdelle, and the La Rochefoucaulds also gripped his attention. Javel found the displayed

Fig. 10.23. This work by Théo Wagner, Désolation, *looks like it could have inspired Munch's more famous* The Scream, *painted the following year (1893)*

sculptures "magisterial," commending the graces of Pézieux, Rambaud, Charpentier, Jean Dampt, Rességuier, and Vallgren. "Nothing there," said the critic, "was banal. There were even works of the first order." He praised for their "imperious or seductive suggestion" Pézieux's *Virgo* and *Virgin and Child,* Rességuier's *Saint John,* Vallgren's *Funerary Urn,* and Dampt's *Virginity* along with the latter's little carved head of a child. Rambaud's *Thought* pleased Javel, as did the "great composition of a beautiful allure," *The Torrent* by M. de Niederhosern, Rodo.

Firmin Javel prefaced his review with a quote from poet and academician François Coppée: "And I have not found this so ridiculous!" Clearly, prejudice against Péladan had suggested it would be otherwise. In the face of beauty, Javel was honest enough to cast aside his preconceptions.

Affiches Parisiennes, April 1892; "Dissolution of Societies" column, dated 24 March:

> Deeds under private signature.
> Order of the Rose+Croix du Temple
> Péladan and La Rochefoucauld
> Annual Salon of aesthetic manifestations
> Seat: 19, rue d'Offémont,[26]

With the breach with La Rochefoucauld, Péladan's dream might have appeared shattered, but Péladan was still ready to live by tooth and claw. He straightened his feathers and took comfort in declaring the *Rose-Croix Catholique* had in Spring 1892 instigated an aesthetic renewal in France of the scale of the Pre-Raphaelite Brotherhood in England.

However, it was not only the count who would be lost to the cause. Erik Satie realized at once that with La Rochefoucauld no longer supporting the Order's official composer, or indeed its aesthetic manifestations, he too must reconsider his position. In June 1893, Satie visited the count. The count sent Satie off to journalist and poet Jules Bois (Henri Antoine Jules-Bois, 1868–1943), soon-to-be editor of monthly review *Le Coeur,* funded for its short life by La Rochefoucauld. Intrigued by the black arts and mysticism in general, Jules Bois would play a considerable part in the next episode to shock Occult Paris.

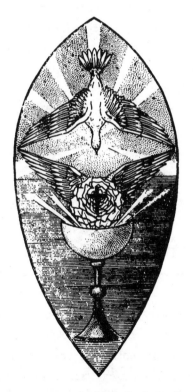

Fig. 10.24. Seal of Péladan's Order of the Rose-Cross, Temple and the Grail

ELEVEN

The Boullan Affair

An announcement appeared in *Le Figaro* 7 January 1893. Antoine-Joseph Boullan was dead: "Boulan [*sic*] was a proud spirit, and as we sometimes find in contentious times, cruelly compromised." He had died in Lyon four days earlier, aged sixty-eight. At that age, no one would have suspected foul play, regardless of Boullan's dark reputation. However, on Monday 9 January, Jules Bois, on page 2 of *Gil Blas,* unequivocally attributed Boullan's death to bewitchment conducted by Rose+Croix magicians, Stanislas de Guaita, Joséphin Péladan, and Oswald Wirth.[1] It should be noted that Péladan's enemy, Léon Bloy also wrote for *Gil Blas* and that the Jules Bois–edited journal *Le Coeur* was funded by La Rochefoucauld.

THE BEWITCHMENT
and
DEATH OF DOCTOR BOULLAN

Decidedly, the mysterious business of poisoning at a distance, or bewitchment in the absence of a better word, which was done in the confusion of the middle ages, has come to be reborn in our practical century, but that the ancient science of the magi illuminates with bloody fires. It is now an incontestable fact, and I believe the proofs carried in this article will leave no doubts about spirits—the abbé Boullan, who came to die suddenly at Lyon, has been hit by invisible illnesses and by criminal hands armed with occult lightnings, by redoubtable and unknown forces.

Having myself spent several days close to the one victimized by hypocritical and unpitying enemies, I feel empowered to pass on here an objective witness and several strange documents.

M.J.K. Huysmans's word of introduction presented me, this same year, to Monsieur Boullan, who having left the priestly robes of the Catholic Church over theological differences with the high clergy, was called by the faithful of his Carmel, Dr. Johannes, a mystic name signifying that the soul of St. John of the apocalypse had been incarnated in him.

L'abbé Boullan was one of the numerous members of Vintras's sect. Vintras has left a controversial and troubling reputation. Prophet perhaps—he claimed to be himself the new incarnation of Elias— medium of sure hand, he levitated before witnesses when he prayed, and crackling sounds manifested in his presence. Untutored, he wrote books of sacred science, complex and incoherent, where, according to Eliphas Lévi's expression, the angel expressed himself in the language of a porter. He professed the sexual act of love, for all people, the most agreeable to God; his doctrine was supported by miracles. When he consecrated, the hosts, before hundreds of stunned eyes, jumped out of the chalice and remained suspended in space; others kept bloody stigmata. They've been preserved in a chapel in Lyon. M. Huysmans, who has seen them, was able to say that despite the blood and the years, they were neither corrupt nor deteriorated.

Abbé Boullan met Vintras, who delegated to him his powers. Inheriting manuscripts of the Prophet, he delayed not in also accomplishing incredible prodigies. He combatted children's diseases, for example, with precious stones and several women— of which one Parisienne most cited in the artistic world—was relieved of a gynaecological sickness—reputed incurable according to the best doctors—by imposition on the ovaries of the consecrated hosts. . . .

I had then a certain hesitation in mounting the tortuous stairs of 7 rue Lamartinière in Lyon, where the thaumaturge lived. I was received by a little old man, lively, eyes aflame, with an inspired face and a pronounced jaw. He put me at my ease straightaway and we chatted with Madame Thibault the clairvoyant and Monsieur Misme, architect and disciple of the "Father."

—You've done well to come, said

Johannes to me, infamous calumnies are accounted against me; they suppose me a black magician: the *Rose-Croix* of Paris, Stanislas de Guaita and Péladan make all this noise. But you will leave Lyon with a clear conscience.

(That which I report now, I can, on my honour, certify it textually, with the attestation of those present: Monsieur Misme and Mme. Thibault.)

"The Parisian occultists, Guaita particularly, came here to seize the secrets of my powers. Guaita even got on his knees before Mme. Thibault and conjured her to give him her benediction: "I am but a child who desires to learn," he cried. For more than fifteen days we treated him as one of the family. Once he departed with a manuscript of the "Sacrifice," the magical book *par excellence,* I awoke with heart pains. Mme. Thibault, in whose home I was, said to me: "It's Guaita." I cried: "I am dead." After her care I was able to get dressed and take myself to the altar. . . ."

—Then Boullan got up and pulled aside the curtain of the alcove where in a simple edifice, in wood, where burnt a nightlight. . . .

"It took all my strength to get to the altar, I intoned the Sacrifice of Glory which confounds the complicity of evil doers, I prayed to the spe-

cial saints and, renewed, went back to bed and slept. . . .

"Guaita himself, biting the hand that fed him, made me know that he had wanted to exercise against me the power that I had granted to him.

"Now I know that he is responsible for all the pains. Beings have disappeared, struck dead by this black magician. And his hatred I believe is so much stronger against me, that only by my sacrifices, me and the director of the *Tromba Apocalyptica* of Rome, can their plots be reversed. When Monsieur Huysmans came here, he assisted with a struggle at a distance, from which I know he has carried away the most tragic memory. Mme. Thibault assisted by clairvoyance sending back blows from Lyon to Paris (Wird [Wirth], Guaita, Péladan had decided to make me die). The host at hand, I invoked the great archangels so they would pulverize the "workers of iniquity."

Strangled cries made me turn my head.

—"Be not astonished," replied Boullan, "these are the birds who carry messages from heaven. They observe the neighborhood and by their rumors, they inform us of our enemies' projects."

I visited the house. It is very simple, a little stuffed with religious nicknacks, but not feeling the least like the world of a sorcerer. Mme. Thibault, a peasant with the look of an eagle, village-like in speech, has only eaten bread and milk for years, goes on pilgrimages on foot very far, and only has to raise her pupils over her glasses to perceive the legions of the invisible; as for M. Misme, an excellent old man, preoccupied with finding again the elixir of Paracelsus.

I left the house, charmed by their hospitality freely offered; and the good laughter of Boullan rang long in my ears.

. . . When I learned of his death today and the suspicions over the acts of the *Roses-Croix,* I ran to the house of Mr J.K. Huysmans.

—You come at the right time, he said to me, and you are going to have the only authentic documents. Boullan died on the 4th. Here is the *Depêche* from M. Misme, and here the last letter from Boullan, note well here, dated the 2nd, the day before the eve, and of the 3rd, the eve of his death. It throws a strange light on this event:

> *Quis est deus.*
> Lyon, 2 January 1893.
My dear friend J.K. Huysmans,
We have received with joy your letter where you send your new-year souvenirs. It was opened under sad presentiments, this fateful year; 8-9-3, figures which together form terrible announcements.

. . .

3 January—My letter was there yesterday evening, to await that of dear Mme. Thibault. But this evening a terrible accident had taken place. At 3 a.m., I awoke suffocating and twice cried to Mme. Thibault "I'm suffocating." She heard, and when she got to me, I was unconscious. From 3 to half past, I was between life and death.

At Saint-Maximin, Mme. Thibault had dreamt of Guaita and in the morning, a bird of death had cried. It announced this attack. M. Misme had dreamed the same. At 4 I was able to sleep again, the danger had disappeared.

DR J.A. BOULLAN

Huysmans resumes:

"As for his agony, as related by Mme. Thibault in a letter addressed to me, with all her naive emotion; just take that concerning the moment when we lost the doctor.

. . . After having drunk a cup of tea, he improved. I relit the fire, warmed a shirt which he put on and returned to his normal state. He got up as usual and wrote his article for *La Lumière* [Spiritualist journal] that Mme. Lucie Grange [its editor] had asked of him, then a letter to a friend, he wanted to take to the post himself. I disapproved and said it was too cold for him.

Dinnertime came, he sat at table and dined well, very gay, even making his daily visit to the dames G . . . and when he returned, he asked me if I would be priest for the prayer; we came to pray. After a few minutes he felt ill at ease, he gasped and said: "What's that?" In saying that, he collapsed on himself. M. Misme and I only had time to pick him up and put him on his armchair, where he could rest during the prayer that I shortened to be able to get him quickly to bed.

His chest had become more oppressed, breathing more strained; in the midst of his struggles he had a sickness of faith and of heart . . . He said to me: "I am going to die. Adieu." I said to him: "But father, you're not going to die; you've got to write your book." He was happy that I said that . . . He requested "water of salvation." After having gulped, he said to us: "That's what saves me." I scare myself too much, we have many times been at the gates of death and recovered a few hours after. I believed it would pass. He spoke to

us up to the last moment of the crisis . . . I said to him: "Father, how do you find yourself?" He sent his last look of adieu, unable to speak. He entered an agony that lasted two minutes . . .

He died a saint and martyr, all his life had only been testing and suffering for the 16 years and more I knew him.

. . .

I expected a sad dénouement from all the writings he compiled for himself and for others. It didn't surprise me. I believe he had fulfilled his task. His death had been shown me for more than six years and at the moment when I was going to take the train to Saint-Maximin to leave the Saintes-Maries, a bird came and made several cries. It wasn't day. It was 6 a.m. I said loudly before several people: "Oh my God! The bird announces a death to me." And I felt it was the poor Father's. I suppressed this inspiration, I didn't expect it would happen five days after my return to Lyon."

—These letters have a secret language, resumed the author of *Là Bas*. I was at Lyon, when one of the letters of the *Roses-Croix* was sent, condemning to death by fluids the one who came to die; one of several saved by Mme. Thibault.

"What I can tell you for my part,

is that Péladan, this display from the Midi, has tried everything against me, before and above all after my novel *Là Bas*. All honest people have been on my side when I unveiled the satanic activities of the Roses-Croix of Paris; but the black magicians beat my skull every night with the blows of fluidic punches; even my cat is tormented, it matters little to me, I'm not scared of them. An evening journal, by a madrigal, advised me that, my magical protector being dead, I risked much now to pass there, but they are assured that my true, my unique shield, beyond their powers, is the saintliness of Mme. Thibault."

I believe that in relating Boullan's strange presentiment, and the prophetic visions of Mme. Thibault and of Monsieur Misme, I present only the facts. The facts indisputably accuse the Roses-Croix Wird, Péladan and Guaita of attacking the man who died.

I am assured that Monsieur the marquess of Guaita lives alone and savagely, that he has manufactured (it must be said) poisons with a great science and most marvelous skill, that he volatizes them and directs them into space, that he has even— M. Paul Adam, M. Edouard Dubus, M. Gary de Lacroze have seen it—a familiar spirit at his home locked in a cupboard and which becomes visible at his command.

What I demand without incriminating whoever, is that someone clarifies the cause of this death. The liver and the heart where Boullan was struck, here are the points where astral forces penetrate.

Now illustrious savants like Messieurs Charcot, Luys, and, particularly, de Rochas recognize the power of bewitchments—should anyone defy their role in furious homicides— I demand the truth. I want explanations as much as Messieurs Joséphin Péladan, Stanislas de Guaita, and Oswald Wird must want them, to alleviate their consciences!

JULES BOIS

The mixture of fact and fiction in Bois's accusations may partly be laid at the door of their chief source, novelist J.-K. Huysmans, whose character "Dr. Johannès" in his 1891 Satanic shocker *Là Bas* was based on personal acquaintance with Boullan. The novel gives a cleaned-up propaganda version of Boullan that suggests how well Boullan had been able to con Huysmans from the start, who wanted to believe in the weird defrocked priest. Boullan's sex-magical rites, fecal "cures," "exorcisms," and abuse of hypnotic speech were all couched in the language of "love." Huysmans never wanted to see the doctor in any other terms than those of the misunderstood prophet, and as such presented him in the form of "Dr. Johannès" in his novel. Since Boullan proclaimed himself "Jean Baptiste" (John the Baptist), preparing the way of the Holy Paraclete, Huysman's "Johannès" was an effective endorsement of Boullan, and Boullan wisely kept close to his celebrated propagandist, while at the same time furnishing him with many details of Satanic practices that gave *Là Bas* its chilling authenticity. This is how the character Des Hermies describes the doctor in *Là Bas:*

> He is a very intelligent and learned priest. He was a community superior and in Paris ran the only truly mystical review. He was also a consulting theologian, an acknowledged master of divine jurisprudence; then he had distressing debates with the Curia of the Pope in Rome and with the Cardinal Archbishop of Paris. His exorcisms and struggles against the incubus he fought in the nunneries lost him his case.

Huysmans even gives a remarkably cleaned-up version of Boullan's "Sacrifice of the Glory of Melchisedek" in chapter 20:

> You are asking more than I can answer. Only Dr. Johannès could tell you. This much I can say. Theology teaches us that the mass, as it is celebrated, is the re-enacting of the Sacrifice of Calvary, but the sacrifice to the glory of Melchisedek is not that. It is, in some sort, the future mass, the glorious office which will be known during the earthly reign of the divine Paraclete. This sacrifice is offered to God by man regenerated, redeemed by the infusion of the Love of the Holy Ghost. Now, the hominal being whose heart has thus been purified and sanctified is invincible, and the enchantments of hell cannot prevail against him if he makes use of this sacrifice to dissipate the Spirits of Evil. That explains to you the potency of Dr. Johannès, whose heart unites, in this ceremony, with the divine heart of Jesus.

Fig. 11.1. Portrait of Joris-Karl Huysmans (1898) by Félix Vallotton (1865–1925), innovator of the modern woodcut and associate of the Nabis

Huysmans had an extremely active and deeply troubled imagination, a point made cleverly in an open letter addressed to him from "M[onsieur] Le'H" on page one of the next day's issue of *Gil Blas* and that called for "miracles in the editorial department," presumably to render trashy articles like that of Bois, invisible. Furthermore, if Jules Bois intended keeping in with Count Antoine de La Rochefoucauld, he needed no reminding that Péladan was *persona non grata*.

The 10 January issue of *Gil Blas* carried a never-before-reproduced letter addressed to the paper's director from de Guaita's friend Edouard Dubus, whose name Bois had also linked to the accusation of death by bewitchment:

Paris 8 January 1893
Monsieur,
I should be obliged to you for inserting in your journal the following explanations:

In the course of Jules Bois's article which appeared this morning in *Gil Blas*, I read: . . . [there follows the account of the familiar spirit kept in a cupboard witnessed allegedly by Dubus and others]. I hold to the affirmation that no one could invoke, without error or abuse, me as a witness to representing M. De Guaita as a practitioner of sorcery.

I have said, it is true, that I have seen at his home an apparition; but have never given to hear that he had anything in common with a "familiar spirit," as entertained by M. Jules Bois.

The house inhabited by M. De Guaita is haunted, as are others: this being the only permissible conclusion legitimately to be made from my account. I only wish it to be established that none of my words have been exactly reported, nor can serve to incriminate an occultist, whose education, books, acts, are, to my knowledge, absolutely hostile to that black magic his enemies impute to him—and the persons of good faith that they have had the license to circumvent.

Please accept, monsieur, the expression of my most distinguished sentiments,
EDOUARD DUBUS
7, rue de Trésor.

Picking up on the immediate journalistic value of Bois's accusation, Horace Blanchon of *Le Figaro* interviewed Huysmans and Bois. Under the headline "BEWITCHMENT" on page 2, Huysmans substantiated the story that the Rosicrucians had a hand in Boullan's death. "It is indisputable," Bois claimed, speaking to Blanchon with Huysmans, "that de Guaita and Péladan daily practice black magic. This poor Boullan was in perpetual struggle with evil spirits which went on incurably for two years, sent to him from Paris. Nothing is more imprecise than these questions of magic; but it is completely possible that my poor friend Boullan had succumbed to a supreme bewitchment."[2] Huysmans then added that he was "certain" de Guaita and Péladan were giving him cerebral pains by magic. Huysmans seemed unaware the two magi had not been in contact with one another since 1891. Nevertheless, Huysmans insisted that the pains had doubled since Boullan's death and that the proof that "the extreme sensibility" of his nervous system was being disrupted by magic was that his cat, at the same time, suffered like symptoms, and were it not for Mme. Thibault, the "dignified lady" he had met at Boullan's home, he should be worse afflicted as she had managed by her efforts to thwart earlier fluidic attacks. The article further stated that "the master romancier" Huysmans claimed to have been suffering from "fluidic" oppression in his head for more than a year, which Blanchon attributed to the magic, not of de Guaita, but of the author of *Le Vice Suprême*. The article described the means of bewitchment, the

Fig. 11.2. Huysmans and Bois: friends

making of an image of the victim, linked to a personal item from the victim, onto which is concentrated the will of the sorcerer to hurt the victim without, says Blanchon, hurting the perpetrator, so long as protected by Kabbalistic formula. Blanchon writes that there is, however, no guarantee of impunity, before adding that he got his information from chapter 43 of Péladan's first novel!

Interestingly, Blanchon comments that Bois, obsessed with mysticism, and Huysmans's experience demonstrates "better than any commentary" how the allegedly most "advanced" literary school has moved a hundred leagues from the materialism and naturalism from which it was born. Blanchon reckoned Huysmans's recitation was most reminiscent of a mystification in the style of Baudelaire. "And we all believed we were living in the century of incredulity and skepticism!"[3]

Blanchon's wry article goes on to give an account of paranormal researcher Col. Albert de Rochas's and hypnosis expert Dr. Luys's scientific experiments into attempting to reproduce "bewitchment," as well as London's Dr. Hart, whose experiments appeared in the *Pall Mall Gazette*. Blanchon concludes that science seems to exonerate Sâr Péladan of bewitching powers of the kind imputed by Huysmans, for were such counter-scientific powers available to the discretion of individuals in the city, Messieurs Andrieux and Delahaye might not last long! The latter reference puts us in the political frame of early 1893, in that Delahaye was a Boulangist deputy who got the government to set up a commission of inquiry into the "Panama scandal" that revealed massive corruption around bonds issued for the Panama Canal Company, which had gone bust, implicating members of the government. In all the papers dealing with the Boullan affair (a minor matter), the word *Panama* occurs very frequently; it was the main scandal of the time.

The chief suspect was Léopold Émile Arton who fled France. MP and former prefect of police for Paris Louis Andrieux was also caught up in the scandal. Blanchon's commonsense approach holds well today. That is, if bewitchment were possible at a distance, those very powerful figures fearful of exposure for corruption in the event of Arton's papers being recovered, would undoubtedly find means to employ it against those whose insider knowledge could unmask the corrupt, compromise the government, and destroy fortunes and high-flying careers! From the editorial perspective then, the Boullan story was simply providing light relief and contrasting intrigue to the heaviness of the ongoing Panama scandal, while enjoying another dig at unworldly Symbolists and occultists.

As for the "magic" sent in Boullan's direction from the R+C+K, it was most likely de Guaita's and Oswald Wirth's belief in particular that Boullan and Julie Thibault were hoodwinking followers with unclean rites binding them to the "healer" and "Father" whose unassuming lair still overlooks the pleasant rue Lamartinière, close to the Rhône in the city of Lyon. The only "fluids" coming from Paris were de Guaita's words inked up and publicized quite openly in the pages of *L'Initiation*.

The review's June 1891 issue had introduced readers to de Guaita's latest book, *Le Temple du Satan* (The Temple of Satan). There they could learn for the first time that on 23 May 1887, after de Guaita had compared his experiences of Boullan with the deeper enquiries of Oswald Wirth, de Guaita's R+C+K tribunal had condemned Boullan for perversions of magic and profanations of the sacred. This being the case, it was extraordinarily unlikely that black magic would have been used to combat the same, for the simple reason that a black magical act by definition requires the cooperation of forces hostile to Christ. If Christ can overcome evil spirits, then the cross, a prayer to "deliver us from evil," and a bold witnessing to the truth should suffice, unless that is, de Guaita believed he and his friends were themselves being subjected to sorcery by Boullan. In that case, they may have resorted to traditional magical measures of spiritual defense. But this is all unnecessary conjecture. Huysmans's testimony, along with its echo in the publicity zeal of Jules Bois, was demonstrably suspect from the start.

Furthermore, it would appear from de Guaita's amusing article in the July 1891 issue of *L'Initiation* "Un Sorcier contemporain" (A Contemporary Sorcerer, p. 61) that de Guaita had, anyhow, scant respect for Boullan's actual magical abilities. In the article, he sarcastically ridicules Boullan's pretenses and weaknesses openly, using Boullan's prophetic name "Jean Baptiste," describing Boullan's attempt to inveigle himself in 1886 into the confidence of a leading lady Theosophist of Paris—possibly Lady Caithness or Mme. Blavatsky, staying at Lady Caithness's home—after having previously inveigled himself into Vintras's confidence, until Vintras's death in 1875, whereafter Boullan had taken over a portion of Vintras's followers. Was it not obvious that Vintras, the self-proclaimed "Elias," would be followed by the one Elias prophesied? Such seems to have been the basis of Boullan's attempt to shore up his position in that part of the "Carmel" community loyal to him. So, it was as Jean-Baptiste that Boullan went to Paris to meet the rich lady, claiming he could heal her of a longstanding disorder, employing his magical "hosts" or other means. De Guaita related how the lady, forewarned—possibly by Canon Roca who would vainly advise Huysmans not to meet Boullan in person—would not see Boullan until he had first submitted to an interview by her guest, a Brahmin adept. The highly educated Brahmin put Boullan through his paces, quickly unveiling the crude nature of the man's knowledge. Declaring Boullan a "cretin" and "an imbecile," the Brahmin informed the lady she might see him if she wished as the man had no real occult powers to offer for

Fig. 11.3. Pierre Eugène Michel Vintras
(1807–1875), heretic priest

good or ill. According to the Brahmin, the man was a dabbler in the "left-hand path." Were he ever *really* to make direct contact with infernal powers, he would run scared. He dismissed Boullan as "innocuous," in terms of power, if not of influence.

De Guaita was clearly unafraid of Boullan, but Boullan had something to fear from de Guaita. Publicity emanating from de Guaita and R+C+K's virtual "house-magazine" *L'Initiation* damaged his following real or potential and ongoing attempts to habilitate himself as a respectable healer, through means such as articles in Lucie Grange's review *La Lumière*. Knowing himself to be up against a group, what else could he, "the victim," do but innocently appeal to his dear, good correspondent, Huysmans, who had used Boullan's knowledge of Satanism so profitably, and whose integrity was doubtless compromised by de Guaita's publicity against his friend, Boullan?

Furthermore, Huysmans himself had reason to feel personally irritated, embittered, or even threatened, by material appearing in the pages of *L'Initiation*. The April 1891 issue (p. 113) contained Papus's

Fig. 11.4. Stanislas de Guaita

long review of Huysmans's novel *Là Bas*. Commenting on an article about the novel in *l'Écho de Paris,* Papus stated plainly that Huysmans had been misled: "The article's author claimed that the character of Canon Docre [in the novel] would have been furnished to Monsieur Huysmans by a defrocked priest from Lyon, l'abbé B, directing a "carmel" [Vintrasian church] down there." Huysmans replied in *l'Écho de Paris* that Docre was in fact based on a priest of Bruges and that the abbé B corresponded to the good Doctor Johannès in whose company Huysmans had spent "several months." The review *L'Éclair* took issue with Huysmans's reply with documentation proving Huysmans was mistaken about l'abbé B. According to Papus, the documentation was "no doubt supplied by one of our most brilliant editors." That brilliant editor, doubtless, was Stanislas de Guaita! And just to add a bit of background color to the story, the same issue of *L'Initiation* that carried Papus's review also noted that the February 1891 issue of spiritist review *Lumière*—to which Boullan contributed—contained its editor Mme. Lucie Grange's accusation that Lady Caithness, Duchess of Pomar, had plagiarized material communicated to the Duchess by Lucie Grange. There were wheels within the wheels of Occult Paris!

It might have been presumed that the Catholic Church in early 1893 could have weighed in with its knowledge and experience of Boullan's dubious career to clarify matters, but that would be to forget that *L'Initiation* was on the Index. The Curia was unlikely to assist de Guaita and his friends; rather, they could, from their own point of view, gloat on the spectacle of the heretics hoisted with their own petard! Huysmans and Bois would have a free hand. The only people who would defend de Guaita had themselves been lumped into the charge. For those who hated the *Roses-Croix,* here was an opportunity to savor.

On 11 January 1893, Jules Bois repeated his main charge in *Gil Blas,* though he denied it was personally motivated: "I hold to affirm that I am not the enemy of M. De Guaita," maintaining that until Boullan's death, he had only ever enjoyed "the most courteous rapport with the magus of the avenue Trudaine." However, it was the duty of "any decent man" in the circumstances, Bois wrote, to affirm that "many times over several years, M. De Guaita had menaced Dr Boullan, who came so mysteriously and suddenly to his death, and that in Boullan's mind there was an obsession that the persecuted one's pain came from these menaces." He then added that on the evening his first article had appeared, J.-K. Huysmans "had been most particularly been afflicted by the fluids." The concept of "fluids" derived from the work of Éliphas Lévi, being the supposed means by which harm could be exercised at a distance by willful evocation.

To the latest accusations, de Guaita replied in *Le Figaro,* denying categorically any exercise of bewitchment. Jules Bois returned to *Gil Blas* on 13 January: "M. de Guaita claims the bewitchments are not his work. *Eh bien,* here is one which is very clearly admitted in his own book *The Serpent of Genesis,* page 477. This bewitchment being the more terrible because it is collective, directed, a long while ago, against Abbé Boullan." He then quoted from de Guaita's text: "From the return of Mr Wirth, examination made of new evidence, the occultists gathered in tribunal of honor, pronounce the condemnation of the doctor Baptiste with unanimous voice (23 May 1889). It was signified to him the next day. . . ."

Bois wanted readers to see the "condemnation," an expression of outrage at Boullan's practices, as an evil spell. On this basis, a court judgment is black magic. Bois imputes the worst motives for any ambiguity:

That M. De Guaita does not say to us that his condemnation was a platonic condemnation [. . .] The inexorable hatred which he had avowed to Dr. Boullan, hatred which he had created as an intense network of menacing fluids in his heart, to Guaita this inexorable hatred closed its grip more and more, like a vice of wrath against the solitary victim. From this condemnation, only one of these conclusions can be drawn: 1. M. De Guaita was joking [. . .] something I do not think habitual to him. 2. M. De Guaita is insensate, condemning someone in the air, without efficacy, without his words having sanction; 3. M. De Guaita wrote in all knowledge of cause and effect, a sentence of which he knew the outcome and which he could direct with disastrous consequences. Condemning Boullan, he was sure, in this case, of executing, of executing this condemnation. And then I leave to readers and to himself, Stanislas de Guaita the care of assessing such cruel conduct.

Seriously riled by Bois's persistent accusations, de Guaita resorted to *Gil Blas* who published the following on 15 January: "For several days now the press peddles malicious gossip about me, ridicule more infamous, in truth, for the ill-wishers or the naive who are lanced by this canard, than for myself." De Guaita wrote that he could no longer ignore the lie that he was devoted to "the most odious sorcery" or that he was Head of an R+C College fervent with Satanism, devoting their energies to the "evocation of the Black Spirit," or that one after another fell victims of their evil works, or that he could himself from a distance slay numerous enemies by bewitchment, "designating me for their assassin." And that was not all. He stood accused of manipulating and dosing the most subtle poisons by infernal art, volatizing them by such means as to project them hundreds of leagues distant, "toxic vapors into the nostrils of those whose face displeases me, I play Gilles de Rais on the threshold of the 20th century; I entertain friendly relations with the redoubtable Canon Docre [the evil canon in *Là Bas*] dear to M. Huysmans; and that finally, I hold as a prisoner in my cupboard a familiar spirit made visible on my order!"

"Is this enough?" asked de Guaita rhetorically. Apparently not! All this nice information is only a preface. Boullan allegedly only succumbed by the combined efforts of the "black confrères of the Brothers of the Rose-Croix." He suggests an autopsy on the defrocked priest so the world could judge for itself the value of Boullan's letters, made public by Huysmans, denouncing him as a magician provoking cardiac arrest in the so-called "King of the Exorcists." "Because it is necessary to say that M. Boullan, whose works and doctrines I unmasked in my last book, with proofs to support the argument, suffered doubly for a long time with ailments of heart and liver. This affliction followed its normal course, with highs and lows. But, with each new attack, our pontiff cried a new bewitchment.

"M. Boullan died: peace on his ashes. . . . The allegations produced in the newspapers, these latter days, would be abominable, if they did not breathe the most intense buffoonery." De Guaita said he most pitied the "authors of these naïve calumnies," since in trying to grab onlookers and alert skeptics, they would only succeed in making them laugh, more at their own expense than at de Guaita's. He had clearly seen the tide indicated in Horace Blachon's article in the *Figaro*.

De Guaita first decided to keep silence in the face of the attacks "from most perfect disdain," believing they were jokes deriving from ill humor that none would credit. However, he observed the stories were even providing a diversion from the great Panama scandal—and might have been so intentioned, journalistically. There was now the possibility of the stories generating menaces that could drag on interminably. His patience had come to an end. Someone had said to de Guaita: "The best persons, in cases like this, give themselves to the meadow [that is the field where duels are held]."[4]

At this first mention of a duel, let us hear the testimony of Victor-Émile Michelet who was personally involved in the proceedings:

Guaita, aghast at being portrayed as an evil sorcerer, sent me along with [Maurice] Barrès, to demand Huysmans's explanation or a recompense by duel. At the same time he sent us to fulfill the same mission with M. Jules Bois, signatory of the interview in question and of several other lively articles written on the occasion. And [de Guaita] also sent me the note below, unedited till today, because before the direction things took, I didn't believe it should be published:

OBSERVATION ON
THE CASE OF MONSIEUR HUYSMANS

All the classics on dueling agree on this point: that when the same offense has been committed by divers individuals against the same person, the offended has the absolute right to choose the adversary from whom he intends to demand reparation. (V. *L'Art du duel*, de Tavernier, pp. 10–11).

M. Jules Bois will also have replied to me with three articles in *Gil Blas;* but I take regarding it first to M. Huysmans who, since publication of his novel *Là Bas,* and after this period, hardly ceased pouring out on occultists in general and on me in particular the most ridiculous calumnies.

He is guilty of the fact of having communicated to M. Bois the text of incredible letters where Boullan the days before and two days before his death was suffering in the heart and liver, accused me of bewitchment, and will demand an explanation for it from M. Huysmans.

Those letters were at the address of M. Huysmans, they have received the publicity of *Gil Blas* from the 9 January; therefore, of two things the one: having fully communicated them, he has done me a grave offense, unless they have been fraudulently taken away from him and he says so.

His rectification in *l'Echo de Paris* of 13 January attenuates nothing, because he only repeats the infamous and absurd accusations. M. Huysmans persists in lancing me with his odious and ridiculous accusation of Satanism, and I consider his allegation a very grave offense, which he must account for.[5]

Michelet went with Barrès to find Huysmans in his office at the Interior Ministry and handed him this letter:

A MONSIEUR J.-K. HUYSMANS   Paris, this 13 January 1893

Monsieur,
Infamous and ridiculous gossips on my account are current in the

Press, and it is you who is yourself in fact their propagator and center.

I demand you account for yourself, not by occult arms with this sorcery you affect to believe in and that I never practice, but properly by sword and hand.

This cartel will be presented by my witnesses to those you make your own.

I have the honor, Monsieur, to greet you,
STANISLAS DE GUAITA[6]

Huysmans greeted Michelet and Barrès as a perfect "galant," appearing deeply put out by the incident. Barrès, with the air of a "chronic boulevardier" or comedian seemed even more put out than Huysmans. According to Michelet: "We were all desirous of an amicable solution, and Huysmans took it all with good grace that honored him. The next day a statement was prepared, based on explanations given by Huysmans to his "witnesses" (or seconds), author Alexis Orsat and Gustave Guiches, novelist and playwright friend of Huysmans and Léon Bloy. Huysmans thus declared to de Guaita's witnesses that he had by no means intended to claim M. Bois's articles as his personal opinion and that he had never deigned to discuss the character of the perfectly gallant man, Stanislas de Guaita. Furthermore, Huysmans declared "that he in no wise hesitates in considering M. De Guaita as absolutely a stranger to the facts which have motivated the polemic on the death of M. Boullan." All four witnesses signed the statement (published in *Gil Blas* 16 January 1893).

On Monday 16 January, *Gil Blas* also published a bizarre turnabout statement from Jules Bois's seconds, Jules Guérin (the paper's editor in chief) and Charles Couïba (alias "Boukay") who with Bois was establishing the La Rochefoucauld–backed review *Le Coeur*. Guérin and Couïba declared that "their friend only intended to convey an appreciation of the philosophical and esoteric order to M. De Guaita, but that these criticisms were not addressed to the character of the perfectly gallant man M. De Guaita and were by no means intended to offend. After these declarations, the four witnesses with common accord, that there was no longer a pretext for an encounter [on the field]."[7] In fact, it wasn't so much a U-turn, it was a question of delicate diplomacy. As Michelet puts it, recounting the episode: "The editing of statements of this type demands a precision and diplomatic subtlety of terms." After reading several drafts, Michelet told Barrès: "I will not sign it." It did not satisfy him. "Barrès turned, his head always raised, with a voice a little barking—*See! Reflect well on what you do. You're going to make us lose our Sunday.* That was because we were there on a Saturday evening. But it was necessary to recommence the foretalk and work to a new formula. Barrès was able to profit from his Sunday. Guaita, who understood that in Barrès the social maneuverer overtook the independent artist, felt painfully his boyhood friend was only accepting involvement in these affairs with displeasure."[8]

That, in fact, was not the end of the affair. Refusing to let the matter rest, in April, Jules Bois attacked de Guaita again in the pages of *L'Evénement* and found himself called to the dueling meadow to face de Guaita, at the Tour de Villebon, south of Versailles. Barrès now backed out as de Guaita's witness and was replaced by anarchist sympathizer and satirical poet Laurent Tailhade, who, according to Michelet "affected to everyone the manners of a gentleman." Tailhade apparently took his duties with great seriousness, and while he was known as an ardent satirist, Michelet noted that in private he was a bravura cavalier of impeccable courtesy. Michelet himself missed the duel as he was abroad when it occurred.

This time, Jules Bois chose as co-witness novelist, journalist, and anticlerical Republican freethinker Paul Foucher (1849–1894), nephew of Victor Hugo. Foucher left an account of strange happenings on the way to the duel.[9] They began with a comment of Jules Bois to Foucher at the moment of leaving for the Tour Villebon: "You will see that something singular will happen." On the way to Versailles, one of the landau's horses halted suddenly, trembled, and reared itself up on its hind legs as if perceiving a demon. They had to change horses. Then, the second horse would not go on. They changed to a *voiture* (covered taxi). The horse leading the second voiture went out of control. The vehicle was turned over. Jules Bois arrived at the field bloody and bruised. Foucher remarked that the devil himself really did seem to have been part of the mêlée!

The two men took pistols. Two balls were fired. Both men left the field unharmed. De Guaita told Michelet later that he held his adversary in esteem on account of his brave conduct on the field. But satisfaction would not be achieved until Bois and de Guaita faced one another later with swords. Skilled in the art, de Guaita wounded Bois in the forearm, whereafter the matter was settled and the two men became friends.

There can be no doubt that de Guaita's assessment of Boullan was correct—and with respect to Boullan's past, not damning enough—and that Huysmans was Boullan's dupe, but nobody came out of the affair well. According to Joanny Bricaud and Mme. Myriam Harry, Huysmans, though a convert to Catholicism in 1892, remained obsessed with Satanism until his death.[10] He must have been a curious Catholic to have gone so far out of his way to support a defrocked, convicted ex-priest in 1893 and to stand by his novel *Là Bas,* so full of heretical notions of the sacraments, attributed to characters he approved of! Then again, Huysmans's conversion has been seen as an aspect of his decadence. He may have suffered more from contact with the mind of Boullan than he knew.

Whilst on the side of the angels, poor de Guaita was doubtless depressed by his brush with public notoriety and the horror of personal exposure and ridicule in the press. He was also hurt by the tarring of his historical work by its being associated, as a detriment, with the flamboyant showmanship of Péladan and the credulity of Huysmans and Jules Bois. Already a near recluse in his apartment on the avenue Trudaine, long since prone to black melancholia, resorting occasionally to opiates and to hashish, overworked and loveless, de Guaita's health and state of mind slowly declined as the R+C+K went to sleep. He had his close friends, such as journalist Edouard Dubus, author of the Symbolist classic *Quand les violins sont partis* (When the Violins Are Gone, 1892), but Dubus would drop dead from morphine addiction in a public lavatory in Paris in 1895. Sick himself, de Guaita would leave Paris for the family home in Alteville, where he died tragically young in 1898, his great work unfinished. After de Guaita's death, Péladan, in a moving dedication to *L'Occulte Catholique* (1899), regretted that it was overscrupulous pride that kept them from making up with one another after their correspondence ceased in 1891: a deadly sin, for sure.

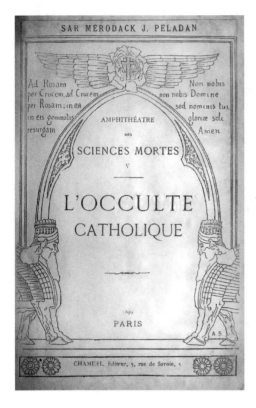

Fig. 11.5. L'Occulte Catholique
(The Occult Catholic), 1899

TO THE MEMORY OF
STANISLAS DE GUAITA

Cher Adelphe,

Thus I called you in the dedication of my third novel, *Sentimental Initiation.*

You had only published Your *Threshold of Mystery,* but I augured that in this path, you were going to march immortally!

". . .The Merodack of the *Supreme Vice,* showed it to you—said I: allow me dear Adelphe ["Brother"], to boast, as of the best glory, to have unveiled in you, the Magus who slept."

Allow me to remember it today, in offering this book to Your memory, tender souvenir of friendship, profound homage: to the Kabbalist. . . .

What vain people, vain things have slowed down, cooled down, apparently extinguished "this thing strong and great" which I

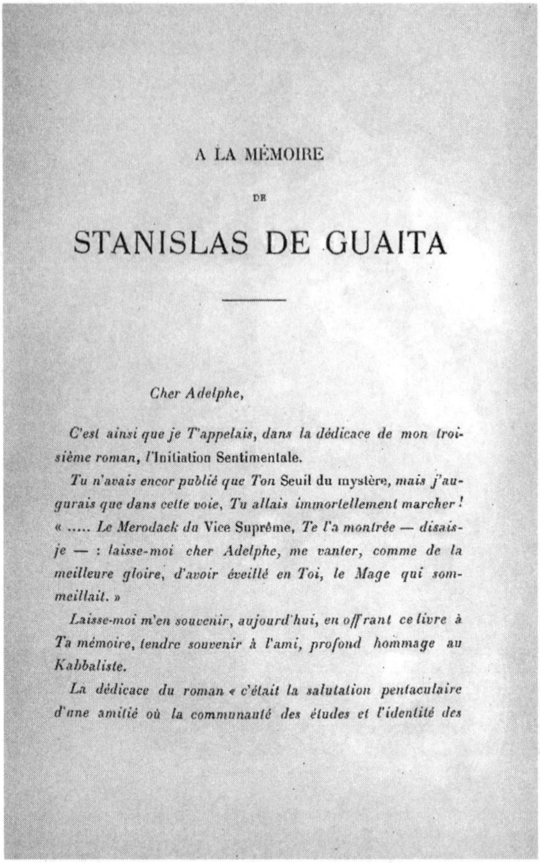

A LA MÉMOIRE

DE

STANISLAS DE GUAITA

Cher Adelphe,

C'est ainsi que je T'appelais, dans la dédicace de mon troisième roman, l'Initiation Sentimentale.

Tu n'avais encor publié que Ton Seuil du mystère, mais j'augurais que dans cette voie, Tu allais immortellement marcher !

« ..... Le Merodack du Vice Suprême, Te l'a montrée — disais-je — : laisse-moi cher Adelphe, me vanter, comme de la meilleure gloire, d'avoir éveillé en Toi, le Mage qui sommeillait. »

Laisse-moi m'en souvenir, aujourd'hui, en offrant ce livre à Ta mémoire, tendre souvenir à l'ami, profond hommage au Kabbaliste.

La dédicace du roman « c'était la salutation pentaculaire d'une amitié où la communauté des études et l'identité des

Fig. 11.6. Péladan's tribute to his old friend Stanislas de Guaita in L'Occulte Catholique, *1893*

proudly bore witness to, our *adelphat?* The several points of doctrine, pretexts that one employed to separate us, were not worth one chat of our friendship.

For You were, a good friend, a noble friend, and Your heart was magnificent, as Your intelligence. To my regret, you have only for company the great Barbey d'Aurevilly and the dear and unhappy Armand Hayem.

To the Renaissance of the dead sciences, Your physiognomy will remain unforgettable, like Your work; You were, for everyone, the gentleman of the Occult.

This is not the place to speak of the distinguished merits of Your work: *The Serpent of Genesis* is one of the monuments of Magic.

I wanted only to write again Your name in my work, because I loved You; and now, I venerate You.

Your premature death has assured all the purification of Your future, and You are, elected, at this hour: I recommend myself again to Your friendship, become celestial, in witnessing that which long united us and which will reunite us, I hope, in eternity.

So be it   SAR PELADAN[11]

TWELVE

SATIE AND DEBUSSY

MOVED BY THE GNOSIS

First came the music.

One boring holiday afternoon—aged fifteen or sixteen—I was trying to lose myself in TV. Finding myself half watching an "Open University" educational program, I was suddenly gripped. It took only a few ascending chords played by the TV lecturer on a piano to rivet me to the spot like Moses before the burning bush. The academic presentation may have been dry, but the content was matchless. Imagination ablaze, I could hardly wait to share the good news with my mother.

Under analysis was Debussy's *La Cathédrale Engloutie* (The Englulfed Cathedral), published in 1910 as the tenth *prélude* of Debussy's first book of twelve. Based on the Breton tale of the lost city of Ys, legend situates Ys in the Bay of Douarnenez, about 50 kilometers northeast of Pont-Aven. The story attributes its disappearance beneath Atlantic waves to its ruler having reverted from Celtic Christianity to lascivious, pagan ways. It may have been Édouard Lalo's opera *Le Roi d'Ys* (The King of Ys), premiered in 1888, that first acquainted Debussy with the legend; perhaps it was one of the Pont-Aven painters. Resonating with Symbolist potential, Ys would also appear in Russian Symbolist Alexander Blok's 1912 verse-drama, *The Rose and the Cross*.

From this legend of Brittany comes the image, or symbol, of a lost cathedral sunk beneath the ocean that at sundry times rises mysteriously to the surface, during which magical epiphanies landlocked

Bretons could hear the bells and chants of Celtic monks of long ago, trapped in time yet somehow able to transcend the constraints of time and space to deliver their plaintive summons before descent into the eternal waves. It is impossible to tell whose grandeur is greatest, the legend or the prelude in which Debussy reflected its power.

The TV lecturer had much to say about pentatonic modes (do re mi sol la), medieval chants, inexact harmonic parallelism (giving mysterious tonality), tempo, and transposition techniques, and the revolutionary character of the music overall. I just loved everything about it. It spoke to something already inside me: a sense of epic, mysterious spiritual renewal, invoking a world the world hardly notices, touching something the world does not see, living beneath the current of common knowledge and temporal events, and that transcends them, weaving through time like a serpent. I knew this profound current was my natural habitat. *What is it?* It is an engulfed cathedral: the symbol says what reason alone cannot.

Soon after this Hierophany, a curious record reached the popular music charts. My mother bought it, realizing that in Debussy we had something we could share, for she had known Debussy's prelude already and kept it to herself, as she did so much. The record was Japanese Moog synthesizer composer Isao Tomita's attempt to express some of Debussy's finest melodies electronically. The editors of *Grammophone* magazine looked down their noses at this way of discovering Debussy, but the music is the music and whether played on a Steinway, or orchestrated by Leopold Stokowski, or extruded through labyrinths of electronic circuitry, it was as clear as day to me that Debussy was in touch with the spiritual sources soon to be identified as gnostic.

Interesting it is how much of Debussy's music was inspired by meditating on the patterns and presence of the sea and of water in general. Leonardo da Vinci was likewise intrigued by the mathematical and geometrical expression of flow structures that energy in apparently amorphous water cannot move without.

In gnostic symbolism, water has a twofold meaning. First, the Primal Father, the unspeakable, unknowable, unnamable *God*—for want of an absent word—is given the moniker, *Bythos,* translated as

"Depth" or "Abyss." The suggestion is linked to the qualities of an infinite ocean, so profound, so deep, so unfathomably dark, who could say what might emerge from it? Conversely, gnostic traditions are inclined to see the material world, always in flux, forever unstable, subject to rot and decay, as essentially aqueous: its forms transient, fleeting, refractive, delusive; its tendency is to overwhelm, to bury, destroy, or drown. Gnostics recognized meaning in stories of Jesus walking on water and commanding waves (as well as particles).

Villiers de l'Isle-Adam once told Catulle Mendès a captivating story of a stone in the Brittany Sea, encrusted with lichen and algae, hidden at the bottom of the ocean, "exiled from all." One day, a very good saint descends into the depths to offer spiritual aid to those who died without unction or were ignored because unseen. Finding the rock, the saint asks it why it is so unmoved by all that goes on about it. The stone replies that its thoughts are directed to the most distant stars in the farthest reaches of the heavens, and when daylight obscures them, he waits for them to light up once more. This gives him the perspective of eternity and then other things don't matter. "A singular way to spend time," sighs

Fig. 12.1. Villiers de l'Isle-Adam:
spiritual mind

the pitying saint: "What is gained by looking at a star?" "Draw back," said the stone, "the lichen and algae which covers me." The man did so and then saw, suddenly, that they covered a diamond whose rays were more luminous than those of the brightest stars in the azure. This diamond, explained Villiers, resembled "the spirit which has left us." It is the "radiant glory of the Ideal." It must be ardent, obstinate, unmovable, so that it may become clear and radiant. We have neglected too long to draw back the lichens and the algae. "But this is death, which, with veiled hand, raises the veils." According to Mendès, Villiers "lived in the dream, by the dream, for the dream. Not for an instant was he unfaithful to the star."[1]

An analogous story was attributed to ancient Persian alchemist Ostanes who spoke of a stone hidden in the Nile that had a spirit (*pneuma*). When the hand was thrust within, its heart could be withdrawn; its soul (*psyche*) was in its heart: probably the first reference to the philosopher's stone and a myth that may have influenced the famous Gnostic "Hymn of the Pearl" in the apocryphal Acts of Thomas.

We may reflect on these symbols when listening to *La Cathédrale Engloutie,* to *Les Jardins sous la pluie* (Rainswept Gardens), and of course, to Debussy's great symphonic work *La Mer,* where he brings together triumphantly the rhythms, the mathematics, the geometry, the poetry, and the awesome spiritual and physical power reflected in the form of "the Sea," which appears formless, but inwardly is not. If I may take a line from an old poem of mine: "A soul so deep embedded further than history, for what they sought was the spirit of mystery."

There was in all of this music a sense of profound nostalgia, or "gnostalgia" as I have facetiously described it on occasion, when old memories come fluttering into one's soul like a butterfly, only to grip one with the iron pang of yearning for a past time to which one is linked by love sealed in mystery, watered by tears.

My mother's favorite composer I think was Ravel, and not long before I went up to Oxford to study theology, she bought me an album whose prime attraction was Ravel's overwhelmingly nostalgic *Le Tombeau de Couperin,* which I would now identify as a Symbolist work and very much to my taste. The LP collection included Satie's *Gymnopédies,* and hearing them for the first time was a quiet revelation.

It was immediately obvious that Satie and Debussy had been drinking from the same Arcadian stream. What I felt then, I know now. Oh, and the cover was by Jean Delville: *Les Trésors de Satan* (*Satan's Treasures*). Had not Lucifer carried into the darkness of matter treasures from above he did not understand, and which in poor hands seduce and entrap the spirits?

The curious thing about the music of Satie and Debussy is that you may feel that you are only hearing a fragment of the music, for the tonal experimentation of these composers, particularly in those pieces composed when the composers' minds were most deeply involved in esoteric sensibilities, aimed at invoking the unseen and the unheard. While the music may be specific to the symbol, the effect is one of suggestion, allusion, and the sense of the slightest brush with that which normally eludes us. Behind the visible church is a hidden church and its choirs may be heard through the prism of nature in echoes and fragments.

Both composers experimented with ancient modes of music, following the unspoken credo of Bailly's bookshop that the purest magical treats lay unseen in the past, only waiting to be brought forth to renew the jaded, faded world with their timeless magic: the aim was, as it were, to raise the engulfed cathedral before it was not *that,* but the civilization around it that would be swallowed up in cataclysm.

A version of the legend current in Debussy's time held that Ys would rise again when Paris was obliterated. We may recall the drawing of the decapitated Péladan on a cross overlooking the utter devastation of Paris under the inscription FINIS LATINORUM in the catalog to the first Rose+Croix Salon of 1892. Listening to the music then becomes a sign of the end of an age and the return of a lost civilization (the Tradition). It is music to confound materialism: to show that even the very poetic image of "matter," the Sea, is understood *à la Gnose,* a revelation of eternal ideas expressed in golden proportions that point beyond the stars. Perhaps this music's ideological attack and dissection of materialism has made it instinctively and reactively necessary for governing academic establishments to inoculate Debussy's music with the diluting adjective *Impressionism* and Satie's early works with words such as *eccentric, humorous,* and *whimsical,* suggesting they were essentially descriptive—

*Fig. 12.2. Design by Alexandre Séon for
frontispiece for Péladan's novel* Le Panthée
(1892), from the 1892 Rose+Croix Salon catalog

Impressionism again! No, these works are profoundly concerned with spiritual revolution. Eternal revolutions do not turn on chanting zealots throwing stones over barricades, or action and reaction. Revolution in Occult Paris meant spiritual reintegration, and with the churches practically silent on the matter, the Arts went ahead under their own halo, foundering now, only for obsession with the algae and the lichen.

GNOSSIENNES—ERIK'S GNOSTIC TWIST

After the little leitmotif appended to Fernand Khnopff's frontispiece to Péladan's tenth novel *Le Panthée,* Satie's next work for Péladan was a hymn for the latter's play, *Le Prince du Byzance* (The Prince of Byzantium), a gender-fixated farce set in Renaissance Italy. Entitled *Salut Drapeau* (Hello Flag) it experiments at the expense of the Sâr's drama with a kind of Greek scale apparent in the *Gymnopédies,* with a melody that goes nowhere but makes its virtue in rarefied stasis, chord

Fig. 12.3. Leitmotif by Erik Satie;
frontispiece to Péladan's novel Le Panthée *(1892)*

based without tonality. Its aesthetic characteristic derived, said Satie, from boredom, but which had hit fortuitously on something "mysterious and profound." It was never performed with Péladan's play.

In 1891, Satie wrote a minute of music only discovered after his death and called *Première Pensée Rose+Croix,* being connected to the music Satie wrote either for ceremonies of Péladan's Order or for the opening of the Rose+Croix Salon in 1892, or for both purposes. *The Sonneries de la Rose+Croix* (Chimes of the Rose+Croix) consisted of three pieces, originally for brass and harp treatment: *Air de l'Ordre* (Air of the Order), *Air du Grand Maître* (Air of the Grand Master dedicated to Péladan), and the *Air du Grand Prieur* (Air of the Grand Prior dedicated to Le Comte Antoine de La Rochefoucauld). La Rochefoucauld apparently paid to have them published, the cover adorned by a red chalk sketch of three mounted trumpeters taken from Puvis de Chavanne's *Bellum,* an idea that could have been either Satie's or Péladan's, for they were both admirers of the painter from Lyon.

Similar to the *Ogives* of 1886 in feel, the three parts take about thirteen minutes to perform, occasionally breaking from medieval chant structures into odd dissonances and unexpected chords that have mystery and a hint of mischief and anachronistic parody, as well as august authority of an almost otherworldly trajectory about them. We may

THÉATRE DE LA ROSE ✠ CROIX

LE PRINCE DE BYZANCE
DRAME WAGNÉRIEN EN 5 ACTES
Refusé à l'Odéon et à la Comédie-Française

LE FILS DES ÉTOILES
WAGNERIE KALDÉENNE EN 3 ACTES
Refusé à l'Odéon et à la Comédie-Française
Représentée, le 19 mars 1892, à la Rose ✠ Croix
L'Androgyne Œlohil a été créé par Mlle Marcelle Josset.
Izel,   Suzanne Avril.
La Courtisane sacrée,   Renée Dreyfus.
L'Archimage d'Ereck, par MM. Maurice Gewal.
Le Palais Goudea,   Reigers.
A été repris, le 7 mars 1893, avec Mlle Nau dans Œlohil,
Mlle Mellot dans Izel et Mlle Corysandre dans la Courtisane.

BABYLONE
TRAGÉDIE WAGNÉRIENNE EN 4 ACTES
Refusé à la Comédie-Française
Représentée, les 11, 12, 15, 17, 19 mars 1893, à la Rose ✠ Croix.
M. Hattier a créé le Sar Mérodack.
M. Daumbbie,   L'Archimage.
Mlle Mellot,   Samsina.
Uruck, An-Ipnon, Sinnakrib, L'ORDRE.

PROMÉTHÉE | ORPHÉE
Trilogie restituée d'Eschyle | TRAGÉDIE EN 3 ACTES

EN ŒUVRE :

LE MYSTÈRE DU GRAAL
MYSTÈRE EN 5 ACTES

Le MYSTÈRE de ROSE ✠ CROIX

LES ARGONAUTES

*Fig. 12.4. Announcement in 1892 Rose+Croix Salon
catalog for Péladan's theatrical productions; Satie
composed music for* Le Fils des Étoiles

feel something radically new is trying to squeeze out of a straitjacket
and assert itself, perhaps a little misshapen by the effort. Not surprisingly, Allan Gray (József Zmigrod 1902–1973) who wrote the music
for Powell & Pressburger's 1946 movie *A Matter of Life and Death*
(U.S. title: *Stairway to Heaven*), seems to have taken them as suitable
for pastiche in a heavenly check-in and courtroom narrative, both comic
and profound. There are hints from Satie's fanfare melodies in Debussy's
"Engulfed Cathedral," especially in the triumphant sequence when the
cathedral manifests fully above the waves and the swell of choir, organ,
and bells resound in understated Wagnerian strokes through the waves.
Debussy's music works better perhaps than Satie's undeveloped but

essential *ideas;* Debussy had the knack of grasping Satie's protean ideas and making more fully realized melodic expressions of some of them, as Satie himself once averred. Satie seems to have been less patient a composer than Debussy.

Performed during the soirées of the first Rose+Croix Salon of 1892, Satie's three preludes to the three acts of Péladan's *Le Fils des Étoiles* (The Son of the Stars) operate above the "Chaldaean" pastoral setting of the play. Otherworldly, the feeling is of hieratic ceremony in a vast temple, preceded by a contemplation of the stars. As usual, Satie's extraordinary economy of sound and duration is striking, as though he had realized that Wagner would have been considerably more effective had he employed a censorious and fearless editor! A café pianist knew quickly when he had bored a restless audience. Satie's economy is not merely pragmatic. His structures show a desire to incorporate ancient geometrical principles of the golden section, of which more anon when we look at Debussy's hidden geometry and musical ecology.

Shortly after the first Rose+Croix Salon, when his role as "Maître de Chapelle" of the R+C+C+ was slipping away on account of La Rochefoucauld's rupture with the Sâr, Satie staked his chances on La Rochefoucauld's continued patronage. It is often supposed Satie's "Rosicrucian" period ended with this rupture, as though involvement with the Order had all been a seduction of Péladan's and a deviation for the "true" Satie: a *folie de jeunesse.* While this narrative may suit musical purists who prefer their Satie demystified, the detailed evidence does not support the supposition. As late as 1893, Satie was working on a *Sixième Gnossienne,* dedicated to La Rochefoucauld whose interest in Satie extended to painting his portrait in oils (*Erik Satie,* 1894, Bibliothèque Nationale de France, Paris).[2] This *Gnossienne* would be known as the *Second Gnossienne* of a total of six composed over a decade, but mostly 1889–93, that is, after becoming an habitué of Bailly's bookshop in the rue de la Chaussée d'Antin. That is to say, Satie's specifically commissioned work for Péladan was very much integral to his developing music and interest in the spirituality and mystery of ancient times and of the medieval period in particular, combined with an idealistic and moralistic will to impose spiritualizing sensibilities upon the materialistic culture of his time. "Rose+Croix" was simply a holdall name for gnostic insight into the folly of materialism, suggesting a body of idealists joining forces in "holy war" against vulgarity. Anyone who has studied Satie's life will realize that he never laid down his arms in this struggle, forever, like a Knight Templar, deeming spiritual privileges to the poorest of society, and especially those, like himself, who accepted poverty rather than succumbed to temptation. The vulgar never understand spiritual values and always try to drag the saints down to their own level.

For those acquainted with the rays of gnostic spirituality, the *Gnossiennes* provide a veritable soundtrack. They simply sound *gnostic,* there's no two ways about it! When British composer Howard Goodall came to write the score for the four-part TV series *Gnostics* in 1987, his music was frequently a pastiche of the *Gnossiennes*—and it was very effective, whether we were uncovering the late antique Gnostics of Egypt, the Cathars, the Hermetists of the Renaissance, or the gnostic world of Carl Jung and modern America.

I had first heard variations on the *Gnossiennes* used to great effect in the extraordinary comedy *Being There* (1979), starring Peter Sellers, a story about a man so unrelated to politics, so removed from the world, so devoted to an infantile perception of life and nature that he miraculously wafts over the worlds of Washington political sophisticates and plutocratic power brokers and by the final frame is pipped as the next candidate for president! His quasi-economic dictum "There will be growth in the spring" utterly floors cynics, TV pundits, economists, the CIA, and the incumbent president himself! In the final scene, as Satie's music drifts over a desolate private lake in crepuscular light, "Chauncey Gardener" actually *walks on water* as the *éminences grises* of Washington gather at a tomb beneath the All-Seeing Eye in a masonic pyramid! It was outrageous and sublime at once: Satie was the perfect choice.

Much has been written of Satie's remarkable *Gnossiennes* and the obvious seems too difficult for many critics to grasp. The title, by that perversity that cannot tolerate the great pursuing the esoteric because the esoteric is great, has oft been linked to Knossos, rather than *gnosis.*

Why?—ostensibly because an excavation at Knossos in Crete was "in the news." Well, while the site had been discovered in 1878, Greek efforts to dig had been blocked by the Cretan Assembly. In 1894—by which time five *Gnossiennes* had already been composed—English archaeologist Arthur Evans paid his first visit to Knossos, having been alerted by his friend, the American William James Stillman, *Times* correspondent in Athens, to some desultory excavation. But the famous digs of Sir Arthur Evans that romanticized the site did not begin until after the twentieth century had begun. *Gnossiennes* have nothing to do with Knossos.

The suggestion is also made that just as the *Gymnopédies* might be linked to a Spartan dance, and Satie's *Sarabandes* are dances (are they?), then the *Gnossiennes* must be a kind of Minoan or Cretan dance, or something like. Dear oh dear! What floundering in the dark!—anything to avoid the obvious.

A casual turning of the pages of Papus's *L'Initiation,* available at booksellers all over Paris, for the precise period of composition of the *Gnossiennes,* shows up the French word *La Gnose* (the gnosis) time and time again: *La Gnose* had become a veritable commonplace of Papus's publications' agenda that "Materialism has had its day" and the collective ideology to supplant it was rooted in the ancient *gnosis.* If you wanted to meet the gnostic bishop of Montségur, you could find him welcoming new members at 29 rue de Trévise most weeks. Never in history had the gnosis been so accessible!—though today Papus and Chamuel's "Bookshop of the Marvelous" has gone the way of the engulfed cathedral.

Péladan agreed with Papus's primary postulate: the *occult* was simply another word for a body of hidden or rejected doctrines expressed in gnostic symbols. Though the Catholic Church had rejected it, and suppressed it, *La Gnose* was still there and only her recovery and practice could save the church from the mire of materialistic vulgarity, liberalism, and cruel moralism into which the "Virgin" had sunk.

Now, while it is plain Satie has incorporated the essential word for "spiritual knowledge," *gnosis*—those things discerned spiritually for they are spiritual, as St. Paul held (I Corinthians 2:14)—the title *Gnossienne* is still not of the academic dissertation type, but is a Satienne pun. Why has Satie used the *-sienne* suffix? Several possibilities immediately present themselves, all with their merits. *La sienne* is French for "hers," where the *la* (feminine definite article) can refer to a female figure or feminine noun, or "La Gnose" itself (viz: la-Gnose-sienne reduces to "Gnossienne," possibly indicating "her gnosis," "gnosis of herself," "gnosis herself," or "her own gnosis").

Now we know that during this period, Satie took an esoteric view of the person of the Virgin of the Catholic Church. Evidence for this comes, remarkably, from a letter twenty-six-year-old Satie addressed to Gaultier Garguille, associate editor of *Gil Blas,* on 14 August 1892.[3] It should be noted the August date tells us that Satie by this time had moved over into La Rochefoucauld's camp where, eager to assert artistic independence, he had become fearful of the consequences of his being seen as a "disciple" of Péladan. Perhaps he had already lent an ear to the hostility of La Rochefoucauld's man, Jules Bois, who six months later would publicly accuse Péladan of murder by bewitchment.

The letter, in the "Propos de coulisses" column of the newspaper is headed: "Monsieur Erik Satie, the good musician, addresses me with the following letter, a marvel," laid out as follows:

Monsieur Editor,
being greatly surprised that me [Satie uses the archaic form *moy*]
poor man who has no other thoughts
than those in my Art, am always
pursued with the title of musical Initiator
of the disciples of monsieur
Joséphin Péladan.
that gives me great pain and disagreement
because if I must be anyone's pupil,
believe I can say that it is of none
other than myself; moreover that I also believe
that monsieur Péladan, despite his
extensive knowledge, couldn't make
disciples, no more in music than

in painting or other things.
Therefore, this good monsieur Joséphin Péladan,
for whom I have great respect and deference,
has never had any authority over
the independence of my Aesthetic; finds
himself *vis à vis* myself, not my
master but my collaborator, also
and in the same way as my old friends
messieurs S.P. Contamine de Latour
and Albert Tinchant.
Before Holy Mary
Mother of our Lord Jesus, Third
Person of the Divine Trinity:
have I spoken, without hatred or malicious
intention, that which my heart feels regarding
this matter; and swears also
before the Fathers of the Holy Church
Catholic, that this question does not
in any way seek to pick a quarrel
with my friend monsieur Péladan.
Would that you receive, monsieur
editor, the humble greetings of a
poor man who has no other
thoughts than those of his Art, and who is
sad to deal with a subject so
painful for him.

ERIK SATIE

Apart from the light this "marvel" of a letter sheds on Satie's relations
with Péladan after the first Rose+Croix Salon, with Satie caught emotionally between loyalties that six months previously had been united,
but now having to make a statement, the thing to notice is what looks
like a detail. Look carefully at the witness to Satie's oath that he is not
seeking a quarrel. "Holy Mary" is described, quite heretically, as the
third Person of the Trinity.

There can be no doubt that Satie was aware of the Egyptian trinity of Osiris, Isis, and Horus, and the pages of *L'Initiation* contained much traditional speculation on a subject that had impressed esoteric circles since at least the Renaissance period. For many esotericists, Mary and Isis were interchangeable: the root-conceit of the "Black Madonna" mystery where the *black* refers to the fertility of Egypt's soil where the child Jesus was preserved from harm and grew—the black soil of Egypt being also the origin of the word *alchemy*.

Satie's brother Conrad related how Erik's *Ogives* was inspired by Satie's sitting in the cathedral dedicated to Our Lady (Nôtre Dame de Paris), where the ogive of the masons' windows represented sacred fire, an image also for the divinely impregnated womb of the Virgin-Mother, both ideas symbolic and redolent of alchemical transformation: the generation in the athanor of the "Son." That is to say that Holy Mother contained a Holy Mystery, the generation of sons of God, and a word for that mystery was the ever-fecund *gnosis*. In Gnostic theogonies, the true Mother of Jesus is the Aeon Barbelo, Virgin and Whore, holder and bringer of gnosis: mirror of God. Hence, perhaps a Gnossienne is on one level, *Her* gnosis, or "knowledge of Her," where divine knowledge is identified as the third figure of a holy trinity.

To add flames to this particular fire, we may note that in 1893, Satie will compose music for Jules Bois's mystical play, *La Porte Héroïque du Ciel* (The Heroic Door of Heaven). Bois of course was at the time dueling—literally—with de Guaita while blaming him, Péladan, and Wirth for Boullan's fatal heart seizure. In Bois's play, Jesus appears before a poet to incite him into replacing the Virgin with Isis, *She* who, before Christ, had uttered the words: "Come unto me."

While this matrix of ideas may have constituted one layer of Satie's imaginative title for his work, we should not, perhaps forget the spirit of playfulness that also trickles through the not-always solemn music, though humor was also an aspect of gnostic spiritual exegesis, and Isis does not put herself beyond pleasure.

The *-sienne* suffix is of course familiar as a common suffix to the city of Paris, when referring to, for example, "La Vie Parisienne" or indeed, a female of the city. A Gnossienne then may perhaps be Satie's musical observation on the *new* gnostics to be seen gathering in the specialized bookshops, cafés, art galleries, studios, and salons of the capital—or perhaps even their female admirers, dressed like Pre-Raphaelite *Dames sans merci.* Will the Gnossiennes overtake the Parisiennes? Will Paris be transformed, as Péladan fervently hoped? Would a new kind of spiritually androgynous citizen emerge in the new Catholic-gnostic dawn? These were all questions hanging in the air during the period of composition. At the time Satie began writing his *Gnossiennes,* discussions were held between Lady Caithness and Jules Doinel over suitable *female counterparts* ("Sophias") for the new gnostic bishops. The Gnossienne could well have been Satie's *Chat Noir*–inspired take on this.

Furthermore, we may ask who was the greatest Parisienne of them all to such as Satie? Surely we have seen already the answer. She is "Our Lady of Paris," the Virgin, Nôtre Dame, *La Parisienne* who looked down on all. For the Catholic Virgin Mary had taken from the gnostics the appellation of Divine Wisdom, *Sophia:* in gnosis, both the consort of Jesus, and also his Mother. Jesus and Sophia together form an androgynous syzygy, while the believer was enjoined to seek "the Mother in Heaven."

We cannot escape the feminine form of the word. But then, we recall the gnostic, *Péladien* ideal of the Androgyne and Gynander, and the love of the feminine and the curve in Symbolist art. In artistic presentations of androgyny, it is the feminine that dominates the image. The curve is, for Péladan, the essential first stroke and principle of Art.

I should say then that a Gnossienne in our context is essentially a piece of music inspired by a gnostic sensibility of loss of the Ideal, dedicated to *Her,* the mysterious female embodiment and giver of the spiritual gnosis, which is Herself. Satie was dedicated to the celestial Virgin, the Ideal, as indeed had been the Knights Templar. She leads men out of this world, as Satie's music does.

And one should not forget, Satie's mother had been taken out of this world already, an unfathomable trauma that would give "gnosis of her" another very special dimension altogether, an emotional and psychological one, emphasizing that Satie's aesthetic was indeed always deeply personal, and always occulted by allusion. A *Gnossienne* is in some sense I suspect, a hymn to his absent, lost mother, an invocation of the Scottish lady born Jeannie Leslie Anton whose spirit perhaps could be sought gazing heavenward through the ogive windows of Our Lady's chapel.

As Villiers taught Catulle Mendès, loss of the Ideal (Mother) is a cosmic predicament for modern man. When in 1905 Satie chose a formal education, having rejected the masculine encroachments of the Conservatoire with its strictures that bound the freedom of art, he opted, against Debussy's advice, for the *Schola Cantorum,* to study harmony and counterpoint the old-fashioned, medieval way. In its chains, he found a new freedom. It would put him back in touch with medieval forms, and what were those forms devoted to?

The Lady.

It was Satie's overwhelming desire to establish his own aesthetic, his own unique reputation that would, I believe, drive him to subsume spiritual commitments in his music beneath concerns with form, for it was questions over form that exposed him most of all to excruciating criticism, since he had the master's desire to break the rules, but his structural iconoclasm prevented mediocre judges from seeing him as a master in the making, but rather as a recalcitrant amateur, like a rural poet.

Écho de Paris critic, Henri Gauthier-Villars described Satie's music for *Le Fils des Étoiles* (1892) as "faucet salesman's music." Satie's sensitive genius directed him chiefly into concerns of musical language rather than subject matter. An artist's work is all one, however, and the tendency to break off Satie's overtly gnostic or so-called Rosicrucian works from the more formal developments of his determinedly secular twentieth-century music is to be regretted. He had a willful desire to distinguish himself, and that would ultimately mean distinguishing himself from his friend Debussy, as he had earlier from his much-admired friend Péladan, and as he would go on to do to the end of his days, even separating himself from such admirers and supporters as Maurice Ravel, who owed so much both to Satie and Debussy, and knew it.

THE WAY OUT

There was then no formal rupture with Péladan and the Idealist Order project; it just slipped away and morphed into Satie's own idealist order project, which surely owed much to Satie's having grasped the conceptual nature of Péladan's R+C+C+ experiment in aesthetic revolution. Magic can be a trick of the imagination and Satie would play it on himself with pitiable consequences. The sequence of events is clear enough if one examines the evidence carefully.

After the first Rose-Croix Salon of March 1892, Satie became increasingly desperate for cash, living as he was at the top of the Butte Montmartre, though he quipped, "well above his creditors."[4] He had written a "Christian ballet" called *Upsud* to a libretto by his friend J. P. Contamine de Latour, for performance at the *Auberge du Clou*, a shadow theater directed by Miguel Utrillo, the axle of a group of Spanish painters lodged in Montmartre: all friends of Satie. Hurt by *Auberge du Clou* punters' criticisms that the music for *Upsud* was rather on the thin side, proud Satie bet them he could get the *Théâtre National de l'Opéra* to accept the work.

By November 1892, Satie had heard nothing back from Paris Opera Director Monsieur Bertrand. Taking this as a personal insult, Satie insisted persistent refusal to deal with him demanded satisfaction "with weapons."[5] Still there was no reply. Writing again in December, Satie gave Bertrand a fortnight to attend to the ballet lest he receive a visit from two of Satie's friends to account for his conduct. Two days later, the letter was indeed followed up by the appearance of Contamine and André Mycho, son of Péladan's portraitist Marcellin Desboutin, at Betrand's house. They left visiting cards and threatening remarks. This worked wonders. The next day, Bertrand invited Contamine and Satie to present their work.

Though not accepted for production, Satie felt the moral victory of getting the director to treat him with respect was well worth the habitués of the *Auberge du Clou* coughing up the cash to have *Upsud* published, with a note on the title page indicating it had been *presented* to the Paris Opera. Acquaintances were called in to subscribe to the project. When little was achieved, Satie tried to haul success-ful Venezuelan songwriter Reynaldo Hahn (1874–1947) into the sub-scription effort. That Hahn's melodies had brought Verlaine to tears mattered little to Satie:

> Erik Satie to Reynaldo Hahn[6]
> In the name of the Rose+Cross
> Curses upon you!
> Erik Satie

Especially noteworthy here is that at the very time the Boullan Affair was exploding between Jules Bois, J.-K. Huysmans, and Stanislas de Guaita's R+C+K in early 1893, Satie still felt sufficiently attached to the *other* Rose+Croix Order to use its "authority" as a means of hexing a fellow musician! On the other hand, it was also a tremendous joke. If de Guaita's R+C+K could make curses effective on Boullan, might not Hahn have something to fear from curses emanating from a repre-sentative of the Catholic Order? Or is it rather that the *collective* term "Rose+Croix" had now become something of a joke by itself, in the wake of the Boullan Affair? That is to say, these weren't real curses at all, but an ironic tail pull on current events. The latter seems the most likely conclusion. Cabaret habitués were doubtless amusing themselves speculating on which "fluids" were best suited to "bewitchment" at a distance—absinthe had its own black magic!

Beside, at this point in early 1893, Erik Satie was deeply in love.

The *Auberge du Clou* shadow theater's director, Miguel Utrillo, had fathered a boy, nine-year-old Maurice Utrillo, on Marie Clémentine Valadon, now twenty-seven. On 14 January 1893, "Suzanne" Valadon began a six-month love affair with Erik Satie. She moved into his lodgings at 6 rue Cortot, Montmartre—a plaque marks the spot today—and Satie embarked on the only serious physi-cal and emotional relationship with a woman of his life. It must have been a spiritual bombshell for him. A trapeze artist before taking up painting, Suzanne Valadon was a character. Puvis de Chavannes, Renoir, and Toulouse-Lautrec all used her as a model. For Satie, she was much more. One can only guess at what unconscious images the pure Catholic heretic projected onto her!

Not surprisingly, the relationship was tempestuous. An echo of the tumult survives in the "novena" of Satie's *Danses Gothiques* (1893). A "novena" is a Catholic means of securing intercessory graces by virtue of nine prayers offered piously over nine consecutive days. Thus there are nine "Gothic" dances each of which is directed to the spiritual need of the penitent. Dance number six is indicated as a prayer "Where it is a question of pardon for insults received." The lovers fight (the Gothic dance?), so the writer, beset by tumults, prays for inner, spiritual peace. Satie tried to establish some kind of control or equilibrium. Unused to passion, or to the forces evoked through sex, or to intimacy with a woman, Satie's dream blew up on 20 June. Valadon moved in with a banker whom she later married; Satie was totally laid waste. What principles could he rely on if human love had failed? He told his brother he would have a hell of a job trying to get a hold on himself again, for he loved her so much and had given his all to her.

And, predictably, we find that it is at this precise point, where a novena had failed him, Satie decided to shore up his identity and surround himself with fanciful medieval battlements and towers by creating a global church with over a billion imaginary communicants, with himself as supreme pontiff or High Priest. He chose to launch the existence of the *Église Métropolitaire d'Art de Jésus conducteur* (the Metropolitary [*sic*] Church of Art of Jesus Conductor), with himself as "Parcier" (an archaic monastic office) and "Maître de Chapelle" in the pages of Jules Bois's review, *le Coeur,* backed by La Rochefoucauld, in October 1893.

A reading of the church's first public statement, courtesy of Bois, does nothing to support Satie's protest of fourteen months previously that his aesthetic was distinct from Péladan's. The "First Epistle of Erik Satie to Catholic Artists and to all Christians" has been read as a kind of parody of Péladan's R+C+C+, but only by those who do not appreciate what Péladan had achieved and what he was trying to do. But to read the following is to feel a little sad for Satie. He has taken Péladan's idea and made his own self-insulating version of it:

We are therefore resolved, in accord with Our conscience and confident in the mercy of God, to erect in the metropolis of this Frankish
nation, which for so many centuries has claimed the glorious title
of Elder Daughter of the Church, a Temple worthy of the Savior,
conductor and redeemer of the peoples; We shall make of it a refuge
where Catholicism and the Arts that are indissolubly linked to it
shall grow and prosper, sheltered from all profanation and in the
complete flowering of their purity, which the efforts of the Evil One
will be unable to tarnish.[7]

A refuge for Erik Satie, more like: a cloister from which he could
promulgate barbed, if calligraphically impressive, ecclesiastical-style
pronouncements against any individual who failed to meet his ideal
standard of Art and conduct. Satie produced two *cartulaires,* a cartu-
lary being a monastic record—or Satie's idea of a review, with himself
sole editor, and reader. In 1895 he accused "Willy" at the *Écho de Paris*

Fig. 12.5. Erik Satie

of blasphemy for treating Wagner in terms appropriate only for God. Willy replied in print with cruel puns at Satie's expense, denigrating his person and his music. Satie dispatched illuminated indictments of the critic so impressive that Colette reported how her husband framed and mounted them on his office wall! The spats went on. In 1904, Satie knocked Willy's hat off, so Willy hit Satie with a stick; a gendarme carted Satie off. While the pair of eternal opposites would eventually shake hands as friends in 1914, Satie's turning inward in 1893 announced a long, harshly difficult, vain, vindictive, poverty-stricken, and above all, uncreative period in his life that dragged on into the early years of the twentieth century: a vast sulk intensified by the self-lacerating, poverty-induced move in October 1898 to a mosquito-ridden room in the working-class suburb of Arceuil, a good 5-kilometer walk south of Montparnasse. Pious indeed was the path that Satie took after 1893, but one deadly sin that poverty could not conquer, only exacerbate, was pride.

After Péladan's death in 1918, shortly before the end of World War I, surviving admirers of Péladan formed a little group to help his widow cope with the legacy. One of these "Friends of Péladan" was Victor-Émile Michelet. On Sunday 23 November 1924, Erik Satie replied to Michelet's letter requesting his presence at a memorial service to Péladan.

> Erik Satie to Victor Emile Michelet[8]
>
> Sunday 23 November 1924
>
> Dear Monsieur Victor Emile Michelet—I am desolate that occupied as I am by an insane amount of work at the Théâtre des Champs Elysées it has been impossible for me to deal with your request. I am in Paris all the time, therefore your second note did not reach me until yesterday morning (Saturday).
>
> What can I do? . . . I would have been very happy to join the friends of Péladan, whose memory is still very dear to me.
>
> What can I do? Please see.
>
> Amicably yours: ES

THE ESOTERIC DEBUSSY

"Tout est nombre. Le nombre es dans *tout.* L'ivresse est un nombre."
("Everything is number. Number is in all. Drunkenness is a number.")

BAUDELAIRE[9]

Claude Debussy destroyed the great majority of his musical sketches, so finding personally written evidence for the impact of esotericism on his musical thinking is somewhat hampered, especially as he followed the Hermetic dictum to keep silent on such matters, nor did he relish the idea of anyone getting inside his deepest thoughts or techniques. However, he left a solitary written clue, whether an intentional leak or not, we shall probably never know.

In August 1903 Debussy wrote a letter to publisher Jacques Durand along with corrected proofs of his work *Estampes*. Its title inspired by artists' concentrated use of potent images in prints and engravings, *Estampes* was written for solo piano in three movements: *Pagodes* (Pagodas), *La soirée dans Grenade* (Evening in Granada), and *Jardins sous la pluie* (Rainswept Gardens). "You'll see," Debussy alerted Durand, "on page 8 of *Jardins sous la pluie,* that there's a bar missing—my mistake, besides, as it's not in the manuscript. However, it's necessary, as regards number; the divine number [*elle est nécessaire, quant au nombre; le divin nombre*], as Plato and Mlle. de Pougy would say, each admittedly for different reasons."[10]

Plato we know; Liane de Pougy (1869–1950) was one of the most famous women in France. *Folies Bergères* star and beautiful courtesan of Paris's demimonde, Liane is famous now for her novelized account of her lesbian affair with American Salon hostess and talent magnet, Natalie Clifford Barney (1876–1972), *Idylle Saphique* (1901). Remy de Gourmont called the no less beautiful Barney, "the Amazon" for her lesbian hunting skills. Symbolist poet Renée Vivien (1877–1909) split painfully with Barney in 1901 over her lover's infidelities while Vivien's neighbor Colette enjoyed a brief affair with Barney after leaving Gauthier-Villars in 1906.

Roy Howat's brilliant analysis of Debussy's use of esoteric

Fig. 12.6. Natalie Clifford Barney (1876–1972)

proportional techniques (*Debussy in Proportion,* 1983) recognizes at once that Debussy's "divin nombre" probably signifies the "nombre d'or" (golden number), the French term for what is commonly called the golden section or golden mean. The joke about Mlle. de Pougy is, he thinks, a pun on the expression for "the divine few," that is the Parisian élite: "le nombre des élus," consistent with her *demi-mondaine,* outside-the-norm, status. Liane had the pick of the gold, so to speak, of the rich and the aristocratic men who courted her. I should suggest Debussy might also have been hinting at same-sex harmonies, since the golden section divides a *single* line into an internal harmony or divine ratio of greater and lesser, analogous perhaps to Liane's idea of a "Sapphic Idyll."

Once the missing bar is put in, *Jardins sous la pluie* does conform to the golden section proportion. Furthermore, since the missing bar referred to by Debussy in his letter to Durand merely repeats the previous one, we can see that the bar's addition is intended specifically to generate Debussy's required internal symmetrical consistency. The means to acquire that internal symmetry was, for Debussy, application of Euclid's *Elements,* Book 5, Proposition No. 30, that is, how to cut a given finite line in extreme and mean ratio. This is how the Divine Proportion is established, and its discovery, before Euclid first wrote it down (ca. 300 BCE), is attributed to Pythagoras and his mystical school, a school concerned with the occult but no less practical properties of numbers.

How does all this affect a piece of music? Revolutionary as Debussy was in so many ways, he still wrote his music out in conventional bars using conventional notes. In the simplest application of the golden section, you may have a piece of music of, say twenty-one bars. If at the thirteenth bar you climax the first movement, since thirteen is the golden section division of twenty-one, the piece then conforms dynamically to a "divine" proportion. What this means is that while a musical statement may not conform to expected or traditional rhythms, repeats, codas, or melodic development, it possesses a hidden, underlying, unbreakable form, an "occult" form of celestial authority and coherence that prevents mere fancy from breaking the bounds of the *internal* laws of nature. While it looks like a constraint, it in fact guarantees a special kind of freedom, and most importantly, it is harmonious. This freedom was dear to a man who was to many ears, initially, "breaking all the rules." Roy Howat is quite right to point out that the combination of the letter to Durand and the analysis of *Jardins sous la pluie* "leaves no doubt that at least on that occasion, Debussy was consciously constructing with numbers."[11]

We might also slip in here the fundamental Symbolist "formula" that the artist contemplate the idea, find its symbol, then give it form. It is on account of Debussy's general, inherent—but not too formulaic—observation of this principle that we must once and for all drop the use of the word *Impressionism* when referring to Debussy. It is painfully misleading, and he rightly hated it, as we shall see. Intrigued by how painters applied geometrical proportion, including golden section proportions, to pictorial composition, Debussy applied the occult principle to music as a means of giving form to ideas perceptible to him *through* nature.

THE MAGIC IN MUSIC

Let us look a little closer at what we mean by the golden section and why it had mystical and magical properties for the ancients, such that from the late 1880s, men such as Papus and Edmond Bailly could promote "occult sciences" as the "high sciences" and the keys to bringing spiritual knowledge in to revolutionize a nonmaterialist *new science,* integrating matter and spirit on a higher plane of consciousness.

The golden section is the point on a given line where the ratio of the shorter part of the length created by the point is in the same proportion, or ratio, to the longer part, as the longer part of the length is to the line as a whole. This is not an arbitrary piece of geometry; nature herself uses the principle in its growth patterns and in their manifestation as organic forms. The rule is inherent to the universe of things; it is an implicit not an imposed idea, and it speaks of transcendent, or if you prefer inherent, intelligence present in cosmic formation. A single line divided into its golden section also exhibits the idea of microcosm—little universe—in relation to macrocosm or greater universe. That is to say, the ratio of the shorter section to the larger section is a kind of microcosm of the ratio of the larger section to the line as a whole. This principle demonstrates the Hermetic dictum: "As above, so below." The harmony of the greater ensures the harmony of the minor, and the two are proportionately and harmoniously interrelated. Recall how important harmony is to music; it is what color is to painting.

The golden section exhibits other, more specific, special properties.

First, the exact figure for the ratio is always *irrational.* That means that the figure for the ratio is always a figure whose decimal places continue indefinitely. Where we measure a given line as 1, the golden section is approximately 0.618034, or a little under two-thirds, but the decimal places ratchet on infinitely.

Another special property, which might be used to show the section's potential to create infinite microcosms, is as follows: say we have divided a line AB at the point of golden section and called that point C. If we now seek the golden section of the longer section AC, and create the point D, we shall find the golden section of AC (at D) is proportionately equal to the golden section of AB, but in the other direction!

However, we really get to grips with what the ancients found so astonishing about the golden section when we look at its relation to the five so-called Platonic solids, and to the pentagon and magical symbol of the pentagram in particular.

Born at Samos circa 596 BCE, Pythagoras initiated a school that perpetuated and developed his doctrines. From that tradition, Plato knew of five solid geometrical bodies that embodied the principles by which the universe was *formed*. Constituted of atoms, these solids represented the four elements: earth (the cube), fire (the tetrahedron), air (the octahedron), and water (the icosahedron). An ultimate fifth element, often symbolized in terms of "spirit," was represented by the dodecahedron. This twelve-sided, three-dimensional figure of regular pentagons completes the creation-palette of the cosmos.

Plutarch (ca. 50–120 CE) recorded the Pythagorean belief that the *heavenly sphere* was formed from the dodecahedron. Jews, Christians, and pagans could see meaning in the 12-fold symbolism manifesting on Earth: 12 tribes of Israel, 12 signs of the zodiac, 12 apostles, the number of the saved: 12 squared (Revelation 7:3–8), and so on. The dodecahedron exhibits a fundamental relationship between the numbers 5 and the heavenly 12, for it is made of pentagons, *and the pentagon is constructed from two lines that are in golden section proportion to each another.*

This is done as follows: take a given line and adduce its golden section. The longer part of the line we call A, the shorter part B. We now take B and use it as a baseline for a triangle, where the base is B and the other two sides are the length of the longer section A. We then construct a circle around the triangle whose three points touch the circle's circumference. We see our isosceles triangle precisely in a circle. We now take the baseline B (the shorter part of the original section) around the circle in consecutive order, marking a point where the line ends on the circumference. These points joined up, we see a pentagon as well as the triangle within the circle. Once we join the points diagonally across the figure, we see a perfect pentagram within the pentagon, within the circle!

This five-sided figure itself has even more properties of a special kind. It has now ten triangles within it (5 x 2), together with a proportionately reduced inverted reproduction of itself heading into the center *ad infinitum,* alternating in inversions. Each point on the circle occurs every 72 degrees on the 360 degree circle, as we should expect, but, surprisingly at first, all of the internal degrees are either 36, its double 72, or its triple 108, and each of these numbers reduces to 9, and all are of course made from an odd and an even number: symbolically speaking, the masculine-feminine harmony in dynamic androgynous union!

Imagine the wonder of the first person who realized all of this! It looked like the Grand Geometer's building formula, revealed by mathematics and geometrical construction. And of course, the Pythagoreans were famous for linking these numerical relationships directly to musical intervals, scales, modes, and proportions.

I have by no means exhausted the mathematical implications of the pentagonal geometry in relation to the golden section, but I hope I have clarified why golden section carried such meaning for Debussy and his esoterically minded friends, and why he had every cause to experiment with it. Oh, and if one should object that the task of calculating the golden section for a proportional number of bars, or, as he did, a proportional sequence of notes, as well as sub-golden sections within golden sections would have been extremely onerous, Debussy could easily have employed Fibonacci sequences to simplify the process.

Briefly, a Fibonacci series is created by taking a number and adding the previous number to produce the next number, viz: 0, 1, 1, 2, 3, 5, 8, 13, 21, and so forth. Take three numbers in Fibonacci sequence and the figure in the middle gives you the longer part of the golden section (to round figures), the figure on the left gives the shorter part of the line, and the figure on the right gives you the length of the whole line, viz: 21, 34, 55.

Roy Howat offered many examples of Debussy's use of, and partial use of, golden section proportions in his works. Not surprisingly, *La Mer* gains much of its force from Debussy's attempt to get really inside the natural dynamics of water to locate its occulted melody, rhythm, and harmonic scope, or as the Greeks would say, its *oikonomia,* or proportional law. The golden section is much in evidence in *La Mer*'s mighty scope.

One of the clearest examples of golden section proportion can be found in the two sets of Debussy's *Images* (1905, 1907) for piano. In the first piece of the first set, *Reflets dans l'eau* (Reflections in the Water), the principal climax occurs at bars 56–61, after 58 bars of a total 94. This is only 1 percent out and that is due to a tempo change. There are other instances of golden section proportion in this piece. Howat recognized that it had often been remarked that the opening phrases of the piece followed a wave shape. He is more specific: "the tops of these 2-bar phrases give each a Golden section shape (5 quavers out of 8), anticipating in miniature the piece's dynamic wave form."[12] In the third piece of the 1905 *Images, Mouvement* has its principal climax at bars 109–110, conforming to golden section proportion. In the first piece of the 1907 *Images, Cloches à travers les feuilles* (Bells through the Leaves), there is only half a bar of *fortissimo* at its climax, and it is at the point of overall golden section, in the second half of bar 31.[13]

Possibly Debussy's most famous piece, *Clair de Lune* (published in 1905, but dated 1890 by the composer[14]) included in the *Suite Bergamasque,* uses the golden section throughout its duration, in the sequence 36:22:14. The much-loved *Clair de Lune* was composed then, at the high tide of the explosion of Occult Paris, when Debussy regularly played at Bailly's *l'Art Indépendant* bookshop, that period immediately preceded by what Howat describes as "arguably the largest evolutionary leap in Debussy's career" (1885–88) when we see "expressive chromaticism suddenly taking a dominating role in their forms, replete with tritonal and other chromatic relationships."[15] Howat marks the leap with Debussy's *Ariettes oubliées* (Forgotten Arias), and the work entitled "Spleen" in particular. From that point, Debussy was particularly open to new ideas that expanded liberty of composition, and the ideas were to hand, presented in a charmed intellectual setting.

The composer experimented carefully, until, from about 1894, "virtually all Debussy's works show proportional organization, although to varying degrees of structural importance."[16] With some works, the pattern is not obvious to locate. For example, *La Cathédrale Engloutie* only revealed its golden section proportion when Debussy's own playing of it was heard on an authentic piano roll, where it was discovered he doubled in tempo some of the bars, demonstrating how he intended the proportions to work, even though this doubling was not present on the published score.

Debussy was struck by natural phenomena such as the pebble in the pool that seem to speak of curious, dormant energies, but it was essentially the spiritual beauty, not the quantity that attracted him. Likewise, golden section proportion is not merely mathematical— though some mathematicians might think so—it has poetry about it; it is suggestive of a deeper, hidden order of subtle intelligence, inherently aesthetic. In other words, we find Debussy full of the Symbolist atmosphere and intellectual fervor of those who gathered, as he did, at Bailly's bookshop. Michelet isn't exaggerating when he tells us that Debussy absorbed the Hermetic universe. Since this universe has been unfamiliar to most commentators on the arts until recently perhaps, it is not surprising it has passed unnoticed, and people have been misled into the Impressionist fallacy. Debussy himself said that he professed "une religion de la mystérieuse nature," *a religion of mysterious nature.*[17] What is this religion but the Hermetic *religio mentis,* the religion of the mind whose axiom held that *mundus imago dei:* "the world is the image of God" (*Corpus Hermeticum*)?

Influenced by Impressionism, Symbolist poet Jules Laforgue (1860–1887) wrote an essay of that name in which Howat is wont to

Fig. 12.7. Jules Laforgue (1860–1887),
drawing by Stéphane Vassiliev (1881)

locate the perceptual eye of Debussy in works such as *Reflets dans l'eau*. According to Laforgue "the basic characteristic of the impressionistic eye" is one of "seeing reality in the living atmosphere of forms, decomposed, refracted, reflected by people and objects in endless variations."[18] I have to say I find this a bit woolly, its being merely descriptive, not revelatory, wholly confined to the visual plane. Nevertheless, Howat considers this reference to "seeing reality" might have influenced Debussy when he described his orchestral *Images* as "*realities*—what imbeciles call impressionism."[19] I should have thought that Debussy's tone and specific denigration of Impressionist categories here makes it abundantly clear that the "realities" he was referring to were not primarily visual impressions, however spun out through enchanting plays of light and color, but the living spiritual principles that animated the perceived universe: the source of the enchantment. The beauty is essentially not in or of the object, but in the mind of the perceiver linking to the beauty of the mind of the creator, that is, *the reality behind the visible reflection of that reality*, not the mere reflection, as in Impressionism, which, when all is said and done, is fundamentally representational and illustrative.

Unfortunately, critics have been easily misled by the poetic titles Debussy placed before and, more significantly, after—as with the *Préludes*—his music. This has had the misleading effect of making critics think the music is purely descriptive of the content of the title, partly on account of the symbiosis between the dapples of color in Impressionist painting and Debussy's gentle and dramatic piano effects, the merging of tonalities in echoes being taken as an aural analog of the Impressionists' blurring of lines. However, it would be well to bear in mind that Debussy shared the specific attitude of Symbolist poets and painters with regard to titles, as exemplified by Debussy's friend, who was also a musician *and* an architect (geometry again!), Odilon Redon. One is to look beyond the obvious; ambiguity is always to be preferred to specificity. If meaning is obvious, one has missed the nature of a symbol. As critic Edward Lockspeiser has put it: "A title is justified only by its vague indeterminate nature, suggesting a double meaning."[20]—to which I should only add that we should not forget triple or quadruple meanings, for a true symbol implies infinite correspondences. However, the image is there, and there is nothing wrong with listening to "The Engulfed Cathedral" and quite naturally imagining an engulfed cathedral. But *what does it mean?* What does it portend? What does it evoke? What does it symbolize? The answer to those questions is expressed in the music, in the spirit, not in titles. Meaning is not exhausted by rational statements or descriptions, but limited by them. Such is the nature of mystery.

Since Pico della Mirandola announced in 1486 in his *Oratio de dignitatis homini* (Oration on the Dignity of Man) that Man the Magus had arrived, the Magus was one who sought in the "hidden recesses of nature" for the transcendent principles that sustained living things that, while accessible to the enlightened man, were closed to the dense. Debussy's beauty is not superficial but ideal and divine. As Debussy would say to Michelet with regard to the success of his opera *Pélleas et Mélisande,* his music was "supported, but not digested." This is still the case, judging by the DJ's sentimental sighs that invariably accompany Debussy's better-known melodies when played on classical radio.

Other than the books and assembled company of Bailly's bookshop, where else might Debussy have encountered esoteric influences? Debussy's education was very inconsistent. Julia d'Almendra interviewed Debussy's sister Adèle in 1948, and from her she learned that many of Debussy's earliest years were spent with his aunt in Cannes where he received training in the cathedral liturgy. D'Almendra wondered if this Provençal period might well have stirred in him a love for old modes as well as an attraction to Palestrina and his contemporaries.[21]

Aged nine, during the events of the 1871 Paris Commune, Debussy and his father met the eccentric Charles de Sivry (1848–1900), whose mother taught Debussy piano. Through de Sivry, Debussy experienced the artistic avant-garde, for de Sivry was Verlaine's brother-in-law, having married Verlaine's half sister Mme. Mauté de Fleurville, who would also teach Debussy music. De Sivry was himself a musician, teaching piano, conducting, and composing songs for cabaret, while maintaining an interest in Kabbalah and the occult sciences. The January 1892 issue of Papus's *L'Initiation* includes Charles de Sivry in its list of "prin-

Fig. 12.8. Charles de Sivry
(1848–1900)

cipal editors and contributors" for its "Literary Section," along with E. Goudeau, Catulle Mendès, Émile Michelet, and others. In the 1890s de Sivry also ran the shadow theater at *le Chat Noir,* where the French *chanson* tradition was born. With this experience, it is not surprising that Debussy entertained disrespect for the academic musical establishment, evinced when he went to the Conservatoire in 1882.

At the end of his student days, Debussy was naturally caught up in the Symbolist movement, enjoying many opportunities to learn about the golden section and kindred occult subjects of harmony and symmetry through his association with painters who were themselves using occult proportional systems to advantage, seeking what Paracelsus called the "divine signatures": the encoded memory, if you like, in nature of the divine source of creation. These interests would manifest in works such as Paul Sérusier's *ABC de la peinture*—see also his oil painting *Tetrahedrons* (ca. 1910). A large part of the work's thirty-five pages is dedicated to proportional techniques, with four pages devoted to the golden section. Though not printed until 1921, the work contained ideas entertained by Sérusier, Maurice Denis, and their Nabi friends since their youth. Denis, you may recall, designed the beautiful cover for Debussy's *La damoiselle élue,* published by Edmond Bailly's *l'Art Indépendant* in July 1893.

* * *

Perhaps the most potentially significant writer on proportion whose works surely did not pass Debussy by was the mathematician Charles Henry, author of *Introduction à une ésthetique scientifique* (Introduction to a Scientific Aesthetic, 1885). Henry's interest lay in demonstrating numerical relationships that related to sensations of harmony, whether produced by shapes, colors, or angles in pictures. He attempted to establish a scientific basis for aesthetic pleasures, happy to think in terms of correspondences more familiar to the world of occult philosophy. He could see how a musical line could correspond to a geometrical angle. He believed proper understanding could help artists avoid disharmonious elements in proportion as well as disharmony in music. His ideas justified the Symbolist search for deeper knowledge of the universe and seemed to put occult insights onto the level of an advancing science of the mind and spirit. Henry's theories on number and proportion were appearing in Parisian Symbolist journals at precisely the time Debussy was composing his *Ariettes oubliées* (1885–88).

During the 1880s and '90s, Charles Henry was mentor to the "Hydropathes," a young men's drinking club devoted to intoxication with drink, poetry, and ideas; de Sivry was an associate. Avant-garde artists constituted the membership, in whose company Henry bonded with Jules Laforgue, thanks to an introduction from poet Gustave Kahn. Laforgue's critical works were much influenced by Charles Henry's scientific approach; Debussy was familiar with them.

Debussy could also encounter Henry's ideas through reading the review *La Vogue,* which Henry, also a poet, cofounded, while contributing articles to *La Revue Blanche.* Neo-Impressionists Georges Seurat and Paul Signac were also interested in applying Henry's theories. According to William Homer,[22] Neo-Impressionism may be laid in part at Henry's door. Camille Pissaro dipped in but was afraid of theory becoming formula: a concern shared by Debussy.

Debussy read deeply and remembered what he read, and let it be said, if it is not obvious, that simply writing a piece of music according to golden section proportions isn't necessarily going to light anyone's candle! Debussy had the essential spark of genius in himself, and like others so gifted, he sought ways of enhancing his talent and taking it via depths and profundities to the heights through inspiration, originality, knowledge, and experience. Given what we now know of the genuine Occult Paris, it would be extraordinary, if not incredible, had a man like Debussy not taken advantage of the spiritual movement of Hermetism that was, for an epoch, alive and radiant in France's capital. That he kept it to himself indicates I think not lack of interest, but depth of understanding, loyalty to its precepts, and innate seriousness about his vocation.

THIRTEEN

THE GNOSTIC CHURCH

On 2 May 1890, Papus's recently founded *Independent Group of Esoteric Studies* opened the premises of 29 rue de Trévise to group members for conferences, lectures, study, and other more recondite purposes: spiritist séances and esoteric ceremonies. A year later, the house journal *L'Initiation* (April 1891) announced that meetings held at the address were now yielding "little volumes" of original work by leaders of the group, works such as Victor-Émile Michelet's "important" *L'Ésotérisme dans l'Art* (Esotericism in Art).[1] Papus's pet publisher and bookshop owner, Lucien Chamuel, had already published, in July 1890, the *Première Homélie sur la sainte Gnose—À l'Église du Paraclet,* the "First Homily on the Holy Gnosis—to the Church of the Paraclete [the Holy Spirit of the New Age]" signed by "T[au] Jules," that is, Jules Doinel, gnostic bishop (*évêque gnostique*).[2]

The confluence of Papus and Chamuel's *Librairie du Merveilleux* in the rue de Trévise with so many apparently distinct esoteric orders is to be noted, for we shall find that whether we are talking about the *Ordre Rose-Croix Kabbalistique, l'Ordre Martiniste, l'Église Gnostique,* or the *Ancient & Primitive Rites of Memphis and Misraim,* we are essentially talking about Papus and his closest associates (Sédir, Barlet, Lejay, Alber Jhouney, de Guaita, Michelet, Marc Haven, Oswald Wirth, etc.) combining forces with existing or novel initiatives. Papus's enthusiastic, but also chaotic, organization simply began absorbing practically anything that was related to occult traditions. Since *L'Initiation*'s opening mission statement never deviated from its war cry: "Materialism has had its day," Papus was bound to be interested in every phenomenon of a mysterious nature that upheld or suggested a mystical theistic belief against the rationalist atheists who were, in his and his colleagues' view, destroying the very essence of civilized life and leading the world into a new dark age.

What motivated key figures in approaching Papus and his friends is obvious. People with esoteric knowledge and interests were attracted to 29 rue de Trévise because first, they received a sympathetic welcome there; second, they acquired a focal point and meeting place; third, they could acquire members and useful contacts; fourth, they could broaden their knowledge base; fifth, they gained access to magazines, publishing facilities, and publicity; and sixth, the shop was slap bang in the pulsing heart of the empire's capital. The operation had a distinct buzz.

By the time the thirteenth volume of *L'Initiation* was published in December 1891, the journal's front cover specified its interests as: "Hypnotism, Psychic powers, Theosophy, Kabbalah, Gnosis, Freemasonry, Occult Sciences." Anyone interested in any of these fields could make contact with anyone else of similar interests, across the world, through the offices of Papus's organization. At its height, during the 1890s, *L'Initiation* constituted the dynamic crossroads of global esotericism. Papus was the Google of the occult.

The reason we find the word *gnosis* prominent on the cover is because Jules Doinel made contact with Papus and his associates through the offices of Parisian occultism's parallel epicenter, the house of Lady Caithness, Duchess of Pomar. How this occurred is a strange story, derived chiefly from records kept by Déodat Roché (1877–1978) who joined Jules Doinel's Universal Gnostic Church in 1899. Following his father's advice to seek in the past for the future, Roché delved deeply into gnostic studies while pursuing a career in law. After bad experiences with the Vichy regime in the 1940s—he was a Freemason and opposed anti-Semitism—Roché would go on in 1950 to found the *Société du Souvenir et des Études Cathares* ("the Society for the remembrance and study of the Cathars"), which society was responsible for the memorial to Cathar martyrs that still stands at the foot of the "pog" of Montségur in the lower Pyrenees. Much of today's great interest in the

Fig. 13.1. Déodat Roché (1877–1978) in 1919

Cathars may be attributed to Roché, however fanciful some of his ideas about them may have been.

Roché kept Jules Doinel's own account of a séance that took place at the home of Lady Caithness in the autumn of 1889, an event that led directly to the "revival" of the Church of the Albigensians, or Cathars, supposed by Doinel to have been the twelfth- and thirteenth-century inheritors of the late antique gnosis of Jesus, Simon Magus, Basilides, and Valentinus.[3]

The participants, who included a Spanish grandee, a gentleman, six foreign mystics, "six curious Eves of occultism," "women of remarkable intelligence and aristocratic nervousness"—gathered in Lady Caithness's secluded oratory, dedicated to Mary Stuart, in the heart of Holyrood in the avenue de Wagram. Dimly lit by a scented lamp burning before an effigy of the Queen of Scotland, everyone felt a curious languishing in a common "fluid," eyes heavy with a hallucinatory vapor, tight jointed with a strain of the heart "not painful but paralyzing." Before the heavy curtains that divided the room from the library and the street noise outside was a huge spherical table on a tripod made of massive spiral feet. It was where evocation was expected. A "powerful medium" served as instrument and channel of the "Powers." It should be stressed that this kind of spiritist channeling was *de rigeur* in practically all occult circles at the time; "communications" so common as to be almost commonplace were granted high levels of credibility and authority.

Doinel recorded that his own state of mind was important to what followed. Certainly it must be said that much of what was in his mind gelled with Lady Caithness's own spiritual-feminist agenda and visionary experiences. Doinel recorded that he was seeking "the religious formula of the Absolute." "My heart avid with infinite feelings, my imagination in quest of idealist visions, my mind, avid for dogmas of light, wanted to realize them and to incorporate them into a superior metaphysical conception, and to condense them into a cult sufficiently grand to replace the catholic religion. In a word, I wanted to resuscitate the Gnosis. . . ."

On behalf of Doinel and the fledgling assembly, the noble *evocatrice* intended to consult the spirits of the distant Albigensian (Cathar) bishops defeated by Simon de Montfort in the thirteenth century. All awaited the "manifestation of the ancient Church of the Paraclete."

Around 10 p.m., after prolonged mental prayer, the heavy table began to tremble under the group's fingers, as if life pulsed through its grain. A vibrating sound was heard that impressed everybody. It appeared to chant: "*Est Deus in nobis, agiante calescimus illo,*" whereupon the medium made a sign to Lady Caithness who seized the wand of evocation—a pendulum—and cast it over the alphabetic frame. The frame contained letters above which the wand would rest. She spelled out the words: "Prepare yourselves. Soon the Bishops of the Albigensian Synod of Montségur are going to appear." Then sparks flew about the oratory and the effigy of Mary came alive. A smile played on the Queen of Scots's lips and her eyes lit up in the dark. Doinel screamed. The "enchanted" oratory was enveloped in a profound, pregnant silence. Doinel felt a soft hand on his lap. His hair stood on end. A countess and princess close by went pale, bundles of nerves as the table assumed vibrating life, beating a rhythm for ten long minutes. At the climax, a huge bang came from the table's center and the wand again ran over the raised letters of the frame, "magically" spelling out the following: "Guilhabert de Castres, bishop of Montségur and the forty bishops of the high synod are here." The circle was seized by an impulse to stand and the evocation commenced with the prayer of the Paraclete, then the salute to the gnostic bishops, then the solemn interrogation.

Doinel could not remember the exact words but the sense he recalled from the magical communication of Guilhabert de Castres, Cathar bishop and debater with the Catholics: "We came to you from the most distant of the two Empyrean circles. We bless you. That the principle of good, God, be eternally praised and blessed, glorified and adored. Amen." "We came to you our dear ones. You Valentin, you will establish the Assembly of the Paraclete and you will call it the Gnostic Church. I announce to you that you will have Hélène as spiritual assistant. You will become affianced to her. You will be her husband, she your wife.

"You will elect your bishops and you will consecrate them according to the gnostic rite. You Valentin, you will be sanctified in this oratory. You will reconstitute and you will teach the gnostic doctrine. It is the absolute doctrine. You will take as your gospel, the fourth, that of John. It is the gospel of love.

"The Assembly will be composed of *Parfaits* and *Parfaites*. The Holy Spirit will send you those males and females that he must send you. We bring you joy and peace, the joy of the Spirit and the peace of the heart. Now, kneel, O you who are the first fruits of the Gnosis. We are going to bless you."

Doinel and the assembled were seized by "an understandable emotion"; tears streamed from their eyes as their hearts were gripped by an anguish at once voluptuous and gentle. Doinel felt fire in his veins. Kneeling down, the table again began quivering to a rhythm while an "aura" enveloped them like a whirlwind and a voice was heard: "That the Holy Pleroma blesses you. That the Aeons bless you. We bless you as we bless the martyrs of the Pyrenaean Tabor. Amen. Amen. Amen."

The noise ceased, the table was quiet, the portrait of Mary appeared dead again and everyone got up shaken. "The manifestation had ceased;

the bishops of the Paraclete had disappeared. Such were the beginnings of the Gnostic Church restored. Jules Doinel."[4]

Revived spiritual bodies usually make claims to some direct contact with a line of tradition. The Gnostic Church was unusual in having bishops but no tradition of laying-on of hands to validate the link to antiquity. It really all seems to start *ex nihilo*. However, there is a clue to Doinel's thinking in this very predicament. The January 1891 issue of *L'Initiation* contains a pious article by Doinel on the Gnostic heresiarch, Basilides (fl.ca. 117–38 CE):

> From an old man called Mathias, who said he was a disciple of Jesus, Basilides had received mysterious teachings that he had confided by the sacred mouth ["la bouche sacrée"] to the élite of his hearers in his esoteric consultations.[5]

We see straightaway the value Doinel placed on direct *esoteric transmission*. This was the principle of authority within the Gnostic Church and Doinel implies here that it was the preferred method both of Jesus and his esoteric followers. We know from a number of authentic Gnostic writings that the Gnostic Jesus conveyed his spirit—that which taught "all things" (John 14:26) and that would come after him (i.e.: the "Paraclete" or "Comforter")—by kissing on the mouth, both male and female apostles. This was not an erotic gesture but a holy means of transmission of breath directly, for breath is spirit (Hebrew: *ruach*). In Doinel's account of the séance that launched the Gnostic Church, this "breath" is conveyed in the "whirlwind," with clear analogy to the experience of the apostles in the upper room in the Acts of the Apostles when they received the Holy Spirit, and with it, courage to launch the new Nazarean assembly in public. The fire the apostles felt on their heads, Doinel felt in his veins.

As for the church's appearance "from nothing," Doinel's article on Basilides shows us the way he understood, or hoped others would understand, the church's mysterious origins. Doinel is at pains to show that Basilides augmented the teachings of the first Gnostic heresiarch

Simon Magus with ideas he received from above and that led, at the next stage, to the complete Gnostic system of Valentinus, the Egyptian poet who nearly became bishop of Rome in circa 150 CE: "It is easy to recognize," writes Doinel, "under the veil of these words, the Abyss [*Bythos*] of our master Valentin."

"When the Demiurge [fashioner of the material cosmos] pronounces the creative word: "Let there be light!—Γενηθητο φως—*whence comes this light?* Basilides responds: *From Nothing.* AND THIS NOTHING CONTAINS THE ALL! Here, we reach the veritable genial conception of Basilides."

> It completes Simon the Magus as it will be completed by his admirable successor [Valetinus]. We must render him this homage. He is one of the fathers of our assembly.
>
> The resuscitated Gnosis salutes in him its most profound precursor. At the same time he has that grand sadness, that painful and chaste Theosophical reserve which always seduces melancholy spirits. At the end of our century, the sick souls and the tired hearts will turn towards him and name him: Master!
>
> Happy our gnostic brothers and sisters, if they understand the providential reappearance of these flames in our night.
>
> T JULES, gnostic bishop.   Jules Doinel.[6]

That which appears to come from nothing, comes from the source of "the All." Doinel pitched his church's claim on the highest peak imaginable.

What do we know of this archivist from Orléans who created a gnostic church from nothing?

JULES DOINEL

Aged forty-six at the time of the séance, Jules Doinel was born into a pious Catholic family at Moulins, Alliers, in the Auvergne near the center of France. Distinguished at school, he was expected to become a priest and, aged ten, he entered the Jesuits' minor seminary at Yzeure near Moulins. At sixteen he entered the novitiate, but by early 1861, eighteen-year-old Doinel quit the novitiate, for the Collège Stanislas in Paris, whereafter he graduated from the École des Chartes on 15 January 1866 having flirted with Protestantism and made a study of the prophets, culminating in a vision of the prophet Nehemiah who, significantly, preached the rebuilding of the Temple. This was not Doinel's first vision. As a student of the Jesuits, Doinel had become passionate about a popular Polish saint, St. Stanislaus Kotska, and experienced a vision of the saint. When Doinel read of the Gnostic of Orléans (Étienne), while working at the archive there, he had visionary dreams of the condemned heretic. Doinel was looking for a solid religious base for his life, something that had the authority of his upbringing but that made more intellectual sense to him and that touched the spiritual visionary in him.

On 20 April 1886, having lived in Orléans since 1875, he was passed Master Mason within the Grand Orient of France and gradually moved, in the spirit of the time toward gnostic ideas, under the influence of Parnassian poet Emmanuel-Adolphe Langlois des Essarts (1839–1909), a friend of Mallarmé. At some point before the critical

Fig. 13.2. Emmanuel des Essarts (1839–1909)

séance, while asleep, Doinel had a dream-vision of being enthroned as a bishop by the "Aeon Jesus Christ." He would later discuss the validity of this enthronement with fellow gnostic Freemasons (Grand Orient), including Parnassian poet Emmanuel des Essarts. While they accepted him as a gnostic bishop by spiritual consecration, other Masons dismissed the visionary assumption of office.

From 1889, Doinel began writing for *L'Initiation* about gnostic teaching, the journal that was also promoting, from its third issue in December 1888, the "principal French Theosophical monthly review, *l'Aurore* ["Aurora"], under the direction of Lady Caithness, Duchess of Pomar and President of the Theosophical Society of the East and the West." The historical gnostics' acceptance of female spiritual ministry (Gnossiennes?) doubtless appealed strongly to the duchess, as it did to mystical feminist Jules Bois. Meanwhile, Doinel could convince many of the significance of the gnosis, writing in *L'Initiation:* "The name of the Holy Gnosis has been forgotten amongst us. Gnosis is the tragic story of the fall of the spirit into matter, and of the painful and providential voyage that makes the spirit remount from the night of the void (the *keroma*) to the clarity of the divine *Pleroma* [fullness], from the material plane of illusions and mirages to the sovereign peace and sacredness of the pure idea, to this unfathomable abyss of Thought, that in their universal language, expressing a unique truth, philosophers have called the Absolute and the people have called God."

"And to operate this voyage and this return, this odyssey of the human spirit, the soul has two wings, Science [Knowledge] and Love, the celestial Christ and the Holy Spirit (*Christos* and *Pneuma hagion*)." Doinel did not pull his punches. His writings were powerful and persuasive, and we know already what happened: on 14 May 1891 *L'Initiation* was put on the Index by the "Holy Office" in Rome, an act that painfully forced Doinel to make a choice, for he recognized that the church was convinced of the "Satanic tendencies" of Papus and feared the revival of the "dualist and emanationist" gnosis of the great heresiarchs, among whom Doinel included Étienne d'Orléans.[7]

It should be noticed also that Doinel's presentation of the Valentinian gnosis conforms fairly closely to doctrines of Louis-Claude de St. Martin, which at the time were much on Papus's mind—he was writing a book on the subject—for Martinism was concerned with reintegration of human beings into the primal, perfect Man before the Fall shattered his capacities, and that the way was marked by the graces of the divine Sophia, which in practice meant advocacy of female spiritual ministry. Martinists thus speak of the significance of the presence of "the Woman": in this context a noun redolent of Mary Magdalene whom the Gnostics took to be Christ's spiritual consort as Helen was Simon Magus's.

A Synod of the Gnostic Church issued a decree on 12 September 1893 that Papus's revived Martinist Order (ca. 1888–89, of which Doinel was a member) was of its essence, gnostic. This identification would enable Papus effectively to absorb Doinel's church into his fold, hardly difficult since Doinel had formed his first Sacred Synod of the Gnostic Ecclesia in 1892 at 29 rue de Trévise from the senior staff of *L'Initiation*. Thus "Gnostic Patriarch" and "Primate of the Albigeois" Doinel consecrated Papus as "Tau Vincent" gnostic bishop of Toulouse, Paul Sédir (Yvon Leloup) as "Tau Paul" gnostic bishop of Concorezzo, and Lucien Mauchel ("Chamuel") as "Tau Bardesanes" bishop of La Rochelle and Saintes. The Duchess of Pomar was elected bishop of Warsaw but refused.

Doinel must have known that the Roman Catholic Church had every reason to regard his "holy offices" as fantasies, since he could not confer what he had not received. However, within the universalist vision of Papus, the aim was for a hidden truth behind *all* religions and religious teachers, which, being a spiritual tradition tending to "right order," was above specific manifest orders of priests and bishops. Nevertheless, one suspects a tension in Doinel, considering his upbringing. It would eventually drive him back, if temporarily, to the Catholic fold. He really wanted both Orders, or the two integrated. In the meantime, Doinel questioned what right the Catholics had to speak of authority, their having exterminated the episcopal order of the Cathars deliberately, an order of transmission that went back, presumably to the primitive church. Hence he called himself Bishop of Montségur, aware of the symbolism that the new church was rising from the flames of the pyres wherein 225 Cathar believers were burnt to death under the eye of the Archbishop of Narbonne in 1244. Besides, no one knew what had happened to the Cathars' line of ordinal transmission; if it was their greatest treasure, it appears lost, though it would be logical to suppose it could be reignited by spiritual means. St. Paul, after all, became an apostle by virtue of a vision of Christ, as he was wont to assert vociferously in the face of his Christian opposition. "We have the *mind* of Christ," he declared (I Corinthians 2:16). Paul disparaged the baptism of John who had baptized Jesus himself—so much for manual ordination!

LÉONCE-EUGÈNE JOSEPH
FABRE DES ESSARTS
(1848–1917)

In December 1888, the literary section of the third issue of *L'Initiation* contained a poem called "*le Sphinx*" by an interesting civil servant (Department of Education) and social idealist named Fabre des Essarts:

> To want is insufficient, to contend is necessary.
> We struggle, but with faith, for triumph is certain,
> And our being freed from the human misery,
> Like the eagle will open its wings towards the azure.[8]

The name Fabre des Essarts will appear again in *L'Initiation,* though in a different if analogous context. July 1890's issue contained a notice that followed news from the *Groupe indépendant d'études ésoteriques:*

UNION THÉISTE

CULTE RATIONEL ["Rational Cult"]	LIBRE DISCUSSION ["Free Discussion"]
Président	Edouard Barme
Vice-Président	Fabre des Essarts
Sec. Gen.	H. Camerlynck
Trésorier	Streiff

"The Theist Union has for its object to gather the believers in God and in the immortality of the soul. Its members only base their doctrines on the more or less precise revelations of the conscience.

"They work to organize a popular and national cult on the terrain where faith and reason meet."[9]

The vice president of the Theist Union was a concerned activist for social harmony, or utopian if you prefer. In September 1894 the Gnostic Synod would consecrate him as Tau Synesius, Bishop of Bordeaux, and when Doinel converted back to Catholicism, allegedly to save his sanity, in 1895, it was Fabre des Essarts who would become Patriarch of the Gnostic Church. How may one account for the rational vice president of the Theist Union's turning to the supra-rational gnostic revelation?

Des Essarts came from an old bourgeois Catholic Legitimist family in the Drôme; his uncle was bishop of Blois (1844–1850). After a seminary education, he devoted his life to teaching, specializing in French grammar and philosophy, while submitting poetry to periodicals and collections, gaining honors at the Toulouse Floral Games and several literary academies. He left teaching after 1878 to work for the Department of Public Instruction and committed himself to the socialist utopian schemes of Charles Fourier (1772–1837). Fourier had attempted to create microsocieties called *phalanstères* (or "grand hotels") where every person did the work for which they were best suited and who were paid according to importance of work, though jobs no one wanted to do were to be well paid. All levels lived in one house, the most significant people at the top. Fourier was practically unique in his opposition to "civilization" and trade; even the word *philosopher* he treated with contempt. Man had fallen into a bestial rat race and the winners called it civilized while the energies of most people were misdirected.

While the project spread to America, des Essarts supported Fourierism in France from the 1880s onward, having met its advocate Victor Considérant early in the decade. In its rejection of man's ordinary condition, one can see how Fourierism chimed in to a degree with the gnostics' contempt for the materialism of ordinary perception. There are also parallels with the Synarchist conceptions of St. Yves d'Alveydre, who owed so much of his social vision to Louis-Claude de St. Martin and Fabre d'Olivet.

In the mid-1880s des Essarts joined the Masonic Grand Orient of France and came under the influence of St. Yves d'Alveydre. This inspired him to try to overhaul the Republican system with councils composed of competent elites while creating a publishing umbrella called the "Little Synarchic Library." Des Essarts also built on his reputation for dedicatory poetry read at the tombs of the famous, on literary anniversaries, or on the inauguration of new buildings and monuments. He was a pure idealist, looking for a brighter future when all men would live in harmony. "Phalansterians" booked him to read his poetry at Fourierist events.

Readers may recall Louis Andrieux MP from Horace Blanchon's interview with Bois and Huysmans in the *Figaro* (January 1893) where, in the midst of the Panama Canal scandal, Blanchon opined that if de Guaita and Péladan really did have the power to bewitch Boullan at a distance, then Louis Andrieux, implicated in the Panama Affair, had better watch out. From 1886 to 1888, Fabre des Essarts was Andrieux's private secretary. Andrieux wanted constitutional reform without going to the extreme of General Boulanger, who was supported by Maurice Barrès. Numa Gilly MP accused members of the Budget Committee (including Andrieux) of corruption. Andrieux sued for defamation, withdrawn when the case reached the courts. When des Essarts wrote a book about the case, Andrieux separated himself from his secretary and des Essarts lost his job in the Education Ministry "for shouting a little too high."[10]

It would appear that Fabre des Essarts's encounter with the rather less worldly idealism of 29 rue de Trévise deeply affected his thinking, coupled with the experience of what actually happened when idealists tried to work together to common ends only to find they did not have as much in common as they thought.

The October 1896 issue of *L'Initiation* featured the third poem from the new Patriarch of the Gnostic Church's *Gnostic Hymns*. Addressed "To the Demiurge," it expresses his conversion to the gnosis directly. Extracts follow:

Demiurge, your work is mad! It is absurd!

. . . .

And to think I once preached your system,
O Fourier, that vowing Malthus to anathema,
I believed in my insanity
That it was enough to put harmony down here,
To model on the plan of the infinite vault
The future Society!

Ah! I came back from it, as one comes out of a dream!

. . . .

O Demiurge, be accursed. Far from the earth.
Beyond time and space, veiled by ardent mystery
. . . World where all is divine, pure, immense and sublime
Paradise of the idea in flower, august Abyss,
Abode of the Word all-powerful!
. . . Thought is the priest and infinity the temple. . . .
Your holy work, O Propator![11]

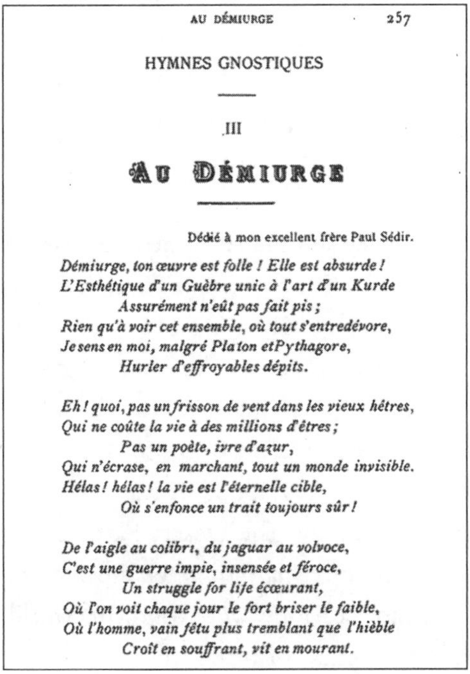

AU DÉMIURGE · 257

HYMNES GNOSTIQUES
———

.III.

AU DÉMIURGE

Dédié à mon excellent frère Paul Sédir.

Démiurge, ton œuvre est folle ! Elle est absurde !
L'Esthétique d'un Guèbre unic à l'art d'un Kurde
 Assurément n'eût pas fait pis ;
Rien qu'à voir cet ensemble, où tout s'entredévore,
Je sens en moi, malgré Platon et Pythagore,
 Hurler d'effroyables dépits.

Eh ! quoi, pas un frisson de vent dans les vieux hêtres,
Qui ne coûte la vie à des millions d'êtres ;
 Pas un poète, ivre d'azur,
Qui n'écrase, en marchant, tout un monde invisible.
Hélas ! hélas ! la vie est l'éternelle cible,
 Où s'enfonce un trait toujours sûr !

De l'aigle au colibri, du jaguar au volvoce,
C'est une guerre impie, insensée et féroce,
 Un struggle for life écœurant,
Où l'on voit chaque jour le fort briser le faible,
Où l'homme, vain fétu plus tremblant que l'hièble
 Croit en souffrant, vit en mourant.

Fig. 13.3. Fabre des Essarts's gnostic "hymn" in L'Initiation, *October 1896*

*Fig. 13.4. Fabre des Essarts as
gnostic bishop Synesius*

He expressed the same sentiments more prosaically in an article for the review *L'Humanité:* "I was in my time, like others, a fanatical Fourier follower. Madly, I believed in the possible social realization of Harmony. . . . Gnosis has completely opened my eyes. . . . But if the world of matter escapes us, that of the Spirit is ours. Harmony!—this we can create in the universe of thought."[12]

Faith in the perfection of the gnostic pleroma sustained des Essarts in his doubts concerning social idealism. On becoming Patriarch of the Gnostic Church, he added the title Archbishop of Paris and as such could sometimes be seen in episcopal garb, with a modest miter, purple gloves, and tie, with the mystic "tau" (Hebrew *tav*) hanging over his chest by a purple ribbon. The tau was the sign above the doors of those saved from the divine judgments against the Egyptians in Exodus. It was also associated with Saint Pachom, the first monk, and the Desert Fathers. For gnostics, it was also the equivalent of the Egyptian *ankh,* or life symbol, as well as indicating a cross whose "head" section was beyond this world, though its message extended into the darkness of finite life.

*Fig. 13.5. Tau Jean: "Joanny" Bricaud (left),
gnostic bishop*

In 1907–08, the Gnostic Church split when Tau Jean or "Joanny" Bricaud, gnostic bishop of Lyon-Grenoble, established his "Gnostic Catholic Church," closely linked to Papus's Martinist Order. Fabre des Essarts continued as Patriarch of the "Gnostic Church of France," incorporating material from other traditions such as the Taoism of Matgioï, while continuing to write poetry for newspapers, works on occult themes, and during World War I, patriotic and anti-German poems, before he died in Versailles in 1917.

DEVELOPMENTS WITHIN THE GNOSTIC CHURCH— THE PALLADIUM CONTROVERSY

In addition to Fabre des Essarts, Doinel spread his episcopal net over several other figures familiar to the rue de Trévise and the avenue de

Fig. 13.6. Louis-Sophrone Fugairon (b. 1846), hydrologist at the Ax les-Thermes spa (1889) and gnostic bishop (1892)

Wagram. In 1892, Louis-Sophrone Fugairon (b. 1846), professor of physics and chemistry at the Collège de Foix, became Tau Sophronius, Bishop of Béziers. Alber Jhouney became Tau Théodotus, Bishop of Avignon, and Marie Chauvel de Chauvignie (1842–1927) became Esclarmonde, Sophia of Warsaw, first consecrated "Sophia," named after famous Cathar *parfaite* Esclarmonde de Foix. François-Charles Barlet and Jules Lejay were also consecrated, and, according to Massimo Introvigne, one of Mme. Blavatsky's close colleagues, the Countess d'Adhemer, was designated as Tau Valentin's "Helen."[13] This was all going on while Péladan was organizing his first Rose-Croix Salon and falling out with La Rochefoucauld.

Doinel regarded gnosis as the absolute religion and Catharism its authentic repository. He reconstructed a "Consolamentum" and "Appareillamentum" partly on the basis of the "Rituel de Lyon" discovered in 1852 at the National Library Medieval Archives, where Doinel's archiving gifts came in useful. He composed a Gnostic Mass he called the "Fraction du Pain" (Breaking of the bread) whose institution was, as we have seen, announced in the pages of *L'Initiation* (May 1894; p. 111–12) and that emphasized the corruption of the world and the perfection of the pleroma.

Doinel accepted Valentinus's spiritual classification of human beings into three types: pneumatics (higher, initiated spirits), psychics (hovering between two worlds and in need of guidance), and hylics (or "materials"). The latter are wholly materialist and as such will perish with that which is perishable. The classes are represented in descending order by the figures Seth, Abel, and Cain.

Matters came to a head for Doinel in 1895 with the eruption of the Palladium controversy and Doinel's return to Rome.

One of the greatest practical jokes of all time, the Palladium Controversy was the cunningly brilliant creation of Gabriel Jogand-Pagès (b. ca. 1854), a confidence trickster in a class of his own. He succeeded in maintaining a series of deepening fictions for some sixteen years under the name Léo Taxil, by which name he was also known to Doinel and to Firmin Boissin as comembers of a small occult circle, *l'Institut d'études cabalistiques*.

In 1881, Jogand became a Freemason, but soon demitted. This was a surprise to all his associates as he had lived a life of extreme anticlerical agitation, fueled by a hatred for authority derived from an oppressive father and an intolerance of the Catholic Church and its constraints; his father had sent him to a penal school in his youth. Having produced a successful anticlerical magazine in Marseilles, Jogand had acquired a great knowledge of publicity. He turned this knowledge to a new cause and began a series of *anti*-Masonic exposures, involving others in his tirades and alienating his old colleagues. He claimed to have undergone a deep conversion, returning to the faith ready to expose the servants of Satan, that is, Freemasons. The Catholic Church was delighted to have him aboard—as it thought—deeming his conversion a prize. Jogand ghostwrote a book with a man called Charles Hacks, known as "Dr Bataille." Hacks was only too easily convinced by Jogand that there was a global conspiracy, led by Lucifer through Albert Pike of the Southern Jurisdiction of the Ancient & Accepted Rite—based in Charleston, South Carolina—to bring the world under Satanic rule through Freemasonry. Published in 1892, their book *The Devil in the 19th Century* was hugely popular, feeding into obsession with Satanism stirred up by Huysmans and

*Fig. 13.7. Gabriel Jogand-Pagès
aka "Léo Taxil" (1854–1907)*

Bois among others. The alleged Satanic organization went under the name "the Palladium."

Jogand decided to top his imposture with the creation of a Satanist arch-priestess he called Diana Vaughan, allegedly descended from seventeenth-century English alchemist and Rosicrucian Thomas Vaughan, of mixed Native American blood and holder of high office in the Palladium. The question was whether Diana might convert to the true faith and show the world how evil Masonry was, and how necessary Catholic salvation was to the future of humanity. For the church, Diana Vaughan would be a bigger catch than Léo Taxil! Jogand created an entire biography for Vaughan, and many were convinced she had been sworn into the Palladium as part of a larger plot whereby she was promised to the demon Asmodeus for sexual services by Pike the Satanic dupe. In order to make it look like she might be about to step beyond the evil grip of the Palladium, Jogand concocted a rival priestess in the Palladium with a great deal of anti-Christian theology and blasphemy to explain it all. A high priestess, Sophia Walder, offspring of Lucifer and her ostensible father's mistress, quarreled with Diana. Matters erupted at a Satanic ceremony in Paris where Diana refused to stab a host or spit on it. She broke away to form her own group: "The Regenerated and Free Palladium." Followers of the story were agog. What next? The theology or "Lucifology" of Vaughan's organization would reach its terrestrial climax with the Antichrist's appearance, set for 1995 when the pope, a Jewish convert, would swear allegiance to Satanism. Concerned persons could keep in touch with developments via Diana's own journal, concocted by Jogand.

It looked like pious prayers for her salvation were answered when on 1 July 1895 a new journal appeared: *Miss Diana Vaughan: Memoirs of an ex-Paladist*. Anti-Masons eagerly lapped up the *Memoir*'s salacious contents, though doubters had started to appear. Jogand kept the ball rolling as well as he could until announcing in February 1897 that Diana would appear, despite danger to herself from a vengeful Palladium, at the Geographical Society in the boulevard Saint-Germain, on 19 April. It was of course Jogand who appeared calmly on stage to explain very pleasantly that all those Catholics, Freemasons, and journalists who had packed the hall expecting to see a convert, instead had the pleasure of witnessing the pleasure of one who held their superstitions as mere toys. He was a confidence trickster and that was what he was. Keeping one card up his sleeve, Jogand insisted Diana was alive somewhere but was in fact a Protestant who had willingly participated in the farce as it made Catholics look ridiculous.

Diana certainly achieved this aim and the sting fell from the anti-Masonic tail for quite a time, while Satanism itself began to look unreal, such that Joanny Bricaud would eventually feel he had to write a book to assert that Satanism did indeed exist and had wormed its way into the mind of J.-K. Huysmans.

Now we must backtrack, because in 1895 when Doinel returned to the Catholic fold, nobody but Jogand knew the truth about Diana Vaughan and the Palladium. For Doinel, the pressure proved all too much. Unstable, he wondered if he had not himself somehow been "taken in" by a Masonic conspiracy and all his gnostic posturing a Satanic perversion pursued in innocent ignorance. He started writing against his old friends' organizations in association with Leo Taxil. In 1895 the Gnostic Church as well as Freemasonry were hit by Doinel's book *Lucifer Démasqué* (Lucifer Unmasked), written under the pseudonym Jean Kostka, recalling the once venerated Polish saint of Doinel's youth. He began corresponding with Huysmans.

In 1900, after the self-unmasking of Jogand, Doinel applied to rejoin the Gnostic Church, after which Huysmans wrote in a letter of January 1902 to Jules Esquirol (Adolphe Bethet) that Doinel had too much pride to accept life as a simple Christian, though I should have thought reapplying to the Gnostic Patriarch Synesius after all he had done showed a remarkable appetite for humble pie.

Fabre des Essarts had been consecrated Patriarch in Doinel's place at the Oratory of Lady Caithness, who died soon after in November 1895. The Duchess's sad demise pretty well left 29 rue de Trévise as the epicenter of Occult Paris, but it was becoming increasingly difficult to establish a clear direction for what in 1888 had appeared a considerably more homogenous movement. Papus found himself trying to focus attention on the successful promotion of his reestablished Martinist Order as a way of integrating the various and sometimes conflicting streams that were washing about the rue de Trévise. There can be little doubt, however, that bringing into the scenario immense issues incumbent on establishing a church was bound to stretch the resources of imagination, accommodation, and tolerance to a degree that even a broad-based agenda like Papus's would find itself incapable of managing effectively. It is also somewhat rare for founders of churches to repent of their having done so, at least while in this world.

As the incense-laden air of the *Librairie du Merveilleux* became more congested, there was still one man who had emerged from the original enthusiasm who still knew exactly what it was he stood for. Perhaps it was because Joséphin Péladan had jumped ship at a critical moment that, at least for a while, he managed to escape some of the dissipation and strain that affected the other companions of the Hierophany.

FOURTEEN

How to Become a Magus

The Rose-Croix Salons 1893–1897

When, in the July 1890 issue of *L'Initiation,* Péladan finally demitted from his role as "Catholic Legate" to the Kabbalistic Order of the Rose-Croix, he made an exception for Papus, who was permitted to attend councils of the R+C+C+ of the Temple and the Graal on the ground that Papus was "the creator and sole chief of the movement for the dis-occultation of the occult."[1] This bold idea, which Michelet came to see as a weakness and extravagance of the movement, was thoroughly Péladanized, that is aestheticized, in a work Chamuel published in April 1892 as the first of seven volumes of Péladan's ironically titled *Amphithéâtre des sciences mortes* (Amphitheatre of Dead Sciences): *Comment on devient Mage* (How to Become a Magus). Its publication marked, in some respects, a new beginning for Péladan: the role of ethical teacher and guide. Having launched the first Rose-Croix Salon, Péladan hoped to nurture its supporters into a new way of life, free from vulgarity and directed to acquiring spiritual mastery in pursuit of the Ideal. He wanted to promote leadership for the New Age of the Paraclete.

His method was somewhat ahead of his time: self-initiation. As a spiritual Catholic, he at once threw out practically the entire panoply of medieval and Renaissance ceremonial magic. He retained some of the theory of Neoplatonic theurgy—such as the "great chain of being" and progressive spiritualization as the soul ascended to "the One"—but dispensed with the ceremonial and placation of demons. There would be no circles on the floor, only on canvas, no intense invocations of angels or evocations of demon-servitors, only the struggle to penetrate the veil and locate the symbol. It was all in the mind. The spiritual powers of the divine were there always to serve the pure in heart and those of pure intention. Magic was the natural consequence of attuning through self-discipline and righteous focus one's innate powers of creativity. The spark was God-in-us, a kind of imprinted memory of lost perfection.

Made originally in the image of God, human beings had every right, indeed duty, to aspire to higher levels of integrated awareness and ability through pure science of the highest order. Our best interest should be our best intention; our "true will" was God's will. The highest exemplar of that will-in-action is Jesus, the aesthetic paragon, restored to the "right hand"—that is, creative will—of God. Satie had grasped Péladan's idea when he established his conceptual Church of Jesus "Conductor." *He* is the conductor; we are the orchestra, and if we will, co-composers. Jesus's life was the paramount work of art. That is why, according to Péladan, it has inspired the highest works of art. As Blake said: "Christianity is art." Magic is the essential art of the artist: the work of creative imagination directed to the highest planes.

Magic, and her sister mysticism, was a process of cleaning the sheet so that newness could come from above. "First clean the inside of the cup," as Christ said (Luke 11:39). "You cannot put new wine in old wineskins." Péladan recognized the Age of the Holy Spirit needed a profound "baggage-check." Simply dragging the past into the present unexamined was of little use. The "Catharism" (purification) of the future was not going to be a duplication of the Catharism of the past. Inspiration was the key: to be in-the-spirit, to be cleansed of the world, chaste. The new holy knight dedicated his poverty to canvas or bronze or wood, and his broadsword and shield was a palette and brush. The Temple was in his soul, not in the Middle East. The soul is the soil in which the spirit may grow. Art itself is the miracle and provides the key to the spiritualization of all other disciplines—architecture, social planning, medicine, psychology, technology, food and drink, everything—since its miracles are so obvious to the eye and its principles universal. Beauty is its own argument.

For Péladan's enlightened view, the arena of magic was social, the worshipper was the visionary sympathizer, able to perceive beyond the frontier, the acculturated perceiver who had a cocreative role.

Péladan's approach was effectively one of exotericizing the esoteric: a plain contradiction to traditionalists with more respect for occult mysticism as inherited. For Péladan, there was no contradiction. The ultimate work of art was Man: his restoration, or redemption, was to be effected by the spirit of creativity that had first created him. Aesthetics and ethics were interchangeable. The "good" was inseparable in essence from the true and the beautiful, for these qualities were absolutely divine. Péladan took it that he was returning to the original science of Man when all Man's faculties were integrated: the Hermetic "man the miracle" who dwelt in the heavens before the Fall. Péladan's fundamental theory then was part Platonist and part Martinist, insofar as Louis-Claude de St. Martin had also broken away from the theurgic practices of his first teacher Martinès de Pasqually and embraced the redemptive Theosophy of Jacob Böhme in quest of an ideal Christianity for the leaders of the world to establish for all.

Comment on devient Mage was divided according to traditionally significant numbers, combining Chaldaean and Catholic concordances, all brought to serve a pristine path, or as Péladan wittily put it: "How to Exit the Century." The first section was subdivided into seven. The seventh subsection concludes: "I must give you a definition of magic: it is the art of sublimation of man; there is no other formula."

The individual must make himself or herself sublime as a creative act *par excellence*. For Péladan, the conscious individual is sovereign. The State must worship, that is respect, its essential component. The state is not God but can only be as enlightened as those who compose its executive. The true individual respects the same principle of divine individualism in others because the aspiring, ascending individual loves God the Ideal and knows it, and therefore loves the best interest of his or her fellow, for there is one universal, that is "catholic," path, even if official Catholic authority often seems ignorant of it.

Men and women then should not treat one another as sexual

chattels to be used as means to selfish ends that exclude the Ideal. Men and women can unite in common devotion to the true purpose, but such unions, or true marriages, are rare. In his short book *The Secret of the Troubadours* (1906), Péladan made it clear he believed the troubadours were worshipping the divine Sophia, the pure and divine feminine, *through* the love of their ladies, and were therefore in spiritual union with the Cathar preachers.

Péladan advocated what he called *kaloprosopia,* an original compound from the Greek for "beautiful" and "personality." The one who would be a Magus would work on himself primarily as a sculptor or actor of his own persona, becoming what the 1960s knew as "a beautiful person," radiating light through example. Péladan really was ahead of his time:

> Do you know what you are hearing in the expression: "That man is a character"? Well, a magus is first that. Up to now the hermetic pedagogy spoke to you of all-powerfulness, of making gold, of talismans and charms: these are impostures, you will only ever be *the spiritual king of a body and a soul;* but if you attain to it, if your spirit [mind] makes of the body a slave and of your soul an integrated minister, then *you will behave toward others according to the same proportion as you would have them behave toward you.*
>
> Seek no other measure of magical power than that of your internal power: let there be no other tribunal for judging a being than the light that he sheds. To perfect yourself by becoming luminous, and as the sun, to warm the latent ideal life about yourself, here is the entire mystery of the most high initiation.[2]

Clearly, Péladan's spring cleaning of the crystal cabinet was too much to take for the editors of *L'Initiation,* who must have seen much of their territory vaporizing into pure aesthetics at the very time they were trying to familiarize new audiences with the collected treasures of forgotten occult traditions and new psycho-medical discoveries. They studiedly ignored Péladan's Rose+Croix Salons—to their discredit I think—and when *Comment on deviant Mage* appeared, the April 1892 edition of *L'Initiation* panned it.

In a review penned by François-Charles Barlet, Péladan was accused of simply providing a rationale for a *culte de Moi:* a "Me culture," a maimed solipsism used to justify Péladan's own postures—one simply cannot help recalling how critics of the neophilia of the 1960s dubbed the 1970s the "Me Decade" some eighty years later! Barlet argued that Péladan's self-initiation theory bypassed what Barlet thought was most significant about the magi of the past, namely, that their message always ensured *social* progress, and that their magic was not centered on the individual. Barlet reckoned Péladan's book should better have been entitled: *Comment on devient sage* (When One Becomes Wise), a biting double meaning that indicated the distance now existing between Péladan and his old colleagues. As if to put a little oil on the troubled waters, Barlet patronizingly declared that Péladan was not a Magus, though he was without doubt "a great artist!" This Art, wrote Barlet, constituted Péladan's Magic and he ought to refrain from narrowing that subject down to suit himself and his ridiculous titles.

That Péladan persisted for the next five years with Rose-Croix Salons was in part to demonstrate his point that the arena for the magic of tomorrow was the public sphere, in short, the art gallery, concert hall, and such places where men and women gathered freely to witness works dedicated to the Ideal, to encourage them and to kindle in them a like pursuit of the highest through the magic of sublime life. In some respects, Péladan's pioneering vision has borne fruit, for today, while many well-intentioned traditional churches find it hard to maintain the presence of worshippers, the palaces of Art have never been so popular or, for so many, so meaningful, ethically and spiritually. We maintain our ancient churches and cathedrals as much out of aesthetic respect for their "creators" as for their original purposes, much of which have been lost. There are no working chantries, but people are excited by recordings of choirs and soloists singing hymns and psalms and sundry works written for the redemption and uncondemned passage of the soul. In short, the artist has become the prophet, as Péladan foretold. On so many fronts, Péladan was a pioneer, not least in the field of heritage and preservation, as we shall see as he tried to develop some of his initiatives through the Salons de la Rose-Croix.

* * *

It is perhaps a sad irony that Péladan dedicated his work on becoming a Magus to Antoine de La Rochefoucauld, who hurt Péladan so badly, but the dedication stood when the money had gone. For the second Rose-Croix Salon of 1893, Péladan would have to foot the bill himself; that he did so is testimony to the altruism of his intentions and his determination that an aesthetic revolution was desirable and possible, despite the incipient barbarism he saw encroaching upon the Latin Decadence.

THE SALON OF 1893

Péladan's agreeing formally to picking up the bill for the Salon Rose+Croix of 28 March to 30 April 1893 guaranteed him an unusual privilege. Thanks to the intervention of influential councilor Maurice Quentin-Bauchart, Péladan was granted use of the last aisle of the Central Dome of the Palais du Champ de Mars, the home of the official Salon des Beaux Arts, on condition the Order did not hammer any nails into the wall. This proviso necessitated the erection of panels; Péladan needed all the help he could muster. Fortunately, sufficient "Rosicrucian" intellectuals rallied to the call.

Péladan's four-act tragedy *Babylon,* featuring Mounet-Sully (1841–1916), *Comédie Française* star and lover of Sarah Bernhardt, was performed five times during the festival of ideal art whose existence was publicized by a poster from Aman-Jean (1860–1935), great friend of the late Georges Seurat. The poster depicted an Italianate arcade through which Beatrice, object of Dante's love, was whisked by an angel, handing a large lyre to a figure out of frame: Dante of course. Above the lyre was a radiant cross, below which was the name: BEATRIX, redolent of Dante Gabriel Rossetti's famous painting celebrating the deceased Elizabeth Siddal's absent beauty. The theme was plainly "inspiration," and much of the inspiration came from the English Pre-Raphaelites.

Listing 378 works, the Salon's illustrated catalog contained 160 reproductions, mostly after old masters from Italy and France. There were thirty-seven esoteric propositions, eleven questions of

Fig. 14.1. Portrait of Edmond
Aman-Jean (1860–1935) in
1918

Fig. 14.2. Alexandre Séon's frontispiece for Istar,
fifth volume of Péladan's Décadence Latine series,
from the 1892 Rose+Croix Salon catalog

initiation, and while repeating much already published, the rules suggested some pioneering innovations, such as the following precursor to organizations such as "English Heritage," though integrated with contemporary art and not merely preservative. "Point XXXV" announced a corporation called the "Militia of the Past." This body would "establish an aesthetician in each city whose job was to inform it of the condition of all monuments and to be the surveyor of all things relating to art. The Militia and the Consul must work together to inform the brotherhood of citizens with artistic or scientific inclinations, among the poor and working class, so the brotherhood could take an interest in their welfare."[3] So much for Barlet's accusation that, as a Magus, Péladan failed to qualify because there was no social benefit from his word!

Armand Point, Alexandre Séon, and Alphonse Osbert all featured strongly in the 1893 Salon, with Osbert contributing his massive pale, pointillist *Vision* of St. Geneviève, a masterpiece. Séon gave another outing to his shocking *Le Désespoir de la Chimère* and Armand Point displayed his talent for portraying women, lost, as critic Camille Mauclair observed, "in the frosts of desire, contemplating the feverish birds of their voluptuousness silently die in sad flights, with their gazes sweet, knowing and cool."[4]

Belgian representation was predictably dominant, considering Péladan's mission of the previous autumn. Delville, Henri Ottevaere, Fabry, and of course Fernand Khnopff sent their work to Paris. Khnopff contributed two of his best works. *I Lock My Door Upon Myself,* like its sister *L'Offrande,* also exhibited, places a self-absorbed female figure close to a classical sculpture (see color plate 19). In the former case, inspired by a Christina Rossetti poem, the young, Pre-Raphaelitish redhead rests her chin and disconcerting face in the cradle of her hands next to a cast of a classical winged head, while in *L'Offrande* we see Khnopff's sister, looking somewhat arrogant and disinterested, her curly red hair in a bun, extend her arm along a marble toward a classical female head. These girls are upper-middle class hippies-in-the-making and their settings suggest both indifferent interiority and the knowledge of death. In the presence of a classical world that seems ghostly while fragments of nature appear mute, faded, and uncanny, these symbol-wise ladies both seem to say: "So impress me!"

The actual title of Christina Rossetti's poem is "Who shall deliver me?" which says pretty much the same thing:

> I lock my door upon myself,
> And bar them out; but who shall wall
> Self from myself, most loathed of all?
>
> If I could once lay down myself,
> And start self-purged upon the race
> That all must run! Death runs apace.

Dark stuff.

In sculpture, a great favorite of Péladan's was represented: Anatole Marquest de Vasselot (1840–1904) whose twelve exhibited works included five inspired by Balzac. When Rodin would come to be embroiled in controversy in 1895 over the *Société des Gens de Lettres*'s Balzac statue commission—the society refused Rodin's now classic work—Péladan insisted de Vasselot was an ideal replacement for Rodin, "sculptor of primates."[5] Not one of Péladan's better judgments, it exhibits his limitations where form was concerned.

Nevertheless it would be many years before artistic taste caught up with the brilliance of Antoine Bourdelle (1861–1929), represented by fourteen drawings and a statue of a *Holy Woman at the Foot of a Cross*. Bourdelle would not become well known until the official Salon of 1909 recognized the brilliance of his *Herakles*.

The decorative arts attracted works by distinguished decorative artists such as Edmé Couty (1852–1931), André de Gachons (1871–1951), and Georges de Feure (1868–1928). One of Satie's few but most treasured possessions was a portrait of him by de Feure.

While very well attended, critical notices of Péladan's 1893 Salon tended to repeat by-now-formulaic praise for Séon, Point, and Osbert, with some consideration for the Belgian contingent. In the public mind, the Salons were bound to public understanding of Symbolism,

*Fig. 14.3. Georges de Feure
during the 1890s*

and Symbolism or "Baudelairisme" was beginning to attract announcements of its imminent demise, usually on account of alleged degeneracy,
an attitude strongly reflected in Max Nordau's now-famous 1893 study,
"Degeneration." For Nordau, mysticism was to modern civilization what
Christianity was to Gibbon's decline of the Roman Empire: symptomatic of a self-destructive retreat from reality. All those pale figures: how
unmanly! All that Péladian androgyny: rank degeneracy! Decadence
was to Nordau and the petit-bourgeois reactionary frame of reference it
appealed to, the cause of Decadence: not only sign, but culprit of decay.
Recognizing ethical nobility in Péladan, Nordau nevertheless regarded
the Sâr as a "higher degenerate," and perhaps more subversive for that.
The attitude spread to Britain and America, crystallized with the trial
of Oscar Wilde, and led to baleful cultural consequences. It was perhaps
not so long a stroll from the muscular Christianity of Baden-Powell's
Boy Scouts to the Somme. The Edwardian era was schizophrenic on
the issue. In 1914, beautiful young men were sent to sacrifice. Who
had made people see "clean limbed" young men at arms as beautiful
Adonises—ripe for Art, not slaughter?

THE ROSE-CROIX SALONS OF
1894 AND 1895

Péladan was not offered the Palais du Champ de Mars again, and Durand-Ruel was too expensive. For 1894 and 1895, Péladan had to make do with rented space in a commercial gallery, the *Galerie des artistes contemporains* in the rue de la Paix, close to the Opéra in the 2nd arrondissement.

The year 1894 opened for Péladan with the publication of his *Comment on devient artiste* (*Ésthétique*) (How One Becomes an Artist). It contained a "Commemoration" of Firmin Boissin, who in 1858 had initiated Péladan's brother Adrien into Rosicrucian mysteries, as Boissin (Simon Brugal) understood them.

Péladan concluded what Pincus-Witten has called an "arcane work" with the notice that anyone who found the discussion obscure could acquire clarity from Péladan's forthcoming *L'Art idéaliste et mystique* (Idealist and Mystical Art): essential handbook to Sâr Mérodack's aesthetic.

Fig. 14.4. Péladan's classic on art theory, L'Art idéaliste et mystique *(Idealist and Mystical Art), 1894*

Despite the number of works exhibited from 5 March 1894 having dropped to about seventy, more than 10,000 visitors responded to Gabriel Albinet's fascinating poster depicting "Joseph of Arimathea, first Grand-Master, in the features of Leonardo da Vinci, and Hugh of the Pagans, first Master of the Temple, in the mask of Dante" forming an escort to "the Roman angel holding the chalice of the crucified rose."[6] Clearly we have here the pictorial origin of the now-famous Priory of Sion imposture of Leonardo da Vinci being Grand Master of a fictional Order. According to Léonce de Larmandie, the flocking of the informed and the curious to Péladan's show interrupted traffic around the rue de la Paix, with crowds having to wait their turn in the vestibule of a small gallery. Péladan's *Babylon* was again performed; this time at the *Théâtre de l'Ambigu*.

The outstanding exhibit was Jean Delville's freaky, but compelling *Head of Orpheus.* Perhaps some of its power, apart from graphic precision and intensity of lighting contrast, derives from the androgynous

Fig. 14.5. Poster for the third Rose-Croix Salon by Gabriel Albinet, 1894

Fig. 14.6. Alexandre Séon's frontispiece for La Victoire du Mari *(The Husband's Victory), sixth novel in the* Décadence Latine *series (Paris: Dentu, 1889), from the 1892 Rose+Croix Salon catalog*

head of the divine poet, having been modeled on Madame Delville. Through androgyny, woman gained access to the Arts' top table.

A new arrival was Louis-Welden Hawkins (1849–1910) whose mystical girls with accessible, country faces and soft bodies decorated the 1894 and 1895 salons with their sometimes weird, sometimes wholesome, and always highly art nouveau fragrance.

The 1894 Salon attracted the usual criticisms that it had but superficial impact on art, being dominated by mannerisms and style rather than epoch-marking substance, and that it might all be part of Péladan's pro-Catholic propaganda. However, *La Plume,* normally hostile to Péladan, went against the grain of the unconscious-acceptable to praise Péladan's achievement in creating a substantial body of valid art criticism and a no less valuable and instructive Salon, before poignantly concluding that in the end "the contemporaries of the Sâr will be severely judged for their indifference."[7] Quite.

In March 1895 the Salon de la Rose-Croix looked like it might have hit the financial skids. Neither a poster nor a printed catalog appeared.

Thirty-six contributors provided about one hundred works. Séon's *Le Désespoir de la Chimère* was exhibited again; was his chimera crowing now, or just yawning? It joined works by Osbert, Point, Chabas, and Cornillier, and yet another portrait of the Sâr, this time by Delville.

Gustave Moreau's student Edgard Maxence (1871–1954) joined proceedings, and remained with the *Salons de la Rose+Croix* until the end. Another new arrival was sculptor Jean Vibert (1872–1942), who had spent profitable hours in Rodin's studio.

As if running out of time, Péladan's literary outpouring continued to be prolific. Interestingly, he dedicated his *Le Théâtre complet de Wagner, les XI Opéras scène par scène* (1895) to Judith Gautier, the lover of Benedictus, composer, conductor, and singer whom La Rochefoucauld had prevented from performing in the first *Salon de la Rose+Croix*. If the latter did indeed hold something against Judith Gautier and her "living in sin" with co-composer Benedictus, it was perhaps Péladan's subtle means of compensation for past injury to a lady and gentleman who had done much to promote Wagner's music and whom Péladan probably first met on his trip to Bayreuth back in the late eighties. Péladan made the significant point that Wagner probably wrote his text before the music, giving rise to a tendency to overwhelm the musician in him. Péladan's insight proved correct when Wagner's autobiography finally appeared.

On 11 January 1896, Péladan married Léonce de Larmandie's niece, Constance-Joséphine de Malet-Roquefort, Countess Le Roy de Barde, a widow and mother. Their engagement and wedding generated thousands of newspaper articles, so much publicity in fact that Péladan's fame required more space for the next Salon. It was held at the *Galerie des Arts Réunis* at 28 rue de l'Opéra, a spacious gallery illuminated by the novel charm of daytime electric light. Larmandie had to take the helm since the Grand Master was honeymooning in Venice, probably discovering that he and his aristocratic wife were not made for one another; the couple would definitively separate in 1900. Whatever the critics may have made of the long-term validity of the Rose-Croix aesthetic, the public was keen to associate with it. Over eight thousand visitors came to the opening day alone, this time alerted by a striking, almost indecent poster and a catalog.

From an Englishman's point of view, at least, the poster was a joint composition of doubtful taste. Armand Point and Dutch pupil Léonard Sarluys each provided a figure for the design. Point drew the Rosicrucian hero, an amalgam of Perseus and St. George, shouldering a broadsword freshly blooded from decapitating realist novelist Émile Zola—provided by Sarluys. Zola's caricatured severed head drips with blood and gore, mixed with titles of Zola's novels. An outcry ensued, answered by Camille Mauclair in the pro-Symbolist *Mercure de France*. Mauclair opined there was nothing to get excited about, just the kind of thing young artists get up to when indulging in a bit of harmless fantasy.[8] The poster proved to be the most noteworthy aspect of the 1896 event, other than surprise at its popularity.

It was art dealer Georges Petit who sought out the R+C+C+ in order to house their next, and last, Salon at his gallery at 8 rue de

Fig. 14.7. Poster by Armand Point and Léonard Sarluys for the fifth Rose-Croix Salon, March 1896

Sèze. It took place from 5 March to 21 March 1897—three months before Queen Victoria's Diamond Jubilee—and 15,000 attended on the opening day, so Péladan must have been getting *something* right, especially as it had become routine to criticize the Salons de la Rose+Croix for snobbery. Snobbery is not necessarily a popular turn-off. Armand Point made a big show of withdrawing since he couldn't abide sharing space with Osbert, for some reason now obscure.

The catalog declared a dictum that could have been very useful for the film industry in the next century: "Man needs neither pure truth nor perfect realization; Man needs Mystery, not to penetrate it but to experience it."[9]

Péladan did not experience it; he was in Belgium and left everything to Larmandie again: 217 works were arranged at the Commander's behest. Petit doubtless had a say in the presentation of Séon, for Petit was now handling Séon's work, and that probably explains why 53 of the exhibited works came from the hand of that artist, mostly drawings. Fernand Khnopff sent his erotically charged portrait of a woman *Lèvres Rouges:* "Red Lips"—and how! (See color plate 21.)

Sculptor Zachary Astruc (1835–1907) delivered examples of sculpture, including a bronze of Barbey d'Aurevilly, a nod back to the heyday of the Decadence. The 1897 show saw some ten students of Gustave Moreau exhibit a year before the great painter's death. Principal among them was Georges Rouault (1871–1958) who would in time be distinguished as a proponent of the *Fauve* (wild beast) style of color for color's sake. Rouault contributed fifteen works, including *L'Enfant Jésus parmi les Docteurs,* a highly evocative work that owes much to his master and that revels in its somber darkness, lit only by the mind of Christ.

It is unclear why Péladan, returning from Belgium, pulled the plug on the Salons and the Order that backed them. Pincus-Witten speculates it may have been irritation with imitations. Jean Delville was organizing Idealist art events in Belgium; another group was doing something similar in Paris. Péladan's marriage was dragging him down and expected funds from the aristocratic pot were not forthcoming.

It is likely Péladan had grown tired of the events, realizing perhaps there was merit in other approaches than his. He did not wish to find himself forever defending one form of the aesthetic ideal at the expense of another. That he could not always like or appreciate the works of certain artists could be a burden. He knew in his heart that there was talent and genius he had missed, that he ought to have encouraged. He knew criticism of his classical taste was sometimes justified. He could himself be an iconoclast and there is some justification for seeing the artist in Péladan rebelling against himself, his prejudices, and even his own image. He had, after all, given it all a good run. He probably felt tired inside; anyone would, especially a creature of imagination, and, despite the self-reflexive peccadilloes, considerable realism. If the wind was changing, he wanted to be ahead of it, but could not quite adjust; he liked to look to the past, to tradition, for inspiration. He had asserted himself sufficiently perhaps and time was getting the better of him.

In 1898, Péladan undertook an extensive tour of the Middle East. The experience of the Holy Land struck him profoundly; he believed he had found the authentic tomb of Christ in the Mosque of Omar. In Egypt, he gazed at the Sphinx and began to ponder whether he had projected his individuality in the best possible manner. He had demanded attention when he could have *commanded* it. Much of the criticism against him had been aimed at his clothes, his hair, and his giving himself titles, all combined with an uncompromising arrogance that often belied his genuine gentleness, sympathy, and sense of understanding. He had believed the individual had every right to assert his unique qualities in distinctive dress and remarkable speech, but it had not brought him the kind of respect his deeper talents deserved. He had muddied his own waters. But then, who *can* rattle the repressive bores and come away entirely unscathed?

On returning Péladan learned of the death on 19 December 1897 of his old friend, Stanislas de Guaita. With sound humility, he recognized it was pride that had separated them. Chastened, Péladan returned to Paris to devote himself to a more realistic manner of life and a deeper commitment to letters. His studies of Rabelais, Don Quixote, Leonardo da Vinci, and of the "Secret of the Troubadours" are all of interest today for those who seek wisdom in these subjects.

His *Nos Églises artistiques et historiques* (Our Historical and Artistic Churches, 1913) is, according to Pincus-Witten: "perhaps his last piece of valuable criticism after which he fell into undignified anti-German propaganda."[10]

Camille Mauclair of the *Mercure de France,* a critic both kind and severe, has left us a picture of Péladan, depressed by neglect and by German aggression, far removed from the gay days of suede boots and velvet doublets and the panoply of the Belle Époque, which had to some extent sheltered him and his ideals:

> One sad winter's day, at the *Petit Palais* among the fragments of "art assassinated" by the Germans . . . I met Peladan, graying, poorly dressed. We chatter for a long time among this piously reassembled débris—and I had the revelation of a very beautiful soul that deception and pain had delivered from all vanity. . . . I cannot render the troubling sensation of pity and of human respect that I carried away from this conversation in that cold and dark room with a defeated person. . . . Leaving, shivering in a too-light topcoat that inadequately protected him from the winter wind, Peladan told me admirable things about the drawings of Leonardo. . . [11]

Having suffered the barbaric bombardments of the Germans for nearly four years, against which he railed violently, Péladan died accidentally on 27 June 1918, aged sixty, at Neuilly-sur-Seine, Nanterre, of food poisoning, less than five months before the Armistice he knew was imminent.

Of Péladan's legacy, Michelet wrote:

> In this world, submitted to a slow but frightful justice, all pays for itself. Péladan has paid dear for the fracas that he made in his youth. He had consented to descend in order to dazzle the vulgar. He was punished hard for it. When he had edified a rich *oeuvre* of brilliant beauties, his contemporaries considered him a clown. Around him he had himself killed respect, discouraged admiration, destroyed friendliness. He died sad and abandoned.

—His *oeuvre* remains. It will enjoy yet the destiny reserved for those who have launched themselves at the peaks. An élite will seek the beauties and will impose them to the respect of the vulgar. Posterity has different floors. Great artists only find their audience at the superior levels. A choice will establish itself between works of which certain ones will not resist the rat-like teeth of the time. Péladan, eloquent and lyrical improviser, wrote too much and too fast. But his hasty word is always brilliant, colorful, ardent, impassioned. In any novel of his, there are always ten pages of magnificent flight. . . . Péladan could write: "Few writers have written on love with such lucidity as I." . . . Ethics and aesthetics are twin sisters: Péladan projects himself into the flower-beds of one and of the other with the same surety. Thus he has spread his torrential propositions, his audacious dogmatism in the series of works he assembled in his *Amphitheatre of Dead Sciences.* The title is inexact: the Sciences he envisages there are immortal, like the gods on whose activities they comment. Without doubt they fall into periods of lethargy, but they always renew themselves and so long as definitive barbarism does not submerge the world, the centuries will resuscitate some minds audacious enough to penetrate them.

In this series of aesthetic predications, Péladan shows himself a *theologian for extravagants*—in the initial sense of the word designating those who go beyond the banal path—a passionate moralist showing aspirants to the disciplines that lead to the feet of Venus, or of Apollo, or even of Hermes Trismegistus. . . . We salute him![12]

So we should.

FIFTEEN

THE MARTINIST ORDER

As ever with esoteric societies, accounts of origins are obscure and often contradictory, frequently as a result of bifurcations and secessions within Orders that leave remnants and dominant strands tinkering with titles and making competitive claims for origin, primacy, and authority. Such is the case with Papus's most enduring creation, the Martinist Order, which in his lifetime maintained a broad unity by dint of his ecumenical instincts and personal charisma.

In his 1899 brochure *Martinéisme, Willermozisme, Martinisme et Franc-Maçonnerie* (Martinezism, Willermozism, Martinism, and Freemasonry), Papus tried to show how it was possible to have integrated the theurgic tradition of Martinèz de Pasqually, the Masonic Templarism of Jean-Baptiste Willermoz, and the Christian Theosophy of Louis-Claude de St. Martin in a single initiatic Order, even when exponents of each of these traditions wanted their emphasis to dominate. Papus's Ordre Martiniste was intended to synthesize the essences of these traditions and function in lodges as a primarily Christian Freemasonry, heir to Pasqually and Willermoz's enigmatic high grade of "Réau-Croix," with an ultimate degree of "Unknown Superior" (*Supérieur Inconnu*, or S∴I∴). The aim of the initiatory process was the restoration of the heavenly Adam within the being of the aspirant.

Most scholarly histories of Papus's Martinist Order date its inception from Papus's resigning from the Theosophical Society and his establishment in 1891 of a Supreme Council of twelve of the Martinist Order with de Guaita, Péladan (temporarily), Maurice Barrès (temporarily),

*Fig. 15.1. The one
and only PAPUS*

Paul Adam, Chamuel, Barlet, Paul Sédir, Georges Montières, Jacques Berget, Jules Lejay, and Augustin Chaboseau.[1] Victor-Émile Michelet would also join the Supreme Council. However, we only have to open the first few pages of the fourth volume of *L'Initiation* of 1889 to find an article entitled "Initiatic Discourse for a Martinist Reception" by a "holder of the Third Degree" and signed by Stanislas de Guaita "S∴I∴" to make us realize that Martinism was central to Papus's plans before either the establishment of the Supreme Council or the *Librairie du Merveilleux* at 29 rue de Trévise.

In the article, de Guaita states that once the three hierarchical grades of "our order" have been passed, culminating in that of "S∴I∴" (occasionally written simply as "S.I."), the initiate becomes in his turn *initiator*, commissioned to establish a group with himself as its "moral Tutor." Whether the initiate considered himself Buddhist, Christian, Idealist, Materialist, or Sceptic was of no consequence so long as the initiate was fired by love of his "human brothers," linked in solidarity to a universal and supreme religion, manifest in multiform ways in the world but essentially identical with itself. According to the Martinist, esotericism is the foundation of "all really true and profound religions," its testimony one in essence: "Love, Solidarity, Altruism, Fraternity, Charity." There is no dogmatic imposition in the Order; essential universal Truth is advocated by persuasion only: "a God defined is a finite god," de Guaita insisted. What the Martinist can know of the Absolute is that "from this unfathomable Absolute emanates eternally the androgynous Dyad, formed from two principles indissolubly united: the Vivifying Spirit and the living universal Soul, the mystery of whose union constitutes the Grand Arcana of the Word."

For the Word, that is "collective Humanity," is considered in his divine synthesis, before his disintegration. "That is the celestial Adam, before his fall; before this universal being became in himself modalized, passing from Unity to Number; from the Absolute to the Relative; from the Infinite to Space and from Eternity to Time."[2]

De Guaita's article shows a synthesis of Pasqually's ideas of reintegration, Böhme's vision of the fall of the heavenly Man, gnostic ideas of emanationism, d'Alveydre's inheritance of the primordial Tradition from Fabre d'Olivet, and Masonic conceptions of "that religion on which all men can agree." This is the marrow of Martinism and the seed from which Papus's initiatic project grew. It is a compelling, positive and spiritual vision of very broad appeal, and will doubtless flower again when the current fixations of global intolerance and bigoted separatism have finally dispersed their energies in futile reaction to the long march through the vegetative life of spiritual evolution, defined by de Guaita as follows: "Evolution, that is the universal Redemption of the Spirit. In evolving, the Spirit re-ascends. But before the re-ascent, the Spirit [or Mind] had descended: that is what we call Involution. . . . Never forget that the Universal Adam is wholly homogenous, a living Being, of which we are the organic atoms and the constitutive cells. We all live one in the others, as ones by the others; and as we are ourselves individually saved (to use Christian language), we do not cease to suffer and to struggle until all our brothers are as saved as we are. . . . Universal fraternity is not a delusion; it is a *reality of fact*." The Martinist mission is adumbrated thus:

> Remember, son of the Earth, that your great ambition must be to reconquer the zodiacal Eden into which you had to descend, finally to re-enter the ineffable Unity, OUTSIDE OF WHICH YOU ARE NOTHING, and in the bosom of which you will find, after labors and torments, that celestial peace, this conscious sleep that the Hindus know under the name of Nirvana: the supreme beatitude of the Omniscience, in God.[3]

Papus's interest in Martinism went back quite a bit further than the establishment of a Supreme Council. Martinism appealed deeply to Papus's inner struggle, as a medical student, with the materialism of many of medicine's most vocal pundits, who said, "I see no soul when I wield the scalpel; life is cells fed by blood. The brain is composed of cells; the individual is cellular activity." Papus's short account of how he became an occultist—in his "Basics of Occult Science"—goes over this ground thoroughly. Little facts suggested to him there was more to it, facts such as: the living human cells are wholly replaced within a three year period. If we meet someone after that time, nothing we see is what was there before, and yet, identification is plain. Individuality is not absolutely identical with visible substance. Papus bravely opposed

Fig. 15.2. Papus's diagram illustrating a Christian synthesis of Masonic symbolism. The seven steps on the right are the traditional seven liberal arts dear to Freemasons; on the left are the seven steps of the mystical Kadosh ladder of the Ancient & Accepted Scottish Rite. The center steps indicate the ascending path from physical, elemental being to heavenly enlightenment: Force, Work, Science, Virtue, Purity, Light, Truth, from Traité élementaire de science occulte *(Elementary Treatise on Occult Science), first edition, 1888.*

the positivist dogma that the brain is like a telegraph apparatus that sends dispatches, whereas to Papus, the brain was a means of transmission, not a source. Put another way, a dismantled piano does not suggest melody but mechanics. The body, a means, is neither cause nor end.

Scholars agree that Papus's introduction to Martinism came through an "initiation" effected by a proponent of Mesmer's "animal magnetism," Henri Delaage (1825–1882) a few weeks before Delaages's death. In an article signed "RA," Pierre-Augustin Chaboseau (1868–1946) is supposed to have maintained he was similarly "initiated" by his aunt Amélie de Boise-Montmart in 1886, initiation consisting in the "oral transmission of a particular teaching and a certain comprehension of the laws of the universe and of spiritual life, which in no sense could be regarded as an initiation in a ritualistic form."[4] This information, however, is uncertain.

Louis-Claude de St. Martin was not responsible for the activities of those who were inspired by him directly or indirectly, and never founded an Order or society with an initiation ritual, though he was personally connected to those who did and who held his works as vital philosophical adjuncts to their ceremonial practices. That being

Fig. 15.3. Henri Delaage
(1825–1882)

Fig. 15.4. Augustin Chaboseau (1868–1946)

a follower of St. Martin required some formal initiation at all seems to have been a supposition endemic to high-grade Freemasonry of the Rosicrucian and neo-Templarist type. Nevertheless, Delaage and librarian Augustin Chaboseau valued their Martinist insights and attributed their spiritual substance to a mind-to-mind or speech-to-ear reception in a direct line of people ("Unknown Superiors") going back to the person of St. Martin who had called himself the "Unknown Philosopher," referring to his isolation from the dominant rationalist philosophers of his day and the spiritual nature of his wisdom discourse. Really, there should have been no need for such obfuscation, but when the transmitters of St. Martin's doctrines were invariably survivors or associates of late eighteenth-century neo-Rosicrucian Orders, or "high-grade Egyptian" Masonic Orders, such was inevitable.

Papus was friendly with both Delaage and Chaboseau, and claimed that in 1888 he shared knowledge of his initiation with Chaboseau only to find his friend had enjoyed the same experience. The experience, whatever it consisted of, inspired the name of the journal Papus launched on an unsuspecting world in October of that year, and most probably the idea of "reviving" a Martinist Order.

L'Initiation served to encourage the "Men of Desire" to come

out of the woodwork. Anyone showing promise was invited to join
the Order and in due course, to establish their own lodges. However,
by what means de Guaita, for example, was able to call himself an
S∴I∴(*Supérieur Inconnu*) is obscure as there were no rituals from
St. Martin himself, only rituals relating to Willermoz's "Scottish
Rectified Rite" that incorporated material from Pasqually's Order of
Elect Priests of the Universe and other sources. Papus himself was not a
regular Freemason, unlike a number of his close colleagues. The desire
of members for formal structures, usually on Masonic lines, created
fissures within the Order, but while Papus was alive, the multicellular
body remained intact despite line fractures in its structure. The three
degrees referred to in de Guaita's article in *L'Initiation* of 1889 would
from later sources appear to have been: *Associé, Initié,* and *Adepte* or
S∴I∴, that is, initiator.

One would like to think that initiation consisted of recognition of
a shared aspirational consciousness, awareness of a desire for reintegration, men known by mind alone, that is, election by consciousness only,
rather than persons imagining they had been truly initiated simply as
a result of having been party to a ceremony and made some declarations, however sincere. One suspects that the election by consciousness
model was Papus's psychological understanding of initiation, that is, a
progressive orientation of spirit, or reorientation if such was necessary.
Unknown philosophers might as such be unknown to themselves, need-
ing just a nudge in the right direction to establish the process of spiritual ascent to the primal glorious state of Man.

With *L'Initiation* as the means of international exchange, it did not
take long for branches of the Order to spread through Europe to the
United States and South America.

To give a sense of mundane reality to what a Martinist affiliation
might have meant in practice in Papus's lifetime, one need only read an
announcement made in the April 1900 issue of *L'Initiation*. At precisely
the time a twenty-five-year-old Aleister Crowley was in Paris taking
instructions from Samuel Mathers to return to London (on the thirteenth) to uphold Mathers's position as Head of the Martinist-friendly
Hermetic Order of the Golden Dawn, threatened by a revolt led by

Florence Farr and W. B. Yeats, Crowley could—and probably did—
read the following announcement on page 90: the context, by the way,
being the 1900 World Exhibition, held in Paris to celebrate a century
of progress:

ORDRE MARTINISTE

During the duration of the Exhibition, the Martinist Order will
hold several formal sessions in Paris, all lodges uniting, and will
invite to these sessions Brethren with passage to rites affiliated to
the Order [such as the Gnostic Church]. A special room has been
prepared for the purpose.

The Velléda Lodge [Michelet's lodge] has inaugurated its obligations by invitations for a conference with projections on *Symbolism*
taking as an example the church of Notre-Dame de Paris. The first
meeting of this kind was a lively success [it was led by Michelet].

The new administrative rituals are at the disposition of our general delegates who will produce them on request.[5]

Papus had created an international, spiritually oriented movement, as
much a part of the real world of 1900 as the World Exhibition.

SIXTEEN

The Boys Move In

It is easy to become a victim of success. When a movement becomes a magnet, who can say what it will attract? After a period of incandescence, new movements frequently see a whole change of actors, if not of scenery. By 1891, Paris was already a magnet for foreign occultists who brought their own ideas to the show, eventually dissipating the tight, mutually conscious, and mostly tolerant world that ran from Montmartre to the rue de la Chaussée d'Antin, the rue de Trévise, then southwest to the avenue de Wagram.

British cofounder of the Hermetic Order of the Golden Dawn, Samuel "MacGregor" Mathers made an exploratory visit to Paris in July 1891, shortly after Papus and Chaboseau's establishment of the Martinist Order's Supreme Council, a not insignificant event for one such as Mathers, leading member of the British Masonic offshoot, the *Societas Rosicruciana in Anglia,* which at the time claimed to be the true channel of Rosicrucian initiation. Mathers informed his Rosicrucian colleague William Wynn Westcott, in London, that his visit to Paris afforded him opportunity to meet several of the "Secret Chiefs" of his and Westcott's relatively new Order. One secret chief in particular, "Frater Lux Ex Tenebris," was later alleged to have been the source for the rituals of the *Rosae Rubae et Aureae Crucis,* the Golden Dawn's interior "Second Order."

While it is significant that of the very few Orders Mathers's Golden Dawn recognized and respected, the Martinist Order held paramount position, it is also significant with regard to this supposed secret chief's identity—if he or she had one—that Mathers's famous description of meeting the Secret Chiefs in the Bois de Boulogne bears kinship with Doinel's account of the spiritual presence of Cathar initiators at the oratory of Lady Caithness in 1889. Like Doinel's alleged encounter with spirit-Cathars, Mathers declared the Secret Chiefs' presence electric, almost unbearable, involving intense pressure on the nervous system. Had these persons "magnetized" themselves, one wonders—if indeed they ever existed outside of Mathers's imagination?

Having greatly admired Lady Caithness's frequent guest, the late seeress Anna Kingsford (1846–1888)—he had, we recall, given lectures to Kingsford's Hermetic Society—Mathers lost interest in the Theosophical Society on much the same grounds as did Kingsford, Maitland, and Papus. Mathers's and Westcott's inspiration to establish the Golden Dawn as a magical society open to women owed much to Kingsford. If one also bears in mind Mathers's personal identification with political Legitimism and with the royal house of Scotland, how could he not have been drawn to the circle of Lady Caithness who held herself to be in spiritual communication with Scotland's last independent queen? Furthermore, Mathers, a man not unknown to embellish facts as he felt inspired, also held that one of the Secret Chiefs was a French initiate of Scottish origin who had some link to the Scottish royal house. This figure he called *Frater Lux Ex Septentriones* (the "Septentrion" being the far northern constellations). "Brother Light from the North" lived in Paris. The "Lion of Septentrion" was a visionary figure of late sixteenth- and early seventeenth-century apocalyptic speculation, dear to those inspired by the Fraternity of the Rose-Cross. The Lion was identified with the northern kingdoms (Septentrion) that would swoop down on the enemies of Christ to establish the age of the Holy Spirit. Lady Caithness was not only related to Scottish nobility but regarded her inspired self, to all intents and purposes, as a kind of manifestation or channel of the spirit of legitimate Stuart, Mary Queen of Scots, and most importantly, held to an apocalyptic theory whose final age would see the spiritual liberation and equality of the divine spirit of Woman. Equally, by association, Mathers's "Secret Chief" could have been Doinel who partook of Lady Caithness's inspirational draft.

Fig. 16.1. Annie Horniman (1860–1937), founder of the Abbey Theatre, Dublin, and the first English regional repertory company, in Manchester

Fig. 16.2. Moina Mathers (1865–1928), feminist artist, wife of Samuel Mathers

Mathers and his French-born wife, Moina, had ample cause to leave London for Paris on 20 May 1892, shortly after the first *Salon de la Rose-Croix*. The previous year, Mathers had lost his museum job working for Golden Dawn member Annie Horniman's father. According to Moina, Paris offered a better lifestyle for less money.[1] Being fond of Moina, Annie Horniman supported the couple. Slade School of Art student Moina wanted to pursue her artistic career at the *Académie Colarossi* at 10 rue de la Grande-Chaumière in the 6th arrondissement, while being closer to her Paris-based brother, now famous doctor of philosophy, Henri Bergson.

Mathers felt instructed by the Secret Chiefs (!) to take advantage of the fact that Belle Époque Paris was the capital of occultism. Mathers also knew that the foundation documents of the Golden Dawn system derived from manuscripts dear to the late eighteenth-century German Asiatic Brethren and the Gold-und-Rosenkreuzers and had doubtless heard it rumored, not only that skeins of these traditions were still active, but that they were linked to lines of Martinist initiation. We should also bear in mind that the name given to Secret Chiefs among eighteenth-century French and German neo-Rosicrucians was that of Unknown Superior. Supérieurs Inconnus had the right to initiate in the Ordre Martiniste, being spiritually not of this world.

It seems fairly clear that Mathers wanted to "get ahead" of his colleagues in the Golden Dawn, establishing his authority over the Order on a surer footing than the basic Order documents themselves. Mathers would spend much time in the *Bibliothèque de l'Arsénal* digging out texts of a kind that had appealed to Adrien Péladan *fils*'s initiator, Édouard de Lapasse, though Mathers favored Kabbalah and magic more than medicine and alchemy. It was there that Mathers translated the seventeenth-century "Sacred Magic of Abra-melin the Mage" a text pivotal to Mathers protégé Aleister Crowley's initiatory system. In the meantime, Mathers brought to Paris authentic British Freemasonry, a Celtic and Scottish legitimacy spin, and the implication of his Order's being a direct descendant of the London Rosicrucian era of Francis Bacon, Robert Fludd, Thomas Vaughan, and Elias Ashmole, a period much respected in French esoteric, and particularly Martinist, circles.

After a brief residence at 79 rue Miromesnil, 8th arrondissement, the Mathers family moved to an apartment at 1 avenue Duquesne, near the Hôtel des Invalides. There the first meetings of the Ahathoor Number 7 Temple took place. *Ahathoor* referred to the Egyptian goddess "Hathor." Its official consecration took place at 8:30 a.m. on Saturday 6 January 1894 (Epiphany) with Mathers as Imperator, assisted by Annie Elizabeth Frederika Horniman and William Wynn Westcott.[2]

Moving west to the suburb of Auteuil the following year, the Mathers family inhabited a very attractive villa with three accesses, and thus three addresses: 87 avenue Mozart (a grand and busy thoroughfare), 43 rue Ribéra (a pleasant narrow back street), and 41 rue de la Source (a quiet residential road), each giving entry to the garden, the temple—a large hall by a marble staircase that served as a dais for the adepts—and the private residence respectively.

Decorated with large paintings of Egyptian deities, the temple swung into action. On 23 March 1895, Papus was admitted as a neophyte at the temple in a ceremony specially conducted in French. Papus

408 ⊕ The Boys Move In

did not proceed with further initiations in the Outer Order. Perhaps he felt he should have gone straight into the Second Order, or maybe he was simply curious to know what they were about. An 1895 document called "General Orders" from the Temple indicated that the Golden Dawn respected other schools of genuine occultism, excepting that of Thomas Lake Harris (which involved sexual magic), Péladan's R+C+C+ ("an ignorant perversion of the Rosicrucian Brotherhood . . . not to be dignified with the name of an occult order"), and the Hermetic Brotherhood of Luxor. The reason for the latter proscription is telling. The HBL is condemned as one condemns "Luciferian and Palladian" teachings. Clearly, Mathers was as taken in by "Léo Taxil" as was Doinel! The Martinist Order, on the other hand, "so long as they adhere to their founder's teachings," will be in harmony with the Golden Dawn's Inner Order: that can only imply that the quality of initiation was held to be in common, for the Inner Order was only for the most serious, committed, and suitable adepts.

Given all we currently know, it is likely that Papus saw Paris as the true "axis of gravitation" for esoteric initiation and was not happy to see competing centers of authority. When all was said and done, the Golden Dawn was a British-based Order that could by extension upset harmony in Paris. What was more, its doctrinal basis was neither, as was the Martinist Order, "Christique," nor particularly Christian. Unlike Papus, who was devoted to expanding the frontiers of science and medicine, the Golden Dawn was committed to ceremonial magic, with a heavy emphasis on talismanic and *grimoire*-based magic with attendant psychological risks. It was not much interested in *philosophy*. Beside, Papus was already committed to what he took to be the revived Rosicrucian Order, the R+C+K. While the Golden Dawn paid great attention to the integration of the tarot with Kabbalah, what need had Papus, an authority of the "Tarot of the Bohemians," with Oswald Wirth and de Guaita and all his other colleagues on his side, for the autodidactic Freemason from Great Britain? *Too many cooks. . .* The most that could be expected then was a mutual tolerance; Mathers had more to gain from Paris than Paris had from Mathers.

As far as the minutes of Ahathoor Temple Number 7 went, while it received visits from England in the shapes of Allan Bennett, Frederick Leigh Gardner, Maud Gonne, W. B. Yeats, Florence Farr, Percy Bullock, Pamela Carden, and Aleister Crowley, the *Librairie du Merveilleux* contingent kept away from it.[3] Victor-Émile Michelet, interestingly, never mentions it once. The only names familiar to Michelet to take an interest in the temple at Auteuil were first, astrologer Ely Star (real name Eugène Jacob) and second, Jules Bois, who continued to weave his own Huysmans-oriented path through Parisian occultism during the 1890s. Among the twenty-seven men and women initiated at the temple, Ely Star was initiated Neophyte on 22 August 1896, raised to Adeptus Minor on 25 February 1898, becoming Hierophant (high priest) of the temple in September 1899, just in time for Aleister Crowley's first visit to the suburb on Golden Dawn business in January 1900.

By the time Crowley visited, Mathers had launched his energies into a new, parallel project, and it appears to have been in pursuance of this that Mathers came to initiate Jules Bois. As a means of broadening the Golden Dawn's appeal, Mathers undertook a semipublic revival of

*Fig. 16.3. Samuel and Moina Mathers revive
the cult of Isis in Paris, 1900*

the cult of Egyptian goddess Isis, with the highly artistic and intuitive Moina as high priestess Anari, and himself as high priest Rameses of the Isiac rite. What began in a suburban street in Passy soon proved so popular it moved to a little theater on the Butte of Montmartre, the *Théâtre de la Bodinière*.

Why had they done it? asked Frederic Lees when he interviewed the "Count and Countess MacGregor of Glenstrae" for *The Humanitarian* (February 1900). The Count replied that it wasn't what people thought: *more decadence!* No! On the contrary, it was to combat the decadence of the time. He and the countess had thoroughly researched the history so that they could strip the authentic cult of accretions and employ it to introduce modern people to a factor of renewal. High Priestess Anari took up the story. It was really all thanks to getting to know Jules Bois, who, as everyone knew, was very interested in understanding the origin of religions and their rebirth.

Bois wrote a fascinating account of the capital's lesser-known spiritual devotees, *The Little Religions of Paris* (Paris: Léon Chailley, 1894), that, in addition to chapters on Swedenborgians and Buddhists, contained a chapter on the "Cult of Isis." While not mentioning Mathers, Bois suggested La Rochefoucauld was a devotee in terms of art. Lady Caithness's name was invoked due to her claim to manifest the Sophia of the Egyptian Gnostics. This rather suggests Mathers got the idea for the enactment from Bois's book, as there was clearly a Parisian audience for the goddess. Incidentally, Bois's chapter on "The Gnostics" opens with an interview with Jules Doinel in which the "modest" Doinel tells Bois: "It was the Aion Jesus himself who in 1867 laid his hands and consecrated me bishop of Montségur." Doinel's date of spiritual initiation is interesting as it precedes publication of Peyrat's history of the Albigensians or Cathars, generally accepted as the start of the Cathar revival.

It was Bois's request that the Mathers's rites be enacted at the Montmartre theater, where Bois had already given a talk on Buddhism and put on a Buddhist religious service. Moina and her "Count" told Lees they didn't want to appear in public, however, and the matter would have rested there but for an intervention from Isis herself. One night she appeared in Moina's dreams to sanction her task of bringing Isiac

Fig. 16.4. Samuel Mathers (1854–1918), high priest Rameses at the Théâtre de la Bodinière

Fig. 16.5. Moina Mathers née *Bergson, high priestess Anari*

worship to a new generation in her own city—for Paris was allegedly a Gallic mispronunciation of the Greek *baris* referring to a boat, the symbol of Isis. *Monsieur* would give his conference on Egyptian magic and then people would see the real thing.

Monsieur et Madame Mathers appeared on stage in spectacular sacerdotal dress: white robes with leopard skin capes, gold bracelets, with Moina's long hair symbolizing the rays of the life-giving sun. On her head sat a little cone symbolizing the divine spirit: life purified by the spirit from above.

The mass consisted of prayers intoned with great solemnity by priest and priestess in turn, with the priest holding the lotus, and the priestess invoking the goddess with great passion. Then a young Parisienne performed the Dance of the Four Elements in a long white robe.

Were they monotheists? "No," replied Mathers. Like their predecessors, the divine spirit could be presented in the form of statues. Was not the universe a manifestation in matter of the divine power, and therefore a "great eidolon"? "We are pantheists. All forces of the universe are directed by a god. Consequently, the gods are infinite and numberless."

The count said their religion shared the general benefit of religions, that is, in showing the Good to humankind and the correct path to live. Despite its antiquity, he believed the Egyptian Book of the Dead more resembled the New Testament than the Old, even though Moses must have seen it when in Egypt and been influenced by it. Mathers suspected Jesus must have been familiar with the Isiac conception; did he not spend some missing years in Egypt? As in the New Testament one speaks of being a "member of Christ," the Book of the Dead speaks of being a "member of Osiris." One of Osiris's symbols was the good Shepherd.

The journalist had also attended meetings at the Mathers's home where he had encountered a large number of Paris's most respectable society, including painters, alchemists, and men and women of letters. The Countess MacGregor, student of the Colarossi Art School and other Parisian academies of art, gave vent to interesting views about religion.

The idea of the priestess had once been central to religion but was now neglected. This was to banish half of the divine nature, the giving and loving and receiving part of Nature. "When a religion symbolizes the universe by a divine Being, is it not illogical to omit Woman, who is the principal part of it, being the principal creator of the other part, the man?" How could the world become more pure, less materialist, if it excludes from the divine, the most ideal and the highest, that part of its nature that has at the same time the faculty of receiving and of giving love, love that is, in its most elevated aspect, a symbol of universal sympathy? And what is Nature, if it is not the assembly of thoughts dressed in matter, ideas that seek materialization? What is this eternal attraction between ideas and matter? It is the secret of life. Even a single flame has an intelligence that animates it. These are the intelligences that are the Elementals or Spirits of Nature. Not a grain of sand is without intelligence. Woman is a magician of Nature, from her birth, because she has great natural sensibility and innate and instinctive sympathy with the subtle intelligences of earth, air, fire, and water.

The journalist felt that Moina's impressive words showed something of the mystical and the occult, as well as of her intelligent nature as an accomplished artist. Readers today may think so too, and wonder why some members of the Martinist Order favored by Papus and his friends argued over whether women should be admitted to their mysteries. The feminist implications of the Isis cult more than explain the interest of Jules Bois in the project. Most of his writings during 1896–97 were devoted to feminism and feminist causes, actively attending the feminist congress in Paris in 1896, and building on the work of Villiers de l'Isle-Adam's book, *The Future Eve*. In 1898 Bois focused his attention on the theater, working in the 1898–99 season at the Bodinière, Montmartre, with the drama critic Sarcey (1827–1899), Gustave Larroumet (1852–1903), and journalist Georges Izoulet. Beyond the opportunity to join feminism to his occult and mystical interests, Jules Bois had no further serious interest in the Golden Dawn.

In early 1900, Mathers's longstanding problems with the London heads of his Inner Order began to accelerate, culminating in a whole new dimension of crisis when on 16 February 1900, feeling desperate for something to uphold his flagging authority, he entertained at the temple a "Mr. and Mrs. Horos." Mr. Horos was in fact American con man Frank Jackson. He and his partner, together with dupe Dr. Rose Adams, had heard about the Ahathoor Temple in New York. What they heard seemed to them an opportunity. They too, it seemed, were seeking to raise funds to promote Isis worship. The clincher came when Mrs. Horos confessed to being the true source of the Golden Dawn inspiration: "Soror Sapiens Dominabitur Astris" (SDA), from whom, Westcott had said, derived the authority to establish the Golden Dawn. Convinced Westcott had been lying when he said that *Soror SDA* had since died, Mathers made the catastrophic error of writing to inform Florence Farr that Westcott had falsified the correspondence with "Anna Sprengel" (Soror SDA) and that the only person with authority to ratify the Order's existence in the new circumstances was himself. From this moment the explosion of the Golden Dawn became inevitable.

Come the summer of 1900, Jules Bois, inspired by his houseguest Swami Vivekananda, journeyed with the Swami to India along with Bois's lover, opera star Emma Calvé, though Emma left the tour at Alexandria to return to Paris. Emma Calvé, by the way, was, like Bois, an S. I. of the Martinist Order and, in that capacity, according to Gérard Galtier, may well have been the source in New York of a supposed ini-

Fig. 16.6. Emma Calvé (1858–1942), performing Carmen *in 1904*

tiation of Harvey Spencer Lewis (1883–1939), founder of AMORC, though Lewis would claim his bona fide initiation occurred in Toulouse in 1909 (picking up, presumably, on a strand of Péladan's claim to Rose-Croix legitimacy). At the very time Lewis was in New York gathering elements for what eventually became the largest Roscrucian organization in the world, Emma Calvé toured the States (December 1914 to June 1916), while Bois, in 1915, worked as a journalist in New York. Since Lewis gave pseudonyms for alleged initiators, Galtier's hypothesis has great merit (Galtier, *Maçonnerie Egyptienne, Rose-Croix et Néo-Chevalerie*, p. 354–357).

Back in 1900, Bois would return from India disheartened and, like his friend Huysmans, convert to Catholicism. Meanwhile, Aleister Crowley, fed up and harassed over the fight in the Golden Dawn—

Fig. 16.7. Aleister Crowley, mountaineer, poet, and magician (1875–1947); Ordo Templi Orientis Archives

London had definitively revolted against Mathers while Crowley's clumsy attempts to retaliate on Mathers's behalf had failed—set sail for the United States in search of love and adventure, the start of an epic tour that kept him outside of Europe and inside Mexico, San Francisco, Hawaii, Japan, China, India, Burma, and Egypt until spring 1903, when he too returned to Paris to make an enviable impression in Montparnasse as explorer, poet, and magician, getting to know artists Carrière, Thaulow, and Rodin as well as the fascinating writer, Marcel Schwob (1867–1905) who wrote brilliantly for the Symbolist haven, the *Mercure de France.*

The Horos scandal and demise of Mathers's relationship with London's Inner Order effectively closed the Ahathoor Temple until 1909. In 1910 Mathers would take Crowley to court for publishing the rituals of the Golden Dawn; Crowley won.

JOANNY BRICAUD (1881–1934)

In 1936, Aleister Crowley's French student, André Pigné, wrote to his teacher for advice on entering Freemasonry, as Freemasonry was part of Crowley's study course, and joining it was recommended. Pigné wrote:

> Let me tell you that it is not as easy as you think to belong to Freemasonry here [France]. I have not succeeded. It is well nigh impossible to obtain Masonic magazines. . . . For the last few years, Freemasonry in this country has been attacked by the *Croix-de-Feu* [a French Catholic, fascist-oriented organization] and idiotic organizations of that sort, as well as in the so-called "right-wing" newspapers and this may be why it is surrounded by more secrecy than in England.[4]

Crowley advised Pigné to make contact with Monsieur J. Bricaud in Lyon, head of the Martinist Order: "he will no doubt introduce you to various Freemasons roundabout." Pigné replied that Bricaud was now dead and that Madame Bricaud was managing her late husband's work from 8 rue Bugeaud, Lyon. This path too proved fruitless and Pigné gave up after a few interviews. One might imagine Pigné would have had a far better chance of entering the Craft in Belle Époque Paris of the 1890s and early 1900s, but even Papus, for all his knowledge, energy, and achievements, could not get into the Grand Orient of France—of which Oswald Wirth and Jules Doinel were members—or any of the mainstream French Masonic Orders, even though there were quite a number of esoterically minded Masons operating within them. It is mainly for that reason that Papus would involve himself in what British Masonry calls "fringe" Masonic Orders, particularly the Ancient & Primitive Rites of Memphis and Misraim. He wanted to show main-stream Masonry that the "real thing" was spiritual, and use it as a means to uniting all esoteric Orders under an essentially Martinist umbrella, an ambition neither Papus, nor anybody else—including Crowley—has ever been able to achieve, on account of that human nature Masonry strives to transcend.

Jean or "Joanny" Bricaud would himself join the Ancient & Primitive Rites, which, after 1908, would in Paris be closely bound to the Gnostic Church founded by Doinel, of which Bricaud would head a split-off, as we shall see. Keen occultist Bricaud was only twenty years old when Fabre des Essarts of the Église Gnostique consecrated him bishop of Lyon in 1901. Bricaud's path to esoteric prominence was colorful and swift.

Fig. 16.8. Joanny Bricaud
(1881–1934)

* * *

Born into a French peasant family, Bricaud entered the Meximieux Catholic seminary northeast of Lyon where his expected path to the priesthood was diverted by fascination for books on occultism and an enthusiasm for the surviving Carmelite heretical—and sex-friendly—church founded by Eugène Vintras. The young, intense, sensitive-faced Bricaud also got to know Lyon chiromancer and bookseller, Gervais-Annet Bouchet (1864–1927), editor of a little review called *The Occult Union,* who with Dr. Marius Boccard, cowrote, under the pseudonym Elie Steel-Maret, "The Secret Archives of Freemasonry, Metropolitan College of France, Lyon, Second Province 1765–1852," published in 1893, having obtained the original manuscripts as a gift from Lyonais Mason Michel Carvanier (or Cavarnier).

A scholarly work, its modest exterior contained vital, truly extraordinary, and long forgotten documents that demonstrated an eighteenth-century Freemasonry animated by spiritual Christianity. It included letters from key continental figures from the archives of Jean-Baptiste Willermoz. In so doing, it helped to revive a "traditionalist" current centered on the Scottish Rectified Rite originally founded by Willermoz, linked by enthusiasts to the philosophy of Louis-Claude de St. Martin.[5] Papus went to Lyon to find Bouchet and took a very serious interest in the work. In fact, he exploited it, employing the material to demonstrate that it "represented the Martinist tradition," which is not the case.[6] As head of the Martinist Order, Papus considered himself uniquely able to appreciate the value of the Lyon archives "miraculously saved," and "Elie Steel," whom Papus had known since 1890, was left in undeserved obscurity, though Bouchet was admitted to the Martinist Order and himself made strenuous, thankless efforts to publicize Papus's *Voile d'Isis* in Lyon before establishing himself at 34 rue de Marseille as a practitioner of magnetic healing, divination, tarot, horoscope, and somnambulism. Papus undoubtedly used the portion of the material he bought from the original archives to justify his sense of authority and destiny, hampered by his not being a Mason. For Papus, the fact that authentic material from Pasqually and St. Martin had come his way was simply "miraculous." It wasn't; it was simply a consequence of Bouchet's attentiveness and generosity.

Bouchet's link to Papus provided Bricaud's link to Paris, for Bouchet introduced Bricaud to Papus's close associate, Dr. Emmanuel Lalande ("Marc Haven"). Marc Haven introduced Bricaud to Papus's "spiritual father," the remarkable healer from Arbresle near Lyon, Nizier Anthelme Philippe (1849–1905), known as "Monsieur Philippe" who would become Marc Haven's father-in-law.

So struck was Papus by Monsieur Philippe's stupendous powers of healing by Christian prayer that he persuaded the wealthy and extremely charitable thaumaturge to establish a school of magnetism at Lyon where Monsieur Philippe taught from 1895 to 1898. Philippe himself never used manual techniques, only the power of selfless prayer. For Papus, Philippe was absolute living proof that spiritual energies were completely real. Materialism was therefore completely false in its premises. Likewise impressed, Jean Bricaud joined the school on 6 December 1897. Bricaud also got to know Lyon-based magnetizer and hypnotist-healer, Alphonse Bouvier (1851–1931). Bouvier had worked at the Salpêtrière hospital, Paris, observing, like Papus, the work of leader in the field Dr. Charcot, while acquainting himself with Lieutenant Colonel de Rochas, the psychic investigator. Jacques Charrot (1831–1911), a surviving pupil of

Fig. 16.9. "Monsieur Philippe"
(1849–1905)

Éliphas Lévi, guided Bricaud's studies in Kabbalah and magic.

As Tau Johannes, Bricaud split with Fabre des Essarts's Gnostic Church in 1907, establishing a body—*l'Église Catholique Gnostique*—more closely tied to the Martinist Order, containing elements of the Johannite Church of Fabre Palaprat and of the Carmelite Church of Vintras. Taking with him Papus and Fugairon (Tau Sophronius), Bricaud produced a new catechism, one that denied a cardinal tenet of Synesius's, namely, that everyone would eventually be saved, as God was love and was above all evil, which is resistance to love. Contrary to Synesius (Fabre des Essarts), to Péladan, and to Abbé Alta (Calixte Mélinge, 1842–1933), Bricaud maintained that even those who wanted to repent at the end when the hylic world was about to be destroyed would be too late; the doors of light would already be shut and forever. This was not agreeable to Déodat Roché's way of thinking. The new body's synod declared Bricaud Patriarch "Jean II" in February 1908, renaming the church the *Église Gnostique Universelle*.

In 1911 Papus's Supreme Council of the Martinist Order signed a treaty of alliance with the High Synod of the Universal Gnostic Church. This alliance, signed by Papus and Bricaud, did not, technically speaking, make Bricaud's church the official church of the Martinist Order, but it functioned as such in effect. Regarding the Martinist Order, Bricaud established it in Lyon in 1914 on Willermoz's Pasquallian-Masonic principles, with himself as "Legate of the Martinist Order for the Province of Lyon": thus, in Papus's terms, bringing the Martinist succession "home."

DÉODAT ROCHÉ

It is fairly curious how from the mid-1890s the influence of Occult Paris begins to extend to Languedoc in a more pronounced manner than even Jules Doinel's calling himself bishop of Montségur, Primate of the Albigeois, might have suggested a few years earlier. After officially quitting the Gnostic Church in 1895 and reconciling himself to Rome—he later explained to Fabre des Essarts that his submission to the Roman Catholic bishop of Orléans, intended to reconcile Rome to the gnosis, was inspired by "demiurgical angels"—Doinel left Orléans and moved far south to Carcassonne for a job as curator and archivist of the Aude department, close to his "old" gnostic-Cathar diocese of Montségur. Coincidentally, Doinel was archiving the region's history in Carcassonne at the very time crooked priest Bérenger Saunière was overseeing final renovations to the church at Rennes le Château, between Carcassonne and Montségur. As far as we know, Saunière, unlike Doinel, had no particular interest in the Cathars, whose presence (or absence) cannot be avoided today by anyone visiting the region. In fact, much of the twentieth century's enthusiasm for the Cathars may be laid at the door of onetime gnostic bishop, Déodat Roché, and his later more circumspect admirer, René Nelli.

Doinel was still working at Carcassonne when twenty-two-year-old law and philosophy student Déodat Roché founded the magazine *Albigensian Awakening* in Toulouse with Doinel's old colleague, naturalist, geologist, philosopher, and medical doctor Louis Sophrone Fugairon, or Tau Sophronius, gnostic bishop of Béziers, who came from Ax les Thermes in the wild Ariège, southwest of Carcassonne. Doinel's successor, Fabre des Essarts, encouraged Fugairon's efforts, recording that the magazine's purpose was to reconnect the "Neognosis" to the "Cathar tradition." By the time the magazine was retitled *Modern Gnosis* in 1904, Doinel had died and there were new kids on the block.

Déodat Roché's father Paul, notary and councilor at Arques, was a Martinist S.˙.I.˙., having committed to occultism in 1894. His son joined Papus's Independent Group of Esoteric Studies in 1896, maintaining a correspondence with "Sédir" (Yves Leloup), entering the Gnostic Church in 1899 when he first encountered Fugairon and Fabre des Essarts. Ordained deacon in 1901, Roché was consecrated Tau Theodotus, bishop of Carcassonne in 1903.[7]

While Roché would lose faith in the Gnostic Church founded by Doinel, he entered the fold with great sincerity. In a letter to Fugairon of 29 August 1899, Déodat stated: "I came to Christ by the Gnosis, I also have a complete confidence in the future of a Church that will convince the psychics by Reason to lead them to the pneumatic [spiritual] state by Love. I have not yet given my stone for the Temple's reconstruction: this will be the work of my life."[8] Roché, in spreading the magazine about the region got to know the people very well who were willing to entertain its ideas. He found liberal Protestants, spiritualists, and Moravian Brethren the most open to the gnostic experience.

On 29 January 1900, Roché requested from Fugairon the addresses of Péladan and Larmandie, adding that Papus was more likely to reply to Fugairon than to himself.[9] Other preserved letters reveal Déodat Roché as a highly intelligent person, grappling seriously with the implications of the gnosis, Valentinian and Cathar, for his own times. He valued Sophronius's gnostic catechism of 1900 and believed it completed the historic task of Fabre des Essarts as Patriarch.

The letters to Fugairon also reveal that by 1901, Doinel was contributing to the effort again. Roché wrote from Toulouse on Thursday, 3 January 1901: "You will receive from Doinel the complete corrected proofs [of "Le Réveil"]."[10] Doinel, however, had very little time left. In March 1902, he died, and the church he created would, as we have seen, bifurcate over issues of doctrine and affiliation.

Roché, regardless, remained devoted to the memory of the Cathars, understood as much by his own spiritual revelations—influenced after 1921 by the spiritual teachings of Rudolf Steiner—as by strict historical methodology.

Roché became a lawyer in 1901, a magistrate in 1906, first in Limoux, then in Carcassonne where he joined Lodge "True Friends United" of the Grand Orient, devoting his spare time to spiritual and moral culture through local history when not attending to judicial offices. His being a Freemason saw him in later life removed from office by the pro-Nazi Vichy regime, some of whose supporters in conjunction with the Gestapo martyred Bricaud's successor, Constant Chevillon, Tau Harmonius, Patriarch of the (renamed) "Gnostic Apostolic Church," Grand Master in France of the Rites of Memphis and Misraim, on 23 March 1944 in Lyon.

After World War II, Roché founded the Association for the Remembrance and Study of the Cathars, without whose pioneering work the region would not be the internationally famous Cathar magnet it is today. His house in Arques has served as a museum devoted to Catharism, a faith practically destroyed by intolerance some 700 years ago, but that stimulates profound spiritual reflection and irresistible fascination today.

THE ANCIENT & PRIMITIVE RITES OF MEMPHIS AND MISRAIM

In many respects it is difficult to understand the attraction for the Masonic rites of Memphis and of Misraim once one has thoroughly removed from one's mind any suspicion that they might once have served as carriers of esoteric knowledge from ancient Egypt, as their first practitioners were encouraged to think. While such a supposition still lingered around the turn of the twentieth century, one suspects their greatest attraction lay in being "underdogs" of official Masonry. All the dominant "regular" Grand Lodges, Chapters, and Supreme Councils in France, Great Britain, the United States, and elsewhere did what they could to prevent brethren from joining them. Other than that, if you had problems getting into regular lodges, access to the condemned rites had the double advantage of giving one Masonic knowledge without too much strain while cocking a snook at the "dogs in the manger," with a frisson of esoteric mystery to boot. And of course, if the idea of "high grade" Masonry attracts, rites numbering ninety degrees or over nearly triples the Ancient & Accepted *ne plus ultra* Scottish Rite figure of thirty-three!

It has been believed that the Rite of Misraim—sometimes with an umlaut over the second *i*—or Mizraim (Hebrew for Egypt) goes back at least to Masonic magician Cagliostro (1743–1795). That would have given Misraim at least the caché of genius, but what appears to have survived of Cagliostro's authentic "Egyptian" rite appears very different, more cogently imbued with alchemical symbolism of regeneration, unlike the smorgasbord of symbolic, philosophic, mystical, and Kabbalistic elements to be found scattered in Misraim's elephantine ninety degrees.[11]

Fig. 16.10. Marc Bédarride (1776–1846),
Masonic innovator

Founded in Milan in 1805 by Joseph, Michel, and Marc Bédarride, the three brothers tried unsuccessfully to establish their Rite of Misraim in France, a failure largely due to the Grand Orient de France's complete resistance to it, though some degrees were worked quietly by the curious. It was persistently accused of having lifted at least five of its degrees from the Ancient & Accepted Scottish Rite, though to objective observers, the history of that rite is somewhat murky as well, and certainly not ancient, even where it was accepted. Misraim has long stood accused of being created because Milan's Ancient & Accepted Rite's Supreme Council rejected its originators. The Rite of Misraim's own Supreme Council was dissolved in 1817, despite Marc Bédarride's 861 page history of the rite!

The Ancient & Primitive Rite of Memphis fared better. It had a fascinating "order history," that is, a moralizing romance cooked up to feel like a legend based in history. A priest of Serapis, one Ormus (Latin for "Elm"), allegedly passed it on from his home in Alexandria through spiritual engagement with St. Mark, founder of the Coptic Church, thus amalgamating the wisdom of Egypt with that of Christ, whereafter it was supposed to have continued in secret until discovered, temporarily, during the crusades when its Rosicrucian-type society illuminated the Templars and continued to illuminate the fortunate thereafter: just the kind of thing for Indiana Jones to get his whip into!

The rite has been linked to the Rite of Philalethes (ca. 1773) of the Marquis of Chefdebien and the "Primitive Philadelphes" ("Lovers of Mankind"). According to one Samuel Honis, he had in Cairo been a member of a Lodge of Philalethes called the "Disciples of Memphis," run by servicemen of Napoleon's Egyptian campaign allegedly hooked up while serving in the East with mystical groups such as the Druze of Lebanon. Whatever Honis garnered he brought to France where, on 30 April 1815, he founded at Montauban a Grand Lodge of the Disciples of Memphis together with Gabriel Mathieu Marconis de Nègre, Baron Dumas, the Marquis de Laroque, and Hypolite Labrunie, among others. Closed less than a year later, its archives were placed at Marconis de Nègre's disposal.[12]

In 1838, a man who claimed to be Gabriel Mathieu Marconis de Nègre's son, Jacques Étienne Marconis de Nègre (1795–1868)—

Fig. 16.11. "Jacques Étienne Marconis de Nègre"
(1795–1868)

and who, according to Emmanuel Rebold's *Sketch of the History of the Ancient & Primitive Rite of Masonry* (London, 1875), was in fact one James Stephen Marconis, a Misraim reject from Paris—revived the Order and was elected Grand Hierophant on 7 July 1838. The Hierophant then arranged the archives and, modeling the rite on the Rite of Misraim, came up with a ninety-degree rite divided into three series and seven classes. Seven mostly administrative degrees were added later, perhaps to "top" Misraim's ninety.

While the Rite of Memphis got off the ground with lodges in Marseilles, Brussels, and London, it suffered constant harassment from regular Masonic bodies, despite Marconis de Nègre's enthusiastic production of magazines claiming its superlative virtue as the most exclusive solar orb of the Masonic universe. It fared better, however, in the United States where David McLellan became the Rite of Memphis's first Grand Master. Establishing the rite in the States proved its salvation, for when de Nègre attempted to revive it in Paris in 1862 by getting it officially recognized, the Grand Orient finally relented, but solely on condition that members accepted its grades were no higher than the three Craft grades. The price of recognition in France was the rite's practical extinction. Back in the States, McLellan resigned his office in favor of flamboyant Harry James Seymour (1821–1883), and under Seymour, claiming the Grand Orient of France had no jurisdiction in the States, the rite persisted through the century with an increasingly checkered, bruised, and controversial career, during which time it was used to create a transposed thirty-three-degree rite, equivalent (by number!) to the Ancient & Accepted Rite, from which Seymour had been expelled.

We now move to Great Britain where the remarkably independent Freemason, John Yarker (1833–1913; United Grand Lodge of England *demitted*) familiarized himself with rare rites, believing them repositories of a suppressed history of true Masonry, while his researches made him suspicious of claims made by established "regular" Orders. Yarker made it his business to join practically every additional Masonic Order, and wherever possible, to acquire charters for establishing, at a nominal expenses-only fee, rare or suppressed rites wheresoe'er there was need of them. Taking intense opposition to his labors in his stride, Yarker's

Fig. 16.12. John Yarker (1833–1913),
Mason extraordinary

resolve only stiffened. Yarker believed he owed a debt to history and was willing to pay it, regardless of being targeted by regular obediences for unmasonic conduct.

And so it came to pass that Yarker found himself, by arrangement with American supporters of the Rites of Memphis and Misraim, in a position to bestow charters upon needy recipients. And there was a timely need. Both Theosophist followers of Besant and Leadbetter, and followers of Rudolf Steiner's Anthroposophy, as well as Martinists like Papus, wanted an arguably bona fide Masonic framework to beef up their operations, legitimize lineage, solidify commitment, and to build fraternal and ideological bridges to the extensive global Masonic network. Living proof that institutions suffer when they reject good men, Yarker had the goods and was generous dispensing them.

THEODOR REUSS, ANCIENT & PRIMITIVE, AND THE UNIVERSAL GNOSTIC CHURCH

While Occult Paris went into quiet convolutions over the sudden fermentation of neo-gnostic activity, Germany experienced corresponding tremors. Chief among exponents of Germanic gnosis were Theosophists

Fig. 16.13. Carl Kellner (1850–1905),
originator of the Ordo Templi Orientis *concept*

Fig. 16.14. Theodor Reuss
(1855–1923), man of
many parts

Theodor Reuss and Franz Hartmann, Reuss's London-based music-publishing Masonic friend Henry Klein, and the man Reuss and Klein encouraged to lead an umbrella organization of gnostic Freemasonry: wealthy industrialist and keen Mason Carl Kellner (1850–1905) who had already demonstrated generous patronage of the "alternative" medical schemes of Franz Hartmann (1838–1912).

Reuss (1855–1923) and Klein (1842–1913) had first met as members of the German-speaking, London-based "Pilgrim" Lodge. Sharing the advantage of being regular London Freemasons, they were well positioned to obtain high-grade masonic charters through John Yarker's and Mathers's Golden Dawn colleague, William Wynn Westcott, Chief Magus of the masonic *Societas Rosicruciana in Anglia.*

In 1902 Yarker bestowed on Reuss, Klein, and breakaway Theosophist Franz Hartmann, charter authority to operate an irregular 33-degree Ancient & Accepted Scottish Rite as well as the Rites of Memphis and Misraim in Germany.

Under Annie Besant's leadership, the mainstream Theosophical Society reestablished itself in Germany, led by Rudolf Steiner and Grand Secretary General Marie Sivers. In 1906, with Kellner now dead, Reuss chartered Steiner and Sivers to form the *Mystica Aeterna* Chapter and Grand Council of Adoptive Masonry: a form of the Misraim Rite open to women. The charter named the parent body as the Order of Oriental Templars (Reuss and Kellner's uncompleted brainchild). The following year Reuss and Klein appointed Steiner Acting Grand Master General of the Rite of Misraim (ninety degree) in Germany.

In 1908, with Papus rejected by regular Masonic jurisdictions and keen to affiliate to the Ancient & Primitive Rite, regardless of source, Reuss issued Papus and his associates—including René Guénon—with a patent to administer the Rites of Memphis and Misraim.

On 29 November 1910, John Yarker appointed Aleister Crowley Sovereign Grand Inspector General (33rd-degree) of Yarker's irregular version of the Ancient & Accepted Rite, with administrative responsibilities for the Ancient & Primitive Rites as well. At this point, Reuss introduced Crowley to his and the late Kellner's idea of an *Academia Masonica:* the OTO, or *Ordo Templi Orientis,* and approved of Crowley's idea to reduce the cream of the Ancient & Primitive Rites into Reuss's ten-degree framework OTO system, a system that had as its highest gift the "IX-degree" of vaguely formulated "sex magic," still in the crudest experimental stage, but obviously linked in theory to early gnostic practices with some very limited acquaintance with tantric ritual.[13] It is believed that in return for Reuss's going to Paris to entrust the A&P Rites to Papus, Reuss received authority, presumably from Bricaud and Papus, as a legate or bishop of the Universal (Catholic)

Gnostic Church in Germany. From that point, the OTO bore within it an affiliation and right of succession to the Gnostic Church that persists to this day, though currently unused since the OTO is now a Thelemic ("Crowleyan") Order.

Reuss understood the secret of the gnostics that most mattered to the OTO was the doctrine that consecrated sexual fluids constituted effective agents of magical, spiritual transformation. This secret doctrine Reuss shared to some extent with Bricaud, who had learned of sexual magic through the Vintrasian cult, and with Papus who was aware of the medical importance of sexual energy flowing freely for psychic health. Reuss understood the doctrine to have been the precious secret of the Templars, deriving, he believed, from Jesus's alleged relations with the "Beloved Disciple" and encapsulated in the words of the eucharist: "This is my body which I give to you." For Reuss, the "body" was the holy seed, Jesus's life-fluid (semen, symbolized as blood since it carried life). This the gnostic savior apparently determined be "sown" and reintegrated to the divine sphere, sacramentally, free of the spiritually enslaving grip of the "prince of this world," the Demiurge who made a fool of the man crazed by lust.

These beliefs were consistent with those of Dr. Ernst Christian Heinrich Peithmann (1865–1943). In 1904, the German Peithmann had composed a *Gnostic Catechism* akin to the "Catechism of the Gnostic Church Explained" of 1899 by Tau Sophronius, gnostic bishop of Béziers, who would become Bricaud's gnostic bishop of Prague. In 1893, Peithmann had joined a Martinist Order of the Grail but felt it lacked the essential gnosis, that is, Peithmann's idea of sexual magic, derived from the Simonian and Sethian gnostics of antiquity, whose doctrine Peithmann condensed into the idea of "the redemption of the

Fig. 16.15. Dr. E. C. H. Peithmann (1865–1943)

seed from servitude": servitude referring to the cycle of birth, death, and rebirth in this world. Health required the redirection of sexual energy toward a lust-free, nonreproductive sacramental sexual practice that had magical health value. Not finding the concept explicit within the Gnostic Church, Peithmann founded his own Old Gnostic Church of Eleusis to promote and safeguard it.

In 1930, Peithmann would ratify the gnostic episcopal credentials of the last of our "boys" who descended on Paris in search of initiatory secrets. Arnaldo Krumm, who hyphenated his father's surname with that of his mother's maiden name, Heller. Krumm-Heller came to Paris in the critical period 1907–09 to study medicine chiefly of the alternative kind. Born in Salchendorf, Germany, Arnaldo Krumm-Heller (1876–1949) went to Mexico to make his fortune. There he worked as the future Mexican president Francisco Madero's private doctor while undertaking secret service and military work for the Mexican and German governments. With charters from the Ancient & Primitive Rites of Memphis and Misraim and the Ancient & Accepted Rites, as well as a gnostic episcopacy granted by James Ingersoll Wedgwood of the Liberal Catholic Church, Krumm-Heller would found the *Fraternitas Rosicruciana Antiqua* (FRA) in Mexico in 1927, heavily influenced by Crowley's Thelema system. Krumm-Heller's tacit acceptance of the Nazis and his residency in Berlin during World War II have made him a figure "out of court" in any assessment of the value of twentieth-century occultism though he still has admiring followers in South America. Spiritually, Krumm-Heller was a world away from the heyday of Occult Paris and arguably represents the decadence of the Decadence. Crowley didn't think much of him (see my book *Aleister Crowley: The Beast in Berlin*), but the Beast could be very black and white.

When John Yarker died in 1913, Crowley was tasked with sorting out the headship of the Ancient & Primitive Rites. A letter of 1914 from Crowley to Reuss shows how Papus's reception of the rites duly paid off for him.[14] As Yarker's death left the rites' honorary 97th-degree—Grand Hierophant—vacant, Crowley was happy for it to "be conferred upon the Most Illustrious S.G.M.G. of France

Dr. Gérard Encausse (Papus) 33°, 90°, 96°, on account of his world wide eminence and his successful labors on behalf of the Rite." That put Memphis and Misraim firmly under the Martinist Order's benevolent umbrella. Other interests, however, now dominated the restless doctor; Papus had changed.

SEVENTEEN

To the End with Papus

Papus was well aware that historically speaking, the greatest influence Martinism had ever enjoyed was in Russia, initially under Catherine II, but from 1801 under Tsar Alexander I ("the Blessed") before, during, and after the war with Napoleon and the subsequent Holy Alliance with Austria and Prussia. In the latter period, the thought of Louis-Claude de St. Martin appeared poised to affect the destiny of the Russian nation. Such commanding spiritual influence was a cause dear to the heart of Papus's "intellectual master" St. Yves d'Alveydre. St. Yves defined history's validity solely in terms of its "volitive" response to the sense of "Mission" afforded by consciousness of the Tradition. Evidence that Martinism's past association with Russia played on Papus's mind can be seen in the October 1896 issue of *L'Initiation*. Its opening pages were dedicated to Papus's "Message from French Spiritualists" addressed to "A.S.M.I. Nicolas II, Emperor of Russia," who had just arrived in Paris for a state visit. The tsar was doubtless gratified to learn that:

> Above all the political discussions, outside all religious communion (although we respect all), we pursue, silently and unknown, our researches whose aim is to illuminate Science by Faith, and it is from regenerated science that we demand positive proofs of the existence of God and the immortality of the human soul. . . .
>
> Now the great secret law of history has been revealed by one of our masters, Fabre d'Olivet, in his "Philosophical History of the Human Species," and developed by another of our masters, Saint-Yves

433

d'Alveydre, in his "Missions." This law, known to Egyptian initiates 1600 years before our era, teaches us that three grand Principles direct the march of all events; these being: divine Providence, Will, and Destiny. . . .

The Empire which takes as its line of conduct the maxim "Force permits the right" banishes by this act all Providential influence, dedicates itself to destiny, demanding of terror, force and all the diplomatic ruses the respect due to God alone before it all shortly comes crashing down, devoured by its own errors. . . .

That Your Majesty deigns to receive with benevolence our Greeting ["Salut"] and that She [*sic.*] immortalize his Empire by total union with divine Providence; such is the dearest wish of those who beg Your Majesty to accept the homage of their most profound respect.

GÉRARD ENCAUSSE (PAPUS)[1]

La reproduction des articles inédits publiés par l'*Initiation* est formellement interdite, à moins d'autorisation spéciale.

PARTIE INITIATIQUE

MESSAGE DES SPIRITUALISTES FRANÇAIS

A S. M. I. NICOLAS II

EMPEREUR DE RUSSIE

————

SIRE,

Nous venons. au nom des Revues et des Écoles spiritualistes françaises soussignées, saluer respectueusement Votre Majesté à son arrivée dans notre Patrie.

Au-dessus de toutes les discussions politiques, en dehors de toute communion religieuse (bien que nous les respections toutes), nous poursuivons, silencieux et inconnus, nos recherches qui ont pour but d'illuminer la Science par la Foi, et de déterminer la Foi par la Science, et c'est à la science régénérée que nous demandons des preuves positives de l'Existence de Dieu et de l'Immortalité de l'âme humaine.

Représentants d'une des plus antiques traditions de l'Humanité, nous recevons, grâce aux fraternités initiatiques, les hauts enseignements des générations passées, et nous transmettons aux générations futures

I

Fig. 17.1. Papus's open letter to the tsar of Russia, L'Initiation, *"Initiatic Section," October 1896*

* * *

Papus now felt in a position to address heads of state in the name of all spiritually minded people in France: quite a leap! In due course this would be backed up by real acts in the historical sphere. Papus had set his sights on Russia.

The April 1900 issue of *L'Initiation* opens with an account of Papus's trip to St. Petersburg recently undertaken: "During a stay of some weeks in Saint Petersburg among good friends whose cordial reception still enchants our memories, we were led to study a medium whose experiences suggested to us several reflections which could interest our readers. This medium, *Sambor* by name [meaning "lonely warrior"], is a man still young, of nervous temperament, lymphatic, blond and who has already produced excellent séances."[2] The account goes on to describe Sambor's feats such as escaping from heavy metal bonds without apparent effort, producing a child's disembodied voice, raising objects with a phosphorescent glow and transporting them to other rooms, and self-levitation. Papus does not tell his readers who his very cordial friends were or what he was actually doing in Russia other than witnessing spiritist séances. The background to Papus's sojourn in St. Petersburg may be found, as usual, in the past.

Between 1802 and 1816, French counter-revolutionary and counter-rationalist philosopher Joseph le Maistre (1753–1821)—he whom Baudelaire thanked for teaching him how to think—was in St. Petersburg where he wrote *Soirées de St Petersbourg* (The St. Petersburg Dialogues), a theodicy on the role of the mystery of innocent sacrifice in bringing men to God in the course of the historical process. Papus was aware that Joseph le Maistre reestablished St. Petersburg as a center of Martinism where its influence still exercised itself a century later. According to Victor-Émile Michelet, it "was the Grand Duke Nicholas, affiliated to Martinism, who in 1900 presented Papus to his nephew Nicolas II. The last Tsar of Russia was also, like his forbear Alexander I, initiated into Martinism. Others knew that that was one of the reasons that kept the Tsar faithful to the French alliance, as against the pressures exercised on him to detach himself from it."[3]

We now come to the nub of the issue: the issue being how, had the French government paid better attention to Papus, the Russian Revolution might have been at least temporarily forestalled, or perhaps its horrors ameliorated. This issue turned on Papus's extraordinary relationship with the man Michelet describes as the "little peasant of the Lyonnais Philippe Nizier Vachod, known as Monsieur Philippe," the man with whom Papus established a magnetic healing school in Lyon in 1895, which Bricaud joined ("Vachod" being Philippe's mother's maiden-name).

Having established Martinist lodges in Russia in 1897—the year after the tsar's visit to Paris—and a Martinist Order there in 1899, Papus took the step of introducing his spiritual master to the tsar and tsarina, Nicolas and Alexandra. At Philippe's first interview with the royal couple at Compiègne, 50 kilometers northeast of Paris, in 1901, the saintly healer made the strongest possible impression. According to Jean-François Var: "Up until his death, in spite of intrigues and cabals, he was treated as a friend and confidant by Nicolas and Alexandra, to whom he had predicted the birth of the much-desired male heir [Alexei Nikolaevich, born 12 August 1904]."[4]

*Fig. 17.2. Tsar Nicolas II and Tsarina Alexandra,
destined for martyrdom*

Michelet takes up the story: "Nothing was decided by Nicolas II and his wife in Russian politics without Philippe's assent."[5] Foolish opponents said Philippe obtained his all-powerful influence by necromancy or a vulgar spiritism. Michelet encapsulates Philippe's power over the sovereigns: "A lady of the imperial court having said, joyfully, to the Tsarina 'I saw Monsieur Philippe' received the reply from the imperiatrix: 'One does not see Monsieur Philippe, he is pure spirit!'"[6]

Concerted efforts by the Russian church, the court, and French diplomacy led to an insistence that Philippe return to France (he made at least five journeys to Russia between 1901 and 1905). The imperial court resigned itself to the pressure, but it went against the sovereigns' hearts. Unfortunately, there was a figure in the shadows ready to seize the opportunity and take Philippe's place at the court of St. Petersburg: "the sinister *staretz* [charismatic monk] Raspoutine," as Michelet refers to the infamous Grigori Rasputin. Papus became embroiled in a "deaf struggle" with Rasputin and tried to get the royal couple to see the monk was not all they thought he was, that to depend on him would be dangerous for the family. Papus prophesied that Rasputin was in effect like a vase, or Pandora's box, that contained all the vices and crimes of the Russian people, warning the couple: "If this vase is broken, one will see its frightful contents spread soon over Russia."[7] Rasputin would of course be assassinated in December 1916, shortly before the revolution erupted. Rasputin himself lost no opportunity in heaping torrents of insults and calumnies on Papus and Philippe. "Better advised than the French government," observed Michelet coolly, "the Germans made Rasputin their instrument."[8] The Germans were plotting to take Russia out of the war by ensuring a Bolshevik revolution. It was the Germans who put Lenin on the train to Moscow. Michelet, who would become head of the Traditionalist Martinist Order after the death of Bricaud in 1934, further observed that in 1914, the greater number of Balkan princes were also Martinists: "The French government, completely ignorant of initiatic societies, did not profit from this advantage."[9] Michelet further believed that the true story of Philippe belonged to "Secret History" for the role he played has not been related with exactitude. "Perhaps it never will be. What is certain is that if the French government and its diplomats had been less foolish, if they had helped Philippe instead of stupidly persecuting him, the last imperial couple of Russia would not have fallen into Rasputin's power, and the inevitable Bolshevik revolution had been retarded."[10]

Philippe returned to France where he remained until his death in 1905. The police wrongly suspected him because he had been called to offer care to Kaiser Wilhelm II of Germany. But there were problems not only with the French police. Papus and Philippe had attracted the hatred of a dangerous informer, General Ratchkowsky, chief of the Russian police in France. Courageously, ten years before the German high command initiated World War I, Papus wrote under a pseudonym and in collaboration with Jean Carrère, a series of articles for a major French newspaper revealing the intrigues that were already brewing at the court against Nicolas II and the tsarina. "Papus dared to denounce the dark works of Ratchkowsky and of the Okhrana [Russian secret police] in Paris."[11] Michelet reckoned Papus ran the risk of becoming victim of some mortal "accident" as not infrequently happens to those who cross powerful persons. Victory went to Papus and Philippe, for the intervention of the tsar's uncle, the Grand Duke Nicolas, led to Ratchkowsky's disgrace.

However, Papus's attack against the informer-policeman had an unexpected result. In an effort to divert the menace at his door, Ratchkowsky tried to make himself indispensable by claiming to have discovered a document that made a great splash: "The Secret Protocols of the Learned Elders of Sion." This document, still bandied about to this day by anti-Semites and Israel's enemies across the world, purports to expose a Jewish plot, using Freemasonry, to dominate the Christian world. Michelet observed that the fake document was simply plagiarized from a pamphlet called *The Dialogue in Hell between Machiavelli and Montesquieu* published in 1864 against Napoléon III by French journalist, Maurice Joly (1829–1878). Meanwhile, Papus's press campaign rendered a strong maneuver of German diplomacy inoperable, while the revelations of an old chief of the Okhrana, General Kourlof, after the Russian Revolution, recounted Ratchkowsky's mysterious end in 1910.

Michelet's account's conclusion should, I think, be read, and read with irony: "It has been said elsewhere that Philippe's death, in 1905, perhaps had political causes. There was nothing that would make you believe it [*Rien ne permet de le croire*]."[12]

Monsieur Philippe's death in 1905 did nothing to lessen the impact the Christian healer wrought both on Papus and upon his close colleague, Marc Haven (Dr. Emmanuel Lalande). Philippe changed both men's lives dramatically.

Michelet noted that Marc Haven's most important works, besides an unedited study of the tarot, were two books on Cagliostro: *Le Maître inconnu: Cagliostro* (The Unknown Master: Cagliostro), and a translation of a little Latin book written by Cagliostro, *L'Évangile de Cagliostro* (The Gospel of Cagliostro). The former book should be read between the lines since it was in fact a portrait of the man whose daughter Haven had married, Monsieur Philippe.

Paul Sédir's life was probably even more affected by Philippe than Marc Haven's. This should give us pause, for these men were among France's leading esotericists, and while there was some grudging respect for intellectual and especially literary occultism somewhere in the mainstream of the French bourgeois establishment, there was not much sympathy for such as Philippe, whom government figures considered a quack, trickster, charlatan, troublemaker, of negligible academic attainment, whose income derived from the folly of a comfortably off woman marrying her idol. His attested record in healing barely elicited a shrug of the shoulders. As Philippe was outside of the medical establishment, his successes were really failures to embrace modern science. If people thought the Philippes of this world were the answer, where would the medical profession or the life of science be? Modern society couldn't rely on one-off strokes than none could account for. Thus the usual explanation of the time for surprising cures was hysteria with a hint of deception. Those who could get cured by such methods as Philippe's must be sick in the head or weak-minded, desperate, or gullible in some way! The sick, after all, are sick.

In fact, Philippe never claimed any special gifts of healing at all.

And that makes it even more interesting to consider his effect on the Hermetists. Philippe declared that he didn't heal; only God could do that. He knew God as a friend and one could only ask for things if one had completely abandoned self-interest or personal pride. The ear of the Lord was open to those who loved their brother more than themselves and who did not judge others. Brotherly love was superior even to faith. Without love for others, there would be no real urge to pray or have faith, or want faith. True faith without charity meant nothing, *was nothing*. One wonders if lurking among the esotericists, there was the old realization that Jesus had the real magic and that it was truly nothing more than spirit, spirit of love, pure and unadorned, expressed in acts that defied reason, for God's reasons are unreasonable to the beings of this world. Philippe was perhaps for Haven, Sédir, and Papus the ultimate human and more-than-human proof that materialism and holding on to things was truly folly and that the miraculous required letting go, and seeing beyond the visible, and desiring with love the welfare of others.

Of course, they must also have been aware that a careful reading of the foundation documents of the "Rosy-Cross" mythology makes it plain that the invisible brotherhood that meets in the House of the Holy Spirit, which the world cannot see, was dedicated above all to healing, and that gratis. They were invisible because the world was blind. You had to be blind to the values of the world to see Jesus, and those addicted to the values of the world would never see, and not seeing, would never believe. This paradoxical dilemma left only one royal way out: resignation to getting on in the world and a dedication to untrumpeted service, knowing the world considers you a fool, while yet, at the suffering center of history, you play your self-sacrificial part in the reintegration of Man to his source, your unlauded part in the redemption of humanity from the grip of what the Gnostics called "the rulers" (archons), who rule the rulers and the ruled, but not the free, who have nothing and, therefore, everything.

It is very fitting then, as Philippe taught that in the gospel all was initiation and no esoteric ceremonial was necessary to be in the divine presence, that Sédir and Papus began to unload themselves inwardly of their many magical accoutrements and embrace the idea of Louis-Claude de St. Martin that the true path was a "way of the heart" and the Order of Martinism, a truly, deeply Christian chivalry, a quest for light in the light of love.

After the First World War, Sédir would practice the preaching and found the association of *Amitiés Spirituelles* (Spiritual Friendships), committed only to the reunion of persons of goodwill, acknowledging Christ as their inner life's sole master, and the gospel as the true "law of conscience and of peoples."[13] Papus's son, Philippe Encausse, whose coming had been predicted by Monsieur Philippe before his mother knew she was pregnant, reported these words of his father's regarding his goodly godfather: "You have brought me to know and love Christ."[14]

Michelet's observation of the change that came over Papus was somewhat cooler and reflective: "Papus had married a lady T., originally from l'Arbresle and an enthusiastic disciple of her compatriot Philippe. Papus, meridional [southern, that is *hot*] spirit in perpetual effervescence, was inclined at this period of his life, towards a sort of christic [*sic*] mysticism. He believed that in Philippe he had found a master, having already commended him to his friend, Marc Haven, a severe and ponderous spirit, as such. Soon he would rely solely on Philippe's judgment."[15] The highly civilized Michelet had as much respect for the genius of art and the intellect enlightened by the spirit aiming beyond the visible universe for the furthest regions of being as he did for the practical apotheosis of ethics. What Philippe was, was what he was. Was he a model for all?

"Who then was this Philippe?" asked Michelet, "A great thaumaturge, a saint, some said; a vulgar charlatan, replied the official world. But the official world understands nothing of that which bypasses the middle stream, or that which enters not the narrow frame of rationalist knowledge. In truth, Philippe seems to have been an excellent man, of a strong ordinary mind, but gifted with authentic abilities of healing and of vision. No doubt he'd have spent his life in his home at l'Arbresle, near Lyon, invaded by crowds of sick people, had not the lively Papus precipitated his launch into political adventure."[16]

* * *

The nobility in Papus's soul was deeply touched by his vision of Philippe as the "father of the poor" giving his healing services freely. Papus followed the example and became more and more committed to joining the life of Paris's streets to offer his medical services to the poor without reward, "save that of knowing that we do thy will."

And then came the warm summer of 1914, when quite suddenly, out of the blue, like a "running dream" that cannot stop, much of the civilized world found itself at war: so it said in the newspapers and soon the street parades of soldiers, drums, and trumpets came out in the sun to prove it.

Péladan had been right about the barbarity that dominated the Germans; Papus had been right to declare to the tsar that those who believed "might was right" cut themselves off from divine providence and would have to rely instead on violence, terror, and diplomatic skullduggery before their world, inevitably, came crashing down, stealing so many futures unlived, unknown. As the Germans came pounding in, the Belle Époque gave up its ghost, indeed millions of ghosts, and with that, Occult Paris vanished in the face of horror.

In the face of the horror, Gérard Encausse volunteered for the French army medical corps to serve the sick, the wounded, and the dying on the western front. Exhausted after two years of carnage, the courageous man known as Papus contracted tuberculosis at a military hospital, and died on 25 October 1916. He was fifty-one years old.

We shall remember the unknown soldier.

EIGHTEEN

THE LEGACY

A FORGOTTEN DREAM

Two years before she died in 1989, I had the good fortune to be introduced to Lina Prokofiev, widow of the famous Russian composer, at one of historian and medievalist Jean Gimpel's memorable salons in Chelsea. We sat in a warm third-floor conservatory overlooking the Thames. What had I, a young writer and filmmaker, to say to a woman who had been sentenced to ten years' hard labor under Josef Stalin in 1948, having already suffered Germany's invasion of the Soviet Union together with her husband, one of the greatest composers in history?

We talked about spirituality.

She told me she missed its presence deeply in modern society and confided to me that her late husband felt his music was spiritually motivated, and that he treasured the conviction that there was more to life than ordinary vision of material things afforded. I observed that in Soviet Russia, spiritual beliefs were taken forcibly away from people, while in the modern West it seemed many "clever" people had jettisoned spiritual beliefs voluntarily, while others suppressed spirituality by influencing education and the media, insisting positivist, so-called progressive secularization was altogether desirable and normal. Madame Prokovief thought for a moment and looked me hard in the eye: "We weren't religious, but we knew spirituality. You can never get rid of it. It always comes back. People will see it again, I believe they will. They will want it. How else can you write music?"

Years later, it was a special delight for me to see the name of Sergei Prokofiev, born the year the Martinist Order's Supreme Council was established, listed in a survey of composers influenced in ways different and subtle by the French Symbolist movement, touched by the mythical and spiritual interests of Symbolist writers and sharing in the modalism developed by Debussy, Franck, and Chabrier. On an obvious level, the overture to, say, Prokofiev's ballet *Romeo and Juliet* undoubtedly serves as an excellent soundtrack to many of Gustave Moreau's grander paintings, and no one would deny that the *Troika* theme Prokofiev composed for the 1934 Soviet film *Lieutenant Kijé* is magical enough to make it a Christmas favorite, but we should recall we're discussing spiritual influence and, as St. Paul said, spiritual things are spiritually discerned. Discerning the legacy of Occult Paris is not always going to be a simple matter.

One thing we can say, where there is a determination to give form to new spheres of feeling, to go beyond, to touch the outer limits, warmly, with passion and depth of feeling, with courage and some intellectual rigor, then we can feel the ongoing legacy of Occult Paris, which itself was part of a greater, ongoing march through history of the gnosis—man's deepest knowledge of himself. Yes, we can hear it in the music, from Brian Wilson and the Beach Boys' pop-music experiments in the mid-60s, to the Beatles, John Barry, the Doors, Dylan, Hendrix, Pink Floyd—all the good stuff you may know better than I, and the many imitators, and all the great unknowns we never hear because the scum also rises.

But I suppose to young people now, though some of them relish a bit of musical archaeology—my daughter likes her downloads but *loves* my vinyl collection!—even what was ultra-new when I was a boy now may seem old and even, God forbid, out of touch. Well, fashions come and go, but the good endures forever.

What then has endured?

A tough question when you get down to it. The movement was pretty much killed by the First World War, and since then we've had another, even more destructive, world war, a cold war, and now a seemingly endless plague of barbarous terrorism, military overkill, and death-cults of one sordid kind or another to unseat our conceit and lock us into our fearful, defensive-aggressive selves. One does wonder whether Papus's strapline for *L'Initiation* "Materialism has had its day" was not a kind of ironic, if pious hope! If materialism has had its day, it's been a long time dying. We consume materialism; we live on it. We like it, and we want it. Like the poor, it seems, it will always be with us. Our idea of freedom is having what we want, or think we want. Having less seems to us like poverty, because in our system, it probably is. And that's no fun. Perhaps we can find some spiritual solace from our own insecurity and greed by at least *valuing* what we have and wanting a bit less, or giving a bit more. Where do we get the inspiration for these little steps in the direction of the Good, the True, and the Beautiful?

I should say there's quite a lot of inspiring material in the story I have told in this book. If it does not encourage us to think a bit more deeply, it will be because we don't like to think any more than we have to.

It's time for a roundup. Let's lasso that Occult Paris legacy and have a look at what we've got so, perhaps, we might better know how we can give.

By the end of World War I, Papus was dead, Péladan was dead (1918), Debussy was dead (1918). And all wars vulgarize the culture of the survivors. Men become *guys,* ladies become *chicks,* that sort of thing. No time for romance. The jazz age was not a hall of aficionados relishing the genius of Charlie Parker or Ornette Coleman or Count Basie; it was largely very smelly and sweaty and mindless—a weekly relief from hard labor. See Chaplin's *Modern Times;* the cog in the machine can only dream of romance, he can't live it.

With Papus dead and the "war to end all wars" still raging, Charles Henri Détré ("Téder," 1850–1918) was recognized as head of the Martinist Order, though the war meant there was very little order to be ordered.

A contributor to *L'Initiation* and director of the Masonic revue *Hiram,* Détré had spent a lot of time in England, where he had been a friend to John Yarker. He had, with Bricaud, been in at the start of efforts

Fig. 18.1. Charles Henri Détré (1850–1918)

to unite Martinism, the Gnostic Church, and the Rites of Memphis and Misraim. But in 1918 Détré too joined the Grand Lodge above. Now the movement began to fissure. A majority recognized Jean Bricaud as natural successor, though he was more of the Martinezist and Willermozist tendency, with a leading stake in his Gnostic Church. Bricaud wanted to exclude non-Freemasons and women from Martinist initiation, continuing Téder's designs for links with regular Freemasonry. The St. Martinist wing, led by gnostic bishop Victor Blanchard (1878–1953), backed by Augustin Chaboseau and other members of the Martinist Supreme Council, broke away on 3 January 1921 to form the independent Martinist and Synarchist Order, with Blanchard forming rival gnostic organizations to rival Bricaud's Lyon-based Martinism directly. As Sovereign Grand Master of the Ordre Martiniste et Synarchique, with the initiatic name Paul Yésir, Blanchard did not recognize Bricaud's Grand Mastership. Since Papus had not left proper statutes for election of his successor, it was impossible to know who was legitimate Grand Master.

Blanchard attempted to advance the esoteric syncretism of Papus, admitting men and women without prior Masonic affiliation. As head of the general secretariat of the presidency of the Chamber of Deputies, Blanchard dreamed of influencing political developments by occult action, and though a dream, opponents imagined a "synarchic plot" operating secretly in the corridors of government. According to Galtier, however, no trace has come to light of Blanchard's ideals influencing political events. His commitments lent themselves to being confused with activities of other persons inspired by Synarchic ideals, as we shall see. Blanchard himself was fully engaged as a senior figure in Grand Orient Masonry between the wars, in addition to episcopal commitments to the Universal Gnostic Church as Tau Targelius, and responsibilities to the surviving Kabbalistic Order of the Rose-Cross—directed by Lucien Mauchel, who died in 1936—as well as to the Fraternity of the Polaires (with its powerful spiritist interest in the Cathar and grail legends of Languedoc) of which fraternity he had been president since 1933. Blanchard was also enthusiastic for the attempted umbrella federation for Western initiatory fraternities FUDOSI, promoted by Harvey Spencer Lewis, founder of California-based AMORC in his search for authentic Rosicrucian lineage.

Lewis's activities with FUDOSI encouraged further splits in the Martinist fabric. Rival U.S. Rosicrucian leader Reuben Swinburne-Clymer opposed Lewis and promoted *his* international federation, FUDOFSI. Bricaud would eventually federate with the latter (Bricaud died in 1934), while Blanchard joined FUDOSI until expelled in 1939 when Chaboseau replaced Blanchard as FUDOSI "Imperator" with special jurisdiction for Martinism in the East. Their argument centered on the apparent absorption of European Martinism by the United States (Lewis). Blanchard rejoined FUDOSI in 1946.

In 1931 Chaboseau had tried to reestablish an Order closer to Papus's intentions with Victor-Émile Michelet, the brilliant man of letters, to whom Chaboseau passed the leadership of the Traditional Martinist Order in April 1932. Victor-Émile Michelet died in 1938. Chaboseau took the reins again, but the onset of World War II in 1939 forestalled any progress. Chaboseau left Paris to live in Brittany where he wrote a history of Britain, and his son went to war. While FUDOSI ceased to exist in 1951, today's members of the Traditional Martinist Order are expected to be in good standing with AMORC, an organization that has had its own share of ups and downs. Today's Traditional Martinist Order is an extremely tolerant, spiritually minded body of people who find their spiritual aspirations for enlightenment encouraged by membership. You can read all about them on the Internet

Fig. 18.2. Constant Chevillon (1880–1944)

without obligation. It's not everybody's cup of tea but what is? *This fish is not for everyone.*

Bricaud's Lyon-based order attracted the most Martinists during the 1930s and 1940s.[1] After Bricaud's death in 1934, Constant Chevillon (1880–1944) renamed the organization the "Martinist Martinezist Order," to distinguish its Pasquallian, theurgic emphasis from Blanchard's St. Martinist priorities. After Chevillon's murder by French Nazi collaborators, Henri-Charles Dupont (1877–1960) carried on, emphasizing the Willermozist Masonic side. Meanwhile, a Martinezist group calling itself the "Martinist Order of the Élus Cohens," committed to theurgical operations, was set up in Paris in 1942 by Robert Ambelain (1907–1997).

Philippe Encausse (1906–1984), concerned for his father Papus's legacy, revived a Martinist Order in 1952, including non-Masons and women with the emphasis on the "way of the heart" of St. Martin. So postwar Martinism continued under the old three forms of Martinezist, Willermozist, and St. Martinist, but there were, according to Massimo Introvigne's account, even more complications than that, though they happily lie outside this book's scope.

When we talk about the legacy of Martinism, we are talking about a sizable web of different traditions and influences on individuals whose esoteric character generally keeps them from public or mainstream historical notice, but those influences are there. One might like to think our finest writers, philosophers, musicians, scientists, and administrators were attracted to such Orders so that the benefits might more readily radiate into the general human condition and so do something about our current woeful cultural wasteland, dominated by melodramatic journalism, uninspiring politics, and spiritually denuded, crude entertainment, while the enemies of civilization subvert ordinary decent behavior and healthy confidence with threats, bullying, and violence. If we fall, we shall fall from within, which is what the enemy is counting on. Clearly, for many reasons, esoteric orders are not as attractive as they once were to the movers and shakers of culture. Not all of the blame can be laid outside them, but where there is spiritual credit, it wants building on.

One cannot leave this strand of the story without mentioning a rather sinister aspect regarding post-Papusian Martinism and Synarchy. While investigating some of the personalities and ideas behind the Priory of Sion hoax in their book *The Sion Revelation: Inside the Shadowy World of Europe's Secret Masters* (Time Warner, 2006), writers Lynn Picknett and Clive Prince learned about some persons who had taken St. Yves d'Alveydre's Synarchist ideas into political forms denuded of controlling spiritual categories, and who were presented as being instrumental in the 1920s and '30s in forming a nondemocratic model for a "United States of Europe" that has now allegedly developed into the European Union with a covert philosophy of hierarchical social control with a socialistic gloss. Putting aside the obvious fact that the vogue for the *Da Vinci Code* type of story, as well as much secret society, neo-gnostic, Magdalenist, and illuminati speculation stems from garbled elements taken willy-nilly from the detritus of Occult Paris, the Picknett-Prince speculation is obviously of some pressing significance.

According to Picknett and Prince, Blanchard's Martinist and Synarchist Order formed a political Synarchic Central Committee (French acronym: CSC) in 1922 to form study groups recruited from the elites of the civil service, the *École Polytechnique,* and financial administrators. Retitled the Synarchic Empire Movement (*Mouvement Synarchique d'Empire,* or MSE), recruitment was by the Martinist chain method, with new members knowing only their immediate recruiter.

Briefly, the MSE produced a secret "Pact" for the eventual and

peaceful replacement of existing orders on Synarchist lines, meaning a bureaucratically controlled system where each person would be
firmly put in his or her place in the hive according to perceived ability,
expected to stay there, while a super-elite ran the Order. One notices
that this idea has no obvious political color and could be presented to
socialists as a form of socialism and to conservatives as a limited capi-
talistic hierarchical order. Areas where voting was fundamentally determinative would be strictly controlled. The effective rulers would be
beyond the elective process, largely out of sight while naturally seeing
it their business to "listen" to public concerns for the sake of order, but
no fundamental change would be permitted, for the sake of "all" on
whose behalf the rulers rule. Naturally, the aim is to prevent anarchy
and uphold tradition. As we saw earlier, St. Yves's idea of anarchy was
any system that did not conform to Tradition. St. Yves's idea of tradition was a spiritual, esoteric understanding, but *what if these terms are
simply politicized?* We very soon find ourselves in the kind of political
philosophy congenial to what was called fascism, that is, absolutist State
control where the individual's identity is subsumed into the will of the
State: uniformed and conformist. You don't have to wear a uniform to
conform. If everyone dresses casually, casual dress is uniform.

Politicised Synarchy is pretty much Plato's famous "nocturnal san-
hedrin" from his *Republic:* always knowing best, wise rulers meet in
secret lest the "rabble" spoil things, and the wise are always at the top,
so if you're not at the top, *ergo,* you are not wise. To oppose such an
order is anarchy: it will not be tolerated. The wise conform.

Naturally, as one observes this version of *Synarchy* ("ruling
together"), one cannot help thinking of the actual functioning of the
contemporary European Union: its curiously mute, limited conception of political representation, state agreements made in secret that
effectively swallow nations for the benefit of leading participants, with
blithe, blank-faced disregard for democratic referenda. We are told from
above that the EU is a kind of "sacred," preordained project that "cannot be stopped," too big apparently for mere individuals to frustrate!
This picture was prophesied, parodied, or even effectively re-created in
the 1960s TV series, *The Prisoner.* If you live in a society where basic

needs are basically provided for—so long as you're easily satisfied—with even a kind of election ("Less work! More money!") but where nothing is allowed to change of any significance and where the limits are felt and guarded strictly, *in what sense is one truly alive?* The people are served but cannot serve themselves. The conclusion of the series was that the genuine individual is Number One and must resist being treated as a number. Take heed. You won't find "them" watching it in Brussels or Strasbourg!

Picknett and Prince related how a Synarchist Empire political scheme became integrated with the thought of French patriots who in the 1930s, alarmed that the country would fall apart into anarchy or to communists, took covert action against perceived enemies. The scandal hit the press, only to go quiet again.

There are conspiracy theories and there are conspiracies. French political history, like most other countries, is full of people conspiring. To *conspire* simply means "to whisper together." Some conspiracies are big, some small. One man's conspiracy is another man's life's work in pursuance of a great ideal. The proof of the pudding is in the eating. Picknett and Prince pick out the names of Robert Schuman, Jean Monnet, Jeanne Canudo, Vivian Postel du Mas, and Louis le Fur among others as persons with hidden agendas involved in the long formation of what was once innocently sold to prospective candidates as "the Common Market," and who all participated to some extent in politicized Synarchy. What is missing from the scenario of Picknett and Prince's book is any hard evidence that Synarchist politics are active today among whoever pulls the essential strings of the EU "project." Do we know who is pulling the strings? May we expect to be informed? *Rien ne permet de le croire.*

It is perhaps natural for English persons, viewing the culture of French politics from without to feel somewhat alarmed at the penetration of philosophy in political thinking familiar to the French. There is precious little philosophy in Anglo-Saxon politics, but that does not mean it is not riddled with secrets or "whispering together." A more informed, nuanced summary of Synarchic politics during and after World War II is provided by Gérard Galtier in his classic on Egyptian Freemasonry, Rose-Croix, and neo-Chivalry (1989), though it may still make us think about what is really going on behind closed doors on the Continent.

EXTRAMURAL SYNARCHY

Galtier describes the triple governing structure of Synarchy in the following terms.

The Synarchists' ideal, or dream, is that cosmic principles may influence and regenerate the problems of state, resolving the fundamental problems that beset society, such as class conflict and social insecurity, that is, not being secure in one's place, or not having a place to feel secure in. Until World War II, "most esotericists," Galtier says, espoused Synarchy openly, so there was no question of clandestine affirmations of the ideal. Barlet had written *L'Évolution sociale* in 1900; Rudolf Steiner's *The Triple Aspect of the Social Question* appeared in 1919.

Generally speaking, Synarchy's proponents propose some kind of federalism: from commune to nation, nation to empire, that is to say from the individual, through society, to a higher power. The higher power ultimately is that toward which all interior will should be directed or should enact, but this need not be spoken of, for its mysterious subtleties require initiation. From the purely terrestrial and practical point of view, the whole is governed not by a national assembly with a senate, but by three councils. These are not elected but considered representative. First: Cultural. This council corresponds to "spiritual authority." It includes responsibility for art, diffusion of information, and scientific research. The second council corresponds to the principle of "temporal power" and may be called the "Judiciary." Its responsibilities include the army, the police, foreign affairs. Finally there is an economic council. In this are represented all professional syndicates of both workers and employers. It decides monetary questions. The aim in this structure is to create an ideal society free of class struggle, and to remove power from politicians, who are partisan, and place control in the hands of truly competent specialists dedicated to the governance of the whole. Behind the pragmatic appearance of the councils is the gnostic theory of the threefold nature of man: spiritual being, astral body (soul), and flesh, or material form. Willing particpants may rise to the highest positions, consistent with the highest dimension of the human being.

According to Galtier, Blanchard had nothing to do with the Mouvement Synarchique d'Empire, which came out of an extremely small number of people of the Kurukshetra branch of the Theosophical Society.

Valentine de Saint Point (1875–1953) was a Parisian idealist artist and theatrical innovator who in 1916 was very close to the main figure in the project, Vivian Postel du Mas (author of *Schéma de l'archetype*). Vivian favored a clandestine political action group, corresponding to his understanding of a secret, invisible governance of the world promulgated in Sufism and in aspects of Western esoteric traditions. The MSE was animated principally by Vivian and the widow of Italian cinéaste Guiseppe Canudo, Jeanne. Their mutual ideals gelled in the mid-1930s amid the desperate challenges to European identity and in 1937, an anonymous document called the "Pacte synarchique révolutionnaire" (Synarchic revolutionary pact) was passed secretly to trusted individuals. This was not only influenced by St. Yves's spiritual reflections on the state of the world but also by the *Fraternité des Veilleurs* promoted by Schweller de Lubicz, influential on artistic circles at the time.

Both Jeanne and Vivian belonged to the Fraternity of the Polaires, launched by the Italian Accomani who called himself Zam Bhotiva and favored communicating with Asian invisibles through mediums. The background was Theosophical, with much enthusiasm for Jiddu Krishnamurti, promoted by Besant and Leadbeater throughout the first two decades of the century before Krishnamurti himself split with Theosophy. When Blanchard took over the Polaires, Vivian and Jeanne Canudo left. Canudo frequented Martinist lodges and Chevillon's "Collège d'Occultisme." The MSE did not, however, derive political direction from any members of FUDOSI. Vivian du Mars imposed ascetic discipline on members of his group and hoped to create a new Order of the Temple dedicated to the spiritualization of politics. The medieval Order allegedly began with less than a dozen founding fathers and the MSE never had more than about twenty members. For such a small group, they had big ideas.

One of their political schemes was the Pan-Eurafrique federal empire, toward a Eurafrica rather on the lines of the prevailing U.S. policy of Pan-America or Pan-Asian ideals. The idea of a federal Europe was also encouraged, drawing freely on the ideas of count Richard Coudenhove-Kalergi (1894–1972), Austrian diplomat and founder of the Pan-European movement.

The MSE was definitely clandestine. No mysteries of an esoteric nature were required since the main ideas were already broadly diffused in the period. Vivian's and Jeanne's taste for secret action was inspired by Theosophical fantasy of secret Masters. Thus the hope and expectation was not rooted in political reality but in the dream of orienting the world's destiny through spiritual means and symbolic living and action. Despite the weakness of working independently of classic political channels, the group had some ideas influential in the long term, such as the assembling of *États géneraux* (States General), as the medium for transcending left-right divides by Synarchic principles. In June 1936 a States General of Youth was formed to attract young people to a sense of mission beyond and above what conventional political parties were urging, whose actions only divided the Continent. The idea of the power of youth, while obviously twisted and exploited by Nazis, fascists, and communists would bear interesting fruit in a more spontaneous manner across the globe two decades after the end of World War II, but in the West, organized youth movements have not been a strong social factor in the wake of the cynicism and disappointments of the 1970s. The vacuum has been partially filled with wildly contradictory social and spiritual enthusiasms. We never seem to encounter middle-aged or aged terrorists.

Between the wars, the SME was unable to fulfill the press image of subversion and a myth of sorcerer-plotters, despite the movement being touted as the source of all evil under the Vichy regime and at the time of the Liberation. Galtier suspected Synarchic revolutionary strains had entered the New Right in France after the 1970s but existed without being named, and certainly without the mystical conceptions of

Synarchy's principal originator, who, I suspect, would have had a traumatic time trying to find a sense of reality in our contemporary world.

While this is all a long way from the day-to-day reality of the European Union, we should at least pause to consider the possibility of what kind of philosophy really informs the peculiar system that currently travels through time under the acronym EU with its peculiarly flat and, to some citizens, lethal currency regime.

If we were to believe that a covert philosophy of a Pan-European social control state was a genuine legacy of Occult Paris, this would be a sad, alarming book. However, to conclude such a thing would be on a logical par with blaming John the Baptist for the Spanish Inquisition. The world of bureaucratic conformity is about as far as can be imagined from the authentically liberating, poetic, courageous antiestablishment spirit, crazy at times, of the authentic Occult Paris.

Once we look into the artistic legacy, we find ourselves practically swamped with reflections, enough for another book, probably! So we must touch on them.

Everybody today has seen something of the wonders of art nouveau. One only has to see the film musical *Gigi*—based on Colette's short story—to see the decor at Maxim and Gaston Lachaille's apartment to feel a brisk frisson of what was so alluring about a decorative art movement that touched so much and so many with its naturalistic, feminine, stylish, and often mysterious abandonment of angular classicism for the joy of *curves*. The development of the "New Art" cannot be fairly disentangled from the Symbolist heyday. We may mention Debussy's friend Alexandre Charpentier (1856–1909) who wanted to put Art into "all" and who designed the *arabesque* decor for *Le Chat Noir* where Satie played, and played. In painting, we must mention Dutch-Belgian Symbolist artist Georges de Feure (1868–1943) who produced a now lost portrait of Satie playing the harmonium, waiting on celestial inspiration. De Feure distinguished himself as an art nouveau theatrical designer inspired by Baudelaire and handsome Belgian Symbolist writer Georges Rodenbach (1855–1898), author of *Bruges-la-Morte* (1892), a writer and a work much loved by Mallarmé and Edmond de Goncourt.

One of the finest, and most fashionable, art nouveau poster design-ers, the Czech Alfons Maria Mucha (1860–1939), was deeply interested in spiritual phenomena, transforming his studio into a "profane chapel" where experts on esoteric symbolism were received. Maeterlinck and Huysmans were counted among his friends.

Art nouveau did not stop when the glamorized exoticism of Art Deco took over. It came back with a vengeance in the 1960s, enlivening countless posters, book and record covers, and main titles for cinema films such as *What's New Pussycat?* (1965) and *Casino Royale* (1967) among many other classics of that very Barbey d'Aurevilly decadent, dandy era that united Paris to California to London and warms the heart of the brighter young today with its style and daring, decadent and genial craziness. TV series like *The Avengers* and *Jason King* (Peter Wyngarde was straight out of Huysmans's *Au Rebours!*) would have been unthinkable without Occult Paris. Indeed, one of the greatest unspoken influences of that era may be seen in countless films, romantic and epic, from D. W. Griffith's re-creation of a Gustave Moreau–style Babylon in *Intolerance* (1916) to practically every Powell and Pressburger movie, the Hammer Horror series, Gloria Swanson's character in Billy Wilder's *Sunset Boulevard* ("I *am* big; it's the movies that got small!"; 1950), and that whole vein of whimsical mysticism and openness to the uncanny that runs right through the history of imaginative cinema and that flowered so delightfully and shockingly in the 1960s and '70s. Only the mediocre resisted.

Which of course brings us to the surrealists. Twentieth-century surrealism would have been unthinkable without its precursors in Symbolism. André Breton, emperor of surrealism and devoted admirer of Rose+Croix+Catholique magnifique Saint-Pol Roux, knew where to look for inspiration. Occult Paris had recognized the reality and power of the unconscious, and Breton realized that true surrealism is a form of initiation profoundly akin to a psychological alchemy. Occult symbols abound in the works of surrealists, and it is fair to say that it is a short step from Redon to Dalí, who himself (Dalí I mean) had recourse to the thoughts of Péladan for his ideal and mystical art, and of course his explicit cult of the androgyne. One need only read *My Life with Dalí* by Amanda Lear to get a flavor of how consistent Dalí's fantasies were with those of Occult Paris's fascination with the androgynous figure.

And while we're on the subject, we can hardly avoid noticing how easily Erik Satie slipped into the Dadaist and surrealist universes during and after World War I. Indeed, it would appear that the very word *surrealism* comes from Guillaume Apollinaire's reflection on Satie's work for *Parade,* a realist ballet produced with Jean Cocteau—who held to a Martinist view of history—and Pablo Picasso. Presented at the Théâtre du Châtelet on 18 May 1917 by Sergei Diaghilev's *Ballets Russes, Parade*'s one-act scenario was written by Cocteau, during breaks from service at the western front, the set design was Picasso's in cubist mode, and Léonide Massine danced to Satie's music. How's that for a team!

The music was punctuated by Cocteau's additions of sounds of the everyday: a foghorn, typewriter, milk bottles, and pistol that were effectively part of a realist score that rather disconcerted Satie. Tristan Tzara had introduced "noisist poems" in Zurich in 1916, saying the noises used in these poems paralleled the objective reality cubists expressed on canvas. This led Cocteau to describe *Parade* cheekily as a "realist" ballet. When Apollinaire was asked to pen an introduction to the program, he wanted to underline this idea of realist elements imposed on abstracted forms with recognizable dramatic elements and came up with the new word *sur-réalisme,* some years before Breton took it up. Of course the combination of Satie, Cocteau, and Picasso alone is already a breathing, orgiastic definition, or surdefinition, of surrealism.

We have probably said enough about the place of music in Occult Paris, but we haven't mentioned Maurice Ravel (1875–1937), surely one of the most influential and evocative composers of the century and himself influenced heavily by Satie, Debussy, and the Symbolist atmosphere pulsing in the air of his childhood. Ravel was a boy in the company of his father when he first met Satie in the early 1890s. Hearing Satie's *Sarabandes* composed in 1887 influenced Ravel to compose his first important work, *La Ballade de la reine morte d'aimer* (1893). True to form, Ravel's interest would annoy and ultimately alienate Satie.

Twenty years after their first meeting, Satie was astonished to find "Jeunes Ravelites" (Young Ravel followers) being encouraged by their musical master to attend a specially organized concert of Satie's work at Paris's Salle Gaveau. The problem for Satie was that after the surprise of Debussy's *Pélleas et Mélisande* in 1902, he consciously changed his style. Satie knew the essential aesthetic that made the opera so new for its appreciative hearers was one he'd created himself. He felt tortured by the fact that the young *Ravelites* were in awe of work he had done twenty years previously (his most gnostic compositions)—Debussy had orchestrated the *Gymnopédies* for public consumption—which meant his recent work, displaying hard-won, sophisticated skills acquired through diligent sweat and toil at the *Schola Cantorum,* was compared unfavorably with earlier compositions that had themselves been criticized as technically inept at the time of composition! To add insult to injury—as Satie felt it—his early works were now being seen as precursors to Debussy! This meant to Satie that however flattering it might have been for people to think Debussy drew on Satie—something Debussy, unlike Ravel, would never admit—Debussy had somehow stolen the lead, taken his ideas, developed them, and run with them far more successfully than he had, all the way to official recognition and glittering prizes. Satie could not avoid feeling bitter about this development, aggravated by poverty and self-imposed asceticism, and it affected many of his relationships. He would get close to talent and then try to escape from it as if proximity threatened to take something away from him. He encouraged young talent then abandoned it. Cocteau, for example, could not understand why Satie seemed irritated by him. Satie found refuge in his imagination, and sleep in his appalling, sad dump of a dusty room in the distant suburb of rundown Arceuil where none visited him—not that he wished them to—like a junky's garret where the only junk was what was left of his furniture and rickety piano and the imaginary career he nearly had.

It was all the more poignant because Satie had been so close to Debussy. "From the moment I saw him for the first time," said Satie, "I was drawn to him and wanted to live constantly at his side."[2] As if to compensate for the critical drubbing Satie received for his *Le Fils des*

Étoiles, performed at the first *Salon de la Rose+Croix,* Debussy inscribed a copy of *Cinq Poèmes de Baudelaire,* dated 27 November 1892, "To Erik Satie, gentle medieval musician who turned up in our century for the joy of his good friend Claude A. Debussy." Satie dedicated his work *Idylle* to Debussy.

And then, when Satie's work started to gain some approval, Debussy made it clear he preferred his friend's earlier pre-*Schola Cantorum* compositions. And Debussy's was the only approval that really mattered to Satie, so Satie stayed away, even from Debussy's funeral. About the time Satie set to music a poem by Lamartine "in memory of Debussy" for a commission, featuring the line "A single being is lacking and everything is empty," in 1920, two years after Debussy's death, Satie confided to his journal: "When all is said and done, *ce bon* Debussy was something else again than all the others put together . . ."[3]

Their relationship leaves open a question that lingers on from Occult Paris. What is more important, the essential idea, or the development of the idea into greater complexity, a more sophisticated form? Minimalists *like* Satie. Satie liked white things. In his *Mémoires d'un Amnesique,* he claimed he lived on white food: "sugar, grated bones, salt, mildew from fruit, cotton salad, and certain fish without skin."[4] Phenomenally revolutionary as Debussy was, altering the landscape of music forever, it is, oddly, Erik Satie who seems most "with it" today: his music has "space"; it's clean. One can see him smile, slyly, and chuckle. He opened a door and we're still going through it.

The best legacy is example. We don't want Prussianism, do we? *Achtung!* Jackboots? Imagine if the Germans of Kaiser Wilhelm II had made it to the moon. What would they have left? Something like this: "Greater Germany has conquered and subdued the moon to our will, in the name of His Imperial Majesty, the Kaiser." They did not come in peace for all mankind. Péladan's fight was not only with barbarians in Germany, it was with the small-minded, frightened, state-sponsored, retreating academic or bureaucratic types that stifle creative life as they rest on rented laurels and publicly paid pensions. All the artists and magicians and writers we have looked at took on an immense opposition, a conceited, surly, aggressive culture of "scientific" certainties, *petit-bourgeois* materialism, and restrictive, hypocritical morality. Stanley Kubrick epitomized it all in *Paths of Glory* (1957).

Péladan fought them with Beauty, the Ideal. I say he won, for the Ideal is what lasts.

Certainly, the magical revival that bloomed in Paris as the Belle Époque galloped to its climax is still with us. Where would Aleister Crowley and all the British, European, Australasian, and North and South American magicians of today be without the source of so much creativity in the field? Papus saw the need of the time and did what he could—a brave try—to dis-occult the occult. He shared his knowledge and himself and maintained an open mind, was willing to change and take on the difficult, even the impossible. But maybe Michelet was right, he might better have observed the rule of the Sphinx to keep silent, as Péladan learned eventually he should rather have commanded attention than demanded it.

And having said all this, and knowing one could easily go "beyond the hour," I believe we have not heard the last of Occult Paris. There is a treasure of great value there, waiting to be rediscovered. May this book be part of its legacy-in-the-making. The dream may have been forgotten, but it is there for the asking. *Can you keep a secret?*

> Take eloquence and wring its neck!
> Once again and always music!
> Let your line be the soaring thing
> Which we feel fleeing from a soul going
> Towards other skies and other loves.
> VERLAINE, *ART POÉTIQUE*

> Because it happens sometimes that the genius
> imposes his presence on men, even those who are
> the most remote from it.
> VICTOR-ÉMILE MICHELET, 1861–1938

N⊙TES

CHAPTER 1.
"MEMORIES WEIGH MORE THAN STONE":
EDMOND BAILLY'S BOOKSHOP 1888

1. Michelet, "La librairie d'Edmond Bailly" in *Les Compagnons de la Hiérophanie* (Author's translation).
2. Ibid.
3. Ibid.
4. Ibid.
5. Ibid.
6. Ibid.
7. Ibid.
8. Ibid.
9. Ibid.
10. Ibid.
11. Ibid.
12. Ibid.
13. Ibid.
14. Ibid.
15. Ibid.
16. Orledge, *Debussy and the Theatre*, 266–68.
17. Michelet, "La librairie d'Edmond Bailly" in *Les Compagnons de la Hiérophanie* (Author's translation).
18. Ibid.
19. Basu, *Spy Princess,* 20–21.

20. Michelet, "La librairie d'Edmond Bailly" in *Les Compagnons de la Hiérophanie* (Author's translation).
21. Ibid.
22. Ibid.
23. Ibid.

CHAPTER 2. THE BUILD UP

1. Valentin Weigel, "Sapiens Dominabitur Astris," from frontispiece to *Astrology Theologiz'd* (1649; repr., London: London Theosophical Society, 1886).
2. Cassou, *The Concise Encyclopaedia of Symbolism,* 279.
3. Ibid., 279–80.
4. Jullian, *Dreamers of Decadence,* 259. Although the quotation is dated 1890, I understand the magazine ceased to be published in 1889.
5. Ibid., 258.
6. Cassou, *The Concise Encyclopaedia of Symbolism,* 29.
7. Ibid., 47.

CHAPTER 3.
MEETINGS WITH REMARKABLE MEN

1. Péladan, *L'Art Idéaliste et Mystique,* 17–18.
2. Webb, *The Occult Underground,* 185.
3. For more detailed treatments of these figures, please consult my books *Gnostic Philosophy* and especially *The Invisible History of the Rosicrucians.*
4. From the opening paragraph of the *Fama Fraternitatis* (1614).
5. Michelet, "Stanislas De Guaita" in *Les Compagnons de la Hiérophanie* (Author's translation).
6. McIntosh, *The Rosicrucians,* 93. Referring to Wirth, *Stanislas de Guaita,* 25.

CHAPTER 4.
THEOSOPHY AND THE TRADITION

1. Knowles, *Victor-Émile Michelet, Poète Ésotérique,* 14–15.
2. Godwin, "Saint-Yves d'Alveydre and the Agartthian Connection," Introduction to *The Kingdom of Agarttha.*

3. Saint-Yves d'Alveydre Sanskrit lessons, Nouveau fonds de manuscrits, MS Carton no. 42, Bibliothèque de la Sorbonne. These were left, along with his manuscripts and books to his stepchildren, Count and Countess Keller, who passed them on to Papus (Dr. Gérard Encausse). Papus's son, Dr. Philippe Encausse, gave them to the Sorbonne in 1938.

CHAPTER 5.
STANISLAS DE GUAITA

1. De Guaita, *Oiseaux de Passage, Rimes Fantastiques, Rimes d'Ébène.*
2. Crowley, "The City of God."
3. Michelet, "Stanislas De Guaita" in *Les Compagnons de la Hiérophanie* (Author's translation).
4. Knowles, *Victor-Émile Michelet,* 16 (Author's translation).
5. *Le Figaro,* 27 June 1886, quoted in Knowles, *Victor-Émile Michelet,* 16 (Author's translation).
6. Charles Berlet, "Membre Titulaire, Discours de Réception" in *Stanislas de Guaita, Mage et Poète 1861–1897,* 10–14. Booklet of Reception Discourse at the Academy of Stanislas, Nancy, 26 May 1932, extracted from *Mémoires de l'Académie de Stanislas, 1932.* According to a sales catalog (see below), Charles Berlet was a militant royalist, a regional writer of the Lorraine, also a member of the Stanislas Academy. To my astonished delight, a copy sold as Lot 18 in a catalog of "Livres modernes" by the Librairie Giraud-Badin, 22 rue Guynemer 75006 Paris, at the Salle Rossini, Paris, 28 November 2011 was autographed: "à Monsieur Émile Michelet, poète, en souvenir de St. De Guaita. Charles Berlet, 1 mars 1933."
7. De Guaita, "Avant-Propos" in *Essais de Sciences maudites,* part 1, *au seuil du mystère.*
8. Péladan, *Le Vice Suprême,* 5.
9. De Guaita, *La Muse Noire,* 27–31.
10. L'Abbé Paul Lacuria [pseud. Abbé Gaspard], *Les Harmonies de l'Être exprimées par les nombres. Paris, au comptoir des imprimeurs unis,* 2 vols.
11. Lacuria, Preface in *Les Dernières confidences du génie de Beethoven,* 2 portraits by Felix Thiollier, 12, 15.
12. Joséphin Péladan, *Prédiction de l'Abbé Lacuria* [a leaflet with the sole identification of the document: "leCri de Londres"] MS 13383, (Paris: Library of the Arsenal, n.d.). Reproduced in *Revue des etudes péladanes,* no. 3

(December 1975): 10–15. This revue is the official journal of the Société J. Péladan. Quoted in *Deux Contes de Lacuria, avec Introduction de Jean-Pierre Bonnerot*, Editions Electronique, November 2004 pour Morgane's World, 14. www.morgane.org/contes_lacuria.pdf (accessed 3 April 2016).

13. Ibid. Quoted in *Deux Contes de Lacuria, avec Introduction de Jean-Pierre Bonnerot*, Editions Electronique, November 2004 pour Morgane's World, 3.

14. Whiting, *Satie the Bohemian*, 133.

CHAPTER 6. THE SÂR

1. Péladan, *Curieuse!*, i.

2. Beaufils, *Joséphin Péladan*, 168.

3. Péladan, Dédication in *Curieuse!*, i–iv.

4. Péladan, *La Décadence Esthétique (Hiérophanie) XIX, Le Salon de Joséphin Péladan (Neuvième Année) Salon National et Salon Jullian, suivi de trois Mandements De la Rose Croix Catholique à l'Aristie.*

5. Eugène Vial, "Adrien Péladan père, journaliste à Lyon (1856–1870)," *Revue du Lyonnais,* no. 6 (1922): 102. Cited in Pincus-Witten, *Occult Symbolism in France*, 16.

6. Adrien Péladan père, *Satan-Renan.*

7. Pincus-Witten, *Occult Symbolism in France*, 22.

8. Ibid., 23

9. Péladan, *Oraison funèbre du chevalier Adrien Peladan* [Funerary Oration of the chevalier Adrien Péladan], 29.

10. Joséphin Péladan, "Le Matérialisme dans l'art," *Le Foyer, Journal de Famille,* no. 300 (August 1881), 177–79. Footnote in Pincus-Witten, *Occult Symbolism in France*, 32.

11. Michelet, "Péladan" in *Les Compagnons de la Hiérophanie*, 51ff., (Author's translation).

12. Barrès, *Un Rénovateur de l'occultisme. Stanislas de Guaita (1861–1898)*, 17. Note that the death date is inaccurate; de Guaita died 19 December 1897.

13. Bertholet, *Lettres inédites*, 51.

14. Ibid., 52.

15. Michelet, "Péladan" in *Les Compagnons de la Hiérophanie* (Author's translation).

CHAPTER 7.
THE KABBALISTIC ORDER OF THE ROSE-CROSS

1. See Galtier's *Maçonnerie Egyptienne*, 219ff. See also de Rességuier, *Éloge de M. Le vicomte de Lapasse*, 261–288.

2. Gérard Galtier, "Les Rose-Croix de Toulouse" in *Les Péladan*, ed. Laurent and Nguyen, 43ff.

3. de Lapasse, *Essai sur la conservation de la vie* [Essay on the preservation of life].

4. Boissin, *Visionaires et illuminés*.

5. Galtier, "Les Rose-Croix de Toulouse" in *Les Péladan*, ed. Laurant and Nguyen, 43ff.

6. Bertholet, *Lettres inédites: de Stanislas de Guaïta au Sâr Joséphin Péladan*.

7. Galtier, "Les Rose-Croix de Toulouse" in *Les Péladan*, ed. Laurant and Nguyen, 44.

8. McIntosh, *Éliphas Lévi and the French Occult Revival*, 166.

9. Ibid.

10. Ibid.

11. Ibid., 167.

12. Ibid.

13. Ibid.

14. Ibid., 168.

15. Galtier, "Les Rose-Croix de Toulouse" in *Les Péladan*, ed. Laurant and Nguyen, 47.

16. Boissin, Firmin [Simon Brugal, pseud.], *Excentriques Disparus*, 69–74.

17. Galtier, *Maçonnerie Égyptienne*.

18. McIntosh, *Éliphas Lévi and the French Occult Revival*, 169.

19. Bertholet, *Lettres inédites*, 106.

20. Péladan, *Théâtre de la Rose+Croix, La Prométhéide, trilogie d'Aeschyle en quatre tableaux*, vii.

21. Lévi, *Dogme et Rituel de la Haute Magie, deuxième edition très augmentée*, vol. 2, 386–91. The source for the Greek text is given by Lévi as Gautrinus, *The Life and Death of Moses*, 206.

22. Wirth, *Stanislas de Guaita*, 23–24.

23. Jean-Pierre Laurant, "Stanislas de Guaïta" in *Dictionary of Gnosis and Western Esotericism*, ed. Hanegraaff, 441.

24. Ibid. Jean-Pierre Laurant names the six known members, in addition to

de Guaita, as "Péladan, Papus, Paul Adam, Barlet, then Sédir and the Abbé Alta [1842–1933]."

25. Michelet, "Stanislas de Guaita" in *Les Compagnons de la Hiérophanie* (Author's translation).

26. Ibid.

27. Michelet, "Barlet" in *Les Compagnons de la Hiérophanie* (Author's translation).

28. Péladan, *Le Théâtre complet de Wagner, les XI operas scène par scène*, xii.

CHAPTER 8. PAPUS

1. Michelet's comments on Papus are from "Papus" in *Les Compagnons de la Hiérophanie*, 31ff., (Author's translation).

2. Papus [Gérard Encausse], "Comment je deviens mystique," *L'Initiation* 29, no. 3 (December 1895). Passage reproduced in McIntosh, *Éliphas Levi and the French Occult Revival*, 158–59.

3. Michelet, "Papus" in *Les Compagnons de la Hiérophanie*, 31ff., (Author's translation).

4. Ibid.

5. Ibid.

6. Ibid.

7. Ibid.

8. Ibid.

9. Ibid.

CHAPTER 9.
ROSICRUCIAL DIFFERENCES

1. Péladan, *Le Théâtre complet de Wagner*, xii.

2. *L'Initiation* 6, no. 5 (February 1890): 97, 101, quoted in Pierrot, *L'Imaginaire Décadent 1880–1900*, 134–35.

3. Pierrot, *L'Imaginaire Décadent 1880–1900*, 137.

4. Vitoux, *les Coulisses de l'Au-delà*, 192.

5. *L'Initiation* 8, no. 10 (July 1890): 384. www.iapsop.com/archive/materials/l_initiation/initiation_v8_n10_1890_jul.pdf (accessed 3 April 2016).

6. Péladan, *La Décadence Esthétique (Hiérophanie) XIX, Le Salon de Joséphin Péladan (Neuvième Année) Salon National et Salon Jullian, suivi*

de trois Mandements De la Rose Croix Catholique à l'Aristie.

7. Bertholet, *Lettres inédites: de Stanislas de Guaïta au Sâr Joséphin Péladan,* 138.

8. Geyraud, *Les sociétiés secrètes de Paris,* quoted in McIntosh, *Éliphas Lévi and the French Occult Revival,* 172 (no page number of source given).

9. Ibid.

10. Lalou, *Contemporary French Literature,* 303.

11. Michelet, "Péladan" in *Les Compagnons de la Hiérophanie* (Author's translation).

12. Ibid.

13. Victor-Émile Michelet, "Décadents," *Le Gaulois,* 29 August 1887, 2. This is a remarkable article in which Michelet described the literary scene of that time, noting de Guaita as poet-magus, working with Péladan and Alber Jhouney. He says that when the Decadents would rather be called Symbolists, they forget that poets have always been symbolists.

14. Michelet, "Péladan" in *Les Compagnons de la Hiérophanie* (Author's translation).

15. Lepetit, *The Esoteric Secrets of Surrealism,* 380.

16. Webb, *The Occult Underground,* 362.

17. Reproduced in McIntosh, *Eliphas Lévi and the French Occult Revival,* 173.

18. Ibid., 174.

19. Reproduced in Michelet, "Péladan" in *Les Compagnons de la Hiérophanie* (Author's translation).

CHAPTER 10. THE SALON OF THE CENTURY

1. Cassou, *The Concise Encyclopaedia of Symbolism,* 50.

2. Kandinsky, *Concerning the Spiritual in Art,* 55.

3. Sar Péladan, "Avant-Propos," *L'Initiation* 10, no. 7 (April 1891). www.iapsop .com/archive/materials/l_initiation/initiation_v10_n7_1891_apr.pdf (accessed 7 September 2016).

4. Reproduced at Pincus-Witten, appendix 1 in *Occult Symbolism in France,* 205.

5. Péladan, *Geste esthétique, Catalogue du Salon de la Rose+Croix,* 64.

6. Péladan, *Constitutions de la Rose+Croix: le Temple et le Graal,* 21–23. On p. 39, it says that the *Constitutions* were first written down in the year 1887, and were set for printing 11 November 1892.

7. Ibid., 39.

8. Pincus-Witten, *Occult Symbolism in France*, 93–94.

9. Ibid., 95.

10. Ibid., 99. (Source: J. Aymé, "Tribune Libre, M.Joséphin Péladan, l'Amour platonicien en 1891," *La Revue Indépendante* 21 [September 1891], 311ff.)

11. Ibid., 99–100.

12. Ibid., 100.

13. Ibid., 101.

14. de Larmandie, *L'Entr'acte Idéal*, 18.

15. Ibid., 24.

16. Ibid., 25.

17. Péladan, *Salon de la Rose+Croix, Règle et Monitoire*, reproduced in Pincus-Witten, *Les Salons de la Rose-Croix 1892–1897*.

18. Pincus-Witten, *Occult Symbolism in France*, 106.

19. Pincus-Witten, *Les Salons de la Rose-Croix 1892–1897*, 18. (Source: "personal papers, Mlle. Yolande Osbert.")

20. Hahnloser-Bühler, *Félix Vallotton et ses Amis*, 177–78; quoted in Pincus-Witten, *Occult Symbolism in France*, 131.

21. Ibid., 178–79.

22. Whiting, *Satie the Bohemian*, 148–49.

23. Pincus-Witten, *Occult Symbolism in France*, 142.

24. Ibid., 143.

25. Ibid.

26. Ibid.

CHAPTER 11. THE BOULLAN AFFAIR

1. Jules Bois, *Gil Blas*, 9 January 1893, p. 2. Bibliothèque Nationale collection: http://gallica.bnf.fr/ark:/12148/bpt6k75191624/f3 (accessed 30 March 2016).

2. Bricaud, *J.-K. Huysmans et le Satanisme*, following n8.

3. Horace Blanchon, "Bewitchment"[in French], *Le Figaro*, 10 January 1893, p. 2. Bibliothèque Nationale collection (online).

4. Bricaud, *J.-K. Huysmans et le Satanisme*, following n8.

5. Michelet, "Stanislas De Guaita" in *Les Compagnons de la Hiérophanie* (Author's translation).

6. Ibid.

7. Jules Guérin and Charles Couïba, *Gil Blas*, 16 January 1893, p. 2. Bibliothèque Nationale collection.

8. Michelet, "Stanislas De Guaita" in *Les Compagnons de la Hiérophanie* (Author's translation).

9. Bricaud, *J.-K. Huysmans et le Satanisme,* following n8. Bricaud says the account comes from Foucher's chronicles of the "Sud-Ouest Toulouse."

10. Myriam Harry, interview in *Revue de Paris,* 15 May 1908; concerning her visit to Huysmans in December 1902, quoted in Bricaud, *J.-K. Huysmans et le Satanisme,* following n12.

11. Péladan [Sar Mérodack Péladan pseud], dedication to *L'Occulte Catholique* [Catholic Occult], vol. 5 of *Amphithéatre des Sciences Mortes* [Amphitheater of Dead Sciences], i.

CHAPTER 12.
SATIE AND DEBUSSY: MOVED BY THE GNOSIS

1. Mendès, *Rapport sur le Mouvement Poétique Français de 1867 à 1900,* 126–27.

2. Davis, *Erik Satie,* 53.

3. Erik Satie, letter to the editor, *Gil Blas,* 16 August 1892. Bibliothèque Nationale collection. http://gallica.bnf.fr.

4. Volta, *Satie Seen through His Letters,* 31.

5. Ibid., 40.

6. Ibid., 42.

7. Ibid., 49.

8. Ibid., 57. Original letter held at the Library of Congress, Music Division.

9. Quoted in Howat, *Debussy in Proportion,* 46.

10. Howat, *Debussy in Proportion,* 6–7. Quotation is from autograph letter in archives of Durand et Cie, first published in *Lettres de Claude Debussy à son éditeur,* ed. Jacques Durand (Paris: A. Durand, 1927), 10.

11. Ibid., 7.

12. Ibid., 7.

13. Ibid., 6.

14. Ibid., 40. The date 1890 is in Debussy's handwriting in corrected proofs locted in the Music Department of the Bibliothèque Nationale, Paris, Rés. Vma MS 286.

15. Ibid., 36.

16. Ibid., 153.

17. Lesure, *Monsieur Croche et autres écrits,* 302.

18. Ibid., 28–29.

19. Ibid., 29. Quotation from autograph letter in archives of Durand et Cie, first published in *Lettres de Claude Debussy à son éditeur,* ed. Jacques Durand, 58.

20. Lockspeiser, *Music and Painting,* 167.

21. Ibid., 163. Information from: Julia d'Almendra, "Debussy et le mouvement modal dans la musique du XXe siècle," in *Debussy et l'évolution de la musique du XXe siècle,* ed. Edith Weber, (Paris: CNRS, 1965), 110.

22. Homer, *Seurat and the Science of Painting.*

CHAPTER 13. THE GNOSTIC CHURCH

1. *L'Initiation* 11, no. 7 (April 1891).

2. *L'Initiation* 8, no. 10 (July 1890).

3. *Déodat Roché et l'Eglise Gnostique, Cahiers d'Etudes Cathares, Numéro Special D, Série No 4 et 5, Dossier par JP Bonnerot* [ed.], Edition électronique Morgane's World, 5ff.; originally published by Roché's *Société du Souvenir et des Etudes Cathares.* www.esoblogs.net/IMG/pdf_deodat-2.pdf (accessed 30 March 2016).

4. Ibid., 8.

5. Jules Doinel, "Basilide," *L'Initiation* 10, no. 4 (January 1891): 310–15.

6. Ibid., 15.

7. *L'Initiation,* August 1891, 143–4.

8. *L'Initiation* 1, no. 3 (December 1888) (Rédaction: 14 rue de Strasbourg).

9. *L'Initiation* 8, no. 10 (July 1890): 468.

10. Notably in *La Presse,* 26 August 1889.

11. *L'Initiation* 33, no.1 (October 1896): 257–60.

12. "The Integral Humanity," *L'Humanité,* December 1897, 219–20.

13. Introvigne, *Il Retorno dello Gnosticismo,* 1993.

CHAPTER 14.
HOW TO BECOME A MAGUS:
THE ROSE-CROIX SALONS 1893–1897

1. "Tiers Ordre de la Rose-Croix Catholique R+C+C," *L'Initiation* 8, no. 10 (July 1890): 486.

2. Péladan [Sar Mérodack Péladan pseud], *Amphithéatre des Sciences Mortes,* vol. 1, *Comment on devient Mage: Éthique,* 27.

3. Péladan, *Catalogue Officiel illustré de 160 dessins du second Salon de la Rose+Croix*, xxvii.
4. Camille Mauclair, "Armand Point," *Mercure de France* December 1893, 331–36, 332.
5. Pincus-Witten, *Occult Symbolism in France*, 155.
6. Ibid., 168 (text from no. 1 in the 1894 Catalogue).
7. Albert Fleury, "Le Sâr Peladan," *La Plume*, November 1, 1894, 445–47.
8. Pincus-Witten, *Occult Symbolism in France*, 188.
9. Péladan, *Ordre de la Rose+Croix du temple et du Graal. VI geste esthétique. Sixième salon, catalogue*, 2–5.
10. Pincus-Witten, *Occult Symbolism in France*, 204.
11. Camille Mauclair, *Servitude et Grandeurs littéraires* (Paris: Ollendorff, [1922?]), 80–81; quoted in Pincus-Witten, *Occult Symbolism in France*, 204.
12. Michelet, "Péladan" in *Les Compagnons de la Hiérophanie* (Author's translation).

CHAPTER 15. THE MARTINIST ORDER

1. Laurant, "Papus" in *Dictionary of Gnosis and Western Esotericism* ed. Hanegraaff, 914.
2. Stanislas de Guaita, "Initiatic Discourse for a Martinist Reception," *L'Initiation* 4, no. 10 (July 1889): 5.
3. Ibid., 8.
4. Saunier, *L'Encyclopédie de la Franc-Maçonnerie*. According to the entry, attributed to "RA" the quote was found in Chaboseau's archive by his son Jean Chaboseau. I can find no supportive evidence for this statement, which appears in Milko Brogaard's website "1891 Supreme conseil de l'ordre martiniste," omeganexusonline.net/rcmo/supremecouncil.htm (accessed 30 March 2016).
5. Papus [Gérard Encausse], *L'Initiation* 7, no. 7 (April 1900): 90.

CHAPTER 16. THE BOYS MOVE IN

1. Jean-Pascal Ruggiu and Nicolas Tereshchenko, "Introduction Historique du Temple Ahathoor No 7 de Paris," meleph.free.fr/introahathoor.htm (accessed 3 April 2016).
2. Ibid., "Les Initiés du temple Ahathoor."

3. Ibid.

4. André Pigné to Aleister Crowley, 22 February 1936, Yorke Collection, Folder 117, Warburg Institute, London. The *Croix de Feu* was dissolved in 1936. Subsequent quotation from Crowley to Pigné also from Yorke Collection, Folder 117.

5. Jean Saunier, "Elie Steel-Maret et le renouveau des études sur la Franc-Maçonnerie illuministe à la fin du dix-neufième siècle," *Revue de l'histoire des religions* 182 (1972): 53–81.

6. Ibid., 56.

7. *Déodat Roché et l'Église Gnostique, Cahiers d'Études Cathares, Numéro Spécial D, Série No 4 et 5, Dossier par JP Bonnerot* [ed.], Edition électronique Morgane's World, 5ff.; originally published by Roché's *Société du Souvenir et des Études Cathares.* Reproduced at www.esoblogs.net/IMG/pdf_deodat-2.pdf (accessed 3 April 2016), see p. 21.

8. Ibid., 24.

9. Ibid., 27.

10. Ibid., 38.

11. For a good treatment of Cagliostro's rite, see Faulks and Cooper, *The Masonic Magician.*

12. Kaczynski, *Forgotten Templars: The Untold Origins of Ordo Templi Orientis,* 139ff.

13. Tobias Churton, *Gnostic Mysteries of Sex.*

14. Aleister Crowley to Theodor Reuss, (undated) 1914, Yorke Collection, Folder NS12 (AC Letters 1913–1914), Warburg Institute, London.

CHAPTER 17. TO THE END WITH PAPUS

1. *L'Initiation* 33, no. 1 (October 1896): 1–3.

2. *L'Initiation* 47, no.7 (April 1900): 1.

3. Michelet, "Marc Haven & 'Mr Philippe'" in *Les Compagnons de la Hiérophanie,* 101–2, (Author's translation).

4. Jean-François Var, "Philippe, Anthelme-Nizier" in *Dictionary of Gnosis and Western Esotericism* ed. Hanegraaff, 948.

5. Michelet, *Les Compagnons de la Hiérophanie,* 102.

6. Ibid.

7. Ibid., 103.

8. Ibid.

9. Ibid., 102.
10. Ibid., 100–101.
11. Ibid., 103.
12. Ibid., 104.
13. Quotation of Papus's son Philippe Encausse, cited in Var, "Philippe, Anthelme-Nizier" in *Dictionary of Gnosis and Western Esotericism* ed. Hanegraaff, 949.
14. Ibid.
15. Michelet, *Les Compagnons de la Hiérophanie,* 102.
16. Ibid.

CHAPTER 18.
THE LEGACY: A FORGOTTEN DREAM

1. Massimo Introvigne, "Martinism: Second Period" in *Dictionary of Gnosis and Western Esotericism* ed. Hanegraaff, 781.
2. Volta, *Satie seen through his Letters,* 144.
3. Ibid., 149.
4. Ibid., 55.

BIBLIOGRAPHY

Ambrière, Francis. "La vie romaine de Claude Debussy." *La Revue Musicale,* no. 142 (January 1934): 20–26.

Barlet, François-Charles. *The Art of Tomorrow: Painting Then and Now.* Paris: Chamuel, 1897.

———. *St. Yves d'Alveydre: Our Teacher.* 1910.

———. *The Synthesis of Aesthetics: Painting.* Paris: Chamuel, 1895.

Barrès, Maurice. *Un Rénovateur de l'occultisme. Stanislas de Guaita (1861–1898).* Paris: Chamuel, 1898.

Basu, Shrabani. *Spy Princess: The Life of Noor Inayat Khan.* Gloucestershire, U.K.: The History Press, 2008.

Beaufils, Christoph. *Joséphin Péladan (1858–1918): essai sur une maladie du lyrisme.* Grenoble, Fr.: J. Millon, 1993.

Berlet, Charles. *Stanislas de Guaita, Mage et Poète 1861–1897.* Nancy, Fr.: Imprimérie Berger-Levrault, 1937.

Bertholet, Edouard, ed. *Lettres inédites: de Stanislas de Guaita au Sâr Joséphin Péladan, une page inconnue de l'histoire de l'occultisme à la fin du XIXe siècle.* Paris: Editions Rosicruciennes, 1952.

Boissin, Firmin. *Visionaires et illuminés.* Paris: Liepmannssohn and Dufour, 1869.

Boissin, Firmin [Simon Brugal, pseud.]. *Excentriques Disparus.* Bassac, Fr.: Plein-Chant Imprimeur Editeur, 1995.

Bricaud, Joanny. *J.-K. Huysmans et le Satanisme.* Reprint, Paris: Bibliothèque Chacornac, 1913.

Cassou, Jean. *The Concise Encyclopaedia of Symbolism.* Hertfordshire, U.K.: Omega Books, 1984.

Churton, Tobias. *Aleister Crowley: The Beast in Berlin: Art, Sex, and Magick in the Weimar Republic.* Rochester, Vt.: Inner Traditions, 2014.

———. *Gnostic Mysteries of Sex.* Rochester, Vt.: Inner Traditions, 2015.

———. *Gnostic Philosophy.* Rochester, Vt.: Inner Traditions, 2005.

———. *The Invisible History of the Rosicrucians.* Rochester, Vt.: Inner Traditions, 2009.

Crowley, Aleister. "The City of God." *The English Review,* Jan. 1914, 161–66 (reissue, London: OTO, 1943).

Davis, Mary E. *Erik Satie.* London: Reaktion Books Ltd, 2007.

de Guaita, Stanislas. *Essais de Sciences maudites: I. au seuil du mystère.* Paris: Georges Carré, 1886.

———. *La Muse Noire.* Paris: Alphonse Lemerre, 1883.

———. *Oiseaux de Passage, Rimes Fantastiques, Rimes d'Ébène.* Paris: Berger-Levrault, 1881.

de Lapasse, Louis-Charles-Edouard. *Essai sur la conservation de la vie* [Essay on the preservation of life]. Paris: Victor Masson, 1860.

de Larmandie, Léonce. *L'Entr'acte Idéal.* Paris: Bibliothèque Chacornac, 1903.

de Rességuier, Fernand. *Éloge de M. Le vicomte de Lapasse.* Toulouse, Fr.: Imprimerie Douladoure, 1869.

Duits, Charles. *Vision et hallucination: L'expérience du Peyotl en literature.* Paris: Albin Michel, 1994.

Faulks, Philippa, and Robert L. D. Cooper. *The Masonic Magician.* London: Watkins, 2009.

Galtier, Gérard. *Maçonnerie Egyptienne, Rose-Croix, et Néo-chevalerie: Les fils de Cagliostro.* Paris: Editions du Rocher, 1989.

Gaspard, Abbé [L'Abbé Paul Lacuria]. *Les Harmonies de l'Être exprimées par les nombres.* 2 vols. Paris: au comptoir des imprimeurs unis, 1844.

Gautrinus, Gilbert. *The life and death of Moses.* Vol. 3. Amsterdam: Laurent Moshé-mius, 1721.

Geyraud, Pierre. *Les societies secretes de Paris.* Paris: Émile-Paul Frères, 1939.

Godwin, Joscelyn. *The Kingdom of Agarttha: A Journey into the Hollow Earth.* Rochester, Vt.: Inner Traditions, 2008.

Hahnloser-Bühler, Hedy. *Félix Vallotton et ses Amis.* Paris: Sedrowski, 1936.

Hanegraaff, Wouter, ed. *Dictionary of Gnosis and Western Esotericism.* Leiden: Brill, 2007.

Homer, William. *Seurat and the Science of Painting.* Cambridge, Mass.: Institute of Technology Press, 1964.

Howat, Roy. *Debussy in Proportion*. Cambridge: Cambridge University Press, 1983.

Introvigne, Massimo. *Il Retorno dello Gnosticismo*. Carnago, Italy: SugarCo, 1993.

Jullian, Philippe. *Dreamers of Decadence*. London: Pall Mall Press, 1971.

Kaczynski, Richard. *Forgotten Templars: The Untold Origins of Ordo Templi Orientis*. N.p.: Printed for the author, 2012.

Kandinsky, Wassily. *Concerning the Spiritual in Art*. Translated by M. T. H. Sadler. New York: Dover Publications, 1977.

Knowles, Richard. *Victor-Émile Michelet, Poète Ésotérique*. Paris: Vrin, 1954.

Lacuria, Paul [Abbé Gaspard, pseud.]. *Les Dernières confidences du génie de Beethoven*. Preface and 2 portraits by Felix Thiollier. Paris: Library of the West, 1902.

Lalou, René. *Contemporary French Literature*. New York: A. Knopf, 1924.

Laurant, Jean-Pierre, and Victor Nguyen, eds. *Les Péladan*. Lausanne: L'Age d'Homme, 1990.

Lepetit, Patrick. *The Esoteric Secrets of Surrealism: Origins, Magic, and Secret Societies*. Rochester, Vt.: Inner Traditions, 2012

Lesure, François, ed. *Monsieur Croche et autres écrits*. Paris: Gallimard, 1971.

Lévi, Éliphas. *Dogme et Rituel de la Haute Magie, deuxième edition très augmentée*. Vol 2. Paris: Germer Baillère, 1861.

Lockspeiser, Edward. *Music and Painting*. London: Cassell, 1973.

McIntosh, Christopher. *Éliphas Lévi and the French Occult Revival*. London: Rider, 1972.

——. *The Rosicrucians: The History, Mythology, and Rituals of an Occult Order*. York Beach, Maine: Weiser, 1992.

Mendès, Catulle. *Rapport sur le Mouvement Poétique Français de 1867 à 1900*. Paris, 1903. Reprint, Genève: Slatkine Reprints, 1993.

Michelet, Victor-Émile. *Les Compagnons de la Hiérophanie, Souvenirs du mouvement hermétiste à la fin du XIX siècle*. Paris: Dorbon, 1937.

——. "Décadents." *Le Gaulois,* 29 August 1887, 2.

Morice, Charles. *La Littérature de tout à l'heure*. Paris: Librairie académique Didier, Perrin et Cie, 1889.

Orledge, Robert. *Debussy and the Theatre*. Cambridge: Cambridge University Press, 2009.

Péladan, *père*, Adrien. *Satan-Renan*. Roanne, Fr.: de Ferlay, 1863.

Péladan, Joséphin. *L'Art Idéaliste et Mystique, Doctrine de l'Ordre et du Salon des Rose-Croix*. 2nd ed. Paris: Chamuel, 1894.

————. *Catalogue Officiel illustré de 160 dessins du second Salon de la Rose+Croix.* Paris: Librairie Nilsson, 1893.

————. *Constitutions de la Rose+Croix: le Temple et le Graal.* Paris: Secretariat, 1893.

————. *La Décadence Esthétique (Hiérophanie) XIX, Le Salon de Joséphin Péladan (Neuvième Année) Salon National et Salon Jullian, suivi de trois Mandements De la Rose Croix Catholique à l'Aristie.* Paris: E. Dentu, 1890.

————. *La Décadence Latine, Éthopée.* Vol. 1, *Le Vice Suprême.* Paris: Librairie de la Presse, 1886.

————. *La Décadence Latine, Éthopée.* Vol. 2, *Curieuse!* Paris: G. Édinger, 1886.

————. *Geste esthétique, Catalogue du Salon de la Rose+Croix.* Paris: Galerie Durand-Ruel, 1892.

————. *Nos Églises artistiques et historiques* [Our Historical and Artistic Churches]. Paris: De Boccard, 1913.

————. *Oraison funèbre du chevalier Adrien Peladan, 1890.*

————. *Ordre de la Rose+Croix du temple et du Graal. VI geste esthétique. Sixième salon, catalogue.* Paris: Georges Petit, 1897.

————. *Salon de la Rose+Croix, Règle et Monitoire.* Paris: Dentu, 1891.

————. *Le Salon XIX, (Neuvième Année), Salon National et Salon Jullian, suivi de trois mandements De la Rose Croix Catholique à l'Artiste.* Paris: E. Dentu, 1890. www.europeana.eu/portal/record/9200365 /BibliographicResource_3000022757244.html (accessed 3 April 2016).

————. *Le Théâtre complet de Wagner, les XI operas scène par scène.* Paris: Chamuel, 1895.

————. *Théâtre de la Rose+Croix, La Prométhéide, trilogie d'Aeschyle en quatre tableaux.* Paris: Chamuel, 1895.

Péladan, Joséphin [Sar Mérodack Péladan, pseud]. *Amphithéâtre des Sciences Mortes* [Amphitheater of Dead Sciences]. Vol. 1, *Comment on devient Mage: Éthique.* Paris: Chamuel, 1892.

————. *Amphithéâtre des Sciences Mortes.* Vol. 5, *L'Occulte Catholique* [Catholic Occult]. Paris: Chamuel, 1898.

Pierrot, Jean. *L'Imaginaire Décadent 1880–1900.* Rouen: Presses Universitaires de France, 1977.

Pincus-Witten, Robert. *Occult Symbolism in France: Joséphin Péladan and the Salons de la Rose-Croix.* New York: Garland Publishing, 1976.

————. *Les Salons de la Rose-Croix 1892–1897.* London: Piccadilly Gallery, 1968.

Saunier, Eric, ed. *L'Encyclopedie de la Franc-Maconnerie.* Paris: Hachette, 2000.

Vitoux, Georges. *Les Coulisses de l'Au-delà.* Paris: Chamuel, 1901.

Volta, Ornella. *Satie Seen through His Letters.* London: Marion Boyars, 1994.

Webb, James. *The Occult Underground.* LaSalle, Ill.: Open Court Publishing, 1974.

Whiting, Steven Moore. *Satie the Bohemian: From Cabaret to Concert Hall.* Oxford: Oxford University Press, 1998.

Wirth, Oswald. *Stanislas de Guaita, L'occultisme vécu: souvenirs de son secrétaire.* Paris: Édition Le Symbolisme, 1935.

Index

Numbers in *italics* indicate photographs or illustrations.

479

BOOKS OF RELATED INTEREST

Aleister Crowley: The Beast in Berlin
Art, Sex, and Magick in the Weimar Republic
by Tobias Churton

Gnostic Philosophy
From Ancient Persia to Modern Times
by Tobias Churton

Gnostic Mysteries of Sex
Sophia the Wild One and Erotic Christianity
by Tobias Churton

The Mysteries of John the Baptist
His Legacy in Gnosticism, Paganism, and Freemasonry
by Tobias Churton

The Morning of the Magicians
Secret Societies, Conspiracies, and Vanished Civilizations
by Louis Pauwels and Jacques Bergier

The Esoteric Secrets of Surrealism
Origins, Magic, and Secret Societies
by Patrick Lepetit
Foreword by Bernard Roger

Lords of the Left-Hand Path
Forbidden Practices and Spiritual Heresies
by Stephen E. Flowers, Ph.D.

Athanasius Kircher's Theatre of the World
His Life, Work, and the Search for Universal Knowledge
by Joscelyn Godwin

INNER TRADITIONS • BEAR & COMPANY
P.O. Box 388 • Rochester, VT 05767
1-800-246-8648
www.InnerTraditions.com

Or contact your local bookseller

PLEASE SEND US THIS CARD TO RECEIVE OUR LATEST CATALOG FREE OF CHARGE.

Book in which this card was found _____

☐ Check here to receive our catalog via e-mail.

Company _____
☐ Send me wholesale information

Name _____ Phone _____

Address _____

City _____ State _____ Zip _____ Country _____

E-mail address _____

Please check area(s) of interest to receive related announcements via e-mail:

☐ Health   ☐ Self-help   ☐ Science/Nature   ☐ Shamanism
☐ Ancient Mysteries   ☐ New Age/Spirituality   ☐ Visionary Plants   ☐ Martial Arts
☐ Spanish Language   ☐ Sexuality/Tantra   ☐ Family and Youth   ☐ Religion/Philosophy

Please send a catalog to my friend:

Name _____ Company _____

Address _____ Phone _____

City _____ State _____ Zip _____ Country _____

Order at 1-800-246-8648 • Fax (802) 767-3726

E-mail: customerservice@InnerTraditions.com • Web site: www.InnerTraditions.com

INNER TRADITIONS & COMPANY
BEAR & COMPANY

Inner Traditions • Bear & Company
P.O. Box 388
Rochester, VT 05767-0388
U.S.A.

Affix
Postage
Stamp
Here